CW00499657

VIRTUE AND THE VOICE OF GOD

VIRTUE AND THE VOICE OF GOD

Toward Theology as Wisdom

Daniel J. Treier

William B. Eerdmans Publishing Company
Grand Rapids, Michigan / Cambridge, U.K.

© 2006 Daniel J. Treier
All rights reserved

Published 2006 by
Wm. B. Eerdmans Publishing Co.
2140 Oak Industrial Drive N.E., Grand Rapids, Michigan 49505 /
P.O. Box 163, Cambridge CB3 9PU U.K.

Printed in the United States of America

11 10 09 08 07 06 7 6 5 4 3 2 1

Library of Congress Cataloging-in-Publication Data

Treier, Daniel J., 1972-
Virtue and the voice of God: toward theology as wisdom /
Daniel J. Treier.
p. cm.
Includes bibliographical references.
ISBN-10: 0-8028-3074-9 / ISBN-13: 978-0-8028-3074-6 (pbk.: alk. paper)
1. Theology. 2. Wisdom — religious aspects — Christianity.
3. Bible — Criticism, interpretation, etc. I. Title.

BT22.T74 2006
230 — dc22
2006016198

www.eerdmans.com

To my parents and grandparents,

for teaching the way of wisdom and making its paths smooth
(2 Tim. 1:5-7).

Thanks to you, *from infancy* I have *known the Holy Scriptures, which are able to make one wise for salvation through faith in Christ Jesus*
(2 Tim. 3:14-15).

Contents

PART III
Education and Interpretation: Synergy

Acknowledgments

During this project, I have often rejoiced in memories of Carl Hoch, Jr., who still seems to stand over my shoulders as I work: may he rest in peace. Thanks for ongoing support to the rest of my seminary teachers (notably James Grier, Jr., who could never have guessed the results of inviting me to read David Kelsey with the faculty); Mark Bowald and the rest of the "Dead Theologians Society"; Allen Sundsmo (who probably recommended and sold to me half the bibliography); the Bolgers, other "Basement Boys" and families; friends from TEDS (notably the Swains and Grindheims), plus at Arlington Heights EFC, along with many others from Grand Rapids. A number of students — notably Matt Bruce, Rob Matlak, Dan McClain, J. T. Paasch, Darren Sarisky, and Scott Williams — have turned into friends, and contributed (at least constructive criticisms!) to the project; moreover, Ben Noonan came to my rescue at the eleventh hour on Greek and Hebrew fonts for a new computer.

Barry Jones efficiently helped with the indexing. Throughout the editorial process, Jon Pott, Linda Bieze, Jennifer Hoffman, and others at Eerdmans have been unfailingly generous and helpful. It is a privilege to publish with such a house.

Without a generous reduction in course load from Wheaton College, completion of this as a dissertation would not have been possible during 2001-2002; since then, the Aldeen Grant and the Alumni Association Grant (with the help of supportive administrators) provided a reduced course load so that I could revise the manuscript. Many colleagues at Wheaton, especially fellow theologians, Mark Noll, and the gang associated with Café Padre, have been unfailingly supportive; additional thanks go to Tim Larsen for helpful comments on select chapters.

Small portions of this book at various stages have appeared in articles for Kevin Vanhoozer, ed., *Dictionary for Theological Interpretation of the Bible* (Grand Rapids: Baker Academic, division of Baker Publishing Group, & London: SPCK, 2005), on which I have spent the intervening years as an Associate Editor, and in "The Superiority of Pre-Critical Exegesis? *Sic et Non*," *Trinity Journal* 24 NS no. 1 (Spring 2003): 77-103. These publishers have kindly permitted reproduction of some material here. Portions also appear in "Canonical Unity and Commensurable Language: On Divine Action and Doctrine," in *Evangelicals and Scripture: Tradition, Authority, Hermeneutics,* edited by Vincent E. Bacote, Laura C. Miguélez and Dennis L. Okholm. Copyright (c) 2004 by Vincent Bacote, Laura C. Miguélez and Dennis L. Okholm. Used with permission of InterVarsity Press, P.O. Box 1400, Downers Grove, IL 60515, www.ivpress.com.

From their days on my dissertation committee up to the present, Linda Cannell and Steve Spencer have been invaluable guides in myriad ways. I am supremely thankful to Kevin Vanhoozer (and his family): for expert supervision with sacrificial timeliness, and in an ongoing way, for his friendship and example; for vocational help and opportunities; for the invitation to argue and tolerance of my stubbornness!

Finally, without the Christian heritage, loving care, and hard-working example of my family, plus the financial sacrifices of my parents, this project could not have been started, let alone completed. Over the years of this project, Amy Black changed from being a fellow rookie professor at Wheaton (whose parties were sometimes neglected in favor of this manuscript) to a close friend and, now, my wife. It is a joy beyond words to celebrate with her the appearance of this book and to share the rest of life so closely with such a wise person.

Preface

This book grows out of a quest for vocational self-understanding. As a seminary graduate, I wanted to understand why theological education had been so vital to my journey of faith, yet simultaneously involved deep frustrations over a series of fractured relationships: between academy and church, biblical scholarship and theology, theory and practice, or even between holistic thinking and specialist detail. Encountering biblical scholarship, in particular, had initially been a liberating and exhilarating experience, but slowly began to seem stifling once I considered what it would be like to play permanently by some of the rules in its guild. As I read about the nature of theological education, and prayed about my future within it, I struggled with more and more questions regarding biblical hermeneutics. Finding answers seemed to involve paying more attention to Christian theology.

Accordingly, this book explores complementary areas of literature: (1) discussion of the nature of theology with regard to theological education, in which the theme of wisdom has risen to prominence; and (2) discussion regarding "theological interpretation of Scripture," in which again wisdom is a key theme — giving rise, in particular, to an emphasis upon the role of virtue in understanding. My project considers these discussions together, as mutually illuminating. A concept of "communicative praxis" helps us to understand the ways education and interpretation shape each other, via the prominence of *phronēsis* (the "practical reason" involved in wisdom) explored in terms of Christian theology.

Characteristic of the recent movement toward wisdom and theological interpretation, the present book blends historical narration to set the scene (chs. 1, 4); engagement with specific Scripture texts and biblical theology (ch. 2); philosophical and hermeneutical discussion (chs. 3, 5, 6); and all of these interwoven with doctrinal reflection (on which see especially ch. 7). I engage in dialogue with a number of prominent authors in the "theological interpretation of Scripture" movement, coordinating their work in some cases but also forging a distinctive path and relating that discussion to literature on theological education.

Part One focuses on the nature of theology as wisdom, an emphasis of such literature. Chapter 1 chronicles the development of wisdom as a unifying concept, to overcome the various forms of fragmentation that characterize theological education. Still debated, however, are the definition of wisdom, and its precise relation to the discipline of theology. Thus chapter 2 undertakes a biblical theology of wisdom by way of theological interpretation of Scripture. The resulting emphasis, on wisdom as involving the every-person communicative praxis of the people of God, raises the question of theology's public authority and truth-status — which is the focus of chapter 3 on the nature of doctrine.

Chapter 4 inaugurates Part Two by reflecting upon the nature of theological exegesis. Chronicling the concerns of this movement likewise raises the question of how *phronēsis* can cohere with the commitment of academic disciplines to the public pursuit and sharing of truth-claims. In particular, my concern is how to fit together the integrity of the Bible as an authoritative divine Word standing over the church, and the illumination of the Spirit who leads people in community to deploy and develop Christian virtues in reading Scripture. Chapters 5 and 6 wrestle with this tension, trying to preserve the integrity and mutual implications of both Christian reading of the Scriptures and critical biblical scholarship. The focus of chapter 5 is on the integrity of theological exegesis of the Bible. Chapter 6 then transitions into Part Three by connecting theological interpretation of Scripture to post-critical understandings of rationality in the contemporary university.

The conclusion in chapter 7, therefore, more explicitly draws together Parts One and Two with their respective understandings of wisdom, which surface in educational discussions of theology and hermeneutical discussions regarding the Bible. Throughout, my effort is to explore theology as a "faith task of the church in the world" (to quote one of my seminary professors), related to character and communal practices, "caught as much as taught" — without ignoring theology's increasingly diverse forms and social locations, or rejecting accountability to the necessary contributions of its (largely Western- or Northern-influenced) critical disciplines. Indeed, it is in the nature of Christian education for the wisdom of its theological interpretation to go public.

Since the initial completion of this book as a dissertation in 2002, newly relevant literature has constantly appeared. The aggregate results of symposia — such as those edited by David Ford and Graham Stanton or Ellen Davis and Richard Hays, in addition to Craig Bartholomew's Scripture and Hermeneutics series — seem consistent either with the direction taken, or else with the types of dialogue represented, herein. So, despite substantially revising the manuscript, I have not continuously updated potential conversation partners, including *The Drama of Doctrine* recently published by my former Ph.D. mentor, Kevin Vanhoozer. Attentive readers will recognize points of both overlap and disagreement in our thinking (yet, probably, it would have been unnecessarily confusing to the reader for me to weave the threads of that ongoing conversation, using only draft manuscripts, into this book).

The burgeoning literary conversation that is relevant to the wisdom of theological education and interpretation of Scripture has made it difficult to let this text out of my hands so that it could finally count as a book. But the wide reach of this dialogue seems healthy. Thus it is the way of wisdom for me to have my say — or, in many cases, to raise my questions — and then to listen carefully for reader responses, especially those that consider how faithfully this text performs the Scriptures.

PART I

Education and the Nature of Theology

CHAPTER 1

Understanding Theology in a Postmodern Context

If theology may be viewed as a pilgrimage, then Christian theologians traveled the same road for hundreds of years. To be sure, the road had its peaks and valleys, and was quite winding at points; nevertheless, the journey was undertaken on behalf of the church. Theologians were in hot pursuit of *sapientia* (wisdom), a kind of knowledge with a teleology: the formation of virtue in God's people.

With the rise of scholasticism, first in its Roman Catholic forms, and later in its post-Reformation Protestant forms, theologians were gradually diverted onto a side road, pursuing *scientia*. By Enlightenment times, this pursuit was undertaken with the "modern" principles of objectivity and criticism essential to a "science"; virtue could no longer be an orienting goal within theology, for it was methodologically excluded on principle. Of course virtue was and is still a desired result (at least for the pious), but it came to be viewed as necessarily external to theology's "best practice" and thus to its epistemic warrant. Friedrich Schleiermacher's proposal for disciplining theology in the university dominated theological study, even if some sectors of the church still refused to equate theology with an aspect of *Religionswissenschaft.*[1] Popularizing the thrust of some predecessors, Berlin's threefold pattern came to epitomize a *wissenschaftlich* approach: theology is a kind of science with historical, systematic or philosophical, and practical disciplines; sometimes a fourth, biblical theology as distinct from historical theology, obtains if the Bible is treated as Scripture, not simply as a community's collection of foundational texts.[2] Undertaken in this new mode, the theological journey followed a different itinerary; thus much of the church, along for the ride, hurtled full speed ahead down the *Wredebahn* to points unknown.

Early in the 1980s, Edward Farley attempted to slam on the brakes. The fragmentation of theology concerned him, particularly in relation to theological education. Chasms lay between the academy and the church, between clergy and laity, and between theory and practice; furthermore, the various theological disciplines grew far too separate from one another, despite their collection in one "encyclopedia." Farley's *Theologia* engendered enormous debate, creating a new specialty with its own literature: the aims and purposes of theological education, with particular concern for the nature of theology itself.[3]

Nowadays, in a sense, the journey has ground to a halt. There sit the travelers at the side of the road, arguing over theology's destination, itinerary, and who should steer. Many claim that the road to *scientia* leads nowhere, and that the road to *sapientia* must be found again. But if *theologia* as *sapientia* was a churchly pursuit, and *theologia* as *scientia* arose from a university context, then Farley's brand — wisdom, a *habitus* (dispositional state or pattern) of reflective inquiry intended for both[4] — may have been unequally yoked. Can a kind of inquiry be appropriate for the church that is disciplined for the university? Can such inquiry pertain to both the church members and their leaders?

As outlined later, this study will address such questions with a Christian account of wisdom. We will relate the doing of theology to the "sanctification" of God's people without neglecting its public context. The topics of *paideia* (Christian education as a kind of transformative enculturation) and the "theological interpretation of Scripture" will enhance this understanding of theology in sapiential terms. Not only will these subjects highlight what doctrines of human being, church, Scripture, salvation, and ultimately God as triune contribute to theological prolegomena; these two discussions also help to connect sanctification with public, critical discourse. For if wisdom — being schooled in virtue as we respond to the voice of God — is our aim, then sanctification may be understood best in terms of education. Furthermore, if such education is to end in true knowledge of God, it must be an undertaking in and for communities of faith that are critically reflective.

First, however, the story of understanding theology must be told in greater detail. Only then can we understand why the current project, with its distinctive contours, is needed. The following narrative is admittedly selective, highlighting representative moments and figures in order to acquaint various readers with the momentum behind Farley's work and the subsequent conversation. While that conversation has been located first in the United States, this book will propose a more globally Christian account of theology and education. Many elements of our story, therefore, might have universal consequences and various cultural analogues.

The story moves through three time periods, or "contexts," by which theologians generalize about their craft. We begin by examining the transition from "pre-modern" to "modern" theology, from a sapiential to a scientific orientation. This requires discussing the relocation of theology from the pulpit and the cloister to the medieval university, and then again into a hallway of the modern university. A second transition, from the "modern" to whatever "postmodern" theology might become, means developing more sensitivity about how language works and reexamining the sense in which theology could be "scientific." The polarity of objective and subjective approaches has been castigated as an unwanted legacy of the Enlightenment, resulting in a turn toward action and practice in defining theology's nature. As we shall see, whether to emphasize theology itself being active and practical, or instead theology's service to action and reflection on practice, remains a crucial issue for us to address.

I. *Sapientia* and/or *Scientia?* From Pre-Modern to Modern

In a standard work on the development of the word "theology," Frank Whaling notes that early Christians adapted that existing term for apologetic purposes.[5] While certain conceptual cousins to "theology" can be found in Paul and other biblical writers, the term itself is absent from the Bible.[6] Thus early Christians used the term in diverse ways, reflecting their contexts. *Theologia* could refer to the Scriptures themselves, or to what is now called a biblical "metanarrative," or to naming, praising, or knowing God.[7] For Clement and Origen, Whaling suggests, theology "was a synthesis of what we would call dogmatic theology and philosophy of religion," yet there also arose a semi-technical, narrower use of *theologia* for theology proper (distinguished from the broader *oikonomia,* which concerned God's relation to creation).[8]

Behind these varied uses, however, lay two basic points in common: first, theology must relate to the divine; second, theology was an aspect of *paideia* or *humanitas,* the Greco-Roman emphasis upon forming people for public life.[9] Christian adoption of this term, therefore, posed no challenges to a sapiential flavor for knowledge of God. Of course, Christians would then alter the *theologia-humanitas* connection regarding the nature of such formation; for Augustine, *humanitas* was a preparation for *theologia,* not vice versa.[10]

A. Christian Theology before Schooling

Indeed, Christianity claimed to be the true *paideia.*[11] People would be truly wise, formed in its cultural virtues, if they participated in the church as the society of truth. Yet, as G. R. Evans admits, in a sense the relation between Christian theology and pagan reason has been a perennial problem; even quite early on, this bothered Augustine despite his sapiential emphasis.[12] However, Augustine's prime concern was to demonstrate the Bible's literary and philosophical excellence among the pagans without disenfranchising the uneducated.[13] Speculative and polemical dimensions of theology developed, to be sure, but until the twelfth century there was no concerted effort to unify and justify these under one scientific, disciplinary rubric.[14] Theology as "marginal notes," then — as commentary on Scripture, and only one contributor to what was central in church life — flourished without much epistemological hand-wringing.[15] Defending Christian theology was largely an apologetic rather than epistemological task, so that theology could be sapiential whatever its public status. The two were not mutually exclusive, because the prevailing (broadly) Aristotelian notion of *scientia* was still connected with a *humanitas* oriented to some greater wisdom.

B. Christian Theology and Schooling: Medieval and Modern

Doubtless the historical complexities in pinpointing the loss of *sapientia* are intricate, beyond the scope and ken of the present work. Nevertheless, the usual narratives contain two decisive time periods, with the key question being how to weight and relate them: the rise of the medieval university, and the rise of the modern university. These narratives raise questions such as the following: When and how did the definition of *scientia* change so as to conflict with *sapientia?* When and how did Christian theology find *scientia* sufficiently necessary to marginalize *sapientia?* And which of these events deserves priority in our explanation?

Yves Congar and Farley illustrate the two emphases. Congar speaks of a definitive medieval "turning point," that with Peter Abelard *theologia* gains its current meaning and then in the thirteenth century its epistemological flavor. Of course, older expressions for Christian theology (such as *sacra doctrina* in relation to *sacra pagina*) linger, in Thomas Aquinas for example.[16] Yet love and knowledge were already fractured long before modernity, many tell us.

Farley, by contrast, freely speaks of two pre-modern senses of *theologia* — which endured the medieval and Reformation periods — over against modern developments: (1) theology/knowledge, "a term for an actual, individual cognition of God and things related to God . . . a habit *(habitus)* of the human soul"; and (2) theology/discipline, "a self-conscious scholarly enterprise of understanding . . . usually occurring in some sort of pedagogical setting." This ambiguity or double reference is tied to a similar ambiguity in premodern Western philosophy over how to speak of a "science."[17] So, for Farley and others, love and knowledge had an enduring connection beyond the Middle Ages and even after the Protestant Reformation, only to be severed with the onset of the modern era.

Each of these narratives can include the time frame of the other, but with different accents. Should the separation of the Christian mind and heart be tied to the early (medieval) schooling of theology which brought about a unified, systematic, less contemplative discipline? In that case the dispute between Bernard and Abelard would be highlighted. Theology as speculation would be distinguished from theology as contemplation of Scripture and the church fathers; theology as schooled *speculativa* would be distinguished from theology as cloistered *activa.*[18] Bonaventure's attempt at synthesizing the two — activity and subject matter, spiritual experience and academic discussion — in one epistemology seems unusual on this reading.[19] Accordingly, Thomas and the Protestant scholastics may still have sought *sapientia,* but their scientific/scholastic methods would have been at cross purposes with that aim. The *lectio divina* (divine reading) so prized in the cloister was out of school, so that grammar and spirituality inevitably flew apart.[20] In addition, rather than the silence that accompanied such listening to God, the schools fostered dialogue and disputation with others.[21] Love and knowledge no longer co-inhered.

Or, on the other hand, should this separation of the Christian mind and heart be tied to the later (modern) schooling of theology, which formalized disciplinary distinctions and opposed philosophy's criticism to theology's church authority? After all, Evans acknowledges that the medieval "fire and energy with which they worked upon the new academic discipline of theology came from something more than mere intellectual curiosity, strong though that was in many of them."[22] Moreover, until at least the seventeenth century, the formula *fides quaerens intellectum* (faith seeking understanding) aptly described how theologians perceived their work in relation to faith.[23] On this explanation, since the frequent accent upon scientific method still served a sapiential aim, the split between love and knowledge must be delayed until *sapientia*'s modern exclusion.

Here evaluative judgments about the ingredients of *sapientia* vis-à-vis schooling intrude upon the historical question. For instance, Bernard saw the contemplative practices of the cloister as ingredient in *sapientia;* their absence from the school meant a spiritually arid *scientia* alone, regardless of scholastic aims and claims. In this vein, even Augustine's *theologia-humanitas* reversal, emphasizing the divine in wisdom, would be instructive in terms of its subsequent overthrow by the Renaissance:[24] those who define *sapientia* by contemplative practices of connection with God (not just virtuous aims) will probably see love and knowledge splintering apart with scholasticism.

Farley, by contrast, hopes for a *habitus* of critically reflective inquiry; his enemy is therefore modern disciplinary fragmentation, not the neglect of contemplative practices which presuppose churchly verities. Fitting this, he cites the reaction of pietism — with its separation of wisdom from theology by making it the end to which theology was instrumental — as an indicator of *sapientia*'s modern, not medieval, loss.[25] Somewhat in the middle, Congar's Thomist sympathies allow him to grant the significance that is due to the medieval developments without seeing *sapientia* and *scientia* (on certain terms) as incompatible.

The historical complexities require nuance, beyond simply chronicling rival schools of *sapientia.* Indeed, Beryl Smalley describes another broad shift that occurred, which is relevant to the present project: "Gradually in the twelfth and thirteenth centuries exegesis as a separate subject emerges. It had its own technical aids to study, and its auxiliary sciences of textual criticism and biblical languages. Even though the personnel of its teachers was still undifferentiated, a scholar distinguished between his work as a theologian and his work as an exegete."[26] However, whereas such large-scale shifts were occurring, nevertheless monks and schoolmen continued to share certain likenesses (especially tied to their common human faculties and functions). According to Luke Anderson, while the cloister favored a rhetorical theology and the schools a dialectical (more philosophical) theology, it was only when this difference seemed to become a contradiction that the larger split occurred between *sapientia* and *scientia.* Indeed, the monks themselves used forms of rational argument, notably the enthymeme, in which premises are hidden or assumed rather than formally presented. Thus the extent of the differences may have been misunderstood at the time.[27] Nevertheless, the social location of the medieval university made a difference in the doing of theology.

C. Christian Theology between Medieval and Modern Schooling

Martin Luther, John Calvin, and the Protestant scholastics are an intriguing midpoint in the time frame at issue. Luther's distaste for scholasticism's "theology of glory" is rather legendary. Indeed, by his time the debate about theology's character had become recognizably Aristotelian: was theology primarily speculative (for instance Thomas) or practical (for instance Bonaventure)?[28] Gerhard Ebeling thinks that Luther burst the bubble of the theory-practice problem altogether by refusing that Aristotelian framework; Luther made theology exclusively practical, in terms of carrying out the life of faith.[29] Calvin, too, might seem bitterly opposed to scholasticism, having used the word as a sort of catch-all for arid intellectualism and useless speculation. Yet he frequently drew from scholastic theologians,[30] and his *Institutes* were sufficiently systematic to lend themselves to a new scholasticism. Indeed, Ellen Charry can appropriate Calvin, following Thomas no less, as a sterling example of a sapiential theologian.[31] For, in terms of aims, there is an abiding connection between knowledge and virtue in these theological giants.

Yet it should be made clear that the character of the theory-practice dilemma has shifted through the centuries. As Randy Maddox notes, during the thirteenth-century debate there is at least one sense in which "practical" meant "dealing with humans and the things humans do, in the light of God," whereas "speculative" meant "concerned with contemplating God per se."[32] Cast in these terms (which seem to parallel the older *oikonomia* and *theologia*) rather than today's popular references for "theory" and "practice," the debate will find a writer such as Bruce McCormack siding with Thomas's theoretical emphasis. Not surprisingly, McCormack also finds properly theoretical echoes reverberating in later giants such as Karl Barth. In a wonderfully ironic twist, he therefore faults the Protestant scholastics for taking the practical side! The very theory-versus-practice debate, says McCormack, is too formal and non-theological, assuming common cause between theology and other kinds of knowledge while neglecting the givenness of theological knowledge, which demands the embedding of the practical within the theoretical.[33]

Thus, ironically, the Protestant scholastics are criticized for losing the priority of God in theology with a "practical" orientation. Meanwhile, Charry's critique is less counter-intuitive: the early Protestant descendants failed to see that "for Calvin, theology is a first-order pastoral undertaking, not a second-order academic discipline."[34] Biblical scholasticism was an attempt to meet an "epistemic crisis" by moving "from immediate knowledge of God to knowledge of God mediated through Scripture . . . to enable theology to position itself to engage both fronts at once."[35] The effort was, however, a huge failure: theology has retreated on both its fronts, becoming "emotionally inaccessible to believers and academically unacceptable to the wider academy." She thinks that "the objectification of scripture meant that theologians now had a subject matter with which to oppose ecclesiastical authority and to harness just as natural science did,"[36] an assertion which lays blame for modernity (at least partially) at scholasticism's feet.

Recently William Abraham has placed the blame for modernity farther back, at the feet of Luther and Calvin themselves, for choosing, at a fork in the medieval road, to walk the path of a *sola scriptura* "foundationalist" epistemology. The foundations of Luther's scriptural clarity and Calvin's internal witness of the Holy Spirit allegedly paved the way for their apologetic parallel in Descartes, and for Protestant scholastic successors.[37]

In some ways, then, we are brought full circle, back to weighing the medieval turns against the modern turns. How to tell the story is bound up with the next step to take today: certain historical judgments seem to coincide with certain strategies for relating (or not relating) theology to contemporary epistemological concerns. Given this coincidence, we should probably be suspicious of proposals that hinge purely on grand narratives of large time periods like "modernity." Instead, firmer historical judgments would hinge on more local narratives of theology's twists and turns, which might then flow into a larger narrative of how *sapientia* and schooling relate. Turning more directly to the modern dilemma, we learn from history only if we do not revise it according to a pre-determined vision of theological renewal.

II. *Scientia* and/or Semantics? From Modern to Postmodern

So far "theology" has denoted an enterprise serving the church, fittingly described as "marginal notes" to Scripture's teaching. Its result was viewed primarily as *sapientia,* for to know God was to be transformed by the good. This *sapientia* was then deemed incompatible with *scientia* by some, though not all, in the late medieval period. At stake was a difference over "the state of Christian life" — to be lived in the world versus a religious sphere — and over the priority of grammar (within the *lectio divina*) versus logic (within disputation).[38] These differences over theology's social location and procedure were actually intertwined: were the practices of the cloister necessary to *sapientia* and would the schools' pursuit of *scientia* entail arrogance, speculation, and disputation instead? Would a worldly cacophony distract from wisdom's contemplation?

Did the primary split between love and knowledge occur right then, or later with the onset of modernity? In the latter case, one might still fault the medieval schoolmen for tying the church to *scientia,* thereby setting up an epistemological fall. Nevertheless, schooling and *sapientia* would not be viewed as natural or necessary enemies; rather, subsequent disciplinary fragmentation — and later oppositions between theology as a discipline, spirituality, and the church — would be the true stumbling blocks for wisdom.

In other words, alterations in *scientia* certainly influenced the love-knowledge relation with the rise of both the medieval and the modern universities. The priority of each can be argued, but for present theological purposes we face two underlying questions. Should theological knowledge bother with the canons of *scientia* at all? And must theology avoid schooling in order to serve God's church truly? Assessing the legacy of scholasticism is an important first step toward answers. One characteristically "modern" way of telling that story is via subject and object in epistemology.

In a sense *theologia* had been defined objectively, in relation to what it produces — the knowledge of God — until the modern age dawned. Upon increasing difficulties for a definition that would orient theology to propositional truth claims about God, turns were made to the human subject. Theology became oriented to dealing with truth claims philosophically, while its proper subject matter became the expressions of religious experience. More recently, the dilemma between propositional and personal foci has turned theology's orientation toward the activity involved in "doing" theology. Eventually this focus upon theology's process, instead of its product(s), has led to discussion of its connection with church "practices."

When first chronicling this trend, from "objective" to "subjective" to "active" to "practical" conceptions of the nature of theology, I found myself searching for appropriate subtitles to match the distinctions as they emerged. Suddenly a strong connection became apparent, between categories for the nature of theology and George Lindbeck's categories[39] for the nature of doctrine: a movement from "cognitive-propositional" through "experiential-expressive" to, more recently, "cultural-linguistic" approaches regarding the connections between Christian doctrine and truth. This could be happy confirmation that the categories of the following narrative are helpful. Of course, Lindbeck's categories are ideal types for a complex history, liable to be unhelpful stereotypes when contemporary nuances of the views are considered; that difficulty pertains to mine as well. Nonetheless, as heuristic devices for dealing with the story of *theologia,* they can highlight important points.

A. Theology Understood "Objectively": "Cognitive-Propositional" Knowledge

Earlier it was noted that Thomas can be construed as a sapiential theologian. He wrote at length on virtues and *habitus*, and was motivated to serve the church. Yet he understood theology in terms of its object on two key fronts: he oriented theology to God as the object of faith, and he construed theological knowledge in terms of propositional statements analogically corresponding to the object.[40] Further, his notion of virtuous activity meant "engaging the objects that perfect human nature according to the measure that right reason sets down."[41] Theology was therefore a highly rational, dare we say theoretical, enterprise, more discursive than contemplative.[42] While Thomas's natural theology remained largely an insertion into a revelation-based enterprise, without significant justification of the biblical revelation on other terms *per se*,[43] his work certainly had an objective, theoretical, scientific cast.

Calvin's work likewise emphasized knowledge of God. Yet Calvin famously connected knowledge of God to knowledge of self, and perhaps should be classed on the practical side of the theory-practice divide.[44] Hence he may somewhat transcend the subject-object polarity, or at least epitomize the best of the objective emphasis. The parallel between Calvin's *Institutes* and Peter Lombard's *Sententiae* is instructive, according to Richard Muller, regarding "the problem of teaching theology in the basic course on Scripture," suggesting a parallel "between the rise of Protestant dogmatics in the sixteenth century and the rise of a more systematized approach to theology in the twelfth century."[45] In each case, though, could we not charge that succeeding generations (e.g., Thomas, the Protestant scholastics) focused on systematizing their ancestors more than on communicating the teaching of Scripture itself?

In any case, the "biblical foundationalism" of the Protestant scholastics, despite their noble intentions regarding theology as a practical discipline, did not withstand the epistemological onslaught of modernity. Abraham relentlessly criticizes their project: he rejects the attempt of Calvin and his followers to stop the "infinite regress" of epistemic justification by insisting "that the Word of God was to be believed merely because it was the Word of God,"[46] and he draws up a nine-point parallel between the "Cartesian project" and the Reformers' "canonical vision." Furthermore, Abraham queries,

> Might it be no accident that the movement which looked back to Descartes as its founding father came to be known as the Enlightenment,

> echoing the original enlightenment of the Holy Spirit in salvation? More boldly and graphically, may we not ask if the light of nature in Descartes does not represent the secularization of the internal witness of the Holy Spirit?[47]

The Reformers' epistemology was inherently and effectively capable of being secularized. Whether or not we accept this graphic history entirely, we must admit that the scholastic project did not hold up in either the modern academy or church.

Once Immanuel Kant played out a critical turn against traditional metaphysics and the church authority long associated therewith, an "objective" or theoretical orientation for theology became extremely problematic. According to Nicholas Wolterstorff, as a result of natural theology's apparently necessary new location at the front of theology's argumentative structure,

> One can make a rough-and-ready distinction between three ways in which theologians have trimmed the sails of theology so as to make it a university-acceptable discipline. Some have adopted the strategy of simply assigning to *faith* those parts of traditional belief which could not be foundationally grounded, thus removing those parts from the scope of university theology.[48]

This first tack, or a variation thereof, is taken by many conservative heirs of the Protestant scholastic legacy. For instance, one writer provides us an "uncomplicated definition of theology as 'the reflection on the truth of God's Word and application of that truth to ourselves and our world.'" On this uncomplicated definition, theology must begin "foundationally" with "the truth of God's Word and, therefore, with the God of that Word, the God of unchanging truth."[49]

Of course this appears to beg precisely the question that modern people ask about the truth of "God." Yet many adherents of the Protestant tradition have persisted in claiming scientific status for their theology. Walter Kaiser, Jr., for example, asserts that theology is a "scholarly enterprise," and that "even though theology carries its own brand of unique methodology, subject matter, and criteria, just as every other discipline does, it must not request a special exemption from her involvement in the full array of methods and disciplines in the academy." He is aware of a ready objection that theology often "comes out at the end of its research at some of the same points where it entered the argument," but charges that other scientific disciplines do so as well.[50] Theology can be scientific so long as a "non-positivist" definition of science is used; while not like an "experimental science," theology is often located in the broader "honored academic tradition" of German *Wissenschaft*, in terms of "systematized knowledge" of an object.[51]

The argument appears to be that theology builds by scientific procedures upon its revelatory foundation; in this sense, a scholastic Protestantism can follow Kant in viewing theology as a "construction"[52] project, for it may have anticipated this in some ways. Oddly enough, conservatives and liberals became frequent allies in labeling use of the word "theology" for everyone's God-talk "superficial";[53] unlike faith and love, constructive "theology" is not everyone's vocation, but is theoretical.[54] Such a stance results in a one-sided theological movement from theory to practice, which becomes all the more problematic once *theoria* is no longer defined in the theological manner we saw above. If theology is theoretical not in pursuing knowledge *of God* but in pursuing *knowledge* of God, then there will be an obsession with critical ground-clearing and foundation-laying that should precede the task of constructing the edifice itself.

Accordingly, for many in the West, an objective theologian "(1) must provide a clear account (2) of exactly what he or she knows (3) and just how he or she knows it," with such an account related to criteria that are not religion-specific.[55] In terms of doctrine, theology finds its *Sitz im Leben* to be "an intellectually vigorous pluralism."[56] To be robustly "critical" reflection on the "validity" of Christian witness for a modern public — the view of the diverse theologians sampled here — entails that "any attempt to make doing theology serve Christian witness directly, by subjecting it to controls that may be properly applied to bearing Christian witness but not to it, subverts its proper service and does away with it as critical reflection, by affirming only its essential unity with Christian witness, in effect denying their essential difference."[57]

In addition to faith-based foundationalism, therefore, and in light of its frequent failure, Wolterstorff names two other strategies for "trimming the sails" of theology in the university:

> Some have adopted the strategy of keeping the words in which traditional Christian belief has been expressed, but giving to those words a new content, until the newly devised content meets the demand for groundedness. Often nowadays the new content is an anti-realist content, constructed in the spirit of either Kant or Wittgenstein. And some have adopted the strategy of reconceiving the very project of theology, arguing that theology ought to be thought of as reflections about the God-talk of

the Christian community rather than as reflections about God, and then developing theology thus reconceived so as to meet the demand for groundedness.[58]

Both strategies apparently concede that theology as a modern, scientific construction project must build with Christianity's traditional "house of [Scripture's] authority" demolished, lying in rubble.[59] Thus, while they might differ as to its social location and task, they seem content that only in a "symbolic" sense can theology start with God; in its "philosophical" dimension theology starts with humanity.[60]

Wolfhart Pannenberg's lengthy *Wissenschaftstheorie und Theologie (Theology and the Philosophy of Science)* epitomized efforts at an "objective" theology on *scientia*-like terms. Pannenberg tackled the relation between the natural and human or social sciences, and the complexities of hermeneutical theory. He sought to rework a notion of "science" that could incorporate the circularity, action, and judgment of (for instance) theology, without excluding hypotheses, testing, and criticism therefrom. Of course, his particular theology and his philosophy of science came together, which, while one might appreciate the concern for theology to remain self-critical and rational, creates certain worries about his proposal.

These worries are perhaps paradigmatic. Namely, does theology become captive to whatever notions of "science" are defensible in philosophical or university domains? Is the "subjective" aspect of theology identical with, or explicable in terms of, the "subjectivity" of all other sciences? Moreover, does one want to say with most moderns that "die allgemeinsten Grundlagen der systematischen Theologie wird man daher in der Anthropologie zu suchen haben"?[61] Does that substitute the spirit of the age for the *sapientia* of Christian theology?

Recent attempts to rehabilitate Pannenberg's project under the label "post-foundationalist" may or may not be convincing; so much hangs on which "foundationalism" is chosen from among a bewildering array of definitions, and then on what is meant by the prefix "post-" (especially in connection with "non-" or "anti-").[62] The temptation is powerful to highlight the word "foundation" *(Grundlagen)* in the above quote and to question where to find the "post," but labels such as "foundationalist" should not be the issue anyway. Rather, the issue is whether "objectively" oriented theologians fall ironically from speaking of God's grace into speaking naturally of human glory.

So, conversely, others broadly labeled "post-liberal" now claim that since modern foundationalism itself lies in rubble, while any theology must use community-specific narrative building blocks, it can still speak publicly.[63] This odd non-foundationalist reconciliation of "Barth" and "Schleiermacher" schools fits awkwardly in Wolterstorff's typology; for that matter, post-liberalism may well fit awkwardly in Western universities. Time will tell. The hard lesson of theology understood "objectively" has been that, on disciplined modern terms, God is hard to speak about. Yet if God is not the "objective" vision of the good that orients theology's "theoretical" dimension, then the theory-to-practice move is thoroughly misdirected away from churchly interests. Furthermore, apart from an orienting object, theology is subject to, and possesses, no authority; theology studies and speaks about God-talk rather than God. Alternatively, when a construal of theology is dominated by its object, frequently epistemology has become an easy preoccupation: how does one know that one knows? What should be joined together — God and Word, love and knowledge, *sapientia* and *scientia,* church and school — tends to be put asunder, despite good intentions.

B. Theology Understood "Subjectively": "Experiential-Expressivist" Knowledge

Problems with an "objective" understanding of theology have suggested a softer claim, that theology might qualify as "rational knowledge" whatever the changing definition of "scientific" might be.[64] Beyond this, however, Farley sought to regain the sapiential character of theology as "primarily the wisdom and critical reflection attending faith. To put it statically, theology is a wisdom that constitutes the cognitive dimension of faith. To put it dynamically, it is wisdom as a reflective activity that should attend the believer's existence and action in the world."[65] Indeed, this is not a Christian-specific definition: "theology is the reflectively procured insight and understanding which encounter with a specific religious faith evokes."[66] A public, rational character still pertains to *theologia,* even as the character of its knowledge is cast more in "subjective" than "objective" terms. That is, Farley wanted to subsume theology/discipline under the unified theology/*habitus,* and thereby to construe the product or object of theology as a kind of knowledge that shapes the human subject. The focus shifts from propositions to persons.

For Farley, *theologia* as "a state and disposition of the soul which has the character of knowledge,"[67] as a theoretical-and-practical "prudence," was in fact the dominant understanding of Reformed scholastics.[68] Such a knowledge-as-*habitus* brings back the *paideia* arising from, and re-forming, the "pre-reflective insightfulness" of faith.[69] Yet this *habitus* is a state of the soul in flux, so that theological understanding "is not simply a timeless instant, a structure, but an activity, a life process . . . a dialectic."[70] That dialectic involves theology's genre as "not citation but inquiry" using appropriate "fields of evidence," a making of "judgments" that leads to "understanding."[71] This elicits the acknowledgment that theological education may generate the dialectical activity more than the *habitus* itself,[72] which is perhaps a pointer toward certain criticisms that have followed.

One has to ask with McCormack, did the emphasis of some Protestant scholastics upon theology's practical character in fact constitute an unhealthy turn to the human subject, which a post/modern project like Farley's would only exacerbate? In losing the specificity of Christian theology, without the Christian God as its "objective" or "theoretical" orientation — without Calvin's knowledge of God, has Farley lost true knowledge of self? Can there be formation without an agent or fairly substantive aim of formation?

Craig Dykstra mentions the further charge that since Farley restricts ordered learning "primarily to the analysis and interpretation of the cognitive products of practices," his educational approach is too cognitive; this criticism Dykstra rejects, only to allege still that Farley misses the way in which cognition and practices are tied together in theology, and that he may have too narrow an understanding of cognition.[73]

These related ways of challenging Farley's "subjective" but modern and public *theologia* are joined by still others. Robert Banks follows Max Stackhouse in asking whether "Farley offers only a procedure for — not the substance of — theological education."[74] Moreover, this procedure itself is questionable if Farley cannot demonstrate how *theologia* can be "both a disposition and a discipline": "The first has its basis in the classical conception of personhood centered on virtue that necessarily involves action, the second in the modern view of personhood centered on self-awareness that does not."[75] Queries regarding theological anthropology have just returned.

John Thiel in fact thinks that Farley's broadside against Schleiermacher's disciplining of theology has missed the mark, that modernity did not lose theology-as-*habitus per se*. Rather, modern theologians refined that notion in relation to theological authorship; no longer is the *habitus* one of faithfulness to traditional sources of revelation.[76] The question arises, for those who follow in Schleiermacher's wake, whether to construe the *habitus* as "the power of divination and guidance" for theological authorship, a position fitting a more positive Roman Catholic anthropology, or as "skill in depicting the present circumstances of faith within the categories of the biblical narrative," à la more pessimistic and protective Lutheranism as in Lindbeck.[77]

Who, in other words, is theology's primary author: God, or the theologian? Efforts at a modern *habitus* all apparently turned to the human subject. This was simultaneously a turn away from "objective" or "theoretical" knowledge of God via revelation. However problematic that traditional orientation was — after all, the "subjective" turn is in some way its unintended progeny — it must be doubted whether Farley can eat the pre-modern "disposition" and modern academic "discipline" cakes simultaneously without dwelling in the "house of authority." The missing category of modern theology has been "response";[78] without knowing God, what changes the human subject, and what indeed would be the object of theological study?

An alternative "subjective" path would be to accept "disposition" versus "discipline" as a distinction between religion as "a way of life" and theology as "critical reflection" thereupon, only to privilege religion or practice over theory.[79] The argument would be that excessive adherence to Western academic standards "fails to take multiculturalism seriously,"[80] that the recently popular hermeneutical orientation for theological education must become ideologically braver, allowing for spirituality and mysticism over systematic thinking.[81] Just as Farley claimed pre-modern roots for his *theologia*-as-*habitus*, so also could this more mystical approach.

However, it is one thing to grant that theology is theoretical (in the popular sense of that term) and simply minimize it; it would be another to speak of "theology's inner character as itself a form of spirituality, and as aptly fitted therefore to articulate the perceptions of spiritual and mystical journeys."[82] We could privilege the religious activity of contemplation either in relation to the language of theology, or at quite a distance therefrom. If we try to recover a traditional "subjectivity" that involves the "objectivity" of God as "acting Subject," must we reject an orientation to God as "scientific 'object of study' for theology"?[83]

This highlights the problematic character of the modern epistemological subject-object dichotomy, precluding theology as a response to God that keeps love and knowledge together. No view of theology is entirely "objective" or "subjective"; using these terms for telling the story highlights priorities and relative emphases, along with the post-Kantian revolution in our thinking. An "objective" focus can quickly fixate on whether and how we know God, know about God, or know about our talk about God. The latter fixation has pushed modern people toward a "subjective" focus, toward regulating the semantics of saintly speech; theology critically reflects upon the meaning, and real truth behind, expressions of religious experience. In that case, religious expression and reflection on or for religious expression tend to polarize — either contemplation or discourse, either private or public, either love or knowledge. The best efforts at transcending these polarities wind up drawing on theological resources, especially concerning knowledge of God and the nature of human being. Farley's magisterial work comes up short because he wants to reunite love and knowledge while remaining preoccupied with critical reflection that is readily acceptable to public discourse in modern Western universities. He criticizes that discourse for losing *paideia,* but retains the assumptions under which *paideia* loses its orienting vision.

One must wonder if "the more general question 'What is theology?' first demands, therefore, a response to a prior question: What is the self-understanding of the theologian?"[84] The pre-modern *habitus* differed from an "activity of inquiry," presupposing "that theological understanding involves not only the manipulation and mastery of objective data, but also the extension and enrichment or even transformation of one's own subjectivity," so that "whether theology can properly be characterized as critical inquiry depends in part on whether the concept of critical inquiry can be broad enough to encompass, rather than ignore or oppose, this aspect of theological understanding, and thus do justice to a central insight of the older tradition."[85] The reason that "theology" could refer both (objectively) to a product (as knowledge of truth) and (more subjectively) to a person-shaping process[86] was due to its dwelling in the "house of authority." A word such as "wisdom" could refer to objective knowledge and subjective *habitus,* and each in terms of the other, because a certain understanding of knowing God through Scripture was presupposed. Hence Charles Wood's judgment is correct that "to attempt to describe theology in terms of a theological *habitus* is to put the cart before the horse, for a *habitus* must itself be described in terms of that for which it is a *habitus.*"[87]

C. Theology Understood "Actively": Second-Order Critical Reflection/Inquiry

Wood, and many after him, have tried switching horses in midstream while staying on Farley's track, defining theology as "critical inquiry into the validity of Christian witness."[88] On such accounts, "as literary criticism stands to literature, so theology, as critical inquiry, stands to Christian witness," as a second-order stands to a first-order enterprise. Wood quickly refuses to separate theology and witness; their distinction is "strictly a functional one."[89]

Theology is indeed theoretical, as reflection on practice; its only practical sense, strictly speaking, lies in the "sense in which any reflective activity is a practice."[90] Lest theory and practice should split, however, Wood finds in theology a union of "vision" (the traditional, embracing thought of theology) and "discernment" (relating to the particular and the practical). A *habitus* is indeed formed in the theologian, yet such a "capacity"-and-"disposition" is that of critical inquiry.[91] The inquiry entails three questions, which correspond to three roughly interdependent dimensions or (dare we say it?) disciplines. Is the witness truly Christian (a historical question)? Is the witness really true (a philosophical question)? Is the witness fit to the context (a "practical" question)?[92] Systematic and moral theology work with the answers to these questions.

There is obvious effort to retain Farley's emphasis on *habitus,* while specifying the activity toward which the formation aims. Further, that specification is intended to serve both the church and the academy, but clearly on post/modern public terms. Indeed, resonances not only with Farley, but with many in the broad tradition of "theological hermeneutics," are apparent.[93] We might say that whereas the "objective" focus has been the propositional and the "subjective" focus has been the personal, Wood attends to the process of theological activity itself.

Although Wood has related to "Yale" post-liberals, comparison with mainline "Chicago" theologians is instructive. Schubert Ogden notes the "systematic ambiguity of the word 'witness,' which refers both to the *what* of witness, in the sense of its expression of its content . . . and to the *that* of witness, in the sense of the act of witnessing. . . ." From the latter Ogden derives a claim of adequacy to content, and another of adequacy to situation; the result is a threefold theology: historical, systematic, and practical.[94] Theology serves Christian witness only indirectly, or else must drop the adjective "critical," so that its historical dimension (viz. especially biblical interpretation) must be subject to no theological controls.[95] Throughout this literature, the similarities are striking: thus Wood's theological hermeneutic ultimately makes only cloistered claims regarding the meaning of biblical texts.[96]

Even some others, such as Chicago's Don Browning, who accept this university-centered picture of theology, Christianity, and religious studies, nevertheless challenge Wood's understanding. Browning thinks Wood's model "becomes something like a theory-practice-theory model," whereas to address the theory-practice movement we need "a more thoroughly practical and hermeneutical model from the beginning."[97] Thus Browning develops — using Hans-Georg Gadamer, Paul Ricoeur, and Jürgen Habermas especially — a "fundamental practical theology *as critical reflection on the church's dialogue with Christian sources and other communities with the aim of guiding its action toward social and individual transformation.*"[98] "Critical reflection" remains the centerpiece nonetheless, for theology's defining public remains the university (and churches that cooperate with its definition of "public").

Banks criticizes such proposals for focusing upon "only one aspect of moral formation . . . on its cognitive dimension."[99] Among subsequent points of agreement in the theological education literature, he notes, are the rejection of a one-way theory-to-practice move, and the relation of theology to all aspects of life.[100] However, theology as "critical reflection" may relate to all aspects of life *only cognitively,* so that regardless of their order, theory and practice still seem dichotomized. For Banks, this suggests that theological thinking and learning need to feel more like a "research project" located in mission activity (fairly broadly defined) than "theory construction."[101]

Likewise J. Andrew Kirk focuses on theology as an activity, asserting that "it is impossible to conceive of theology apart from mission."[102] This assertion arises from his understanding that theology's object is God, who is an acting Subject and whose action is missional.[103] On these proposals theology remains "reflective" (though perhaps less strictly so for Banks); reflection is more strongly shaped by a particular context and end, due to theological notions that inform accounts of theology itself.

For this process-oriented set of positions, the "objective" component restored to theology is, as previously seen with some contemplative emphases, oriented toward God as an acting "Subject." Hence distinctions such as "doing" versus "studying" theology,[104] or religious experience versus theology, are not so hard-and-fast. Indeed, still other candidates besides mission vie to shape theological activity in context. For instance, Geoffrey Wainwright retains theology as "reflecting on faith and doctrine,"[105] but finds that faith and doctrine overlap, and that "belief and action meet in the liturgy."[106] Worship therefore functions as a "hermeneutical continuum" to orient theological activity.[107] In a somewhat similar vein, Martin Thornton had proposed to situate theology in prayer as the pattern of the church's life.[108]

Oddly enough, at least some praxis-oriented liberationist proposals also fit under the heading of theology-as-activity, but construe that activity with a strongly theoretical thrust. Clodovis Boff, for example, makes theology both autonomous from and dependent upon practice.[109] Theology remains scientific, as critical reflection or theory with its own logic and needing the social sciences, despite its concrete situatedness; the theory-praxis dialectic involves not just their *perichoresis* (interpenetration) but *chorismos* (difference) as well.[110] For all the attention to praxis, however, the activity basic to theology remains critical reflection in a "scientific" mode.

The strengths and weaknesses of construing theology as an activity have therefore generated considerable reflection on its orientation and context. Jaroslav Pelikan has famously and shrewdly observed that

> During the years 100 to 600, most theologians were bishops; from 600 to 1500 in the West, they were monks; since 1500, they have been university professors. Gregory I, who died in 604, was a bishop who had been a monk; Martin Luther, who died in 1546, was a monk who became a university professor. Each of these life styles has left its mark on the job description of the theologian, but also on the way doctrine has continued to develop back and forth between believing, teaching, and confessing.[111]

This truth about theology and context has focused the discussion about theological activity more sharply on "practices" and their relation to reflection. As we shall see, a follow-up question arises quickly: whose practices? Which rationality?

D. Theology Understood "Practically": Knowledge of/for "Cultural-Linguistic" Action

Earlier we noted that Luther, and some others who dwelt in the "house of authority," nevertheless tried to circumvent theory-practice tension simply by designating theology as "practical." More recently, Maddox has argued likewise for theology as a "practical" discipline, with these accomplishments: unifying theological concerns around a focus on praxis; being holistic, transformative, communal, and contextual.[112] Indeed, if opposing "speculation" is the target, this practical choice might well make its mark. Alternatively, we might dispense only with the linear move from theory to practice, retaining differentiation between them. Regardless, the effort has been to link more closely theology and practice, guarding against excessive systematization on the one hand, while on the other hand still granting theology a cognitive orientation and guarding against too narrow a focus on the present context.[113]

If the older theory-practice tangle arose partly from understanding theory in terms of speculation, then the more recent divide suffered from understanding practice simply in terms of any individual, instrumental action. The little discussion of "practices" by Alasdair MacIntyre thus struck many chords amid the cacophony of voices speaking to theological education. If theology is at least partially about formation, then MacIntyre's rediscovery of classical virtue means rediscovering a notion of "practice" as

> any coherent and complex form of socially established cooperative human activity through which goods internal to that form of activity are realized in the course of trying to achieve those standards of excellence which are appropriate to, and partially definitive of, that form of activity, with the result that human powers to achieve excellence, and human conceptions of the ends and goods involved, are systematically extended.[114]

In this sense, practices provide the arena in which virtues are defined and also exhibited.

Practices not only have outcomes but also produce goods internal to their processes.[115] Accordingly, "practices central to Christian life are conditions under which various kinds and forms of knowledge emerge — knowledge of God, ourselves, and the world; knowledge that is not only personal but public."[116] We must no longer be "burdened by a picture of practice that is harmfully individualistic, technological, ahistorical, and abstract," simply as "someone doing something,"[117] which tends also to downplay or neglect the moral and spiritual dimensions of life.

What then is theology's relation to such a rebuilt understanding of "practice"? At minimum, some aspects of theology will study church practices, both describing them thickly in the present and aiming theological theory toward their future.[118] More than that, theological understanding will partially occur through some kind of participatory engagement with these church practices. Stanley Hauerwas, for instance, can claim that "if theological convictions are meant to construe the world — that is, if they have the character of practical discourse — then ethics . . . is at the heart of the theological task." Theological claims, for Hauerwas and his followers, "are already ethical claims."[119] So we have progressed from focusing on the proposition, the person, and the process, to this more holistic concept of practice that might hold them together.

The point that remains murky, however, is whether theology merely serves "practices," after a new practice-to-theory-to-practice fashion, or whether in fact theological education is such a practice, or whether even theology itself is a practice. Already we have claimed that any reflective activity is a practice, but should we take this in a mundane or a meaningful sense?

One option would be James McClendon's dubbing theology a "secondary practice," specifically located in the church's teaching ministry.[120] Doctrines are developed by church "practitioners," and as "convictions" they are deeply "self-involving."[121] While they are sometimes "discrete means" of the church's teaching ministry, doctrines often are *"presupposed* and *exemplified"* in the rest of Christian practice(s).[122] Again, we see effort to maintain theology's critical function, but tied ever more closely to the practice of all God's people, acknowledging their participation in shaping its content.

At least until very recently, though, probably the most ambitious effort to revamp a construal of theology "practically" was David Kelsey's. To start with, he has noticed widespread agreement about the aim of theological education — a kind of wisdom. Yet its definition remains up for grabs: "This wisdom concerning God embraces contemplation, discursive reasoning, the affections, and the actions that comprise a Christian's life. But the ways in which these four are interrelated vary enormously."[123] Indeed, each of the four elements dominated a definition of wisdom long before the modern age:

> For third-century Christians *sapientia,* contemplative understanding, might here and now yield human fulfillment in vision's union with God. For Thomas Aquinas *scientia,* understanding by discursive reasoning, might help prepare us for a future intellectual vision of God. For Bonaventure understanding of God might start in reason's contemplating *(sapientia)* but then must go on beyond reason to the completion of understanding in will's affectionate union with God. But for Scotus, because understanding God culminates in precisely will's love of God, it must begin here and now neither solely in reason's *sapientia* nor solely in its *scientia,* but in will's deliberate and conscious action, that is, in *praxis.*[124]

The general lesson of this history is exceedingly important to learn: agreement on the aim of theology or theological education is often formally achieved around "wisdom" vocabulary. However, there has been longstanding disagreement about its material content. The interplay between schools of sanctification, doctrines of human being, and of course epistemological approaches, is always complex.

As Kelsey emphasized in his more descriptive work on the theological education debate, choosing between the two types of post/modern schooling — "Athens" versus "Berlin" — is related to the choice about how to envision wisdom. Most specifically, if one envisions Christianity itself as a kind of *paideia* (Athens), then the modern university's *telos* of formation (namely, Berlin's critical inquiry) will not seem to fit the wisdom of Christian theology. Yet Kelsey himself is unwilling to choose *paideia* over *Wissenschaft.* Instead, though admitting that the two types of schooling will constantly face inherent tensions,[125] he seeks a definition of theological "understanding" that will keep them together. This "understanding" of God consists in a "set of practices," or "capacities for action" in relation to God. Theology must understand God "indirectly *by way* of . . ." other activity. A *habitus* is involved, but its disposition to act — or, to engage in certain practices — involves intention and therefore self-critical thought. Hence theology is not itself a practice, but is the cooperative "self-critical reflection" that is "an integral part of a practice."[126]

The indirect nature of understanding God, the necessity of thoughtfully and critically engaging in particular practices — which are, on recent definition, communal and traditioned — means that the "horizon" of theological understanding is the particular Christian congregation.[127] One indirectly grows in capacity for relating to God by engaging with congregational practices, an aspect of which is the self-critical reflection called "theology." In this portrayal, "'theology' is not some one enterprise and may have no single core 'essential structure,'" being practiced during congregational life "in a piecemeal and ad hoc way."[128] Nevertheless, Kelsey's three-part breakdown of theology has remarkable affinities to some proposals already seen, such as Wood's: "constructive" (how to construe "the Christian thing"), "critical practical" (what speech and action in the congregation are faithful to a construal), and "apologetic" (how to assess the truth of the Christian thing in a construal).[129]

Therefore, "theology" is, like philosophy according to Stephen Toulmin, not a "discipline," but "field-encompassing."[130] Its "understanding" is neither theory-formulation nor research, but the acquisition of capacities for action.[131] The theological *habitus* must relate people to God indirectly rather than directly, formation involving Berlin's critical thinking as well as Athens's *paideia.*[132] This forces Kelsey's concession that his proposal stresses action and discursive reasoning, but he claims not to exclude contemplation and affection: all that the proposal does require is "that the capacities are capacities for what is in principle *public* action."[133]

Now this option for a "practical" construal of the nature of theology exemplifies the priority of anthropology once again. Kelsey explicitly rejects the notion of human being underlying traditional *paideia,* a notion which he dubs "something like an ahistorical and universally self-identical essential self."[134] Moreover, his proposal is explicitly developed in service to committed pluralism, regarding the diversity of Christian congregations and their construing what it means to understand God. Their diverse religious experiences are not merely "alternative 'symbolic expressions' or 'thematizations'"; they are "genuinely and profoundly pluralistic."[135]

Yet this pluralism, ironically enough, is vulnerable to critique on its own grounds. Kelsey's proposal hinges on the university divinity school — probably on an American version — as its defining social location. Despite a claim to countenance pluralism, in fact his "theology" thoroughly reflects the commitments of mainline American Protestantism. Ironically, therefore, Reinhard Hütter subjects Kelsey's "pluralistic" construal to ideology critique.[136]

Hütter's own proposal then offers another variation of the "practical" turn (in densely theoretical prose). He takes theology to be itself a practice, and not in a secondary sense. With Kelsey's, his intricate work must be engaged in some detail throughout the chapters that follow. For now, the affinities between Hütter's orientation and other critiques of the current scene should be noted. The orientation missing in the modern academy, theology as first of all "response" to God, is central for Hütter. Indeed, we have already voiced a major concern about a "practical" focus — that the God of the gospel will not initiate and influence theological reflection, that accordingly Christian doctrine's value will be assessed in isolation, "on outwardly observable human behavior."[137]

Between Kelsey's America and Hütter's Germany lies David Ford's Great Britain, where theology and religious studies cohabit more peacefully in public life than they do elsewhere. Already this chapter's chronicle of theological education has highlighted the importance of its social location and the identity of its practitioners. Surely, therefore, the differences are significant between the intellectual culture of German and British universities, given their historic interconnectedness with state churches, and the American commitment to separate church from state *and* university. The "theological education debate" began and continued largely in the United States for a time, since its seminaries and/or university divinity schools have functioned in distinctively-created modes. These American problems and possibilities have been somewhat unique, although this is perhaps symptomatic of a need for Christian wisdom that characterizes the entirety of "the West."

In any case, Ford maintains that religion "is about the whole shape of living," while theology "deals with questions of meaning, truth, beauty, and practice raised in relation to religions and pursued through a range of academic disciplines."[138] He has a keen interest in wisdom as "the most satisfactory overall 'interest' for a theologian," namely "the good shaping of understanding and of life in the midst of the multiple overwhelmings. . . ." Dealing with "the whole ecology of reality before God," such wisdom is a "universal pursuit" enabled by the discipline of theology.[139] Theology has a corresponding "ecology of responsibility" which Ford develops from Rowan Williams: the "celebratory," "critical," and "communicative" dimensions or "styles" of theology embrace the "publics" of faith community, the academy, and society, respectively.[140] That is, theology arises from and addresses the church's concern for its worship before God, its nurture of its people for witness, and its encounters with others — even criticism from outsiders.

III. Theology as Pursuit of Wisdom: Prospectus

Each of these developments in defining theology "practically" makes welcome contributions. Undoubtedly effort to recover theology-as-wisdom is evident. Nevertheless, one has to wonder if there lingers a characteristically "modern" notion of speaking public truth — privileging the detached, dispassionate research ideal of a Western university public, with corresponding critical distance between religious practice and theology, between church and academy. While the inadequacies of the objective orientation to theology with its "cognitive-propositional" view of doctrine must be acknowledged, the subjective, "experiential-expressivist" approach has also been problematic and become passé.

Farley's noble effort to recover theology-as-*habitus* remains within that broad tradition. Subsequent efforts to reform that approach through theology as an "activity" (e.g., Wood) and theology as reflection related to "practices" (e.g., Kelsey) have been fruitful, but even these "cultural-linguistic" approaches — with theology reflecting upon and regulating Christian speech — can remain entrenched in forms of the reflection-action, theory-practice, academy-church divide. So this introductory chapter has developed the dialogue over theology and theological education via narrative form for a reason: theologians have made particular moves in relation to their prior dialogue partners. Several of those moves seem promising. Nevertheless, they are only mid-course corrections on a mistaken pathway, if the narrative indicates that a decisive detour put us in this wandering condition to start with. We will not meander back to wisdom; our quest will be satisfied only if, while appreciating how much we have learned along the way, we reconsider our fundamental direction and rediscover the main path. Core considerations of Christian sanctification and of human beings' relation to God must re-orient us.

At the root of contemporary dialogue on the nature of theology, this chapter's narrative suggests, lies the following tangle: do *sapientia* and *scientia* remain apart as far as the "knowledge" in various versions of "wisdom" is concerned? Specifically, do Western university criteria for what constitutes public knowledge, or what constitutes religious activity, commit people to, at best, indirect encounters with God — and can such knowledge be suitably constitutive of wisdom? How should theology be described if we take truly Christian wisdom as our starting point?

Answering that question is the goal of what follows, a project which this chapter has introduced with a narrative about understandings of "theology." Once theology was sapiential, then strove to be scientific as the very notion of "science" greatly changed; now scientific, theology can at best function semantically for some saints. But is that the same as a sapiential theology? In response, the story has three morals so far.

First, historical judgments about the loss of theology's sapiential character are bound up with theological judgments about what sapiential theology would be, and vice versa. Neither historical nor doctrinal commitments can be naively privileged in construing theology as wisdom.

Second, social location can also dominate how sapiential theology is construed, or even whether one seeks a sapiential understanding of theology at all. Is theology an inescapable enterprise for all people of faith, a particular enterprise for either ecclesiastical or academic professionals, or somehow both? Can theology be both sapiential and scientific? If so, whose science? Whose wisdom?

Third, therefore, theological questions are inescapable, from the start, when seeking to understand what theology is. Attempting to allow for a plurality of starting points — or, what kind of pluralistic prolegomena to allow — is itself a theological decision, tied to certain social locations. Aside from the ecclesiastical-doctrinal question just raised, the most pressing theological questions apparently concern the knowledge of God, the character of human being, and their relation.

Despite the local realities of institutional life, we might step back and seek a more global Christian construal of the pursuit of wisdom. This construal would best be global in two senses — first, in acknowledging a biblical and theological tradition of wisdom that holds treasures for all Christians (hence universally binding in one sense, however complex must be the particularity of its local cultural expressions); second, in accounting for the contexts of Western academic theology as themselves traditions (hence not always richly beneficial to all communities, and not necessarily binding at all points — even for Western theologians).

The recovery of sapiential theology seems tied to a form of *paideia* in which communities of the virtuous are formed, as they envision responding to God's communicative action. If the "house of authority" has so crumbled that divine communicative action and human selves cannot be recovered at all, then wisdom probably lies in ruins. The only rational *habitus* available would concern life in the hallowed halls of the university, with knowledge located solely in the laboratory of critical inquiry.

The present work, though, is not so pessimistic — setting off instead on a quest for the building blocks of "theology" in Christian wisdom, which means taking seriously the biblical admonition to lay no other foundation than Jesus Christ. The three morals above generate three questions that will initially guide inquiry. The first question concerns that "house of authority":

can we still speak about the knowledge of God in a way that acknowledges and identifies prevenient divine action? After all, the various church practices of recent focus all presuppose that somehow the church responds to, and engages with, God therein.

In chapter 2, this first question of divine action is addressed in tandem with a second: in theology as wisdom, would "theology" concern everyone or some particular group? What should be its social location? The goal of chapter 2, an account of Christian "wisdom," has entailments for this second question. Theological interpretation of Scripture will demonstrate that sapiential theology must include not merely a select few, but everyone in communicative action concerning God. Such communicative action is a response enabled by the transforming Holy Spirit, a response of seeking Wisdom in God's Son Jesus Christ, who is the Word that Scripture communicates.

Chapter 3 then places a third question in dialogue with the first: how does theological knowledge relate to "theory" and "practice"? This question surely surfaces once theology is related to the church and doctrine. If theology is defined so that everyone participates via praxis, then does reflection on doctrine lose out so that we cannot lay claim to knowing truth? If so, how can the church speak publicly about God's communicative action?

Chapter 3 faces this challenge. So by the midpoint of the study, tying theology to wisdom will have suggested (1) that the primary social location of theology is what I shall call the every-person "communicative praxis" of the church in the world, and (2) that theology is not so much a discrete practice as the practice-encompassing effort toward virtuous communication concerning God, although (3) like wisdom, theology is a term with multiple uses, able to refer secondarily to a practice of Christian teachers who intensify its doctrinal and critical dimensions. The ensuing theological knowledge, while defined as *sapientia,* still involves truth claims open to "scientific" criticisms.

Theology like wisdom is able to denote both a kind of knowledge and an activity; involving dialogical, communicative action, theology and wisdom can embrace varied audiences for communication and intensities of inquiry. Every effort should be made not to privilege unduly either the "objective" or "subjective," the "theoretical" or "practical," dimensions, indeed to escape the very (modern) terms of these dichotomies. The more objective and theoretical dimension of defining "doctrine" in chapter 3 is balanced by the more subjective and practical-formative dimensions of theology in chapter 2. The payoff for theological education will be an understanding, informed by Christian doctrine, that theology itself must be viewed with reference to educational process. Theology is the development of *phronēsis* (the practical reason, or virtuous judgment, of wisdom) in Christian *paideia.*

Still, learning the virtue to understand God's voice in Scripture should not exclude certain kinds of critical inquiry and public dialogue, which are essential to Christian wisdom. For we must acknowledge that "at the heart of the enormous churchly, curricular, and systematic problem that presently confronts theology is the issue of hermeneutics,"[141] of what uses of Scripture may count as "public." And that is the reason for chapters 4 and 5, which take up the recent move toward "theological interpretation of Scripture." Many in this movement emphasize how wisdom, or the Christian virtues, should determine the Bible's interpretation in theology. Others, if they allow for the virtues at all, limit what theological interpretation may claim publicly about the "meaning" of biblical texts. Moreover, some who advocate theological interpretation happily concede this point, remaining dubious about the possibility of public truth, or about *the* "meaning" of Scripture at all, and locating theological interpretation squarely in the church, according to its interests.[142] The "easy polarizations"[143] of this debate are a synecdoche for the question of theology-as-wisdom: is public *paideia* possible?

Thus chapter 4 will chronicle the movement toward theological interpretation, paralleling chapter 1's narrative regarding the recovery of wisdom in defining theology. In other words, our prime question about knowing God, and the possibility of identifying divine action, is further specified with relation to the interpretation of Christian Scripture.

Chapter 5 then, in parallel to chapters 2 and 3, responds constructively. At this point the interrelated concerns over social location and doctrinal criticism can be refocused from the complementary angle of theological hermeneutics, while learning from prior labors to define Christian wisdom. In the final chapters, we can seek an understanding of *paideia* and the public, of how Christian transformation and critical inquiry can walk together, that is fostered by properly theological interpretation of Scripture. "Figural reading" of the Bible, to be defined and defended with a Christian version of *phronēsis,* will help to capture the possibilities and pitfalls of sapiential theology.

Thus the contribution of this project is to connect two conversations that have hitherto run parallel but stayed apart: the nature of theology has been sought in connection with the virtues of wisdom; meanwhile the place of virtues in the interpretation of Scripture has become important to conversation about theological hermeneutics. Perhaps each would advance with aid from the other: that is my aim. Linking virtue and the voice of God in Scripture, theology is an every person, transforming, communicative praxis, subject to a chastened understanding of public criticism.

CHAPTER 2

Wisdom: Knowing God and Living Virtuously in Communion

Toward the end of the introductory chapter, recent attempts at making theology wise unto practice were surveyed, attempts which have left unclear in what sense theology is itself practical. Is *theologia* (a term used for "theology" when defined by theological criteria) practical as reflection on or for practice, as reflection embedded in a practice like education, or even as a practice itself? A related challenge is David Kelsey's comment about the varieties of Christian wisdom, how its four components (contemplation, discursive reasoning, affection, and action) are weighted and united. An understanding of "wisdom" must therefore be sought that can link "theology" and "practice" appropriately.

Any account of wisdom is inextricably bound up with a social location for theology, and with presuppositions about God, human beings, and their interaction. Whose wisdom? Which theology? In order to address the problem of theology and practice through the questions detailed in the previous chapter, *theologia*, church, and doctrine must eventually be related (in chapter 3). However, to avoid co-opting the term "wisdom" for a "theology" that has already determined its social location and its prolegomena, an extended biblical-theological consideration of wisdom itself is needed. Otherwise, we will continue to correlate theology's first things with whatever epistemological commitments happen to be the current fashion, cloaking such prolegomena in the contemporary language of "wisdom." As this second chapter will demonstrate, however, a truly Christian account of wisdom has plenty that is distinctive to say about the social location of the knowledge of God.

I. Shall Wisdom Be Found?

"Where shall wisdom be found?" asks the Book of Job (28:12), as do many from a postmodern age. Before setting off on a search for wisdom, however, we must consider the propriety of seeking this holy grail. Indeed, "wisdom" may be too popular in our postmodern context, easily covering for any number of glib convictions already held by a knowledgeable elite.[1] Moreover, the Bible's praise of wisdom is ambiguous, and this ambiguity is particularly stark when reading two passages about the tree of life. In Prov. 3, wisdom is an alluring tree of life with fruit that God invites us to savor. On the other hand, Gen. 3 seemingly walls us off from that tree of life for lusting after "wisdom." At this point we might wonder not where wisdom shall be found, but whether it shall be sought at all. Or, perhaps, the ambivalence of these texts indicates that different kinds of "wisdom" entice us, so that the proper question is "What kind of wisdom shall be found?" A fruitful answer to this query might get our search off on the right foot, by clarifying the appropriate destination.

The ambiguity of wisdom in relation to the tree of life[2] is a helpful starting point for several reasons. First, a biblical theology of wisdom can begin in the Old Testament (hereafter OT), rather than quickly skipping to New Testament (NT) material without its canonical context. Second, the tree of life is important for creation theology, appearing in Genesis and in Wisdom texts, as well as for eschatology, appearing in Ezekiel and the Apocalypse. So the project does not fall prey to an exclusive focus upon Christian redemption simply from the start, but takes account of nature in concert with grace. Third, by treating particular texts in canonical context, a model of theological exegesis can be undertaken, the "best practice" of which Parts Two and Three will develop. In connection with the tree of life, there will be postulated neither a particular setting or tradition history for Prov. 3:13-18 or Gen. 2–3, nor a direct literary dialogue between them. Rather, attention will focus upon how each discourse addresses our theological query. Other material from the Christian tradition, particularly regarding Augustine's two cities, will be relevant in addition to the Scriptures themselves. The movement of this section will not simply go from context to context, but will also correspond roughly to a move from theological "discipline" to "discipline." Yet while moving from OT to NT studies, then to historical theology and to constructive synthesis, we must listen carefully *throughout* to how the various texts address our theological query and so, moreover, to how they dialogue with each other.

A. Reading Prov. 3:13-18 within Prov. 1–9

On, then, to wisdom and the tree of life: in fact, according to Prov. 3:18, wisdom *is* a tree of life. This saying supports the larger unit of 3:13-18, lauding the value of wisdom for successful, secure living, and thus enticing the proverbial son to accept the exhortations of surrounding units.[3]

These exhortations resonate with Deuteronomy, with themes such as wearing divine instruction (vv. 3, 22),[4] finding favor with people (v. 4), fearing YHWH (v. 7) and thereby enjoying blessing (or vice versa; e.g., v. 33), plus experiencing divine discipline (vv. 11-12). The point is not that wisdom rivals the Torah, but that wisdom can be lauded on the Torah's terms.[5] This is so because, as we read in vv. 5-7, wisdom is only obtained by receiving it as God's gift: as the text stands, "we should come to the reading of vv. 13-20 already primed with the assumption that human insight comes from and is accountable to the LORD."[6] Such a perspective is certainly hospitable to the fear of YHWH, a dominant notion in Prov. 1–9.

Beginning at 3:13, we read אַשְׁרֵי אָדָם, a phrase that quickly evokes Ps. 1:1 and a hymnic aura. חָכְמָה and תְּבוּנָה are unequivocally extolled in stylistic tandem: in finding them one has divine favor. The harmony between vv. 12-13 and 8:32-36 is unmistakable: the son who listens to Wisdom and keeps her ways will be blessed and find life.

Divine blessing suggests, according to vv. 14-15, that Wisdom possesses incomparable value, greater than jewels or any other object of desire. This judgment regarding Woman Wisdom's surpassing value has echoes in 8:11 and in 31:10.[7] Moreover, personification of Wisdom is evident in v. 16. We are on firm ground, therefore, to take the pronouns of these verses personally: as McKane translates, "she is more profitable than silver, and gives a higher yield than gold. She is more precious than jewels, and nothing you desire bears comparison with her."[8]

Now the surpassing value of Wisdom has a twofold explanation in v. 16, in terms of long life and success. Wisdom is alluring, but properly so. Taking hold of her will bring stability and success (vv. 17-18; compare v. 2), whereas being taken hold of (the word in both 3:18 and 7:13) by the adulteress brings destruction. Wisdom is a trustworthy guide according to v. 17, so that she now adopts YHWH's role (compare v. 6).[9] Rejecting one's own תְּבוּנָה; does not entail rejecting תְּבוּנָה altogether: indeed, to grasp תְּבוּנָה is to grasp YHWH, and vice versa.

Wisdom's value for a stable and successful life is grounded in her involvement with creation. Verse 19 again parallels חָכְמָה and תְּבוּנָה; this time, according to McKane, we should not see in תְּבוּנָה a "colourless synonym," but the tinge of Isa. 40:12-31 regarding YHWH's creative wisdom.[10] The thrust of these verses evokes Prov. 8 once again; here, though, wisdom is instrumental to creation rather than the personified onlooker of ch. 8.[11] The comparison with that chapter could entangle us in a mire beyond our ken, at least for this project, concerning the nature of Wisdom's personification.

For the moment, it can be asserted with Murphy that "one does not have to choose between God and creation in Woman Wisdom, as von Rad does. Ultimately the revelation of creation is the revelation of God."[12] By way of qualification, creation neither simply reveals itself nor nakedly reveals the divine, but rather Wisdom mediates God's presence as he speaks in creation.

The nature of this mediation is contested. R. N. Whybray argued that the point is not bridging a gulf between humanity and a transcendent God, but between the "wisdom tradition" (with its sideways glance outside Yahwistic piety toward other cultures) and Israelite religion.[13] Such an assertion is problematic if allowed to pose an either-or dilemma. However, it points out a both-and relationship between the challenge posed for Israel by her God's transcendence, and the challenge posed by the apparent wisdom which other cultures possessed without allegiance to YHWH. If Wisdom could stand in both these logical gaps at once, then her mediatorial role would be most alluring.

It is not quite the Proverbial view to say that "Wisdom is unknowable for humanity, since humanity does not fully participate in God's creative process."[14] Instead, like God wisdom is both transcendent (or inaccessible) in one sense, and immanent (or accessible) in another.[15] Human limitations do surface in Proverbs, and thus complications arose for an Israelite upon seeing the wisdom of other cultures and religions: how could s/he know that wisdom lay in fearing YHWH if external wisdom seemed appealing? So in Proverbs Wisdom must come near and call out, with a divine invitation for the YHWH-fearer to share her company on the path of life.

Then, and only then, could there be "a similarity, perhaps an actual kinship, between the human thirst for knowledge and the childlike freedom of the Godhead."[16] This mention of childlike freedom is especially rich when we read chs. 3 and 8 together. On one view Wisdom is a wide-eyed child when YHWH creates in ch. 8,[17] but she is certainly a grown woman elsewhere in that chapter and in ch. 3. Like the Proverbial son, then, Wisdom has come of age in YHWH's family: who better for the son to embrace as a life partner? If he does, he can freely delight in discovering the wonders of creation, within an order made safe by YHWH, whom he fears.

It is in this context, therefore, that we may speak of Wisdom as a tree of life. Such life is, like Wisdom herself, a gift rather than a wage, which is not incongruous with the necessity that the son embrace discipline and obey instruction. Wisdom calls (Prov. 1–9), but humans must respond (Prov. 10–31).[18] In fact, the givenness of Wisdom is what invites the human seeking that, by fearing YHWH, will find (compare 8:17 with 1:28-29 and 2:5-6).[19] Yet life is not given quite so certainly as Wisdom; at points YHWH himself takes Wisdom's place in offering security (3:25-26).[20] Indeed, 3:11-12 tacitly acknowledges that divine favor must take various forms.[21] Appropriate qualifications of retribution theology need not be stated ubiquitously in order to pertain; Wisdom offers a life of shalom, but that life may take various forms within YHWH's freedom and the world's complexity.[22] The cosmos has the potential for chaos, though YHWH oversees this deluge to shower blessing upon the wise (3:19-20).

What then is the nature of this life that, all things being equal, will be the fruit of Wisdom? Perhaps physical life only, or perhaps a quality of life as well, is in view; it is true that some obscurity might be poetic and intentional.[23] However, more may be said: given the context, both length of days (v. 16a) and quality of life (vv. 16b-17) are apparently involved. Yet should the quality of life be seen exclusively in terms of the here-and-now?

External parallels only complicate the matter,[24] while the immediate context of Proverbs should be more helpful anyway. Unfortunately, no additional mentions of the tree of life occur in Prov. 1–9. In 13:12, the tree of life is connected to fulfilled desire; in 15:4, a soothing tongue is a tree of life, in contrast to a perverse tongue that crushes the spirit. Both have in view a quality of life on this present earth. In 11:30, the situation is more ambiguous, with difficulties in translation and with 11:7 apparently addressing the afterlife of the wicked; still, the surrounding verses seemingly relate to the present earthly order.

Thus we return focus to the immediate context, which does address the quality of earthly life. Proverbs 3:18 can certainly have a share in whatever hints or ambiguities exist throughout the book about the ultimate recompense for wisdom or folly, for righteousness or wickedness. In this way such life-giving texts are allowed to offer possibilities "by remaining vague as to the ways in which morality is better."[25] Nevertheless, we must not leave unsaid what the text does say: that Wisdom offers a successful and secure life here-and-now, even if the modes and manifestations of success and security might vary. This Wisdom clings to YHWH, albeit somehow connected as well with what is cosmically consistent, with what would be successful even for other cultures (though this goes largely unsaid).

B. Reading Prov. 3:13-18 within the OT

Strictly speaking, this "tree of life" is found canonically only in Proverbs, in Gen. 2–3, and in the NT Apocalypse (2:7; 22:2, 14, 19). Nonetheless, the core image springs up elsewhere: in Ezek. 31, for example, where the glory of Assyria is portrayed as that of a well-watered Lebanon cedar, its majesty evoking jealousy even from the trees in the Garden of Eden. The restored temple of Ezek. 40–48 relates to a river banked by trees in ch. 47, a vision that certainly underlies the hope of the Apocalypse. Barred from the Edenic tree in the Pentateuch, and awaiting the new Jerusalem in the Prophets, we might be tempted to defer such flourishing to the eschaton. Yet the Writings will not allow this: we are bidden, not forbidden, to eat of the tree, via the path of Wisdom in Proverbs, via the path of Torah in Ps. 1:2-3. It is popular to relegate the convergence of these paths — Law and Wisdom (e.g., in Deut. 4:6) — to the later post-exilic Yahwism of writers like Ben Sira. But whatever the historical location of their convergence (and assumptions behind any proposed consensus are vulnerable to challenge), its theological geography is more significant.

The OT's growing prominence of Torah should not displace creation as revelation, "for the wisdom used by God in creating and sustaining the world now resides in nature and the text of the Torah (cf. Psalm 19)."[26] However, understanding the revelation of creation seems quite problematic: if we are barred from Eden, then is it not a hubris, a "leaning on our own understanding" (Prov. 3:5), to seek wisdom in the created order? Would not the Torah underscore this? To answer "what kind of 'wisdom' shall be found?" while facing the angel's flaming sword requires us now to read Gen. 2–3. Can we really eat from the tree of life via wisdom, or is seeking "wisdom" what got us expelled from Eden in the first place?

To start with, the mythical, sapiential, and salvation-historical cast of the Genesis narrative should be noted. Acknowledging each of these elements is not unfaithful to Scripture (John of the Apocalypse authorizes such a reading!),[27] although the word "myth" is hardly useful given its endlessly competing and confusing definitions in relation to "history." At any rate, acknowledging literary complexity does not entail denying that historical claims are made by this unique text. Rather, its learned use of "mythical" themes characterizes sapiential literature.[28] Indeed, here sapiential motifs — such as knowing good and evil, the serpent's cunning, the rivers[29] — and vocabulary (עָרוּם) are clearly present. Thus we encounter Everyperson in this story, while the classic sequence of salvation history is also apparent: "God's initiative in giving, categorical precept, rebellion, punishment, mercy, and then the continuation of history."[30] Israel's covenant story of being given a task and blessing, but then falling into a curse, is Adam's story, and vice versa: the Gen. 2–3 account is both "paradigmatic" and "prototypical."[31]

Many readings of Gen. 2–3 occur in layers, so that 2:9 and 3:22-24 are not assumed to cohere in how they depict the tree of life. For instance, Karl Jaros thinks that "während nach dem vorjahwistischen Text von Gen 2–3 der Mensch die Früchte des heiligen Baumes gegessen und ein Leben ewiger Jugend verspielt hat, differenziert J: Er redet von zwei Bäumen, dem Lebens- und dem Erkenntnisbaum." Thus for "J," humanity ate from the tree of knowledge, seeking total autonomy but experiencing powerlessness instead. If s/he had eaten from the tree of life, a total break with YHWH would have occurred, resulting in our self-destruction. Being barred from immortality is for our own good. The snake deceived the woman first, because Israelite women were more vulnerable to the wiles of the Canaanite fruit-bearing cults.[32]

The snake functions quite differently for Paul Kübel. He discusses the snake's shedding its skin for rejuvenation, in connection with the nakedness of the first humans. Unlike other animals, the snake was clever not merely in its ability to speak and to tempt, but also in its ability to stay forever young. This obviously puts the עָרוֹם־עָרוּם wording in a new light:

- Die Schlange ist "klug" im Reden.
- Es ist "klug" von der Schlange, sich verjüngen zu können.
- Die Schlange ist "nackt", damit sie ihre Haut abstreifen und sich so verjüngen kann.[33]

The tree that deceived our ancestors would then be, in part, the tree of life; they fell for the prospect of rejuvenation, of ongoing youth. Kübel thinks that the literary unity of Gen. 2–3 cannot be maintained this way, for such a view runs up 2:16-17 against 3:22: had they eaten from the tree of life or not? Thus what to do with the final, canonical text would get complicated.[34]

But that is the text we have, and its layers are very difficult to peel apart. So how, according to the person(s) responsible for the text as it stands, should the story be read? First, let us identify the serpent. Relating it to Baal and the Canaanite fertility cults is a popular move, but YHWH's creation of the serpent makes that direct association unlikely.[35] Divination (Deut. 18:10) is another explanation,[36] but does not seem very pertinent to the story. Or the language could be symbolic regarding what we know as the devil.[37] The most to be said for certain is that among all animals the serpent would be the archetypical unclean enemy of God.[38] Moreover, the עָרוֹם־עָרוּם wordplay is intriguing. Perhaps we could posit, not that Adam and Eve were duped into eating from the tree of life and securing immortality (to the contradiction of 3:22), but that they sought a rejuvenated life the wrong way, via the wrong tree.

So, secondly, what is that other tree, the tree of the knowledge of good and evil? Unlike the tree of life, this tree is without parallel, inside or outside the OT.[39] Various views are proffered, including sexual awareness, comprehensive knowledge, cultural knowledge, wisdom (taken negatively), and moral autonomy. The possibility cannot immediately be dismissed that wisdom, prized so highly in Prov. 3, is here condemned. When this "fall" is juxtaposed to that of Ezek. 28 (esp. vv. 6, 17-19), but also to the Torah's redeeming role (Ps. 19:7-10), the notion of trumping תְּבוּנָה with Torah seems plausible to many. The Yahwist is accused of driving "a wedge deep into the heart of wisdom," "splitting knowledge from life with the ax of the law," stressing "the primacy of law over wisdom, of community over material blessing or beauty."[40]

Other considerations, however, spare the Yahwist's tree from this ax. First, note the other OT instances of knowing-good-and-evil: Deut. 1:39; 2 Sam. 14:17, 19:35; 1 Kgs. 3:9; Isa. 7:15-16. In each instance, the accountability of authority, or authorization for moral judgment, is at issue. Undoubtedly this motif is closely related to wisdom, but moral autonomy rather than wisdom is the forbidden fruit. Second, this interpretation is confirmed by the woman's attempted autonomy implied in aping God: she "saw" that the food was "good," she "gave" to her husband, she "said," etc.[41] Then it may be noted that the first humans sought to be "like" God in order not to be under God.

Therefore, a third query concerns the relation of this autonomy to life and death. In a sense, of course, the tempter spoke truth: the half-truth was that humans now wield a sort of independence over their conduct, and that the first humans did not drop dead on the spot. Our dying is ambiguous, complex even in its telling. Independence, however, is a death-sentence, incompatible with life: the angel wields the sword of God's judgment for our own good, as Genesis soon testifies. Sin, like the Proverbial adulteress, is now a predator lying in wait for us (Gen. 4:7).[42] The irony of Balaam's later encounter with the sword-wielding angel should not be lost: the person with eyes now open can do nothing but follow divine command.[43]

Moreover, it is scary to read the Gen. 11 story of Babel and today's newspapers in the same sitting. Why is autonomy incompatible with life? Because God's provision is despised: now ungrateful humanity does not enjoy the garden's unbroken communion with God, or even communication with each other. Yet according to the prophets, the tree of life still exists, and not without reason! The primal "covenant" is followed by Israel's covenant; constantly renewed life, by which to enjoy the garden and all its gifts, was not for the taking, but is for the receiving. Much of the imagery in 3:22-24, where the angel guards the way to the tree of life, is connected to Israel's sanctuaries;[44] fearing YHWH is the approach to life.

Now many have thought that the tree of life granted immortality upon one taste; so Adam and Eve obviously had not partaken, whether or not they were permitted to do so. It is alleged that our forebears reached for the tree of life only after they were fallen; apparent confirmation of this comes from the גַּם of 3:22, taken as "also."[45] Yet there is good reason to think otherwise, to think that God's worry was their eating "again" from the tree of life, which had already been their sustenance. The narrative never proscribes eating from the tree, and does regard immortality (though not in the Greek sense) as the graced state from which Adam and Eve fell. The clause in 2:16 implies, in fact, that they would have eaten from the tree of life; moreover, the text never even hints that immortality would be permanently secured upon one taste.[46] To see their eating from the life-giving tree as periodic is consistent with other parallels,[47] and with the symbol's use in the Apocalypse. Communion with God is "the inexhaustible source of life." This is why there were two trees in the midst of the garden, and without contradiction between 2:9 and 3:3. Not only does the language allow it, the symbolic usage demands it: one cannot have life and autonomy both.[48] Doubting the goodness of divine provision means rejecting the life that God offers; autonomy is alluring, but alienating and deadly.

So, finally, where does wisdom fit into this narrative, if not condemned in itself? What about the serpent's cunning, and the human desire for wisdom that made autonomy so alluring? Does not seeking wisdom in creation mean trying to be like God, thereby breeding autonomy? Surely wisdom is that behind which sin crouches; can Woman Wisdom really clothe herself in garb distinct from that of the alluring adulteress? In the Genesis narrative, does seeking wisdom mean spurning Wisdom?

The answer is to put scare quotes around some uses of the word "wisdom," uses of the term for a purely instrumental knowledge set free from God. Vocabulary usage, while notoriously open to abuse, gives us one way into the current subject. The דַּעַת disparaged by Gen. 2–3 is an autonomous knowledge, related but not equivalent to wisdom. Now two other terms require treatment: the serpent was עָרוּם, and the woman desired the fruit for becoming שָׂכֵל.

Concerning the former, some offer no condemnation, thinking the word in this context to offer a neutral designation for the clever prudence of the serpent's approach;[49] others find in it "a cleverness that is opposed to the works of God."[50] The term appears nowhere else in Genesis; in Job (5:12; 15:5) its sense is pejorative, of people whose machinations God easily thwarts. All its positive uses — and they are substantial — appear in Proverbs. It could be that uses of עָרוּם are purely instrumental, with its moral assessment defined by the propriety of the end being sought in a particular context. An additional implication, though, could be that successful ends may not be sought independently of God; Job accords with this, and Proverbs would too if the fear of YHWH envelops the entirety of its wisdom. Our Lord enjoined us to be as shrewd as snakes, as innocent as doves (Matt. 10:16).

Accordingly, what should one make of the woman's desiring to be שָׂכֶל? The idea is, again, an instrumental one: "effective knowledge," if you like, "the kind of wisdom that leads to, among other things, prosperity and happiness."[51] At stake is "the way humans acquire wisdom," whether they acknowledge God its giver.[52] Additionally, however, the end is subtly perverted by a means independent of God: "the tree represents a form of intellectual capital that can function in self-serving ways, depending on the aim of the wielder of wisdom," who ought not seek a prosperity equated with "mastering life." The serpent presented the tree of knowledge *as* the tree of life.[53]

So, where does our quest for the appropriate kind of wisdom stand? The bridge between Prov. 3 and Gen. 2–3 is left with two admittedly brittle planks. Must the Torah master wisdom? And must we beware when wisdom offers life, lest we be seduced into mastering our selves?

The patriarchal narratives tell of blessing for pre-Torah obedience, upon listening to God's voice, and of the curse for cunning that schemes apart from God's giving.[54] Moreover, Ps. 19 lodges both the revelation of creation and the revelation of Torah in the speaking of the same God. These are steps in the right direction; does the rest of the canon further strengthen the planks on which we can stand?

C. Reading Prov. 3:13-18 with the NT

In the NT, the tree of life appears in Paradise, in the new Jerusalem. Its healing leaves sustain the saints as they enjoy endless Edenic blessing, basking in the light of God's presence. Fruit from the Proverbial tree of life grants long days of secure, flourishing temporal existence. Fruit from the prophetic/apocalyptic tree of life grants immortality — someday; eating its fruit is deferred. These differences not only highlight the tree's symbolic usage, but also raise the question: can these gifts of God be envisioned together? Indeed, at first glance the NT replaces Woman Wisdom with Jesus Christ, and her offer of a long, lovely life with an eternity expected only after suffering. Moreover, the "wisdom" of this world is subject to Paul's unrelenting critique, lest it supplant Jesus Christ (e.g., 1 Cor. 1:18–2:16); meanwhile, through creation God says little, barely enough to condemn (e.g., Rom. 1:18-32; 2:14-16).

This dimension of NT teaching should not be ignored, but neither should it be overemphasized, which post-Reformation Protestants have tended to do. After all, Paul (for example) does incorporate prudence into his ethics, as his prayers and the *Haustafeln* testify.[55] Granted, this is practical reason patterned on Christ and enabled by the Spirit; still, it is not wholly unconnected to secular virtue and vice (e.g., 1 Cor. 5:1; also 2 Pet. 1:5-11). As for its Christ- and Spirit-centeredness, that might be the Proverbial refrain "fear YHWH" transposed into a higher key.

And wisdom is certainly interwoven with life in the Book of James. There the vocabulary of blessing appears (cf. Prov. 3:13, 33). There the theme of trusting God wholeheartedly, refusing to be dubious and lean on one's own understanding, also appears (cf. Prov. 3:5-8). There wisdom triumphs over desire (cf. Prov. 3:14-15). There wise people are known by lives of good deeds, particularly by their uses of words and wealth (cf. Prov. 3:9-10). They are generous when able to help their neighbors; they are not merely well-wishers (cf. Prov. 3:27-28). Nor do they plot against their neighbors. They do not quarrel and fight with them out of self-interest (cf. Prov. 3:29-30). They do not envy the violent/rich (cf. Prov. 3:31-32), upon whom the Lord's curse rests (cf. Prov. 3:33-35).

Whether or not James and Prov. 3 are literarily related, surely they are theologically. Proverbial reason is here retained by the NT. In James we glimpse the reality of deferred "life" benefits, the fact that seeking those benefits wisely sometimes means waiting, and always means planning in subjection to God's freedom. James' earthly "wisdom" is the selfish, unfaithful autonomy condemned in Genesis; James' heavenly wisdom has room for Proverbs' tree of life. Living in a hostile society, the NT writers emphasized shalom with God, and patience for some of its benefits. Looking at the created order, in a society (that was supposed to be) ordered by God, the OT Wisdom writers emphasized that shalom with God should bring the benefits of life. These words must be read together; both instruct us that our Lord is merciful, but sometimes we will need the patience of Job (Jas. 5:11).

D. Reading Prov 3:13-18 in the City of God

Briefly, then, we glance at the communities that have read these wisdom texts as Scripture. After Prov. 3, as already noted, Judaism (which is, at points, an anachronism) would increasingly equate wisdom with the Torah, and the penchant for seeking life — survival, even — in the Torah cannot be unrelated to Israel's tragic exilic and post-exilic history.[56] Wisdom thus became increasingly particular, and when this coupled with the expectation that the Messiah would teach final wisdom, a possible pattern for NT Christology emerged.[57] Indeed, Christian tradition would allegorize the tree of life as the cross of Christ, following the irony of an antitypical tree of life, in the bronze serpent of Num. 21 and 2 Kgs. 18.[58]

Augustine, in Book XIII of *City of God,* saw Christ as the tree of life, amidst his discussion of divine Wisdom in the work of creation. He depicts the two cities "as being defined by two loves which determine the kind of wisdom possible to both cities."[59] His own life story vividly bears this out, especially as told in *Confessions* using Eden's two trees: the pear tree (the tree of the knowledge of good and evil) in Book II, and the fig tree (the tree of life) in Book VIII: "At the pear tree Augustine came to an experiential knowledge of good and evil; under the fig tree, he received the power to obey what he took to be the command of God. . . ." Throughout each following set of five books (III-VII, IX-XIII), "the theme of the frustrated knowledge of God or the satisfied knowledge of God is pervasive. . . ."[60] Thus did Augustine, that great champion of the prototypical fall saddling us with original sin, recognize its paradigmatic significance for Everyperson struggling to know God: lust and ignorance are paired against continence and knowledge.[61]

Shall wisdom, therefore, be found for a biblical *theologia?* What exactly are we looking for, and where shall we find her? The winding canonical road has begun to point in a definite direction. First, it must be emphasized that wisdom involves divine communication, God's speaking presence.[62] "The metaphor cluster of divine word was very significant in the wisdom tradition," and wisdom's emphasis on proper human speech analogizes this.[63] Small wonder, then, that creation, the Torah, and the Christ all relate to, and become identified with, wisdom: they are each God's words.

The second and corresponding truth is that the Creator's language "is embodied and disseminated by the community."[64] The intriguing similarities between case law and proverbial sayings, between apodictic law and instruction, indeed between Deuteronomy and Proverbs, make sense in this light.[65] So does the rapprochement between the created order and law, for "knowledge of the world and knowledge of God were not sharply differentiated in wisdom's epistemology."[66] The Words of wisdom are heard and spoken in a social order. Furthermore, "die Torah ruht nicht in sich selbst, auch nicht bloß auf göttlicher Anordnung. Sie verweist auf den Gott, der für Israel da sein will."[67]

This is not to dump Wisdom literature and other OT literature into one large cauldron, stirring them into a thoroughly homogeneous mixture. However, it is, in the third place, to make an argument about the fear of YHWH and the center of Wisdom literature, an argument that will return the several cauldrons to one table. In the past, there was assumed to exist a wisdom institution, a house of sages if you will, in Israel. The many scholars who take this line usually put creation at the center of wisdom's distinct theology, and then try to organize the material around anthropology, cosmology, theodicy, or a dialectic between anthropology and cosmology.[68] Theological particularities having to do with Israel's salvation history, and the rest of the OT, are seen as post-exilic Johnny-come-lately's to Wisdom theology. On that reading, Wisdom influence upon other OT texts manifests not so much common ground, as those texts' later arrival on the Yahwistic scene.

Now the present work cannot deconstruct this reconstructed history in one fell swoop, nor is that necessary. What *is* necessary is reclaiming the canonical common ground, however the historical development of its topography is explained. The sapiential literature displays "an approach to reality which was shared by all Israelites in varying degrees," and this approach was "not alien to Yahwism" for the average Israelite.[69] In days to come, more scholars may join the recent agnosticism or even antagonism toward the existence of a "Wisdom tradition" and its peculiar preoccupation with creation. They may decide that "God's acts as a national God are what impose an obligation on Israel, but it is his role as Creator and controller of destinies which must influence the actions of the individual."[70] Both these ethical contexts, however, are marked by a history of salvation and divine speech.

Thus wisdom gives the fear of YHWH, a seemingly cultic notion, "a strong psychological character."[71]

Admittedly, this could generate another version of the perceived conflict between Wisdom and other OT literature, namely between the corporate and the personal. However, if "character" is taken to be the central or unifying theme of Wisdom literature, yet the communal and cosmic ethos of its formation is recognized,[72] then perhaps canonical wisdom will become an area of fruitful tensions instead of fragmented theologies. For, additionally, the Christian canon sees in Jesus Christ both God's acting for Israel and God's transforming persons worldwide; in him lies the fulfillment of their reciprocal obligations. He is God's final Word of Wisdom to which the Law and Prophets point.

So far, then, a threefold assertion: wisdom involves (1) divine communication, ordered in various forms, (2) appropriated in a community for its people to enjoy life (3) as they are characterized by fearing YHWH. Now a fourth angle: what about the connection between wisdom, the order of creation, and worldly success? For the OT incorporates instrumental wisdom material from outside Israel. Yet certainly the OT intends for such wisdom to involve a moral, even theological, dimension, and in Proverbs not just Genesis; the wisdom in creation may not involve the historical particularity of revelation, but does come as God's speaking presence (e.g., "the heavens declare the glory of God"): it is not simply there for the taking.

Accordingly, we should probably seek a vocabulary by which to describe particular aspects of wise persons, related to the complex ways the word "wisdom" can be generally used. Sometimes a skill or craft that secures success is in view, which has often been designated by *technē* since Aristotle. Other times *phronēsis,* Aristotle's higher-order instrumental virtue of practical reason, is meant. The prudent person knows what to do — how to regulate other virtues, criteria, and skills in a situation — for making moral judgments.[73] But the OT can use similar vocabulary for independently achieving an evil end (its closest word/concept, עָרוּם, is used for both the crafty, vicious snake and the prudent human, in a sense), and this encourages us to define Christian *phronēsis* very carefully later on. The instrumental dimension of "wisdom" should make readers of Gen. 2–3 uneasy; achieving evil ends, or good ends by purely human means, makes "wisdom" unworthy of the name. The Christian story and doctrine of the fall lends itself to a healthy suspicion of sophistry replacing wisdom, of all knowledge turning scientific for the merely technical utility pursued on behalf of human autonomy.

Proverbs too lauds a wisdom of character, character that reveres YHWH in response to the welcoming divine speech. Eventually I will call this biblical knowledge of God *sapientia,* in line with Christian tradition and with its manifold character, since *phronēsis* is indispensable therein. For the moment, however, *sophia* — Aristotle's term for the unchanging ultimate, but a term which the NT connects to Jesus Christ — will be the focus.

Now the Proverbial problem is that "as a credit to their pedagogical ingenuity, the sages successfully lodge the rigors of wisdom within an ethic of self-fulfillment."[74] Wisdom in Proverbs seems to embrace ultimately what Christians will mean by *sophia* (in connection with fearing the Lord), but *phronēsis* and even *technē* are incorporated as well, their usefulness readily acknowledged. So back to the two fragile planks in the bridge between Proverbs and Genesis: it seems possible for Proverbial *phronēsis* and *technē* to grant a measure of success (1) apart from the Torah and (2) via independent human agency. Would the urgency of Christian *sophia* be minimized thereby?

No, the following assertions modify that portrayal. For one, blurred boundaries between moral virtues and skills for success are a potential danger of misconstruing wisdom, but are not positively constitutive of the concept. True, much popular literature is currently guilty of exactly that dangerous misconstrual. William Brown adduces the works of Stephen Covey such as *Seven Habits of Highly Effective People* to highlight our cultural confusion between virtue and instrumental skills;[75] hence the canonical significance of Gen. 2–3. Still, this confusion is not a necessary entailment of appealing to wisdom; hence the canonical significance of Prov. 3.

Likewise, we are often guilty of misconstruing success. For Proverbs success means, preeminently, shalom; riches, honor, physical security, family, and the like are derivative. As was asserted much earlier, Proverbial "life" remains ambiguous about the particular shape it will take for a wise person. That means, moreover, acknowledging God's sovereign freedom to grant life rather than assuming an automatic, bluntly causal, domino effect between wisdom and success. "Life" is a gift, and wisdom has its limits; hence the Wisdom literature's tension over the questions "Does retribution really work?" and "Is it really possible for human understanding to discover the orderly purpose of God in the universe?"[76] Wisdom listens in response to God's self-given presence, yet realizes that such presence is (in the words of Samuel Terrien's famous title) "elusive." Therefore, canonical wisdom hears other diverse wisdom voices "within the traditional, *revealed* faith of the Torah."[77] If Gen. 2–3 wields an ax against worldly wisdom's tree of knowledge-and-life, then Proverbs does too.

E. But What About the City of Humanity?

So *technē* and *phronēsis* may take up with *sophia* wherever in the world wisdom is found. "Life" has no guarantees, but the One who graciously gives wisdom thereby gives true shalom to those who fear God. Genesis and Proverbs both acknowledge mere *technē* and also *phronēsis*, but deny them the power to confer life fully upon their autonomous users.

Nevertheless, the city of humanity builds a pretty tall tower. The derivative elements of life apparently do follow around *technē* and *phronēsis*. The created order speaks volumes to those who cannot or will not identify the voice. What should be made of that: a natural theology or ethic?

Not quite: many agree that OT wisdom is not natural theology.[78] Oliver

O'Donovan helps us to understand that there is an "ontological" ground for a natural ethic, an "objective order to which the moral life can respond": in Christ's resurrection God affirms the created order of which Wisdom speaks. Alternatively, "the *epistemological* programme for an ethic that is 'natural', in the sense that its contents are simply known to all, has to face dauntingly high barriers."[79] The outworking of this ontological-epistemological distinction accords remarkably with the surrounding context of Prov. 3:13-18. In line with Prov. 3:19-20, we can see the utility of non-Yahwistic *technē* and *phronēsis:*

> The universe, though fractured and broken, displays the fact that its brokenness is the brokenness of order and not merely of unordered chaos. Thus it remains accessible to knowledge in part. It requires no revelation to observe the various forms of generic and teleological order which belong to it. An unbeliever or a non-christian culture does not have to be ignorant about the structure of the family, the virtue of mercy, the vice of cowardice, or the duty of justice. Nor does such a one have to fail entirely to respond to this knowledge in action, disposition or institution.[80]

Yet, in line with Prov. 3:5-12, that utility has limitations: "Knowledge of the moral order is a grasp of the total shape in which, if anything is lacking, everything is lacking."[81] Whether such a grasp could accompany faith in YHWH "that is not explicitly related to a particular historical revelation of God"[82] is an important question, but a slightly different one (and beyond the scope of the present project). At minimum it must be noted that biblical virtue is enjoined with awareness of God's judgment, with a sense of (redemptive) history.[83]

At this juncture, enough has been said to maintain the propriety of finding wisdom for theology, and to mark off the boundaries and pitfalls of that quest. But we have scarcely reached the end of the road: how might biblical, Christian wisdom be defining for the nature of theology? Hence the next leg of the journey looks at the relation of *sophia,* and knowledge of God, to the formation of Christian virtue and *phronēsis.* That means turning from a focus upon the Old Covenant story to fix our eyes upon Jesus Christ. For the New Covenant involves the Word of *sophia* becoming flesh, and then pouring out the Spirit of Wisdom upon all flesh, so that the new humanity is transformed, learning a *phronēsis* patterned after Christ.

II. Where Shall Wisdom Be Found? Virtue and Knowledge of God

Already in Gen. 3 surfaced a theme that recurs throughout Scripture: skepticism concerning human wisdom. Part of Eve's seduction by the serpent was her longing for a creaturely wisdom (Gen. 3:6). Rather than being told by God what was good and evil, she would decide as much herself (or so the serpent falsely advertised). Thus the creation and fall narratives presage a later theme: bearing God's image means obeying and discovering, not deciding good and evil for oneself. The latter was all too tempting for the prototypical humans, and now affords manifold temptations for the rest of us. Accordingly, we cannot yet ascribe to renewed humanity the scope of opportunity, and the wisdom of stewardship, that was enjoyed before the fall.

Yet there is an affirmation of post-fall cosmos rather than mere chaos, and a related affirmation of prudence's life-giving value. The caution of Gen. 3 is that such prudence should be exercised by those who serve the true God of the living. The NT claims that this God is now known and served through the ultimately revealed Wisdom, Jesus Christ, a Wisdom granted by the Holy Spirit. Moreover, the NT claims that the power to be wise, and the paradigm for exercising wisdom, are found in Christ and the Spirit, not in the Torah which they fulfill. How then does wisdom factor into the formation of virtue via the knowledge of God? Or, since wisdom shall be found, where and how?

A. The Wise Christ

Christians confess that the fulfillment of OT hope was inaugurated at our Lord's first advent. The New Covenant texts of the OT were crucial to the early Christians' understanding of Jesus, a fact readily apparent from their frequent appearances in the NT. Jesus' fulfillment of the OT legitimated his role as teacher of the Torah. He fulfilled its requirements as the faithful son that Israel never was, and he also knew its core (Matt. 23) and its far-reaching significance (Matt. 5–7). Therefore, Jesus the Christ embodied Wisdom and taught a restful wisdom, in contrast to the burdensome wisdom of proto-rabbinic Torah observance (Matt. 11:25-30; note the contrast to Rom. 2:20). Christians are now aware that this contrast between rest and burden must be applied very cautiously, certainly not to "Judaism" *per se*, which would be an anachronism in any case.

Nevertheless, whatever its exact nature and extent,[84] Wisdom Christology overturned Israel's self-understanding in terms of the Torah. Her national identity, as manifest in Deut. 4:5-6 for example, was wrapped up in Torah observance; this pattern continued into the days of early Christianity and beyond. The Christ, however, was wise and understanding as Israel never was; therefore he could identify with and deliver her from exile. He redefined, in his person and word, how to be wise and understanding.[85]

1 Corinthians 1–2 is crucial in this regard. There Paul makes both claims: Christ *is* our God-given wisdom (1:30), and Christ *enables* us to become wise as we have his mind by the Spirit (2:7-16). These claims, here and also in Colossians, express the OT critique of human "wisdom" against new dangers such as Hellenistic philosophy, particularly with an ascetic bent. Thus Paul seems ambivalent about "wisdom" on the whole, and uses σοφία negatively in particular.[86] Aristotle had used σοφία of a "combination of Intelligence and Scientific Knowledge . . . a consummated knowledge of the most exalted objects."[87] The Corinthians, centuries later, were infatuated with thinking creation apart from Christ, and instead of him were exalting the human "wisdom" they sought.

This infatuation betrayed a lack of understanding about the working of God's power. Greek "wisdom," ultimately unlike Jewish and Christian, was a possession of a heroic few; Greeks aspired to the necessary recollection of the divine from within. The self-giving action of Jesus Christ would seem foolish in that light, and the judgment which his action implied upon the world would seem preposterous.[88] In the New Covenant wisdom is not just communal, but cruciform as well; therefore wisdom is a gift of God to people who have lived foolishly together and would never find it on their own.

So Paul, having Isa. 11:2 in the background along with Jesus' self-understanding, must reveal the eschatological mystery of Christ by the Spirit.[89] True wisdom is mediated by revelation, an orientation that also underlies the Gospels.[90] Biblical wisdom's personal dimension in the New Covenant answers the human problem of which Israel's failure in the Old Covenant was one manifestation. This answer is first Christocentric; then, as we shall soon see, the NT corporate ethos incorporates the Holy Spirit and a distinctive communal praxis as well. But pneumatology and ecclesiology follow Christology, lest they authorize merely effective, autonomous rhetorical strategies for spirituality. For Christian sanctification is not merely pneumatic but cruciform.

B. The Spirit of Wisdom

To advance our understanding of NT wisdom, that pneumatology must now be developed further. If the Christ fulfills the Torah as the embodiment of wisdom for us, then the Spirit also fulfills the Torah, as the enablement for wisdom.

Space prevents a detailed consideration of this theme in the Pauline corpus, with all the complexity added by Paul's view of the Torah in particular. Clearly, in Gal. 5 and Rom. 6–8, Paul opposes walking by, or being led by, the Spirit to being led by the Torah. The latter is enslaving, the former liberating; the latter is fleshly, the former fruitful. The contexts are recognizably similar to that of Ps. 143:10: at stake is how the believer shall be instructed to render covenant obedience to God. In my view, Paul's polemic is not against the good Torah *per se*, but against its (mis)use in the new epoch after Christ. After Israel's Old Covenant failure, her promised renewal would be through a New Covenant, not another attempt at the Old. Torah observance as the covenant rule would now be inimical to the gospel of Jesus Christ, both in walling off Jew from Gentile and in walling off covenanters from the Spirit's mediation of God's presence — the fulfillment of the New Covenant that Israel should have anticipated all along. As Scripture the Torah remains a spiritually profitable manifestation of the divine character and will. But, as the newly prominent covenant mediator of the divine presence, the Holy Spirit is the persistent source of discernment or understanding that Paul prays for his people.

In James, despite a certain prominence of the Torah, deeds that demonstrate wisdom spring from divinely-enabled virtues (3:13-18), and that divine enablement (at least implicitly) could involve the Spirit (4:5; who seems to have, moreover, a corollary in wisdom). Good deeds are only sufficient as opportunities to embody wisdom (1:2-4; 2:14-26; 3:13-18), and that wisdom is a matter of grace received in faith (1:5-8; 3:17; 4:6-10).

In the NT teaching about the Torah as related to wisdom, then, there is a basically harmonious, albeit tense at points, development. The New Covenant's inauguration means that the Torah is both replaced and fulfilled by the Spirit (Rom. 6–8, especially 8:4): replaced as an identity marker and mode of knowing God; fulfilled, in terms of its ethical end, by Spirit-led obedience. The Spirit forms persons and communities of "righteousness, joy, and peace" (Rom. 14:17): thus (negatively) they do not transgress the Torah's prohibitions, and (positively) they obey the Torah of Christ-like character.

Good and evil are still distinguished partially on the basis of divine command. God does value human discovery and decisions in the created world; doing good, however, must be empowered by the Spirit, and knowing the good to do involves mostly character-concerned exhortations that inculcate virtue. Now more specifically to the moral of the story: how does prudence — the Old Covenant way of knowing the good to do, in relation to God's commands — pertain in the New Covenant?

(1) The Need for Practical Reason

Further consideration of the Torah-Spirit relation in the NT suggests that the pattern of prudence[91] does still hold for the New Covenant, albeit in a somewhat modified form. Two arguments may be adduced here to support this contention, before exploring practical reason itself.

The first argument is a material one: "the prudential ethics of the wisdom traditions has its New Testament counterpart in the *Haustafeln* and the Epistle of James."[92] Already it was noted that James develops wisdom somewhat analogously to the OT. Wisdom concerns living righteously, forming in believers the character to obey God. So, for instance, prudence addresses justice (Jas. 1–2), speech (Jas. 3), and economics (Jas. 4–5). Upon moving to Paul, there we also discover paraenesis that is roughly analogous to wisdom, focused on the formation and embodiment of godly character in relationships.

A second, formal, argument supports New Covenant prudence as well: the NT enjoins its development. Upon discovering the general, virtue-oriented character of New Covenant stipulations, the need for practical reason is already established: how else, unless human choosing were to play no appreciable role due to the Spirit, shall one determine how to embody these stipulations? Indeed, Old Covenant prudence is located precisely at this point: sometimes one response is called for, sometimes another (for example, Prov. 26:4-5; compare Gal. 6:2-5), and the moral agent must decide.[93] Plus prudence can draw support not only from need, but also from command. Two passages will suffice for this: Rom. 12:2 urges us to δοκιμάζω the will of God, and Eph. 5 instructs us to walk as wise (5:15), understanding what the Lord's will is (5:17), and thus capitalizing on our moments of opportunity (5:16).

Yet one might argue that the NT material on practical reason is fairly limited, while worries over worldly "wisdom" are extensive. In response, it should be noted that the critique of worldly "wisdom" merely echoes the OT critique of same[94] — or sometimes quotes it — in a Christocentric key. Additionally, wisdom vocabulary actually frequents the NT. Granted, σοφία (the usual equivalent of חָכְמָה)[95] is downplayed or avoided, for reasons mentioned previously. Still, the σύνεσις family (often related to the בין family in the LXX), and "knowledge" vocabulary, abounds; the need for judgment or discernment (δοκιμάζω, αἴσθησις) is acknowledged. Finally, the NT does emphasize the character of wisdom as a gift, not received (in the first instance) by the fear of God in Torah observance but by the Spirit and prayer. Admittedly there is a measure of discontinuity between Old and New on this point, but this discontinuity simply regards the Holy Spirit's New Covenant newness which the Torah anticipated.

(2) The Nature of Practical Reason

From an OT perspective, prudence is being so oriented toward the covenant community and the created order, that one has good sense about how to live and the impetus to live that way. In the LXX, aside from σοφία (the dominant wisdom term), the important prudential word is φρόνησις. Aristotle's distinction between the two may be particularly helpful for renderings of the Proverbial material where φρόνησις is more central, and so Aristotle must be explored in more detail first.

He distinguished "five qualities through which the mind achieves truth in affirmation or denial, namely Art or technical skill [τέχνη], Scientific Knowledge [ἐπιστήμη], Prudence [φρόνησις], Wisdom [σοφία], and Intelligence [νοῦς]."[96] The prudent person is "able to deliberate well about what is good and advantageous for himself, not in some one department, for instance what is good for his health or strength, but what is advantageous as a means to the good life in general."[97] Prudence is indeed "a truth-attaining rational quality," but is "concerned with action in relation to things that are good and bad for human beings."[98] Such prudent knowledge is necessary as a higher-order regulative virtue, appropriating rightly the procedures, rules, skills, and virtues that an occasion warrants, none of which would be sufficient in themselves for a proper, balanced judgment.[99] This notion of practical reason apparently held sway for quite some time, if Plutarch, Clement of Alexandria, and other writers from the early Christian period are any indication.[100]

Back to the OT, a variety of Hebrew terms are rendered in the LXX by φρόνησις vocabulary (the חָכָמ family, the בין family, etc.), and φρόνησις surely overlaps with other Greek terms to an extent. Again, one should not conclude too much based on vocabulary, confusing words with concepts or concepts with theological judgments (as discussed in subsequent chapters). Nevertheless, there does seem to be a biblical niche for a concept of prudence or practical reason, as good sense tailored to contextual particularities.[101]

What of such terminology in Paul and the rest of the NT? The relevant nouns are quite limited (φρόνησις in Luke 1:17 and Eph. 1:8; φρόνημα, of the faculty involved, in Rom. 8 exclusively; αἴσθησις or αἰσθητήριον in Phil. 1:9 and Heb. 5:14). The adjective φρόνιμος has a wholly negative use in Rom. 11:25 and 12:16, and derisively so to the Corinthians (1 Cor. 4:10, 10:15; 2 Cor. 11:19). The verb is often used of a "mindset" or orientation to life, also of a viewpoint (Acts 28:22; Gal. 5:10), or self-appraisal (Rom. 12:3).

Despite the initial appearance that it is conceptually peripheral to NT theology, φρόνησις is apt once it is characterized Christianly in two important ways. The first Christian qualification of φρόνησις concerns humility or selflessness. The Greeks did not include this virtue within φρόνησις, for they did not see it as virtuous: such a view of humility is distinctly Christian. In this vein, note that φρονέω the verb saturates Philippians (2:2, 5; 3:15, 19; 4:2) where Christ's low-mindedness (as both humility and self-sacrifice) should be the mindset of wise Christians, thereby unifying the church. The same emphasis holds true in the contexts of Rom. 12 (vv. 3, 16), 14:6, 15:5, and 1 Cor. 4:6, among others. Where Paul does appropriate the φρόνησις vocabulary, therefore, he may well be forceful rather than reluctant, accomplishing a "renewal of the mind" just as we saw with σοφία. Colin Gunton reminds us that "only by a radical transformation of meaning can this action [the cruciform model] be motivated by anything that is recognisably [Greek] *phronēsis*."[102]

A second Christian qualification of φρόνησις follows on this emphasis, in that the Pauline version has a different teleology than the Greek version. Aristotle's φρόνησις serves the human good life rather generally, arriving at each particular context almost void of criteria, a virtual *tabula rasa*. Moreover, the virtuous Greek is individually heroic by acting in spheres of tragedy and conflict, as John Milbank has emphasized. By contrast, Christian φρόνησις has its pattern in Christ and thus its animating principle is love. Christian virtue is enacted against the viciousness of this present evil age (a point on which Milbank could perhaps be clearer), but does not presume an "ontology of violence."[103] Instead, those who are transformed by the Spirit, adopting the mindset of Christ, anticipate an ontology of peace.

Does New Covenant φρόνησις perhaps differ subtly from Proverbs as well as Aristotle regarding an aim of human fulfillment, but our frequent failure to realize it without conflict? OT wisdom did puzzle over the failure to realize shalom in the midst of faithfulness, and contrast with the NT may be a function of context instead of theological conflict. For, on the one hand, Job proved to serve God in spite of suffering while, on the other hand, the NT retains a role for joy in life. True, OT wisdom's overall paradigm, and even her puzzlement over theodicy in places, presumed a link between loving God and loving life, whereas the NT disciple saves her life by losing it. Yet this life is saved from violence through forgiving relations with God and others, which could be initially enjoyed even if deliverance from evil is only hoped for at a particular moment. Hence New Covenant φρόνησις is a markedly Christian fulfillment of its Old Covenant counterpart in two ways: its orientation is self-less, and its criteria are not only situation-specific, but Christocentric.

(3) The Nurture of Practical Reason

Having established the need for prudence, and its nature under the New Covenant, we develop its acquisition and exercise. An intriguing starting point is actually the New Covenant foil, the Torah, according to Rom. 2:18. There Paul summarized Jewish self-understanding in relation to the Torah:[104] they thought that by Torah instruction they could know God's will and approve (δοκιμάζω; a form of judgment) what is excellent or essential (τὰ διαφέροντα).[105] And surely they could, to an extent; Paul acknowledged the Torah's revelatory value (in Rom. 3:2, for instance).

The NT emphasis on the Spirit does not minimize the role of God's Word — preeminently Christ and then the Scriptures witnessing to Christ — in moral formation (John 17:17; Col. 3:16). Furthermore, Christian teaching is commended for its nourishing effects (1 Tim. 4:6). Such teaching should center upon Christ, but also be derived from the Scriptures (2 Tim. 3:14-17, where Scripture, wisdom, and salvation/sanctification are linked). Paul had no hesitation about the OT's ongoing provision of exemplars for moral formation, both negatively (1 Cor. 10:1-11) and positively (Rom. 15:3-5). His own practice substantiates this, for he appealed to the Torah authoritatively, though typologically and analogically out of due regard for epochal changes in redemptive history (note 1 Cor. 9:9-10, in relation to 10:11).

So, firstly, Christian φρόνησις must be bounded and nurtured by Scripture. Yet the mode in which this occurs must be carefully specified. The best evidence suggests that a great majority of the early Christians were largely illiterate, but "it did not prevent them from participating in literacy or from becoming familiar with Christian texts."[106] How so? The answer must center upon the public reading of Scripture (1 Tim. 4:13; also consider Col. 4:16; 1 Thess. 5:27; Rev. 1:3), and upon teaching in Christian assemblies. No doubt the literate ascended frequently to teaching roles; in addition, the early Christian appropriation of Scripture may have differed markedly from our own. Often theirs would have been an auditory, and perhaps more selective, encounter with Scripture.

Now the point is not to denigrate or deny "the priesthood of all believers." In preparation for a complicated use of the Scriptures (ch. 7), Hebrews chided readers for their immaturity (5:13-14), expecting that they could (should) have been sufficiently learned to exhort one another, as needed, apart from intervention (3:12-13).[107] That the audience was Jewish, and thus (potentially) more biblically literate, would not mitigate need for Scripture on the part of all God's people.

Still, the ramifications of this historical tidbit ought to be considered for the development of φρόνησις. For early Christians, Scripture's role in φρόνησις would have entailed forming their "worldview" or habits of thinking and perception, telling them of Christ, and exhorting them to follow him. Even the NT (then apostolic) literature, as it addressed particular exigencies within these congregations, could be characterized in this fashion. What we know as Scripture does not, in other words, provide a complicated and comprehensive calculus for scientific, topical application to every judgment. Rather, Scripture and its derivative healthy teaching are to form us wisely as Christian persons and communities, enabled by the Spirit (within certain commanded boundaries) to discern how the "logic" of the gospel fits particular circumstances. We see this pattern inside the Scriptures themselves.

The Hebrews text instructs us, however, that discernment is not merely a product of sapiential Scripture-learning; it is nurtured, secondly, by habit and growth. Our competence for relating Scripture and situation has moral-spiritual roots. Given its emphasis on human faithfulness, Hebrews naturally advocates training and discipline as the necessary nourishment for those roots.

By contrast (though not contradiction), Paul focuses fruitfulness upon the Spirit, thus adding a third ingredient to the nurture of φρόνησις. While training and discipline are not absent from Pauline teaching (1 Cor. 9:24-27; 1 Tim. 4:7-8), φρόνησις finds its true home in prayer, as a spiritual gift: according to Eph. 1:17, a prayer for God to give the Ephesians πνεῦμα σοφίας καὶ ἀποκαλύψεως ἐν ἐπιγνώσει αὐτοῦ; in Col. 1:9, πληρωθῆτε τὴν ἐπίγνωσιν τοῦ θελήματος αὐτοῦ ἐν πάσῃ σοφίᾳ καὶ συνέσει πνευματικῇ; in Phil. 1:9, ἡ ἀγάπη ὑμῶν ἔτι μᾶλλον καὶ μᾶλλον περισσεύῃ ἐν ἐπιγνώσει καὶ πάσῃ αἰσθήσει. That Christian practical reason comes as a gift, connected particularly to the Spirit's ministry, is clear.

Some other passages provide the rationale for its God-given character. 1 Corinthians 2:7-16 relates having the mind of Christ to the revelatory ministry of the Spirit, who discloses gospel wisdom. In harmony with Jeremiah's anticipation of the New Covenant (31:34), 1 John 2:27 highlights the Spirit's teaching ministry, in a context of discernment that is first Christocentric, but also has moral overtones related to love. Later, at the end of 1 John (5:20), there is a connection between understanding (διάνοια this time) and knowing God in Jesus Christ.

This New Covenant knowledge of God, and its gift-character, underlies Paul's praying about φρόνησις. God must ἔλαμψεν ἐν ταῖς καρδίαις ἡμῶν πρὸς φωτισμὸν τῆς γνώσεως τῆς δόξης τοῦ θεοῦ ἐν προσώπῳ Χριστοῦ (2 Cor. 4:6), if he is to φανεροῦντι τὴν ὀσμὴν τῆς γνώσεως αὐτοῦ . . . δι' ἡμῶν ἐν παντὶ τόπῳ (2 Cor. 2:14). We are taught by God to love one another (1 Thess. 4:9), and that both by adopting the mindset of Christ (φρονέω in Phil. 2:2; 2:5; and 3:15, in which note its revealed character) and by abounding in discernment that is God-given (ἐπιγνώσει καὶ πάσῃ αἰσθήσει εἰς τὸ δοκιμάζειν in Phil. 1:9-10). Whereas in the Old Covenant eyes were enlightened by the Torah commandments (Ps. 19:8), in the New Covenant eyes are enlightened by a spiritual grasping of our great salvation in Christ (Eph. 1:18).[108] Again, this does not exclude Scripture and discipline altogether; for instance, consider how James holds all these elements of wisdom in harmony (as gift in answer to prayer, 1:5; with a role for Scripture and discipline, 1:4, 1:19-25, etc.).

Practical reason, then, has been a need for both Old and New Covenant members. Prudence is often translated, and is captured well, by the Aristotelian concept φρόνησις once it is duly Christianized. This φρόνησις is a type of knowledge and a regulative virtue, standing at the intersection of ethics and epistemology within an ethos of divine creation and command. φρόνησις is nurtured by the Spirit in response to prayer, who hones it through habits of obedience, and informs it by Scripture and Christian teaching. This combination of gift and nurture — indeed grace given by various means of communal nurture — strongly implies that wisdom is not a possession for a privileged few, but a privilege for all who live in God's New Covenant. And that will have implications for defining theology sapientially.

(4) The Norm of Practical Reason

A final aspect of φρόνησις needs further detail, though. What are the criteria for Christian judgment, the application of which φρόνησις regulates? What does φρόνησις enable the Christian to know, understand, or judge, and thereby enact?

The most relevant passages for this inquiry, because they connect discernment or judgment to a virtuous *telos,* are four: Col. 1:9-12, Eph. 5:15-17, Phil. 1:9-11, and Rom. 14. The first passage has God's will (θέλημα) as the object the Christian knows, and specifies a *telos* for knowledge: περιπατῆσαι ἀξίως τοῦ κυρίου . . . καρποφοροῦντες καὶ αὐξανόμενοι τῇ ἐπιγνώσει τοῦ θεοῦ . . . δυναμούμενοι . . . εὐχαριστοῦντες. . . . Such vocabulary is clearly reminiscent of what the Spirit produces in Christians through New Covenant knowledge of God. The prayer aims for a context-specific embodiment of Christian virtues, not merely that readers would learn Scripture, or even that they would become capable of applying Scripture.

Colossians 1:9-12 in context fits a pattern, that the fruitful, obedient Christian is divinely enabled and informed to choose the right enactment of the right virtues in the right proportions in the right contexts. Such is the wisdom that knows God's will, and Eph. 5:15-17 accords with this view. The *telos* (5:16) there is ἐξαγοραζόμενοι τὸν καιρόν, to live as lights that shine therein. As for the object of understanding, τὸ θέλημα τοῦ κυρίου (5:17) is connected to spiritual fruit (5:9), so that its rough equivalent is successfully discovering what is pleasing to the Lord (δοκιμάζοντες τί ἐστιν εὐάρεστον τῷ κυρίῳ in 5:10).[109] Consequently, God's will is tied to Christian character and "vocation" in an evil age, the latter accomplished by a specific rendering of the former as God gives opportunity.

In a similar context (ἀγάπη abounding in ἐπιγνώσει and αἰσθήσει), the Phil. 1:9-11 passage puts a twist on this approach. On top of blamelessness (1:10), here again the *telos* concerns fullness (from πληρόω) and fruit-bearing (καρπός) unto God's glory (1:11). The object of knowledge and discernment, however, is explained differently, in terms of successfully discovering (δοκιμάζω one more time) τὰ διαφέροντα, what is supremely important (1:10).[110] Remember that this very phrase described the product of the Torah for the Israelite (Rom. 2:18). The former attitude could be summed up, as *T. Naph.* 8:10 would put it, "So be wise in the Lord and discerning, knowing the order of his commandments, what is ordained for every act."[111] That is, wisdom was defined in terms of Torah. Now, however, under the New Covenant, God-given judgment is exercised to accomplish the goal of most effectively loving (as obedient fruit, or fruitful obedience), unto God's glory. "God's will," in these NT contexts, concerns what "sacrifice" would please the Lord, on such teleological terms.

We come, then, to the tangle over *adiaphora,* most especially in Rom. 14. Forms of κρίνω abound therein, signifying a sort of judgment that the Christian should not undertake in relation to another; such judgment is reserved for God. And what shall be the standard? God's judgment will be κατὰ ἀγάπην, by which we are to walk (14:15; consider the parallel: to walk by the Spirit is to walk according to love). Romans 14:17 highlights the Pauline ethical *telos:* "righteousness, peace, and joy in the Holy Spirit." According to the next verse, the person who serves Christ in that fashion is pleasing (εὐάρεστος; note the sacrificial overtones, especially after 12:1-2) to God, amidst acceptance before God in Christ (προσλαμβάνω; 14:1, 3), and should have the approval (δόκιμος) of Christian brothers and sisters. They should not κρίνω one another, but should μὴ ὑπερφρονέω themselves (12:3) and δοκιμάζω those who fruitfully love Christ. Regarding the controversial matters, the beatitude of 14:22b is a commendation of the strong, while 14:23 permits — exhorts, actually — the weak to continue their current practice, until they should change their convictions. And the underlying rationale here is significant: the believer's "faith," as a response of conviction and loving service for Christ (consider the "measure of faith" in Rom. 12:3 in this regard), is all-important for God's judgment. So, in one sense, there can even be a right-or-wrong answer as a rule (here, the strong were right about what was permissible), yet that answer can be tangential. For what pleases God is the believer's faithful effort to serve Christ by loving others.

Without claiming to have solved all the interesting problems, we can draw some conclusions. First, the *telos* of φρόνησις is effectively bearing spiritual fruit, preeminently love, which displays the glory of God to the world. Second, the object of φρόνησις is God's will, or what might be pleasing in a given instance. Sometimes the search for God's will is misdirected, in terms of act and rule: is it always right or never right to eat food sacrificed to idols, or to observe special days and other elements of Jewish spirituality? Such decisions are *adiaphora* in terms of applying a universal moral rule (from the Torah) to the act. They are in a sense *not adiaphora*, regarding motivation and outcome, when measured by love.

A third point: in some cases, the motivation and outcome *might* determine the proper decision; if there is a loving act to do or not to do, there would be a choice that does or does not please God. Or, in other cases, there might be good, better, or best alternatives in light of love. The specificity of God's will might be indexed to the teleological clarity of the options.[112] Indeed, most of our choices require some level of φρόνησις; few are reached by straightforwardly applying God's moral will as command. Conversely, few have absolutely no relation to God's will in terms of effectively displaying Christ-like character for Christ-honoring reasons.

C. The Wisdom of the Faithful

We have now taken up the Christology and the pneumatology essential for Christian wisdom. Jesus Christ is, in a very important sense, "our wisdom"; we then communicate wisdom as the Spirit reveals to us the mind of the crucified and risen Christ. This transforming revelation entails the *paideia*-unto-*phronēsis* being sketched here, but raises two critical questions as well. Does the linkage of *phronēsis* to *sophia* — opting for a sapiential understanding of knowledge that correlates with divine revelation — lie in the rubble of a demolished "house of authority"? Moreover, if knowledge of God and knowledge of self co-inhere, then is the Christian tradition tied to an old-fashioned (proto-modern and then modern), unbelievable, individualist and essentialist anthropology?

The former question about revelation and knowledge of God is reserved for the next chapter, when the significance of Christian wisdom for *theologia*, church, and doctrine is spelled out. The latter question, however, is addressed here, because NT wisdom implies not just a Christology and a pneumatology but an ecclesiology as well. By encountering the anthropological problem at the point of wisdom's ecclesiology, we may find resources to help in time of need. We will discover that since imaging God occurs in Christ, *phronēsis* is linked to *sophia*, knowledge of human self to knowledge of God, and anthropology to ecclesiology. The narrative unity of a Christian life is discovered dialogically, emerging through storied judgments about encounters with God and others, encounters in which we come to have the mind of Christ.

Romans 12 can help these pairs to come together. There Paul's exhortation is to virtuous living with others, as a sacrifice offered gratefully to God. The renewal of the mind(set) — which results in Christian *phronēsis* or judgment (12:2) — involves both knowledge of self (12:3) and knowledge of God's will (12:2). But is this self "something like an ahistorical and universally self-identical essential self — a substantial soul (Plato) or consciousness-as-such"?[113] Paul should not be pressed so far. In fact, the subsequent verses (12:4-8) make clear that self-evaluation concerns God-given *capacities for action,* and such evaluation is conducted vis-à-vis free, joyous service to others in community.

Paul's notion of personhood is thoroughly Christian: in the near context he exhorts us to "put on" the new person that we are in Christ (13:14); more distantly he speaks of our eschatological hope as "being conformed to the image" of Christ (8:29), the *telos* which the renewal of 12:2 anticipates; this point could even be argued from similar conceptual patterns outside Romans. So if our identity is in Christ and still becoming in Christ, and if the uniqueness of our identity concerns how Christ gifts us for others via the Spirit, what sort of personhood is suggested?

The words "narrative" and "dialogical" come to mind, two words that underlie notions of selfhood in hermeneutical theorists such as Paul Ricoeur and Anthony Thiselton. Both address the sometimes radical postmodern challenges to modernity's autonomous or essentialist self. Ricoeur refers to "the amazing oscillations that the philosophies of the subject appear to present," asking wryly if we should say of "the 'I' of these philosophies, as some have said of the father, that there is always either too much or too little of it."[114]

His response is a reworked notion of identity, what he calls the *ipse*-identity of selfhood (of being subject in a story) as opposed to the *idem*-

identity of exact sameness (which forces an all-or-nothing choice about whether or not "I" am the same person "I" was).[115] The latter notion has been easily caricatured by many postmodern thinkers but, as Charles Taylor points out, they proclaim impossible what no one would currently claim anyway — "belief in a kind of total self-transparent clarity, which would make even Hegel blush."[116] This *ipse*-identity recognizes a "dialectic of *self* and the *other than self*," because such a reworked self arises in answer to four questions: Who is speaking? Who is acting? Who is recounting about himself or herself? Who is the moral subject of imputation?[117] The recognition that we "do things with words"[118] brings the first two inquiries — philosophy of language and philosophy of action — closer together before moving more directly to complicated questions of personal identity.[119] So we find our selves over time through interpretation, interpretation that works via narration, ascribing actions to agents. We find our selves through interpretation because our selves are constituted in relation to the constitution of actions. Our own agency and *ipse*-identity is discovered indirectly through stories of our selves and others — indeed, of our selves as others.[120]

This recourse to the "narrative unity of a life" takes Ricoeur back to Aristotle, meaning that he converges significantly with the work of Alasdair MacIntyre.[121] Once again an appropriate oscillation is established between large-scale life plan and local situation, between the "good life" and particular choices, between rule and case. This oscillation bears likeness to the famous "hermeneutical circle" between part and whole of texts; incidentally, the oscillation also parallels Wood's vision and discernment (discussed in chapter one).

Thiselton, likewise, argues that "a close relationship of analogy and interaction may be proposed between hermeneutics of texts and hermeneutics of selfhood and of human life,"[122] so that the loss of self-expression in the public domain is accompanied by the loss of any meaning or truth, and vice versa. His stinging critique of postmodern anti-realists (regrettably, at times he seems to equate the two terms)[123] not only faults them for birthing a "*new Fundamentalism*" by losing the possibility of "rational dialogue," but also for being inconsistent: they try to keep the modern, autonomous agent at play while simultaneously describing the self as "a passive product of language, history and society."[124]

Following Jürgen Moltmann, Thiselton opts instead for a view of personhood as "being-in-relationship."[125] Whereas Ricoeur's understanding of selfhood is derived philosophically and is not specifically Christian (or so he claims, at any rate), Thiselton claims that Christianity reconstitutes the self through love. The category of "promise" is one defense against charges of wishful thinking on this point: there are both a finality or fixedness to our hope of being transformed into Christ's image, and an openness or newness as to what exactly we shall be.[126] Here, in broad strokes, is the necessary mediation between Ricoeur, or MacIntyre et al., and Milbank. Ricoeur, for instance, speaks of "the inevitable place of conflict in moral life"[127] as it seems at present, whereas Milbank could be construed as leaving aside the tragic and conflicted reality "between the times," having already realized too strongly a future ontology of peace.

A Christian *phronēsis,* though, as opposed to a purely philosophical one, must pass through Christology, pneumatology, and ecclesiology, *and* thereby through eschatology for its *telos.* A Christian *phronēsis* has a vision of the good that is fixed upon Jesus Christ, who is our *sophia.* Yet our conformity to the mindset of Christ is only partial; our transformation by the Spirit is an ongoing quest to envision Christ properly and to manifest his image in particular situations (e.g., 2 Cor. 3:18–4:6). We know one day we shall be conformed to that image (Rom. 8:29), yet what we shall be has not yet been made known (1 John 3:2) so that we see through a glass darkly (1 Cor. 13:12). In the meantime, we must ever be realizing our identity through identification with the Crucified and Risen One.

By taking "image of God" verbally rather than nominally — as what we are by way of what we may and shall become — and relating this to Christ, we link *phronēsis* to *sophia,* knowledge of self to knowledge of God, but also anthropology to ecclesiology. The narrative unity of a Christian life emerges dialogically through storied judgments about encounters with God and others. Christian shalom is envisioned as being-in-communion, which both manifests (in a creaturely analogue) and participates (ultimately as the church) in the love of God's triune life. This vision of the good enables prospective judgments about one's particular gifts or "communicative capacity"[128] (Rom. 12:3), and proper communicative actions (Rom. 12:2) to realize one's vocation — which is, ultimately, constituted ecclesially (Eph. 4). In this way Christian *sapientia* is thoroughly dialogical, involving communion with God and others, both receiving and passing on wisdom — a wisdom that oscillates between its encompassing vision of *sophia* and its enactment via *phronēsis.* Far from requiring or presupposing either an outmoded or modern, individualized concept of selfhood, Christian *paideia* in fact means recovering the social nature of human character as well as a vision of creation's restoration to goodness.[129]

Perhaps, then, we can navigate between radically modern and radically postmodern selves, by narrating *ipse-* rather than *idem-*identity — who we are over time and in communion. To be sure, we should not overdo a dialogical emphasis, lest people be rendered powerless to act, or at least subjugated, by their social networks.[130] Paul's exhortations in Rom. 13:8–15:13 speak of our loving others as a pursuit, which the Spirit has empowered us to undertake. Apart from this measure of faith is a measure of judgment that we are not allowed to undertake: others are responsible for their own actions as well. Paul envisions a loving community of mutual admonition and acceptance (15:14), of plural voices that harmonize to God's praise because all can be heard (15:6). Again, the pattern for such communal life is in Christ (15:7): for all its situational specificity, Christian *phronēsis* is guided by the love of Christian *sophia.*

The narrative and the dialogical dimensions point further to a corporate dimension of Christian discernment. Acts 15 narrates an example of corporate *phronēsis,* of the congregation making a judgment about how the gospel and the Scriptures related to a particular case. A combination of narrating human lives and apparent divine action (15:7-11), of interpreting Scripture (15:15-18), and of seeking consensus (15:19-29), resulted in judgments that "seemed good to the Holy Spirit and to us" (15:28). This story of dialogue about gospel narratives does not simply concern personal but corporate identity: *phronēsis* can result in public judgments about God's ways in church and world. The process of *phronēsis* can take up from *sophia* and bring not just understanding of the case but of the rule; in this case the virtue of *phronēsis* was that the church's vision of its very quest, the aim of God's action in Christ and in the Spirit, was transformed. Here is a concrete instance of judgment touching both the epistemological and the ethical at once — to make explicit a subtext of our quest in this chapter, a sapiential, *theological* judgment with *sophia* and *phronēsis* entangled. On this basis wisdom and *theologia* may be linked when discussing the nature of doctrine in pages to come.

III. Wisdom, *Phronēsis,* and Being-Sanctified-in-Communion

These extended biblical-theological arguments have mined the Christian tradition's original treasures for a core of wisdom. To that end, I first argued that biblical teaching affirms the pursuit of wisdom, with cautions. Seeking moral autonomy, or worldly "life" independent of God, is deadly and diabolical, bearing only a formal similarity to wisdom's instrumental (but truly fruitful) dimension. So I specified, secondly, not only what kind of wisdom is to be found, but where and how. New Covenant knowledge of God involves transformation by the Spirit so that we have the mind of Christ. Thus wisdom unto salvation means wisdom unto sanctification, being called into a community that offers to God a harvest of loving virtue.

Since, as commonly acknowledged, a concept like *theologia* in some sense dates to the apostle Paul,[131] and "knowledge of God" bound up with *paideia* is its closest antecedent therein,[132] we have explored the transformation of moral life and judgment which Paul related to knowing God. Accordingly *phronēsis* has seemed vital for wisdom, with its acquisition and exercise not simply communal, but communal in a distinctly Christian way.[133]

How then should we move from wisdom to *theologia?* On the one hand, exemplars of the Christian tradition, even "pre-moderns" such as Hugh of St. Victor, have tended to distinguish theology as a higher wisdom from the practical wisdom of ethics.[134] And this tendency to keep *sophia* and *phronēsis* rather distinct is right-headed, insofar as Christian doctrine must provide *phronēsis* its distinct *telos* and structure, keeping it humble after the loving pattern of Christ. Moreover, the distinction allows us to preserve *sophia* in relation to the truth claims of Christian doctrine, as developed in the next chapter. Once again Charles Wood's interplay of vision and discernment appears to be helpful.

On the other hand, *sophia* and *phronēsis* are mutually implicated, as are knowledge of God and knowledge of self. R. W. L. Moberly says correctly that the point is not "to concede to the suspicion that talk about God is, at heart, only a coded projection of talk about humanity." Rather, the affirmation is "that an understanding of God, as the Bible depicts God, and a self-understanding of humanity, with corresponding implications for how people live, are necessarily interrelated dimensions of a complex reality."[135]

The proper relation between *sophia* and *phronēsis,* between theology's encompassing vision of the Good and the ethical discernment of good judgment, is that of relative distinction but not separation. The distance between such Christian wisdom and our usual Western notions of academic "theology" apparently proves Ellen Charry's point about how different modern, scientific "knowledge" has become from the *sapientia* of a truly Christian *theologia.* But is this Christian wisdom tenable for theology anymore, or must we be content with wisdom as a somewhat glib metaphor that tries to reconcile theory and practice, religion (as first-order) and "theology" (as second-order)?

Two considerations make Christian wisdom eminently suitable for *theologia.* First, we have seen that wisdom is communicative from first to last: from God to humans, from humans to one another, and from humans to God, wisdom issues in speech or, more broadly, communicative action. With our dialogical understanding of personal and corporate identity, and with an understanding of communication as action, we can now understand that all four of wisdom's components — contemplation, discursive reasoning, affections, action — have linguistically related aspects. How fitting this is for a concept tied to the word *theologia* itself (mildly etymologizing to make the point): careful communication with regard to God!

Second, the word "wisdom" — just like the word "theology" — is ambiguous in an important respect. Does "wisdom" vocabulary denote a kind of knowledge (a product), a reflective/communicative activity (a process or practice of a "tradition"), or a quality (say, of a person or a judgment) — does "wisdom" denote what is communicated, or its communication, which (along with the communicator) can be called "wise"? Already we have noted such ambiguity. Indeed, do we not use "theology" to talk of each element: of a discursive product that is seen as knowledge, of a process or practice involving reflective, communicative activity? And are not the products and practices dubbed "theological," with the practitioners called "theologians" who are formed by these?

While Wood rightly highlighted this shared ambiguity, he drew the wrong inference. He should not have concluded that Edward Farley was confused; Farley was on to a traditional Christian understanding (even if his understanding of the activity itself departed radically from the tradition). Theological activity results in a transformative sort of knowledge that, in turn, results in fresh theological activity. Seeking wisdom results in gaining wisdom, which makes one the wiser for seeking wisdom. And so on.

Wood worries about the inconsistency, and Farley fails to capitalize fully on the ambiguity as intentional, because of their commitment (shared by Kelsey and others in the discussion as well) that we cannot directly know and speak about God — reflection and action remain separated. Whether, therefore, "theology" is second-order reflection on Christian witness or practices (Wood, Kelsey), or a *habitus* of reflective inquiry undertaken critically (Farley), some separation of theory and practice, of cognition and action, of knowing God and knowing self, pertains.

Instead, full capitalization on the gains of the recent discussion requires a true integration of *theologia* into Christian practice. That integration cannot occur so long as theology is almost exclusively critical reflection (according to a narrow definition of "criticism," at least), and this explains the present interest in Christian wisdom's involving communicative action — in recognizing the linguistic and hence dialogical character even of reflection. Since reflection is a species of communicative action (or, as the next chapter further specifies, "communicative praxis"), true fellowship is discovered between *theologia* and practice. That fellowship is heightened, though, when theological understanding is not just reflection on practice (Wood), or a set of mostly reflective practices indirectly related to God (Kelsey), or even a *habitus* for reflective inquiry (Farley), but involves communion with God and others.

An important objection could intrude, though. Charry notes that "since most people do not have the leisure to sit quietly and think through the beliefs of the faith, most Christians have relied on those who have been fortunate enough to do so."[136] That is for good reason; later she urges that "discernment is not one's first thoughts about God, but one's considered and reconsidered thought."[137] Does this not suggest an academy-church, theory-practice, first order–second order separation? If Charry is right to resist such dichotomies elsewhere, however, then what is the solution? Before retaining these (modern?) separations, perhaps we should consider, in the reverse, whether Christian communicative praxis ought to be made more discerning! Indeed, that is an important mandate, or subtext, in the rest of the project, allowing for some occasional distinctions without separation.

The importance of this evaluation may be seen in two additional construals of "wisdom." Ford insightfully recognizes OT wisdom's identification with God, its "political and economic" not just "personal and religious" character, and its "strongly self-critical and revisionist" stance.[138] Ford's understanding of wisdom "is long term and social, an achievement of generations . . . involved in the good shaping and reshaping of character, of patterns of life, of institutions and of discourses."[139] Despite wisely relating wisdom to questioning and listening, however, he stops short of making it fully active (as opposed to intellectual in a particular sense): "theology at its broadest may be defined as a thinking relation to religions. . . ."[140]

Moreover, Ford's conclusion is helpful that "the challenge, in the hopeful pursuit of wisdom, is to keep together magnanimity without presumption and humility without despair."[141] But he fails to tie this challenge of wisdom's self-critical questioning adequately to the Christian conviction that wisdom is embodied in Jesus Christ. The most profound magnanimity and humility about human wisdom are to be found in that cruciform conviction; most importantly, however, this wisdom may seem foolish in the world because it is not offered merely to an elite few. Ford could extend his insights if the inclusion of all God's people in forgiveness and transformation were acknowledged to imply their involvement in Christian wisdom — and if that involvement influenced more fully the understanding of theology.

Similarly, Peter Hodgson's account of wisdom in relation to education is commendable in many respects. But in his case the account is only haltingly Christian. His *paideia* yields a "life-enhancing" wisdom that takes the form of "critical thinking, heightened imagination, and liberating practice," and thus can fruitfully relate to "transformative pedagogy."[142] In this vein, Hodgson catches the significance of the biblical Torah-to-Spirit shift, as a shift of emphasis from wisdom as God's teaching to Wisdom as God the teacher; he develops "God's pedagogical presence in the world" in terms of the Spirit.[143] He also recognizes that "Christian theology does not simply graft Christ and the Holy Spirit onto an essentially unchanged Greek paideia," for Christian *paideia* is not about overcoming ignorance of what is already immanent within humanity. No, Christian *paideia* is about overcoming idolatry and self-centeredness, so that "the remedy for this problem is not recollection, but salvation, conversion, transformation."[144]

Just here, though, Hodgson balks; he is worried that *scientia/Wissenschaft* (Greek *epistēmē*) will drop out, eclipsed by a privatized or specialized *gnōsis.* Rejecting "revelatory positivism"[145] and retaining "the critical methods of religious studies" so that appropriating wisdom will be "*theological*" rather than "simply the act of faith itself,"[146] he wants to "articulate the idea of God as teacher nonmythologically, that is, without thinking of God as a supernatural being who controls everything in the world and directly reveals sacred truths."[147] So we may characterize the Christology that informs his project as one of incarnation without crucifixion — a type of incarnation, that is, without divine intervention to overcome idolatry by forgiving and reforming people of God.

Richard Hays's essay on wisdom in Paul, especially in 1 Cor. 1-2, is a useful caution.[148] The relative weight of the above sections devoted to pneumatology and ecclesiology, over against Christology, could slide toward Hodgson's conclusions. Yet Hays reminds us of the Christian conviction that our pneumatological-ecclesiological ethic, and transformative pedagogy, must be cruciform. What is more, their realization became possible only once the risen, victorious and ascended Christ poured out the Holy Spirit upon all flesh. Following Christ's pattern is possible only with the Spirit's empowering presence that we receive upon being forgiven: we love because God first loved us. Before and apart from Christ, the wariness of wisdom exhibited in Jer. 8–10 (especially 9:23-24) was required due to the folly of idolatry.

With the "magnanimity" and "humility" more specifically implied by Christ's cruciform wisdom, we can then follow Christian wisdom in relating *theologia* to everyone's communicative action regarding God, to both the communicating (including the dialogue involved in understanding) and the communication. The next chapter addresses this move concerning theology's social location to the question of its relation to the practice of Christian doctrine. Not only will the gains of relating theory and practice be consolidated, but I hope to minimize liabilities concerning theology's public truth claims. For a simple distinction between religion as first-order and "theology" as second-order reflection means proclaiming inadequately the wisdom found in Jesus Christ. Such notions have grains of truth, after their husks have been shed; ultimately, though, we must grow in our understanding of how the church's praxis responds — and corresponds — to the communicative action of the triune God.

CHAPTER 3

Doctrine: Learning to Speak of God

The previous chapter pursued a theological account of Christian wisdom, especially by interpreting Scripture theologically. The canonical witnesses were heard in both their distinction and their direction toward Christ, in dialogue with tradition and the context of our present query. The ensuing account of wisdom responded to questions raised by the narrative in chapter 1. Specifically, if theology's sapiential character is to be recovered, what must be held true regarding knowledge of God as response to prevenient divine action? And what should be the prime social location for *theologia?* In answer to these questions, a Christian account of wisdom maintains that a sapiential *theologia* would involve not a select few, but everyone in communicative action concerning God. That communicative action is a response enabled by the transforming Holy Spirit, a response which contemplates the only wise God revealed in Jesus Christ.

The question of prevenient divine communicative action must now be put in dialogue with a third question, that of theory and practice, picking up where chapter 2 left off, with the move from wisdom to *theologia.* As noted earlier, recent discussion has left unclear in what sense theology is itself practical. Is theology practical as reflection on or for practice, as reflection embedded in practice, or even as a practice itself? A biblical-theological account of wisdom has started toward an answer, but the move to *theologia* raises the complication of doctrine. If a quest for wisdom means defining theology practically, does critical reflection on the church's teaching lose out? If that is the case, do we have doctrine that cannot claim to be true? And if *that* is the case, how can we speak publicly about (and in response to) the communicative action of the triune God?

I. Defining Theology "Practically": Doctrine as "Cultural-Linguistic" Grammar?

Current discussions regarding the nature of doctrine have largely been reviews, often pro and then only slightly con, of George Lindbeck's *The Nature of Doctrine.* Indeed, part of chapter 1 has already narrated varieties of modern theology's "knowledge" in connection with Lindbeck's three views of doctrine: the "cognitive-propositional" (early modern and conservative), the "experiential-expressivist" (later modern and liberal), and his own "cultural-linguistic" approach (postliberal). While somewhat open to criticism, this scheme does capture broadly perceived shifts of doctrinal definition. Modernity saw theology split into two rather separate and identifiable camps, liberal and conservative. Their theological visions differed at least over the possibility or particularity of divine action, the ground and character of knowledge, and the nature of religious language, which Lindbeck's scheme clearly addresses.[1] So, while both liberal and conservative writers have criticized Lindbeck for presenting the propositional approach in a brief, outmoded, and unsophisticated light,[2] his scheme has still shaped the contours of subsequent discussion.

A. The "Cultural-Linguistic" Approach and Public Practice

This characterization of modern "doctrine" did not arise out of mainly historical interest, nor directly out of an Edward Farley–like proposal for reconciling fragmented theological disciplines, the academy and church, or theory and practice. Rather, Lindbeck wanted to explain and enhance his own experiences at doctrinal dialogue and ecumenism.[3] In John Milbank's words, "for Lindbeck, apparent divergences among Christians can often be exposed as mere over-estimations of the importance of conceptual articulation in different cultural settings."[4]

Thus Lindbeck took up (among others) Ludwig Wittgenstein on religious language and cultural anthropologist Clifford Geertz on religion, proposing that the Christian religion (for example) be viewed in terms of a culture with its sign-system. No longer should one follow liberalism in assuming a pre-reflective or pre-linguistic religious experience that is brought to expression in language. Nor should one opt for the older propositionalist view that doctrine brings truth or external reality (as opposed to experience) to linguistic expression. Both approaches presume what cannot be presumed, namely the pre-reflective or pre-linguistic. All religious experience (for that matter, all truth?) follows on the structuring of life by language, the sign system of one's culture.

If religions are like cultures, each having their languages which shape thought and experience before reflecting and expressing them, then they need grammars also. And that is the function of doctrine: to be the second-order grammatical rules for proper, culturally literate first-order religious communication. On this point there are both similarity to and dissimilarity from prior voices: similarity in terms of a first-order/second-order distinction (that concerns both religious language and the associated theological activity), with dissimilarity in terms of what occurs in the second order.

As previously detailed, for Charles Wood, whose position is basically representative of revisionist American mainline theology, the second order's "theology" is critical reflection on the validity of Christian witness, and hence concerns not only its Christian authenticity but its public truthfulness. For Lindbeck, the second order's "theology" is primarily about Christian authenticity, teaching Christians to follow their culture's rules. Many "postliberals" then eschew apologetics and fundamental theology almost entirely; those who do not would presumably have to speak of a third order behind the second, doctrinal order of discourse.[5]

A definition of doctrine not only has an attendant view of theology; a view of the church's public role vis-à-vis truth also comes along. So Roman Catholics such as David Tracy,[6] and many Western university-related mainline Protestants, tend to retain some kind of fundamental theology or apologetic task within the second order, and they will be concerned with the public validity possessed by a particular aspect of Christian witness. A cluster of cultural-linguistic concepts, by contrast, has Lindbeck viewing apologetics basically as nothing but communal praxis and catechesis.[7]

Regarding Lindbeck's view of truth, one must assess the "categorial" adequacy of the Christian (or any other) religion as a whole, not in doctrinal parts. A religion functions like a giant proposition that can be true or false. Particular statements within a religion are assessed for their coherence with the whole ("intrasystematic truth"). Their correspondence with some nonlinguistic reality ("ontological truth") cannot be directly at issue, although Lindbeck claims that rejecting a correspondence theory of truth is not necessary, except with regard to statements of "doctrine." The correspondence of particular statements to reality involves their cultural-linguistic coherence, not simply correspondence to reality in a narrowly linguistic or propositional sense. Accordingly, statements as doctrines are a matter of intrasystematic truth or not; only when made in religious practice (e.g., adoration) *could* statements put ontological truth at issue.[8] So Lindbeck provides his infamous example of a Crusader claiming "Christus est Dominus" while cleaving an infidel's skull: was the claim "true" or "false"? Here the mantle of truth-or-falsehood speaker has been passed from the theologian to the religious practitioner.

In this way, Lindbeck might seem to reconcile theory and practice, doctrine and ethics, within the Christian "language game." The truth of religion lies in ethics or praxis; doctrine is its grammatical substructure. As for an outsider who must choose whether or not to participate in the Christian game, that outsider cannot measure the correspondence of the Christian proposition to reality using some universal rational standard.[9] Particular Christian statements or practices may well make no sense to outsiders; language games are incommensurable, logically independent. Hence the need for catechesis: an outsider needs to be socialized into how Christians live and speak, with the hope that our community life will prove more winsome than other options.

What about this chapter's query regarding theology's relation to practice? In his prospective chapter "Toward a Postliberal Theology," Lindbeck is not entirely clear on this point, which is not the focus of his discussion. Theology seems not to be a church practice itself,[10] but operates via what is a church practice: reading the Bible "figurally" or typologically (canonically, narratively, post-critically) — doing theology "intratextually." The theologian's task is not "extratextual," correlating biblical meanings with more public and universal categories as in liberalism. Instead, theology is about finding one's place in the biblical story as one reads. Theology is "intratextual," with "the text absorbing the world" rather than the other way round.[11]

Such a view suggests that "theological competence" involves religious commitments, "a supportive environment, the tutelage of expert practitioners, and assiduous practice in a complex set of unformalizable skills that even the best theoretician cannot adequately characterize." Oh yes, and "genius" would not hurt! History's theological greats affirmed reason but not in a modernist way; even Thomas Aquinas and Schleiermacher, claims Lindbeck, were "more intratextual in their actual practice than their theories would seem to allow."[12] The church's "best practice," in fact, is a key argument for intratextuality; Lindbeck admits that he has not built his case theologically, though he could have done so (he claims) with help from not just Thomas but the Reformers, Barth, et al. Yet, for all the talk about its recovery, there has been a recent lack of truly intratextual theology.[13]

So, in its initial exposition, the cultural-linguistic view of religion and doctrine did not take up theology as a church practice, but its call for intratextuality certainly could have incorporated church practice in the doing of theology. Here Wood's 1985 understanding of theology as critical reflection on the validity of Christian witness can be usefully compared with David Kelsey's understanding of theology in the 1990s. Pace Lindbeck, Kelsey retains a component of critically assessing public truth claims, but he sees theological understanding as a set of practices or capacities for action in relation to something (say, God). So "self-critical reflection is not a separate practice in its own right; it is an integral part of a practice"; accordingly, "theology is no one inquiry" but an *ad hoc* dimension of congregational practices. Because these can be "theological" rather than there being any one such inquiry labeled "theology," Kelsey rejects the notion that one recognizes theology by a "distinctive method of inquiry."[14] Despite, therefore, a rather Lindbeck-like understanding of religion and even doctrine, Kelsey has to spurn intratextuality. In a 1990 evaluation of Lindbeck, then, he accepts the cultural-linguistic paradigm so long as its limits are acknowledged — limits dealing precisely with the relation of God to the church's public witness.[15]

B. The "Cultural-Linguistic" Approach and the Meaning of Truth

The truth of what the church says about God, with its obligation (or not) to listen to others, has probably been the most contested issue in evaluations of Lindbeck's approach. One of his early defenders (and, some might say, revisers) is Bruce Marshall, whose recent *Trinity and Truth* bears on questions about theological truth and church practice.

Marshall's chapter "The Triune God as the Center of Christian Belief" argues from "the liturgical centrality of the Trinity" that the doctrine's "communal centrality" requires its "epistemic primacy." And this pattern holds for all communities: "On pain of forfeiting its identity and dissolving the ties which bind it together, *any* such community must, according to this argument, regard its own most central beliefs as true, and revise or reject other beliefs which conflict with those central convictions."[16] A recognizably cultural-linguistic pattern holds: discovery and maintenance of communal identity go by way of communal convictions, which are manifest most easily (though not exclusively) in Eucharistic worship, the communal practice reserved for church members.[17]

However, for the church to privilege Trinitarian belief as true on the basis of its own practice seems to beg the questions asked by a modern public. So Marshall must labor toward an account of truth which not only retains the Trinity's epistemic primacy but also accounts for other truths and, ultimately, for what to do with other communities' rival claims.

Marshall distinguishes between the definition of, and the criteria for, truth.[18] Something like correspondence to reality is retained in what truth is: truth ties language to the world.[19] But Marshall admits that there may be no non-theological way to retain such correspondence against modernity's onslaught of skepticism. Rather, the triune God is the end of the infinite regress that is evoked when skepticism convinces people about the necessity of epistemic "subordination" and the "dependence" of beliefs upon other beliefs.[20] Truth links language and world, but ultimately is a matter of correspondence between beliefs.[21] For Christians, Marshall claims, a true belief corresponds to reality, strictly, in terms of what God the Father knows; someone has the right to believe conferred upon them by God the crucified and risen Son; someone then actually believes as enabled by God the Holy Spirit.[22] The triune God enables the definition of truth to involve correspondence with reality even though skepticism would force us toward only a coherence approach — because from the human side beliefs must be compared with, and correspond to, other beliefs.

So much for definition: what about criteria for truth? Further explanation for now must be confined to two main points. First, the aforementioned Trinitarian structure of "the act by which we come to have true beliefs concerning the divine persons"[23] pertains not just to those true beliefs, but then to all true beliefs. Marshall takes the Col. 1:17 injunction "in Christ all things hold together" very seriously: even or especially truth — the community's central convictions — must hold together in Christ.[24] Therefore, "the chief standard for justified beliefs, we have argued, is that they at least be consistent with the narratives which identify Jesus and the triune God."[25] How then may we know, or justifiably believe, the truth? The church's Trinitarian convictions banish skepticism, so that

> beliefs justified according to these standards will generally be true just in case the triune God — and especially, in his distinctive way, the risen Christ — undertakes his truth-bestowing act (1) with regard to belief in the narratives which identify him, (2) with regard to no belief inconsistent with these narratives, and (3) with regard to beliefs which there is otherwise good reason to hold.[26]

So if first we decide — made willing by the Spirit — that truth holds together in Christ's revelation of the Father, then we seem to have embraced Christianity's "categorial" adequacy and "ontological" truth, to follow Lindbeck. But, secondly, we must decide what to do about other beliefs and other communities. Regarding other beliefs, having rejected the (modern) need for a thoroughgoing epistemic "dependence," Marshall suggests that "holding beliefs rationally requires not only the ability to give reasons, but the ability to distinguish between those occasions when we need to give reasons, and those when we do not." And he finds his view no worse off against charges of "fideism" than anyone else's.[27] Positively, he grants the possibility and importance of "giving reasons" for beliefs — though "without creating epistemic subordination and dependence"; negatively, he grants that "our epistemic responsibilities do seem to require that we be open to changing any *one* of our beliefs if given sufficient reasons to do so."[28] Moreover, he finds that "the imperative to take in alien beliefs" comes from within Christianity's embracing worldview, not from external pressure.[29]

Marshall further claims that "the epistemic novelty of the church's central beliefs does not depend on the apparently hopeless suggestion that the gospel is opposed to most or all of the beliefs which the rest of humanity holds true, but only on the contrast between the gospel and the epistemic *priorities* human beings are otherwise inclined to have."[30] This claim heightens the significance of the church's encounter with other communities. Alien beliefs, Marshall seems to say, are not usually problematic (criterion two above) once skepticism is vanquished (in criterion one). But what about that criterion, our Trinitarian truth that has rivals?

To the degree that Marshall represents a legitimate extension or development of Lindbeck, the relevance of his book appears just here, in two ways. First, the third criterion, concerning external beliefs that have good reason, does not give specifically Christian convictions or sources much work to do. Perhaps that could be viewed as a strength; from a Trinitarian account of creation and redemption, we have gained a healthy opportunity for human life and discovery in God's world. There might be a downside, however: are we really "taking every thought captive to Christ" in this fashion? The broader question this raises for a "cultural-linguistic" approach is whether theology becomes marginal to a secularized space, having become too parasitic on specifically religious linguistic practice (for which theology exists to set the rules). Conversely, does the secular space get marked off in a thoroughly nontheological way, with theology having ceded the turf to others?

Second, returning to the first criterion and prime claim of Marshall's work we must ask, what about the central beliefs of rival communities? How should the church dialogue with outsiders? In response, we are told "the Spirit will not persuade by adding something to the totality of belief, by giving us reasons or evidence we do not already have, but by eliciting our assent to a way of structuring the whole."[31] This persuasion is related, shortly thereafter, to the gift of wisdom, a gift that "goes hand in hand with that love for the Trinity which the indwelling Spirit sheds abroad in our hearts — the love which tastes, however faintly, the supreme goodness of the Father, and so by the Spirit's grace clings to the crucified and risen Jesus in spite of everything."[32]

Marshall's account "of how the Spirit persuades people to hold these beliefs true" is an extension of his account "of how the Spirit's action fixes the contents of central Christian beliefs."[33] In both cases, the church's communal life is central. Throughout, one reads about meaning as the bond between belief and truth, and also that "perhaps one important epistemic link of practice to belief lies not in the direction of evidence, but of meaning."[34] Lindbeck's turn against modern apologetics shows up again, as does his famous example:

> However one thinks of what truth is for sentences and beliefs, whether a sentence is true depends on what it means. Thus the suggestion that the practices of speakers fix the meaning of the sentences they utter cannot be equated with, nor does it imply, a 'pragmatic definition' of truth. If this suggestion is correct, it is quite compatible with the claim that the truth of sentences depends, as Davidson rather loosely formulates the point, on 'how the world is arranged.' To indulge the theological suspicion that because the world is arranged in such a way that Christ is the Lord, no one can ever say 'Christus est Dominus' and have it come out false, is therefore either to claim that this sentence is true regardless of what it means — which is absurd — or to claim that the practices of the people who speak it cannot make any important difference to what it means.[35]

Lindbeck's distinction between a religious statement and a doctrine, between speech and grammar, does not rule Marshall's work. But his distinction between "ontological" and "intrasystematic" truth (albeit refined) does pertain. As non-skeptical Christians our beliefs do have "ontological" pretensions to truth, whether they are central or less central or alien. But the meaning of our beliefs is very much an "intrasystematic" and "cultural-linguistic" matter. Christian practice was Marshall's means for identifying central beliefs; likewise, such practice is the Spirit's means for fixing the content of Christian beliefs. Not only that, such practice is the Spirit's means for persuading us to believe:

> If a share in the Father's creative and definitive knowledge is the end of the epistemic road, and the narratives which identify Jesus crucified and risen — not all alone, but as they are used to order the whole field of belief — are the road itself, then we traverse this road from beginning to end by partaking of the communally embodied love the Spirit imparts.[36]

Finally, note how the criteria for truth work back on its definition. Sharing in the Father's knowledge via the Spirit makes us bearers of the Son's image: "bearing the image of another is obviously a relation of correspondence." We correspond to the Father (even his knowledge!) as we bear the image of Christ. If this is the intended goal of the triune God's revelation, then "that believers bear the image of the risen Christ itself belongs to the concept of truth for whatever beliefs this relation requires, and similarly for the sentences which express those beliefs."[37]

Dialogue with outsiders, therefore, does not simply concern alien beliefs, or even what beliefs the Christian community is entitled to hold as central. No, at issue is not just the content of truth (what is true) but the definition of truth (what truth is). Christians are committed to a unique kind of realism, or truth's correspondence to reality, by virtue of the very beliefs that identify who they are.

Underlying the importance of practice shaping the meaning of Christian speech is the significance of language, of course. On this basis David Cunningham criticizes Lindbeck for ignoring "certain questions about context and commitment." By this he means that Lindbeck's view "reintroduces a strict dichotomy of subject and object — and in a form particularly alien to Christian theology," by rooting a doctrine's authority in its instantiation of a "rule." This is a failure, claims Cunningham, because the equivocity and dynamism of language do not allow the rules to come clear in expression or to act like rules. The significance of language and hence of interpretation means that doctrines are "shaped much more by the character and predispositions of interpreter and audience than by an imagined univocal definition," so that one must speak of the *"politics of doctrine"* and opt for dialectical instead of analytic modes of inquiry.[38] Perhaps ironically, given prior worries about Lindbeck's "cultural-linguistic" turn, Cunningham locates its escape from complete relativism in context — in rhetorical contexts of Christian practices and practitioners.[39]

II. Defending Theology's *Theoria:* Doctrine vis-à-vis Church, Language, and Truth

Yet, since some kind of realist definition (of truth involving correspondence to reality) seems essential to Christian faith,[40] many theologians are troubled by the irony just mentioned. In evaluating the cultural-linguistic turn, therefore, we must evaluate two corollary issues: the church's truth claims, and the language-ridden character of our relation to reality. Already, though, any hard-and-fast distinction between theory and practice has broken down, because the meaning of truth is expressed linguistically so that cultural practice impinges upon it. This entails rejecting linear moves either from theory to practice, or from practice to theory, as well as dialectical moves that take theory and practice to be discrete entities (whether or not they eventually are fused).[41] So what is the way forward?

A. Eschatology, Epistemology, and Testifying of Divine Action

John Webster acknowledges the worry of many concerning post-liberalism's odd Wittgensteinian fusion of Barth and Schleiermacher: "The emphasis on Christianity as culture can lay too much weight on the immanent realities of Christian believing and belonging, and give insufficient space to discussion of divine action (perhaps most of all in postliberal talk of scripture as the church's store of meanings rather than as testimony to divine revelation)."[42] Indeed, Kevin Vanhoozer follows Alister McGrath in questioning the sheer givenness of the Christian tradition, and its practices, that is found in Lindbeck. Vanhoozer wants to insist that the church follow "the communicative practices of the canon, rather than those of the interpreting community, as the primary locus of the meaning and truth of Christian faith."[43] Presumably Marshall's work would be a bit troublesome on this score as well: to identify the Christian community's core convictions, Marshall eschewed examining Scripture in favor of examining church practice.

The worry can, in fact, be taken farther than Vanhoozer does: why and how should one look to the communicative practices of the canon rather than the community? Does a "canonical-linguistic" approach still accept too much Christian particularity in concert with the "cultural-linguistic"? For doctrine does not simply serve, but is reciprocally involved with, other identity-giving functions of the Christian community.[44]

We must avoid a doctrine of revelation that "appears to be nothing more than a description of the faith of the religious community . . . not a doctrine of *revelation* at all."[45] So when it comes to Scripture, "God's prior initiative must be distinguished from the response of the community of faith. God's prevenience must be established not only as an intelligible category within the discourse of the text but also as a reality which confronts the reader *through* the text."[46] For many, this means turning to eschatology, prioritizing "promise" over "knowledge," thus avoiding the epistemic metaphor of sight which traps us in the modern problem of either full presence or else absence.[47]

As previously suggested, Wood's oscillation between "vision" and "discernment" does seem useful for describing how one's theology, informed by Scripture, might function as the "spectacles of faith" (in Calvin's famous phrase). Accompanying a frequent use of visionary metaphors, however, would be the danger of an overrealized eschatology when it comes to epistemology. Faith involves what is not yet seen, as a kind of knowledge that confesses we see through a glass darkly. The prominence of the Word metaphor in Scripture prioritizes the verbal over the visionary; indeed, it is with hearing that the biblical concept of faithful obedience becomes intertwined, not with sight. Hence an eschatological turn seems promising.

Yet the "eschatological realism" of Stanley Grenz, who takes the cultural-linguistic turn in this direction, may illustrate an opposite danger. For him, theology "explores the world-constructing, knowledge-producing, identity-forming 'language' of the Christian community," articulating the community's "belief-mosaic" or linguistic "framework."[48] That "belief-mosaic" is a vision of the eschatological world or community being constructed by the Holy Spirit, the world that is really "real" or "actual." Then we shall know fully, even as we are fully known. However, on this view, can we now know in part?

In the strictest sense, the answer seems to be no. Grenz raises the question that Lindbeck so often faces, of whether Christian theology articulates merely a particular tradition's interpretative framework or anything more "public." He acknowledges a certain "givenness" to the universe, but thinks that since reality is not static, the only object of which we can speak objectively is the world "as God wills it to be."[49] Hence "promise" has almost become exclusive of "knowledge," rather than simply a prime consideration in articulating theological epistemology.[50]

The resulting danger is that an account of the Bible's authority will become almost exclusively functional, in terms of how individual Christians or Christian communities happen to read the text for their future identity. Such a purely formal account would issue in irreducible material diversity.[51] Grenz, again, emphasizes the authority of the Spirit speaking "through" Scripture to construct the eschatological linguistic "world." He does not want to set Word and Spirit against one another: the Spirit's speaking "does not come as a speaking against the text." Yet the Spirit's speaking "is always a contextual speaking; it always comes to its hearers within a specific historical-cultural context."[52] The rub lies in what we make of this truism: in what way do we take culture to be a theological "source" or hermeneutical force? We must answer the question of how Christian doctrine can claim to anticipate the truth, given the particularity involved in cultural-linguistic practice.

For if the cultural-linguistic turn entails that linguistic worlds are thoroughly incommensurable, what about the possibility of understanding what God says we should teach? How can Christian communities testify to outsiders, and how can present-day Christians understand God's voice in the canon? No doubt Vanhoozer's "canonical-linguistic" emphasis and Grenz's "eschatological realism" both reflect a commitment to God's revelatory action through the Word of the Son and Spirit, even as Marshall discovers the primacy of this action in core Christian practices and the convictions they imply. Nevertheless, one wonders if Marshall and Grenz attend sufficiently to Scripture's authoritative witness, or if Vanhoozer and Grenz attend sufficiently to the linguistic question — to the significance of traditioned Christian practice "between the times."[53]

Related to postmodern suspicion about commensurable language is suspicion of "immediacy to experience," which seems to mean that "George Lindbeck's critique of what he calls the cognitive-propositional conception of theology is in effect an attack on the notion of revealed religion."[54] If a culture's language shapes experience as Lindbeck thinks, then his ecumenism is only a mixed blessing: do different conceptual articulations mask an underlying unity of cultural-linguistic practice (as he would often like to suppose), or do the different articulations actually pre-structure different practice (in which case ecumenism is potentially disastrous, because someone might break the doctrinal rules)? How would one know the difference? Is Christianity as religion a cultural-linguistic system, or is Christianity actually embodied and entangled in a host of such systems, both linguistic-doctrinal and cultural-practical?

Indeed, according to Philip Kenneson, we should doubt whether "Christianity" qualifies as a language game, given Wittgenstein's examples.[55] Accordingly, Miroslav Volf doubts the viability of Lindbeck's proposal on the question of agency: "Who or what is doing all these wonderful things Lindbeck says the Christian 'cultural-linguistic system' is doing?"[56] Again, the point is not to disavow Lindbeck's work but rather to advance the discussion with more careful handling of questions he has raised.

So Colin Gunton counters with the claim that the immediacy of revelation "is in some form biblical" — intratextually necessary! — and that apart from modernity "for all their variations, for all their requirement of the exercise of theological judgement and discussion, [creedal forms] are fundamentally *stable*."[57] We seem to need, therefore, an understanding of theology that respects *both* the stability of doctrine rendering a reality, *and* the importance of practices in linguistic context, for Christian identity. Such an understanding must work in tandem with a doctrine of revelation that is not obscurantist when it comes to the public, yet does not neglect the particular action of the Son and the Spirit — just what Reinhard Hütter seeks to provide.

B. Ecclesiology, Pneumatology, and Practicing Theology

In order to address the present-day truth status of Christian doctrine, Hütter contrasts "praxis" with "the quite distinct, theologically structured notion of 'practice,'" involving a "multiplicity of distinct and interconnected practices that cannot simply be subsumed under the rubric of a comprehensive 'praxis' but must be considered each in and for itself and with regard to their variously specific interconnections."[58] So he follows Luther in "explicating the church from the perspective of certain constitutive core practices which, as the work of the Spirit in its mission of the triune God's economy of salvation, simultaneously participate in the being of the Spirit itself," thereby participating in God's own freedom[59] to unfold redemption as a drama.

(1) Redefining "Practice" via the Pathos of Theology

The church is presupposed to be a distinct public sphere with its own integrity, with a redemptive *telos,* only then encountering other public entities.[60] This requires a reworking and careful use of certain Aristotelian categories. *Theoria* concerns the eternal and unchangeable, in contrast with praxis and now also with poiesis. Praxis deals with the natural and changeable involving both the action itself and the agent's character, whereas poiesis is evaluated on the quality of the work alone. Praxis is founded on *aretē* (virtue), poiesis on *technē* (skill or craft).[61] Hütter argues for theology as "one church *practice* among others within the comprehensive *praxis* of faith," but ties these to God's own poiesis.[62]

Faith is *vita passiva,* a life actualized in certain responsive activities, a "distinct comprehensive praxis"; some of these actualizing activities or "practices" are constitutive (e.g., sacraments), some are necessary (e.g., theology), and some are neither necessary nor constitutive (e.g., Christmas on December 25).[63] While Alasdair MacIntyre's larger Aristotelian aims are left behind by Hütter, the basic structure of MacIntyre's "practice" is maintained, in which the products that result (e.g., a sermon) are evaluated internally to the practice, from the perspective of its aims — aims that are distinct from the products. There is something essential happening internally to the Eucharist; that activity is not merely instrumental to an end that could be realized by another means. This ties together human and divine action, if God characteristically works through such practices in particular ways. Hütter wants to relate the practice of theology to the original sense of the term pathos, which is translated by the Latin *passio,* of "suffering" or "undergoing" as opposed to "doing." Neither the human affections, nor the pathos of rhetoric — nothing simply Aristotelian, therefore — is in view: "The reference is rather to the 'other' of action, that which determines or defines a person prior to all action, in all action, and against all action, that which a person can only *receive.*"[64] We "suffer" or undergo God's goodness via the hearing that is faith; this pathos corresponds to God's own poiesis, *"the poiesis of the Holy Spirit to which all theology is subjected and which is presented to theology in a quite specific way,"*[65] namely, dependence upon word, sacrament, and the church.[66]

While appreciative of the *"inseparable juxtaposition of faith actualization and faith content,"* Hütter maintains that Lindbeck's failure of a gospel ecclesiology leaves pathos purely formal and external to Christian practice in a sense.[67] As for Lindbeck's understanding of Christian truth claims, Hütter thinks that critics have repressed the real theological question at stake in favor of "old metaphysical concerns" over truth as correspondence or coherence.[68] What should matter is that *"if Lindbeck's distinction between church doctrine and theology really is to function, it implies theological discourse as an independent church practice between church doctrine on the one hand and the (ongoing) acquisition or learning of faith on the other"*; if the pathos of faith is to be truly central in the theological enterprise, then we cannot simply undertake theology-as-ethnography.[69]

While Barth long ago returned pneumatology to the discussion of theological prolegomena, Hütter questions his particular way of doing so. A focus on revelation seems to land the Holy Spirit in the subjectivity of the individual believer. In this way theology cannot have the necessary "unequivocalness of faith," but is tempted toward either the "unequivocalness of eschatological perception" or the "equivocalness of a dialectic that must also behave as if God takes with one hand what he gives with the other." We are easily impaled on the horns of the post-Reformation Western dilemma: institution versus charisma.[70]

Hütter's response is to suggest that if, in one sense, appropriate human action either anticipates, or responds to, divine action, we cannot stop with that. An "absent center" would follow: "if God's action in principle has never nor will it ever tie itself to any human action, then God's actions can be conceived only as becoming evident as God's self-manifestation in the interiority of the believer."[71] So we must not simply address theology, church, and doctrine; we must clarify the relation of the Holy Spirit and the church theologically, understanding "both the church and church doctrine rather as the work of the Holy Spirit,"[72] in which case "the incompleteness of theological statements is then to be understood not from the perspective of some *epistemologically* explicated eschatological reserve and then addressed in the form of dialectics, but from the perspective of the incompleteness of God's salvific work and of the attendant reality of concrete contradiction to God's salvific activity."[73]

(2) Suffering Divine Things and the "Practice" of Theology

Hütter opens his own proposal for accomplishing this with "the theological assertion that in order to be a church at all, the church needs binding doctrine."[74] All the church's core practices, he notes, "imply a normative standard, a *regula fidei* . . . a concern with the *correct* gospel proclamation, the *correct* administration of baptism, the *correct* performance of the Lord's Supper. . . ." Yet despite the need for such a rule, "in a reverse fashion, 'doctrine' isolated from the core practices can all too easily be reified, that is, become ersatz metaphysics in isolation from the soteriological telos."[75] Accordingly, he claims to take up from Luther "the theological insight that the *doctrina* and the core practices *together* actually constitute the indissoluble union of the work of Christ and of the Holy Spirit."[76]

Now because doctrine must be accessed via language, "to express the *doctrina evangelii* ever 'anew' without saying something 'new' in the process, or to express the one truth in variously new ways, theology as a church practice needs the horizon of canon, the core practices, and doctrine."[77] Doctrine's linguistic expressions, then, are a pathic horizon, along with the resulting praxis and consensus, by which the church participates in God's own exclusive freedom, including God's double hiddenness. Hütter thus maintains that "any immediate knowledge of God collapses before the eschaton."[78] And so, "it may sound paradoxical to modern ears, but Christian theology acquires and preserves its freedom exclusively as *church* theology."[79]

In that case, how does the church speak truth to worldly publics? Hütter advocates not a "*historicizing of the Holy Spirit* of the sort genuinely expressed in modern hermeneutics," but the "*pneumatologizing of history,*" in which "certain forms and articulations are appropriated by the Holy Spirit at certain times, acquiring thereby a form of permanence in the life of the church." Of course, like Scripture itself, these forms are linguistically expressed and thus will need translation; they will be more or less contested or helpful, as they cross contexts. Such truth remains, however, pathic as the poiesis of the Holy

Spirit's eschatological work. The correspondence to reality involved is uniquely Christian, not "part of a universally accessible metaphysical reality" but the promise of the gospel.[80]

This does not preclude theology's having a public place in society and the university. However, no public is neutral, so that theology "can acknowledge the binding principles constituting these publics only insofar as they can be qualified by the telos of the church." Theology is not, therefore, to be bound up either in religious studies or civil religion.[81]

If on the one hand we insist on the necessity of binding church doctrine, recovering the horizon of its gospel promise, on the other hand this "*theoria* of theology is utterly inaccessible without the horizon of the core practices constituting the church":

> The *theoria* of theology is thus neither theory in the classical sense as the free perception of the divine and of the divine order, nor in the early modern sense of the Cartesian knowledge of reflection, nor in the emphatically *modern* sense of a Hegelian mediation of the unity of theory and praxis through historical-philosophical speculation in which world history becomes the locus of the realization of reason.
>
> Rather, the *theoria* of theology always presupposes a nexus of distinct practices and is itself a distinct practice within this nexus.[82]

The resulting "theology" can be described in three essential aspects: (1) as a practice of argument and discourse, (2) as a practice of perception and judgment, and (3) as a practice of communication, albeit with each of these aspects oriented toward the next, so that communication is theology's "all-encompassing telos."[83] It is precisely the fixity of the *regula fidei* which allows that "its portrayal or presentation can be different, depending on the situation, completeness, method, and teacher."[84]

The communicative aspect of theology is simultaneously final in theology's *"substantive order"* yet first in theology's *"teleological order."* This ultimate aspect of theology oscillates between two poles, (1) catechesis or "initiatory acquisition," leading new believers into Christian pathos, and (2) "ongoing learning" which allows for poiesis within pathos, doing justice to theology's "context of discovery."[85]

So then, theological discovery amid Christian praxis must have "a specific and binding horizon (biblical canon and *doctrina*) and . . . specific and binding configurations of language and activities (the core practices)."[86]

There is a properly Christian theoretical aspect to theology; formulations of church doctrine can become binding via the Spirit rather than being left behind as mere contingencies.[87] Nevertheless, Hütter balks at theology's every-person character, upon which my project has heretofore insisted, still separating church doctrine and the New Covenant knowledge of God discussed in chapter 2. Theology itself is a practice related to the church's teaching, as in the work of James McClendon. For Hütter, though, theology is undertaken by only a select few on the church's behalf. But neither is theology a matter of its teaching authority directly. Therefore, we must consider the rationale behind this, as well as a possible reform of his proposal.

III. Redefining Theology "Practically": Doctrine as Instruction in Communicative Praxis

At this point recapitulation and crystallization of this chapter's argument is appropriate. First I described the "cultural-linguistic" turn in theology and doctrine that has resulted from the work of Lindbeck. On this account, doctrines function as grammatical rules for proper religious speech; theology is a second-order "intratextual" activity of an ethnographic sort, centered in "figural reading" of Scripture to adjudicate the doctrinal rules.

Some inadequacies of Lindbeck's rule-theory of doctrine have been uncovered in opposite directions at once. On the one hand, Lindbeck does not adequately account for the doctrinal rules requiring linguistic instantiation. Evidence of this problem surfaces frequently in reflection on contexts of Christian practice and their rhetorical importance for theology. If the rule-theory promotes ecumenism by allowing for multiply-stated rules, it could also highlight the need to get right the language that structures experience and praxis.

On the other hand, both "cognitive-propositionalists" and "experiential-expressivists" (who, indeed, still find doctrines to be propositional truth claims, only after a different fashion)[88] worry about Lindbeck's intratextuality. However appropriate is concern about "extratextual" frameworks controlling biblical interpretation, Lindbeck's proposal does not adequately account for the truth claims that Christians suppose themselves to make vis-à-vis other publics. In other words, he does not help us to explain *why* a doctrine is regulative; as the assertive form of his exemplary rules signals to us, doctrines are regulative *because* they are informative or expressive, and so on. He forces upon us an "unacceptable choice" by proffering intratextuality "instead of" what is essentially a natural theology.[89] In between there may lie more sensitive possibilities for theology to involve conceptual re-description in context.

The cultural-linguistic turn threatens to charge theology with talking about talk[90] rather than talking about God, a conception that flies in the face of Christianity's character as a revealed religion. That the modern revolution mandates a very careful doctrine of revelation as we sift through the rubble of the "house of authority," should not be disputed. That postmodern turns have complicated and contextualized linguistic reference also should not be disputed. Yet the work so far has necessitated some theoretical aspect to Christian theology and some fairly stable, binding dimension to Christian truth claims. Hence the question of theory and practice must be considered alongside the question of prevenient divine action.

I therefore engaged, secondly, the recent work of Hütter, who locates theology as a church practice between the first order — the core Christian practices — and the second order — binding Christian doctrine or dogma. From this pathos of undergoing the Holy Spirit's poiesis, theology finds its truest freedom in the public with a redemptive *telos,* the church. Hütter's "pneumatologizing of history" can be affirmed in response to the shortcomings of Lindbeck's proposal: the linguistic instantiations of doctrine are necessary actualizations — the Holy Spirit's poiesis — for their context and are instructive for other times and places as well. They address the correctness of core Christian practices because they are concerned with the truth claims of the gospel itself.

However, two related worries point to modifications of this proposal. First, the "who" of theology: Hütter sees theology as a practice for a select few, in a complex relation to the church's teaching authority. Second, the "what" of theology: Hütter's notion of doctrine avoids traditional metaphysics by focusing upon gospel formulation to regulate core Christian practices. However, theology's oscillation between the first and second orders could undercut doctrinal engagement with both worldly reality and virtuous Christian praxis. That is, each Christian practice involves the argumentative, judgmental, and communicative aspects of theology that Hütter describes; moreover, wise Christian teaching itself is bound up with a quest for how to live in the world. Hütter's discrete location for theology threatens to set these too far apart. The underlying issue, I will claim, is that he has inappropriately institutionalized the church's teaching authority over against Scripture.

A. The "Who" of Theology: Everyone's "Priesthood"

The last chapter argued, from scriptural antecedents, that *theologia* should be seen in terms of everyone's communicative praxis concerning God, bound up with *paideia* of the Spirit oriented toward New Covenant knowledge of God in Jesus Christ. Hütter's proposal, by contrast, makes *theologia* a distinct practice of a select few vis-à-vis church teaching authority. The university's pattern of separating religious practice and theology is of course prevalent as well. Do the chief arguments for such a distinction overturn our presumptive case for relating *theologia* rather directly to the *paideia* of Christian faith?

(1) Church Teaching

Oswald Bayer's position, against which Hütter argues, bears some structural similarities to my own, for Bayer sees academic theology differing from "theology within the normal actualization of faith" only in degree, not in kind.[91] But many cannot abide this perceived loss of "second-order discourse." For Bayer charges theology, Hütter suggests, with "binding and loosing," so that theological debate is "crippled"; theology cannot be a "scholarly discipline"; ultimately, the "logical primacy" of doctrinal content to performative speech is lost.[92]

A major theme of my first chapter, that setting theology loose as a scholarly discipline is precisely to engender the loss of *sapientia,* already counters such a claim. Then there is the biblical-theological counterpoint from chapter 2. Moreover, these arguments may be supplemented with two additional counterclaims, about the church's teaching ministry. First, to connect theology with "binding and loosing" is to add sobriety and significance to its task, but not necessarily to "overtax" it "hopelessly." The distinction for which Hütter fights strongly suggests that theology does not speak directly about God, in the first instance; he sets theology too free.

Conversely he sees "binding and loosing" too narrowly. NT patterns for (e.g., Matt. 18:15-20; 3 John; Jude), and instances of (e.g., 1 Cor. 5:1-13; Acts 15:1-29), disciplining theological judgments are not simply cases of clerical leadership, involving isolated spheres of theological discussion. The initiative of leadership seems indexed to the maturity of the discerning congregations, but undertakes the education and involvement of all God's people in the decisions; the truthful witness of all God's people is at stake. Moreover, both the canonical and post-canonical periods of the church suggest that theological discussion is stimulated by, and accountable to, precisely the questions of "binding and loosing," of who may teach and what may be taught with concern for the communal identity.

Second, a similar pattern holds for teaching. That the exalted Christ gives the gift of teachers to the church, or the special gift of teaching to particular people within the church, is undoubted. The relation of these gifts to church office could bog discussion down in a quagmire of competing ecclesiologies with no escape. However, while conceding that both "binding and loosing" and church teaching are topics worthy in themselves of whole monographs, I would nevertheless claim that biblical connections of "teaching" to every member of the church are frequently neglected in theological prolegomena.

The New Covenant, again, involves the diffusion of the Holy Spirit, who previously was connected to special task or office, upon every member of the church. Everyone, it is hoped, will "speak the truth in love," growing competent to exhort one another (Rom. 15:14; cf. Heb. 3:12-13 with 5:11-14). The variety of aspirations to, and actualizations of, what constitutes "teaching" in the NT is further corroborating evidence (e.g., Jas. 3:1-3, 13-18; Titus 2; 1 John 2:20-27). Whatever the exact church polity, the "priesthood of the believer" was an important theme recovered in the Protestant Reformation.

Granted, there is irony in criticizing Lindbeck and Hütter — who have recovered the significance of church practice for theology — on this point. Nevertheless, it is intriguing that Hütter's proposal may possess sufficient ambiguity to transcend the Protestant–Roman Catholic divide between institution and charism.[93] Is such ecclesiastical ambiguity necessarily a virtue, depending on how the bridge between the two is constructed?

Ephraim Radner has poignantly highlighted the crucial interface between ecclesiology, pneumatology, and theological authority. He accepts Richard Popkin's thesis that Protestants and Roman Catholics, after the Reformation, "were set against each other in a dizzying and always fruitless effort to justify their canons of interpretive criteria," a "circularity" of "criteriology" which led to "methods of discourse that, all sides agreed, reeked of skepticism."[94] Adopting a figural interpretation of the church's division being tied to the Israelite kingdom's division, Radner concludes that we must acknowledge "pneumatic absence from the church." Scripture cannot speak the gospel to its divided hearers "except insofar as it unveils our deaf incomprehension."[95] Churches may attain "particular understandings" of biblical texts, but not a "true hearing" that involves "the general understanding of Scripture as the Gospel of Christ manifest and perceived."[96]

Arrogance, of course, is the danger in either the Protestant or Roman Catholic side claiming Israel's "faithful remnant" texts as their own.[97] Yet both must do so, in a sense, and not only due to mutually exclusive understandings of "one, holy, catholic, and apostolic" church. For ingredient to the gospel is some contrast between Old and New Covenants regarding the work of the Holy Spirit in personal lives. Admission of our personal and corporate sinfulness, not least in theological epistemology, cannot entail disavowing this. Division can require the disavowal of apparently false teaching, the NT shows; even if one hopes that Protestant–Roman Catholic disagreements increasingly avoid that category, Radner's portrait of NT commitment to church unity appears one-sided. Moreover, it is a socio-historical reality that division can be associated with spiritual renewal, and the NT seems aware of its possible coincidence with the Spirit's presence (e.g., 1 Cor. 11:18-19).[98] Whatever our ecumenical hopes and possibilities, the divisions of the past may have been needful. Or, at the very least, we should avoid all-or-nothing evaluations of competing ecclesiastical claims to grasp the gospel.

History bears out that neither "institution" nor "charism" is an unqualified good. However, at least one may claim that New Covenant fulfillment of OT expectations makes some space for personal judgment within the church: the Spirit speaking in Scripture to the church, an anointing that enlightens the eyes of believing hearts, must retain a certain *extra nos* character, outside the church as well as the individual.

This necessity arises soteriologically; because we do not have the will to love as we ought, institutional Christian practice must not become so routine and all-encompassing that no room is left for interruptive or freely justifying divine grace.[99] Such interruptions need not preclude God's commitment to church practices as prime means of grace, but there remains a practical necessity: divine transcendence can serve as a potent critical principle for theology,[100] yet if Scripture simply becomes a storehouse of meanings ruled immanently by church interpretation,[101] the force of that critical principle seems lost.

Likewise, loss or lack of dogma may have "helped generate the undisciplined disorder" of Protestantism, but giving up a careful version of *sola scriptura* may not be the solution; perhaps it is "the excessive uniformity sometimes imposed by Rome that has encouraged the rebelliousness of many theologians."[102] The very real danger, and sad reality, of Protestant individualism and fragmentation should be seen as a selective and mistaken appropriation of Luther and Calvin, rather than a necessary entailment of their basic position. Neither "institution" nor "charism" alone can guarantee the stability of a truly faithful Christian identity.

Both, in fact, can work with a fairly hard-and-fast distinction between first-order religious speech and second-order doctrinal discourse. Such a distinction, however, is difficult to square with a vital connection between doctrine and practice. Yet its breakdown does square with the present worry that Hütter makes theology and doctrine excessively institutional. This tends to correlate with the second-order statements of a grammar really being "talk about talk"; consider, for example, "subjects and verbs must agree in number."[103] That does not seem to be a fitting paradigm for thinking about doctrine, especially since many doctrinal statements can double as religious ones in talking about God (which Lindbeck admits). The fact that second-order statements somehow transcend their particular cultural-linguistic frameworks also belies a hard-and-fast distinction; at the least, we would have to say that such statements imply indirect or intermediary first-order statements.[104] David Ford relates the first/second-order distinction to Lindbeck's use of three "ideal types" regarding the nature of doctrine, and thinks this vulnerable to "one-sidedness and misinterpretation" which ignores the possibility of a "more thorough integration of rules, categories, and content."[105]

The upshot is that Hütter's pathic horizon of "canon, the core practices, and doctrine," and his partially-institutionalized theology, are coordinates. He simultaneously neglects the every-member knowledge of God given in Scripture as the prime horizon of accountability for the core practices, as well as the implications of the potential for every church member to live and teach the truth of Christian wisdom. Knowing that the Spirit works through binding doctrine is important for the *possibility* of church identity and theological practice, but we still face the question of recognizing the Spirit's *actual* work. Were Hütter to see doctrinal formulations binding us as vital but subordinate instantiations of what God has said to the church in Scripture, he would neither have to institutionalize "binding and loosing," nor free theology to be a "scholarly discipline," quite as he does.

(2) Communicative Praxis

Once again, an account of theology must address not only the special and general aspects of Christian teaching, but also the hermeneutical dimensions of ordinary Christian living. The concept of "communicative praxis" assists in explicating this.

A useful starting point is Calvin Schrag's recognition that "theory, scientific as well as philosophical, is itself a form of communicative praxis,"[106] that is, partaking in "the interplay of presence and absence" which may be described ontologically in terms of "temporality, multiplicity, and embodiment."[107] Discourse and action are "*about* something" and "*by* someone" yet their various subjects are "not *foundations* of communicative praxis . . . but are rather implicates of it, emerging within its history and modified by its changing scenes."[108] Schrag's development of the subject via "implicature" seems to be a good analogue of Charles Taylor's "best account" principle, namely, that we should develop the best possible account of what is implied in the practices of ordinary life and especially moral agency.[109]

Communicative praxis involves both "expressive discourse" and "expressive action," each including both events/actions and histories/systems (of language and social practices).[110] We use the terminology of "communicative praxis" instead of "communicative action" in order to "indicate that the normative 'action' is never totally objectified or expressed."[111] Applied to theology, this concept would suggest a strong interrelationship between doctrine and practice. Thus theology's rhetorical aspect should "deformalize truth as the manipulation of propositions and reinsert it into a hermeneutic of everyday life, where truth is more a matter of disclosure than correspondence, making manifest the dynamics of the social world as a web of human affects and interests."[112] Emphasizing truth as disclosure means that "the discovery of truth is indissolubly linked with its communication . . . expression, reference, and persuasion unfold in a developing reciprocity."[113]

Without relinquishing all the aspects of truth as corresponding with reality, we can acknowledge Schrag's broad claims: if even theology's theoretical aspect of doctrine partakes of the rhetorical, so that "a complementarity of speech and action" is involved, then theological rationality "slides into ethics." The primary category for hermeneutical reflection will thus be "fitting response" or "*responsiveness,*" following a logic of questioning.[114] Varying intensities of critical reflection, and uses of academic skills and tools, between university or ecclesial theologians and parishioners, will be matters of degree rather than kind.

In communicative praxis, ideas are recognized to be embedded in practices and "articulate practices as patterns of dos and don'ts."[115] The notion of a "concept" developed later in this chapter suggests that the patterns are actually present in reality, or should be; all is not left to church whim. But the important recognition is that many shared Christian beliefs live in the "tacit background of objects of reliance"[116] until some situation or other evokes their expression in discourse/action. The evocation might be the worship or witness of the ordinary believer, or it might be the challenges encountered in the special vocation of teaching the church. These situations offer new opportunities to realize expressions of Christian communicative praxis, even as these realizations will often "say nothing new," simply bringing the background to articulation. In Schrag's words,

> The present is understood not as a punctual now but as the opportune moment for decision. The response to the past is one of recollection, occasioning a preservation of the discourse and social practices of the *polis.*

> The response to the future is that of a projection and anticipation of new possibilities for redescription and reinterpretation, setting the stage for novelty and invention.[117]

To what, if any, notion of "objectivity" can this model hold? Intersubjectivity seems crucial to answering that: not only "participation" but also "distanciation and critique" will be required undertakings,[118] to render judgments about — and which serve as — "*transsubjective* validity claims."[119] Jürgen Habermas's work on this point is important and worthy of much more ink than we can spill here, as is the debate regarding whether or not Hans-Georg Gadamer emphasized participation to the exclusion of distanciation. For now, only this brief comment can be made: transsubjectivity and sought-after consensus are vital to the truth claims Christians make, and this suggests that criticism of those truth claims ought to be faced. But the possibility of defending truth claims — or the need to offer reasons — should be distinguished from Habermas's requirement (yet impossibility?) "that a communicatively achieved agreement must be based *in the end* on reasons,"[120] at least narrowly conceived as the exclusive basis of agreement. Perhaps Habermas betrays a nostalgia for the Enlightenment on that point, although his distinction between purposive activity and communicative action remains important: Christian witness ought to seek after understanding rather than using manipulation. In that sense reasons certainly do not drop out, but a suitably broad, whole-personed notion of "understanding" them is necessary.

The call is for all to recognize the sense in which their communicative praxis is theological — as Christian witness it concerns God — so that they take responsibility for discernment in embodying, and discovering afresh, a Christian vision. If liberation theology has made possible this recognition of every-person theologizing, nevertheless the grudging admission of that truism has scarcely influenced theological prolegomena to date. The call for every-believer theologizing does not trivialize the word "theology," but heightens responsibility. Nor does that call deny the special gift or office of teaching the church, in which the intensity of discernment — and usually of engagement with scholarship — is heightened. However, the difference concerns degree, not kind.

B. The "What" of Theology: Doctrine and Communicative Praxis

One might still counter that the above proposal loses any binding aspect to doctrine. This could occur in at least two senses: in opting for a version of *sola scriptura,* we could easily be ensnared in Protestant individualism and theological fragmentation of interpretative making; or we could lose any means of retaining canonical unity through a *regula fidei.* With Thomas Jefferson, might everyone pick the parts of the Bible that seem right in their own eyes? Such charges are common enough in our day, and they raise the larger questions regarding "theological interpretation of Scripture" that will be addressed in succeeding chapters.

The truth-teaching aspect of doctrine, however, must be addressed now. Can we have the best of Hütter's "pneumatologizing of history" without the institutional privilege he accepts? For Maurice Wiles has often held forth the difficulty of doctrinal "development": on the one hand he claims that "the concept of the Spirit's guidance *by itself* can be used to legitimate anything, which means that it can be used to legitimate nothing"; on the other hand, he thinks that "we cannot lay down any rules about the relation of contemporary doctrine to the affirmations of the past which will not be so general as to offer no practical guidance at all."[121] Indeed, criticizing the classic formulation of John Henry Newman, he suggests that a doctrinal development be judged true or false based on "continuity of aim."[122]

Admittedly in quite different ways, both Hütter and Wiles leave a lot riding on the church's judgment about which developments instantiate the gospel doctrine. Just what sort of permanence do doctrinal forms have: how are they binding, and what is their relation to the church practice of teaching as well as theology? Must we choose between a static doctrinal unity across time and place (that would deny the significance of practice for the meaning of Christian beliefs), and such a dynamic diversity of practice that doctrines' biblical and traditional formulations have no permanence? In my judgment, a more robustly normative role for Christian Scripture is needed, as that linguistically-instantiated canon by which various doctrinal statements can be measured (hence the focus of succeeding chapters on Scripture's relation to the *Regula fidei*). Otherwise we fall back into the problem of finding rules too separate from linguistic form. Thus the relation of "canon" and doctrinal "concept"[123] returns us to issues of language and truth once more.

(1) "Relative Adequacy" and "Critical Realism"

The linguistic incommensurability accepted by many theologians after the language games of Wittgenstein and the paradigm shifts of Thomas Kuhn is open to challenge simply in terms of general theory. Scientists, yea theologians, from differing traditions seem to achieve a basic level of communication across boundaries; within various traditions, Kuhn's revolution may confuse the "rate of change and the degree of change" in the movement of scientific paradigms.[124]

Furthermore, the significance of good translations from one language to another, which is granted only grudgingly by some, should not be understated. If it is admitted that languages can be translated, but language games cannot,[125] then we could grant that claim by definition. Still, however, the danger lurks of freshly bifurcating practice and language, losing the priority of "meaning" as use. Commitment to a "basic logic" and "other substantive beliefs" seems to accompany the possibility of translation;[126] people must recognize, at least, that their language games are different.

Aside from the vicissitudes of general theories, however, the theologian may have quite particular reasons to forswear any staunch linguistic incommensurability. Christianity's monotheistic truth claims and associated divine revelation would seem to demand realism of some sort; at least we must be able to communicate with other publics. Christianity also needs a relative adequacy of its doctrines' truth, and a relative stability of its doctrinal formulations across time and place.

Can such adequacy and stability be claimed without denying the significance of contextual practice for linguistic meaning? Befitting an emphasis on rationality as involving argument within the frame of conversation or dialogue, David Tracy provides the appropriate tool with a notion of "relative adequacy." He follows Bernard Lonergan in suggesting that a judgment is not "absolutely unconditioned" but "virtually" so, "since it answers the questions relevant to the subject, the criteria and the evidence now available to competent inquirers." Yet in this way judgments are "by definition open to further revision as further questions emerge. And further questions will always eventually emerge."[127] Sometimes the questions will have to do with the content of the judgment itself, whereas other times its formulation or articulation in a context of practice will be at issue.

So then, if adequacy is defined as having no more relevant questions to answer, a kind of critical realism can ensue. There can often be confidence and conviction regarding the truth of Christian doctrine, regarding its description corresponding to what has been revealed about the reality over which God rules, or about its anticipation of what God will bring to pass in the new creation. Yet such confident conviction will not — or at least should not — lapse into arrogance. For faith is not sight; because we await the consummation of God's kingdom rule, we do not have the clarity of eschatological vision (1 Cor. 13:12). Additionally, the realism will be critical because life in the present cosmos will generate new questions for theologians to answer in formulating doctrinal statements. This is not philosophical "occasionalism"[128] but principled acceptance of a connection between theology and the pilgrimage involved in Christian *paideia.*

The contention should be made explicit that particular doctrinal statements involve a definition of truth as correspondence with reality, not just with Christian doctrine as a whole. Nevertheless, the coherentists are entirely correct to suggest that, in terms of criteria for truth, Christian beliefs interrelate — indeed, they interact with non-Christian beliefs still often held by Christians — in all kinds of ways. Christian doctrine can function as a whole, in both propositional and cultural-linguistic terms, because particular doctrines engage in a sort of perichoretic dance, around a core *regula fidei* — Trinitarian belief.[129] The resulting Christian view of truth, whatever the general theory terms used for its articulation, will involve correspondence not simply in defining truth, but also partly in testing for it. Correspondence to Jesus Christ can mean, positively, believing (and living!) what God says in Scripture; negatively, beliefs may be falsified by contradicting what God says in Scripture. Yet this is, in another sense, quite a coherentist approach, involving the relation of beliefs to other beliefs — instantiated or implied in the Bible. Christ-centered doctrines of creation and revelation give Christians a potent solution to skeptical problems about language and world.

Our notion of adequacy is related to the question of doctrinal stability: how close must the various correspondences be? As in chapter 2's discussion of Christian selfhood, so also, with regard to church and doctrine, we need an *ipse*-identity (narrative continuity) instead of *idem*-identity (exact sameness). Doctrinal identity will be discovered in relation to multiple "others" at once; applying a reworked notion of self-identity to this problem is especially appropriate because doctrine functions as a social demarcator for the church's identity.[130] After all, doctrine is a matter of personal and social agency, of both divine and human action over time.

For this reason, several scholars are following in the footsteps of Hans Urs von Balthasar, and formulating notions of theology and doctrine in terms of drama. They do so in different ways, often without pursuing the power of drama as an analytic tool very deeply. Nevertheless, their move seems fundamentally correct. For, as Richard Heyduck points out, cognitive-propositional approaches arguably derived from a preoccupation with relating theology to science; experiential-expressivist approaches derived from a preoccupation with relating theology to art; and a dramatic version of a cultural-linguistic approach can relate theology to action.[131] Drama is a fitting way to pursue a notion of theology that is biblical by being salvation-historical and eschatologically-oriented,[132] and also to plot the relationships of divine and human action in their necessarily diverse ways.[133]

For the prime "otherness" involved in negotiating the church's identity by the Spirit will be the action of God in and through the scriptural canon. Yet a thoroughgoing "intratextuality" is impossible on two fronts: there is a kind of diversity internal to the canon, and there is the cultural-linguistic context in which the doctrinal statement is formulated.[134]

(2) "Relative Stability" and Narrative Identity

First, the otherness of the canon must be considered in connection with the diversity of its own voices. Vanhoozer has addressed the tension between "canon" and "concept," between "sameness" and "otherness," by arguing for the possibility of "conceptual mimesis" involving "creative imagination." His specific query was the diversity of biblical genres, diversity that invites conceptual re-description while also forestalling any absolute sameness within that re-description. The very diversity of genre is bound up with *necessarily* diverse, imaginative ways of truth that relate language and life.[135]

To this query about canonical diversity must be added the various conceptual patterns within a literary form; David Yeago provides a helpful example by countering arguments for multiple, widely differing, NT Christologies. Yeago demonstrates the possibility of similar theological judgments taking different conceptual forms.[136] Both these aspects of canonical unity-with-diversity deserve further attention when addressing theological interpretation of Scripture; for now, the need is highlighted for an *ipse-*, narrative concept of identity that utilizes multiple conceptual forms in rendering like judgments.

Second, then, the otherness of the canon must be addressed vis-à-vis any subsequent cultural-linguistic context. While "concepts" require a degree of theory-independence to achieve relative stability of judgments across such distance,[137] this does not force us thereby into an antiquated understanding of language. Linguist Kathleen Callow suggests that for explaining translation we need "a mental correlate of words which is not language specific."[138] She tackles the difficulty of defining such concepts and concludes that they should be understood as "habitual events" acquired "by participation" in activities.[139] Concepts have "firm cores" of meaning with vast amounts of detail, some of which we draw upon in any particular thinking event, in any action of referring.[140] So "concepts are not what we think about; they are what we think with."[141] Concepts are "instruments of understanding,"[142] understanding that consists of theological judgments which have "intersubjective availability" and are thus communicative.[143]

(3) "Concepts" as Habits of Christian Practice

Could this view leave us with concepts as merely "social skills"[144] so that the Christian language game is unintelligible to the outsider? On the one hand, contextual "otherness" should not be overemphasized to the point of a hard incommensurability or unintelligibility. John Milbank points out that all of us live with a sort of fragmentation, with multiple subjectivities;[145] or, put differently, we indwell a plenitude of language games. Yet, whether or not we lack an "essential" self, we do not fly apart into utter schizophrenia either. This strongly suggests the possibility that meaning can transcend cultural-linguistic barriers. Often we recognize *when* something seems lost in translation, even if we do not know *what* all is lost; we can work toward understanding, even as we strive for personal integrity despite our various social roles. In addition, Christian theology often involves "communicative" and "critical" styles that respond in catechesis and apologetics to stimuli from other publics;[146] in this fashion "doctrinal discourse has as its only *Sitz im Leben* an intellectually vigorous pluralism,"[147] a pluralism that elicits communicative engagement rather than enclosure.

On the other hand, we must learn to appreciate that Christian practices *do* affect the understanding of doctrinal meaning and thereby capacity for theological judgment. As socially-formed habits of thinking, the concepts of Christians are shaped by a variety of interactions. The point of Christian teaching or doctrine is to norm these habits by the mind of Christ through Scripture, then freeing them for the church's creative contextual use as led by the Holy Spirit.

If the significance of Christian practices does not suggest a hard incommensurability in which Christian language is utterly unintelligible to the world (or to Christians as they live in various worlds), nevertheless the primacy of conversion is highlighted.[148] The Holy Spirit, Christians believe, elicits a new way of viewing the world as a whole, beginning to find wisdom with the fear of God in Christ. Moreover, once *sapientia* is made possible, its actual growth involves the learning of Christian habits, all of which are bound up with theological understanding. Doctrine is not statically reified, due to a redemptive *telos;* however, it must be added that the gospel promise offers not only forgiveness in Christ, but also the Spirit's enablement for virtuous living-in-communion — including the development of relatively stable understanding.

By seeing concepts as habits for thinking events, "social skills" formed amidst practice that refers them to reality, we may understand both the permanent and the performative aspects of doctrinal statements. It is not that doctrine instantiates a theological judgment in the only way possible. Nor need we act as if the Bible is simply a storehouse of concepts uniformly connected to particular words. But doctrine does instantiate a theological judgment with relative adequacy, and because concepts form habits of Christian communicative action, doctrinal statements are a way for the Spirit to maintain the church's relatively stable identity, to link the story of the church's theological judgments with the canonical Rule of faith.

Merold Westphal rightly worries, therefore, that fixation with propositions has preoccupied theology with "facts" for theoretical reason. By thinking rather in terms of communicative praxis, we strive for the modest "double holism" — "semantic" and "practical" or "pragmatic" — necessary to recover practical reason in theology. Practices "play a constitutive role in generating our meanings and truths, but our cognitions feed back into our practices as well."[149] Christian theology may maintain that, while truth is public and communicable, modes of knowing and engaging that truth are not always entirely accountable to the reigning epistemological canons.[150]

C. Theology as Practice-Encompassing Meta-Discourse

Having considered theology's relation to church doctrine in concert with its relation between theory and practice, what may we conclude? Doctrine is indeed easier to describe than to define.[151] Jaroslav Pelikan has suggested that like "tradition," "doctrine" can refer simultaneously to the process and the content of communication;[152] this dual reference fits the pattern of "theology" and "wisdom" in prior chapters. Christian teaching or doctrine is properly construed as instruction in wisdom, conferring imaginative (though not just humanly imposed) "designs for living."[153] This means, on the one hand, that doctrine cannot be separated from ethics; doctrine is sapiential in that the *theoria* of Christian truth claims always (at least) implies praxis, a way of life.[154] On the other hand, we must allow for the biblical critique of hypocrisy; there exists the possibility of knowing the truth without doing it (consider especially the book of James).

A certain distinction, without separation, between confession and conduct can therefore be made.[155] Just as wisdom involves *sophia* and *phronēsis*, however, so doctrine involves both the theoretical and the practical; occasionally necessary distinctions — that explain the failure to live out confessed convictions — must not push the two apart.

Christian practices hold these dimensions of wisdom, the *sophia* and *phronēsis* of Christian teaching, together. Because the teaching that makes wise unto salvation embraces the whole of living, such teaching is communicable to the world. However, the Holy Spirit must elicit the fear of the Lord — a conviction that elicits conformity to Jesus' way of life — in order for true understanding to occur. Thereafter participation in Christian practices aids growth in understanding of Christian convictions. If doctrine is instruction in communicative praxis, like wisdom it incorporates both a general communicability of "vision" and the particular situatedness of "discernment."

Despite linguistic and conceptual diversity, a narrative *(ipse-)* identity of personal constancy for theological judgments is possible through the church's Spirit-given continuity and growth. Moreover, the implications of the canon's normative theological judgments may foster additional renderings and even additional judgments evoked by the questions of other times and places, a subject explored in chapters to follow.[156] These theological judgments, and the capacity for them, are learned not only by reading Scripture, but through church teaching. Doctrine, as the matter of this teaching practice, utilizes an *ipse*-identity of conceptual forms — utilizes habits of thinking, in other words — to pass on, and enable the formation of, like judgments. The narrative identity of doctrine serves the learning of Christian truth by instantiating in particular ways the normative canonical judgments.

The following chapters will explore how such judgments are reached through theological interpretation of Scripture, since this discussion of doctrine has highlighted that theology must be "prepared to integrate a 'performative' mode into its work."[157] Analogies with music and drama incorporate both a measure of stability and faithful improvisation, which will be important for theological interpretation of Scripture. The notion of performance accords nicely with Hütter's "pneumatologizing of history," in which doctrines are truth-judgments instantiated in particular conceptual forms.

Still, we are left to decide how these conceptual forms function. Theology is not a discrete practice *per se*, but is performed within a host of Christian practices as people engage in communicative action concerning God, as people seek to live wisely — they "understand," or exercise capacities of relation to God.[158] Such understanding makes theology practice-encompassing,[159] although — in line with the activity-versus-content ambiguity I have emphasized — theology is what Milbank calls a "meta-discourse" as well.[160] That is, due to its subject matter referring to God, theology both embraces and is constituted within a variety of communicative practices. Theology is a discrete discourse, in a sense, yet not a discrete practice. It is the communication concerning God which occurs in teaching, preaching, sacramental life, Christian hospitality, and so on.

Theological understanding involves the habits called "concepts." The Christian practice of teaching or doctrine is perhaps the most directly theological practice, in association with the reading of Scripture. These practices are about the formation of Christian communicative judgment; they instruct Christians in, and actualize, communicative praxis that conforms to Jesus Christ via scriptural norms. Particular doctrinal statements, when they are in narrative continuity with canonical judgments, are binding as the Spirit's way of linking Christians across time and place to apostolic testimony. They build a bridge, one plank at a time, from the "canonical-linguistic" world, across the various "cultural-linguistic" worlds we all inhabit, to reach the eschatological "world" for which we hope.

When theology is seen as a discrete practice of a particular group, the *theoria* of biblical truth, life in the "real world," and hoped-for eschatological praxis can seem disconnected. Moreover, doctrinal "binding and loosing," without being subordinate to Scripture by actualizing and imitating its thinking habits, can foster institutionalism to the detriment of ecclesiastical humility. Because the practices of teaching and reading Scripture invite both every-member participation and God's gift of leadership — subject to the Spirit's interruptive communicative action — and because other church practices affect understanding of Christian convictions, both individualism and doctrinal fragmentation can in principle be avoided (although frequently this has not been the case in practice).

Theological responses — using the conceptual habits of doctrine — should be seen not as *"dictated"* by circumstances and therefore dying with them, but as possibilities "which the circumstances gave us occasion to realize,"[161] fitting the *sophia-phronēsis* pattern of Christian wisdom. The former circumstances will connect in various ways to common aspects of human and ecclesial experience. Doctrine means instruction in communicative praxis, using conceptual habits to instantiate Christian vision and teach communicative judgment. The link between *theoria* and praxis is inextricable because of the pathos of Christian practices with which theology is bound up. Imagination and rhetoric will be incorporated into the resulting theological rationality because of this practical pathos. Yet, if God must first teach us, a prime means the Spirit uses is Holy Scripture.

IV. Prospectus: Theological Interpretation of Scripture

Accordingly, the focus of our inquiry will now turn to theological hermeneutics, a different although related literature base. Inquiry into the possibility of sapiential theology began with concerns raised in theological education. As those notions of wisdom were surveyed, three interrelated questions surfaced to guide the inquiry. Can we still speak about the knowledge of God in a way that acknowledges and identifies prevenient divine action? Would sapiential *theologia* concern everyone or some particular group: what would be its social location? How then would it transcend not just the academy-church divide, but the divide between theory and practice, without losing the public claims to truth that are made by church doctrine?

Chapter 2 engaged the first two questions together, and argued that if Christian wisdom is to guide our conception of theology, then its primary social location is the every member "communicative praxis" of the church in the world. The corollary, with regard to the question of theory and practice in chapter 3, is that theology is not a discrete practice *per se* but the practice-encompassing endeavor at wise communication concerning God.

Still, we have discovered ambiguous reference for "wisdom," "theology," and even "doctrine" — all these terms refer not only to activities of discourse but also to the matter of these discourses, to knowledge communicated. Accordingly, *theologia* often refers to a discourse undertaken by teachers who intensify the doctrinal and critical dimensions of every Christian's discernment. This intensification, however, is a matter of degree rather than kind, of gifted leadership rather than binding institutional authority; otherwise sapiential *theologia* is lost, for *theoria* begins to drift off as "critical reflection on" Christian practice, or as merely the regulation of Christian language.

Viewing theology as practice-encompassing suggests that theological understanding consists in a set of communicative practices related to God; theology is (reflective) Christian witness, not reflection on Christian witness that engages God only indirectly if at all. Christian convictions entail that the habitual instruments (concepts) of these practices are normed by God's communication in Scripture. Theological judgments can conform to this norm with "relative adequacy" across time and place despite various conceptual forms. However, the "relative stability" of doctrines, as habitual conceptual instantiations of theological judgments, is crucial to the *paideia* of Christian communicative praxis. Christian doctrine, and the associated reading of Scripture, are especially significant practices tied to *theologia* because of their role in Christian learning; they link the church's instruments of understanding "between the times" to the normative biblical world(s) and the aimed-for eschatological world. This linkage occurs through teaching and learning the habits of virtuous Christian practice.

The need to address theological education together with theological hermeneutics, reinforcing and refining the conclusions reached so far, should now be clear. Using wisdom to understand *theologia* has highlighted the importance of how Christians read Scripture. This is especially so once the Bible is seen not just as the "trigger of some immediate experience" but as "the mediator of teaching,"[162] although of course we should understand such teaching to involve encounter with God.

Surely it is no accident that much recent literature concerning "theological interpretation of Scripture" speaks in the language of wisdom or especially "virtue." Indeed, considering these trends together could foster a mutually-enriching dialogue. Understanding how *sophia* and *phronēsis,* vision and discernment, relate in Christian wisdom should be important for the relation of biblical texts and readers. Furthermore, our understanding of *theologia* faces questions of identity or correspondence — between canonical voices, and between the canon and other contexts — that require theological hermeneutics. In both discussions, we face the ongoing challenge of how to understand *paideia,* "publicness," and their polarization.

PART II

Interpretation and the Nature of Wisdom

CHAPTER 4

Understanding Biblical Interpretation in a Postmodern Context

Doctrine, wisdom, and theology run parallel. Each can refer to an activity or practice and to its product, to discourse; each is in principle open to everyone but also incorporates particular leadership to help everyone learn Christian vision and discernment. Doctrine is a particular practice whereas theology is practice-encompassing, because doctrine is strongly catechetical and its habits can have binding implications. Doctrine aims to teach what ought to be; theology seeks the "ought," but is also constituted by what the church's witness "is."[1]

The communicative praxis of theology involves certain habits for thinking and speaking, often functioning as "concepts." The particular linguistic formulations of Christian doctrine are to shape these habits and assist the church in recognizing bad or even perilous ones. Doctrine embodies wisdom's respect for tradition so that theological discernment can enact wisdom's dimension of questioning.

This understanding begins to return theology to the public square. Theology makes truth claims by enacting Christian witness, not simply by reflecting on it. Yet these truth claims are open to criticism, first, with reference to the church's identity, which doctrine passes on and puts at stake. Moreover, because doctrine involves designs for living, Christian truth claims may be criticized with reference to lived experience — both regarding the fit between

> Christian witness and the church's proclaimed identity, and regarding the fit between Christian witness and life in our world. A wisdom model fosters both the stability of Christian communities and the possibility of further inquiry amidst life experience.

Nevertheless, at this point in the proposal, Christian theology could still seem secluded from academic life and criticism. Perhaps the university is so wed to outdated "modern" understandings of rationality that it cannot embrace any quest for wholeness, but must preach dogmas such as naturalism and procedural reason. This should be assessed and treated on a case-by-case basis, as the differences between the United States, Great Britain, and Germany, let alone non-Western contexts, suggest. Perhaps in some cases theology, defined with reference to the redemptive *telos* of the church as a public, will find itself so opposed to the practices of a university public that it must feel at home elsewhere. Nonetheless, whatever one's hesitations about the current health of the academy, some of its epistemic practices and procedures remain useful and even essential to theology.[2] Utter exclusion from the scholarly world, and seclusion from its criticism, would constitute a serious objection to the *theologia* of this proposal.

So my preliminary thesis, and the inquiries of the first three chapters about theology as wisdom, must be further specified with reference to "criticism." Nowhere has this issue been more hotly contested than on the battleground between the church and biblical scholarship. Since theology may be more, but is certainly no less than, a higher order form of biblical interpretation, this battleground requires careful reconnaissance.

Accordingly, the present chapter examines an emerging movement that advocates "theological interpretation of Scripture." By surveying some of its proponents and detailing its central claims, I will uncover objections to the shaping of biblical scholarship by *Wissenschaft.* While specifying the disagreements between some of these hermeneutics, I will claim that theology's prime epistemological challenge is understanding the role of Christian practical reason, or *phronēsis,* in biblical interpretation for the Word of God.

The centrality of *phronēsis* for both major subjects of this book — the nature of theology as wisdom, and theological interpretation of Scripture — strongly supports linking them, so that they can be mutually enriched. On the one hand, the character of theology as wisdom, with an interplay of *sophia* and *phronēsis,* will be further specified by examining its core practice, appeal to Scripture. On the other hand, the role of *phronēsis* in biblical interpretation will not merely address the nature of theology, but will be further specified with reference to Christian wisdom. In succeeding chapters, *phronēsis* will continue as a central theme because it is both indispensable to human rationality in general and ingredient to Christian wisdom in particular. Before constructive discussion of *phronēsis,* though, its centrality must be established for the advocates of theological exegesis.

I. The Critics of Critical Biblical Scholarship

"Theological interpretation of Scripture" is often defined in opposition to the reigning practices of academic biblical scholarship. Admittedly, to speak of reigning practices within that guild is increasingly problematic; a kind of plurality or even chaos is ascendant. Yet Walter Reed is probably correct to generalize about the "centrifugal tendencies of historical analysis and the centripetal tendencies of theological interpretation."[3] Historical criticism is perceived as fragmenting the Christian canon, whereas theological interests are perceived as foisting false unities upon it. The extremes result in biblical-theology-as-archaeology and systematic-theology-as-philosophy.[4]

Plus a critical mindset makes reading Scripture for edification difficult.[5] Richard Muller even claims that a disciplined approach to theological study, such as a classic fourfold model (biblical, historical, systematic, practical), could still serve the church if criticism did not stand in the way by turning upon Scripture itself.[6] The quite diverse critics of biblical criticism worry that its legacy is a focus upon technical knowledge, professionally defined by the scholarly guild, so that students of theology study precious little of the Bible.[7]

E. David Willis claims that efforts to solve this problem "can finally be grouped under two basic responses: (a) faith is not vulnerable to historical research because its material is of another order than that of historical science, and (b) faith is dependent on historical knowledge and this tells us as much about historical knowledge, positively or negatively, as it does about faith."[8] Perhaps the former approach becomes attractive when historical criticism is hegemonic; Werner Jeanrond suggests that the real issue about historical criticism is "whether it is the *only* legitimate approach and whether the only alternative . . . must necessarily be a dogmatist reading."[9] He has urged that to speak of "theological" interpretation "heißt hier nicht, daß der Leser selbst gott- oder christgläubig sein muß, um den Text verantwortungsvoll zu lesen, sondern es heißt, daß jeder Leser, ob gläubig oder nicht, den Textanspruch, der letztlich ein theologischer ist, gelten läßt."[10]

Yet allowing the text to validate its theological claim apparently is not tantamount to making a religious move.[11] More staunchly, in fact, Schubert Ogden maintains that one can interpret theologically without making theology formally normative for interpretation, and if one does not make the Bible's meaning purely a matter of interpretative validity, then the approach is not critical.[12] Not to be critical would, for this school of thought, mean a retreat from the public to a private world.

Is theological interpretation of Scripture such a retreat, an instance of Willis's first strategy (making faith invulnerable to historical research)? Some would answer affirmatively, but others would adopt a form of the second strategy (making faith dependent upon historical knowledge while then using faith to learn about what historical knowledge is). Regardless, Robert Morgan's generic definition of "theological interpretation" as distinguishing "a religion's critical reflection on its scripture or tradition from other modes of interpreting the same texts, such as purely historical or literary studies"[13] does not capture adequately the specificity of this Christian movement. Instead, we must explore three further themes in particular: (1) emphasis on the role of virtue in interpretation, especially Christian charity; (2) recovery of the Rule of faith in Christian interpretation of the Bible; and (3) reorientation toward reading the Bible as Scripture. While there is broad agreement on this third theme, the aim of reading the Bible for the Word of God, different understandings persist regarding the implications of the second theme, "Ruled" reading. Does such a pre-modern approach entail, regarding the first theme, that communal understandings of virtue should be a norm for faithful interpretations? Or should virtue be an aim that we realize upon reading the Bible as the Word of God?

II. Practice over Theory: Interpretation and Christian Virtue

Stephen Fowl's book *Engaging Scripture* can serve as a fine introduction to central claims of the movement toward theological exegesis, first illustrating a certain priority of practice over theory. Interpretation of Scripture belongs in the church, and "needs to involve a complex interaction in which Christian convictions, practices, and concerns are brought to bear on scriptural interpretation in ways that both shape that interpretation and are shaped by it. Moreover, Christians need to manifest a certain form of common life if this interaction is to serve faithful life and worship."[14]

Second, practical reasoning will be needed if Christians are to bring "appropriate convictions, practices, and concerns to bear on specific texts, in the light of particular circumstances, so that the prospects for faithful life and worship are enhanced rather than frustrated."[15] Fowl not only argues for this; he also exemplifies it by repeatedly providing extended theological interpretations of biblical texts. This distinctive writing style, in which an argument develops *ad hoc* through the hard work of exegesis, again characterizes the larger movement.[16]

Third, for Fowl these claims about practical reasoning and the priority of the church imply that Christians are not compelled to accept the reigning practices and ideologies of critical biblical scholarship. This is most especially true with regard to the discipline known as "biblical theology."[17] Critical scholarship tends to splinter the practice of theology into discrete disciplines[18] and the biblical canon into discrete Testaments, or worse.[19] Christians may make *ad hoc* use of critical biblical scholarship, but should do so very, very carefully.

A. Stories of Interpretation

Fowl's particular model for making these claims, however, does not represent the entire movement, as he acknowledges. His "three stories of interpretation"[20] are, in my judgment, contestable, not so much in advocating "underdetermined interpretation" as in obscuring actual disagreements about what is underdetermined.

In Christopher Seitz's terms, Fowl's "called-for shift in 'engaging scripture' entails matters in front of the text: virtues, habits, community ethos and the like, assuring, it may be hoped, on-going, proper engaging of biblical texts as a sort of end unto itself."[21] Actually, though, the phrase "end unto itself" must be qualified: Fowl would say that engaging biblical texts is a practice with internal aims, yes, but a spiritually formative practice that aims to produce spiritual fruit.

Given his focus on matters in front of the text, the contrasts drawn by Fowl between his own work and that of Brevard Childs, Francis Watson, and Jeanrond become fairly obvious.[22] For Jeanrond, revisionist-liberal, Chicago-style theological hermeneutics intend to embrace much of the biblical scholarship that others criticize. He chronicles twentieth-century efforts, traceable especially to Barth and Rudolf Bultmann, toward giving biblical interpretation a theological slant and recognizing theological claims in the texts.[23] But his chronicle is still in the interests of a public broader than the church; in fact, he strongly advocates special hermeneutics only following, *then* contributing to, general hermeneutics:

> Our narrative of the history of philosophical hermeneutics began with a theologian, Friedrich Schleiermacher, who discovered that theological interpretation needed a thorough foundation in philosophical hermeneutics. Now the development of philosophical hermeneutics by Ricoeur has revealed the need to include the interpretation of religious texts in an adequate human existential reflection. The symmetry between the theological endeavours of Schleiermacher and the philosophical enterprise of Ricoeur is striking![24]

Accordingly, Jeanrond celebrates the work of David Tracy and others who follow in Schleiermacher's footsteps and lean heavily on Paul Ricoeur. Meanwhile, he criticizes not only Barth but also the likes of Gerhard Ebeling for their failure to interact with, or contribute to, philosophical hermeneutics.[25]

Childs and Watson, likewise, retain a much more integral role for biblical scholarship than would Fowl. He criticizes both for advocating "determinate interpretation" or at least, in Childs's case, for trying to hold onto some notion of Scripture's literal sense. Eight representative characterizations of "determinate interpretation" will make Fowl's counterclaims clear.

(1) The aim of determinate interpretation is to "render interpretation redundant."

(2) "Determinate interpretation views the biblical text as a problem to be mastered."[26]

(3) "Determinate interpretation sees the biblical text as a relatively stable element in which an author inserts, hides, or dissolves (choose your metaphor) meaning."

(4) Determinate interpretation operates with the assumption "that matters of doctrine and practice are straightforwardly determined by biblical interpretation and never the other way around."[27]

(5) Determinate interpreters "trump others" by showing how "opponents have allowed theological concerns, prejudices, or preferences to determine their interpretation, rather than rigorously mining the text for its meaning and then letting that meaning shape their theology."[28]

(6) Determinate interpretation is often linked to the word "method,"[29] implying that its proponents seek one method which can specify in advance how all reader-text interactions should work. Besides being impossibly naive, this implies a "professional ethic"[30] that snatches the Bible from the hands of ordinary Christians.

(7) Determinate interpretation is also linked through biblical scholarship to "various forms of historical criticism."[31]

(8) Determinate interpretation always ends in "question-begging" to undergird its theory of meaning.[32]

Instead of determinate interpretation or its parasitic opposite, "anti-determinate interpretation," which is especially connected to uses of "deconstruction" among biblical scholars, Fowl advocates "underdetermined" interpretation. This he defines as believing "there is no theoretical way to determine how these interactions [of Christians and biblical texts] must work in any particular context," avoiding use of "a general theory of meaning to determine interpretation," so that critical biblical scholarship is only occasionally useful, but certainly not necessary, for theological interpretation.[33] With such an *ad hoc* approach he links the need for practical reason.[34] Earlier Fowl and L. Gregory Jones had claimed to follow the apostle Paul in a "doubly pneumatological" interpretative practice: "On the one hand, the interpretations themselves are Spirit-inspired. On the other hand, the confirmation of the interpretation is found in the presence of the Spirit in the community." This pneumatological emphasis becomes the basis for the need to exercise practical wisdom.[35]

Of course emphasis upon Christian virtue for the evaluation of biblical interpretations can appeal to precedent in the Christian tradition. Augustine, for example, staked the rightness or wrongness of interpretations partly upon whether or not they led to charity. In an oft-quoted passage from *De doctrina christiana,* the "double love of God and neighbour" is first a negative criterion: its lack signals lack of understanding. Positively, its presence signals that the interpreter is not a liar, even if s/he has misunderstood the writer's meaning.[36] Yet Augustine was not cavalier about the verbal sense, lest such misunderstandings eventuate in greater error; moreover, not only the Rule of faith but also context serves to resolve ambiguity.[37]

Subsequently, the three non-literal senses of Scripture would correspond to the three theological virtues:

> The allegorical sense taught about the Church and what it should believe, and so it corresponded to the virtue of faith. The tropological sense taught about individuals and what they should do, and so it corresponded to the virtue of love. The anagogical sense pointed to the future and wakened expectation, and so it corresponded to the virtue of hope.[38]

To put the point about tradition negatively, Hans Frei claims that general hermeneutics and historical criticism came into being together, at the dramatic modern fissure of the pre-modern world. Their chief difference lay in the fact that general hermeneutics would be apologetically motivated,[39] whereas historical criticism was not; crudely put, the former protected biblical truth by changing its meaning. By contrast, any historical criticism, whether its conclusions about the Bible be positive or negative, seems, from a certain outlook, to be "an admission of the discernment that the real world in which we ineluctably exist is not the biblical stories' world. . . ."[40]

B. Postmodern Interpretation: Engaging the Community

We should therefore highlight the decidedly postmodern character of many appeals to Christian practice and the virtues as criteria for interpretation. The appeal of a position such as Fowl's lies in using postmodernity to rejoin what modernity put asunder. But Watson makes a striking point about that strategy:

> There is room here for both 'radical' and 'conservative' theologies. If, with seeming consistency, we identify intratextuality with non-realism or relativism, the resultant theology will appear to be a 'radical' one. The same will be true of ethically-oriented theologies which highlight the problem of exclusion. If, on the other hand, we emphasize the sheer givenness of the community, its narratives, texts and language, the result will be a 'conservative' theology — orthodoxly trinitarian, perhaps. But these radical and conservative theologies are perhaps not so very different after all. They all derive from the discourse we have identified as 'postmodern hermeneutics' and from the concept of 'community' that lies at its heart.[41]

Indeed, Luke Timothy Johnson claims that to follow the apostle Paul, we should make "edification" the church's "formal" criterion for discernment, and "sanctification" her "material" criterion.[42] This follows upon his earlier claim that the biblical texts themselves are so diverse that they resist "any single unifying principle," whether from without or within — not "salvation history or justification or liberation or kerygma or *regula fidei* or narrativity or existential decision."[43]

By contrast, others do not primarily engage matters "in front of" the text. Watson, for example, tries according to the subtitle of his *Text and Truth* to "re-define biblical theology." Appeal to Christian practice is not at all absent from his work, since biblical texts are the sort of "object" that demands our participation.[44] Kevin Vanhoozer, likewise, appeals to the need for interpretative virtue.[45] Both, however, would claim that Christian virtue is an interpretative necessity (through which the Spirit opens us to the theological claim of the text) and an interpretative aim, but not the interpretative norm.[46]

Whither then this impasse over the role of practicing Christian virtue in theological interpretation of Scripture? To answer, first we must clarify the actual shape of the impasse; then we must retrace the steps leading to it.

C. Retelling the Stories of Interpretation

Regarding the shape of the impasse, Fowl's narrative could be misleading. First, in attacking determinate interpretation, particularly as he describes it, he does not successfully preclude the "authorial discourse interpretation"[47] advocated by several in theological hermeneutics. While many of Fowl's descriptions pertain to some, the composite can only describe traditionally modern biblical scholarship or even a worst-case scenario, not the goals of Watson, et al. Second, authorial discourse interpretation has recently garnered support from George Lindbeck, who at the same time would probably see interpretation as underdetermined and Christian use of biblical scholarship as *ad hoc.* Third, several advocates of authorial discourse interpretation emphasize practical reason, yet they would not accept Fowl's construal of the ways in which interpretation is underdetermined.[48]

In my judgment, therefore, we must spin a different yarn, tying together a broad parallel between three modes for post-critical canonical interpretation chronicled by Lindbeck, and three approaches to hermeneutics and biblical authority chronicled by James Buckley: (1) advocates of authorial discourse interpretation (Lindbeck excepted, probably) tend to be "revelationalists" (emphasizing God's presence related to the Bible's subject matter); (2) advocates of interpreting for witness to Jesus Christ (e.g., Childs) seem to be "textualists" (emphasizing the Bible's final form); and (3) advocates of interpreting for narrationally structured symbolic worlds (e.g., consider the links between Richard Hays and David Kelsey) are "functionalists" (emphasizing the interpretative context).[49] What happens when we try to fit Fowl into this picture? It seems that he is quite explicitly functionalist — in repeated definitions of the church's interpretative interests; in acceptance of Stanley Fish's location of "meaning" (if there were such a thing) in the reading community; and in utter lack of discussion concerning divine inspiration when defining "scripture."[50]

The nuances between the various positions occur because of different weights and placements within the triads. Almost no one anymore (at least among advocates of theological exegesis) accounts only for author, text, or reader — or, only for subject matter, text, or context. Fowl, though, seems to be at the extreme of functionalism, leaving author, subject matter, and text largely to the reader. The possibility should not be overlooked that theological interpretation of Scripture is underdetermined but that authorial discourse is important to it — not in permitting an exhaustive theoretical account or singular interpretative procedure, but simply some reflection on the work practical reason has to do. The real impasse, then, might concern the contours of such practical reason, and how the aims of theological interpretation relate to the Bible's authorship.

Regarding what leads to such an impasse, two different habits of mind are the obvious candidates. First, apparently Vanhoozer and Watson accept a fairly traditional doctrine of biblical inspiration whereas Fowl does not: earlier Fowl and Jones said that all we need for biblical authority is a doctrine of providence,[51] and the point seems to be that Scripture functions as proto-tradition, as the identity-giving text about which the Christian tradition is an extended argument, à la Alasdair MacIntyre.[52] Second, Vanhoozer and Watson (plus others, as we will see) are far less enamored of Fish than Fowl. These two issues, doctrines of biblical authority and general theories of hermeneutics, are linked: Fowl denies not only that texts have meanings and ideologies, but also that the biblical texts have authority *per se*.[53]

If simply these are the habits of mind at stake, then we face an impasse indeed. Doctrines of biblical authority and theories of hermeneutics are dearly held, defining personal, vocational, and institutional identities. Before despairing of further discussion and agreement, however, we should consider the possibility that other habits of mind lurk behind these two. In fact, I shall argue for another set of differences being at stake: pre-modern versus modern interpretation, and the unity of Scripture.

Fowl does not think that "biblical theology" as usual — focused on the human authors of the Bible — allows for Christian readings of the OT[54] or for a unified Bible, and he worries about doctrines such as the Trinity — both regarding its derivation and defense from the NT, and its relation to reading the OT.[55] This is consistent with Johnson's sweeping rejection of canonical unifiers, whether from within the Bible or without.

Brief mentions of two biblical passages illustrate the point. Fowl quotes David Steinmetz's now famous rhetorical question:

> How was a French parish priest in 1150 to understand Psalm 137, which bemoans captivity in Babylon, makes rude remarks about Edomites, expresses an ineradicable longing for a glimpse of Jerusalem, and pronounces a blessing on anyone who avenges the destruction of the Temple by dashing Babylonian children against a rock? The priest lives in Concale, not Babylon, has no personal quarrel with Edomites, cherishes no ambitions to visit Jerusalem (though he might fancy a holiday in Paris), and is expressly forbidden by Jesus to avenge himself on his enemies. Unless Psalm 137 has more than one possible meaning, it cannot be used as a prayer by the Church and must be rejected as a lament belonging exclusively to the piety of ancient Israel.[56]

And, following Johnson, Fowl discusses Acts 10–15 in the context of "reading with the Spirit." There certain OT commands are dispensable according to a "sense of the faithful" who are led by the Holy Spirit, and Fowl finds this pattern suggestive for today: we must be open to the Holy Spirit's present activity leading us to read against what the biblical text says. So, for example, if the Holy Spirit seems to be active in the lives of Christians who engage in homoerotic behavior, this might be sufficient warrant to welcome them fully, whatever their practice, into the church, despite apparent biblical proscriptions.[57] Apart from the specifics of that issue, Acts 15 has become a crucial test case for talking about the Holy Spirit in theological hermeneutics.[58]

Now Watson has also acknowledged biblical diversity, or a complexity to biblical unity. But he has used law-gospel hermeneutics to address the issue,[59] claiming that this does emerge from the text itself — which is a different warrant than Fowl's approach claims. Of course, the Christian tradition has never agreed on a canon-within-the-canon (the Rule of faith will be discussed later), but long discussions of this do have a track record.

So the issue of canonical unity is obviously quite important, and vexing. Hence a transition necessarily arises, from commitment to incorporate Christian practice in theological interpretation of Scripture to the challenge of what to do with theory in interpretative procedure. Disagreements about critical biblical scholarship and its preoccupation with the texts as humanly authored, I am claiming, concern not just doctrines of biblical authority and theories of hermeneutics, but also stances toward the pre-modern church and understandings of canonical unity. Thus we turn to surveying the claims of the theological interpretation of Scripture movement concerning the role of the church and the "Rule of faith."

III. In and for the Church: Interpretation and the Rule of Faith

It is intriguing that the history of biblical interpretation and the history of "theology" suffer similar disputes. Chapter 1 showed that the split between love and knowledge in theology is attributed, on the one hand, to the medieval rise of *scientia* or, on the other, to a modern fissure between *sapientia* and *scientia*. The Protestant Reformation is sometimes blamed in both directions, as an exacerbation of the medieval mistake (epistemologizing the faith), and as a forerunner of modern mistakes (building an untenable, individualistic epistemic foundation).

Likewise the history of biblical interpretation tries to understand the Protestant relationship to pre-modern and modern exegesis. Many argue that theological exegesis, to be done in and for the church, must be "ruled reading," undertaken in deference to the church's Rule of faith or tradition. Often they advocate a return to allegorical interpretation as well: allegory is permissible and even desirable, so long as interpretations (1) bear the fruit of Christian virtue, and (2) cohere with the Rule of faith. The warrant for this ruled reading is deceptively simple, appealing to (1) the edifying practice of the premodern church, and (2) the impossibility of canonical unity on terms of the determinate interpretation practiced in the academy. To exaggerate only slightly, such ruled reading produces the readings the church needs, while critical biblical scholarship does not. In the words of Steinmetz,

> The defenders of the single meaning theory usually concede that the medieval approach to the Bible met the religious needs of the Christian community, but that it did so at the unacceptable price of doing violence to the biblical text. The fact that the historical-critical method after two hundred years is still struggling for more than a precarious foothold in that same religious community is generally blamed on the ignorance and conservatism of the Christian laity and the sloth or moral cowardice of its pastors.
>
> I should like to suggest an alternative hypothesis. The medieval theory of levels of meaning in the biblical text, with all its undoubted defects, flourished because it is true, while the modern theory of a single meaning, with all its demonstrable virtues, is false. Until the historical-critical method becomes critical of its own theoretical foundations and develops a hermeneutical theory adequate to the nature of the text which it is interpreting, it will remain restricted — as it deserves to be — to the guild and the academy, where the question of truth can be endlessly deferred.[60]

Are the warrants for such a hypothesis adequate as it stands?

A. Historical Warrant: For Pre-Modern Ruled Reading

Exegesis from the patristic age to the Reformation usually permitted and incorporated allegory, reading the text with the use of an interpretative key from outside, other than the text itself. Whatever its excesses, advocates say, the basic pattern bears repeating. For instance, Augustine practiced both literal and allegorical interpretation; since he tied even the latter to the Bible's verbal sense and to the church's Rule, interpretations were not limitless.[61]

The first crucial point is that Augustine, typical of his predecessors and contemporaries, saw biblical interpretation as fundamentally a religious activity. Later even Thomas, for all his focus on the Bible's literal sense, continued this pattern, according to Eugene Rogers, Jr.: "The *Summa theologiae* can be read so that the *sensus literalis,* far from promoting one predeterminate meaning for a text, promotes instead a certain ordered diversity of readings, and that the evaluation of readings belongs largely elsewhere than in hermeneutics."[62] This ordered diversity means neither that anything goes nor that an encompassing method or procedure for adjudication could be provided. Rather, "the marshaling of scientific and literary evidence for interpretation does require the virtue of prudence, about which Thomas has much to say."[63] Such prudence is a virtue "because it specifies the good of a product," but not merely an intellectual one (in the sense of an art or skill for making things).[64] Its moral tone led Thomas to prioritize prayer, so that he would primarily address the danger of interpretative prejudices via providence instead of hermeneutics.[65]

Second, Rowan Greer typifies those who claim that "the argument from Scripture and the argument from tradition are regarded as identical by the Fathers," so that "since the creeds are thought to represent the 'scope' of Scripture, interpretation is always concerned both with the biblical text and with the credal key to its general meaning."[66] It might seem a small step from this to construing the literal sense "as that which a community of readers takes to be the plain, primary, and controlling signification of a text. . . ."[67]

If allegorical interpretation with the Rule of faith allows exegesis to be a religious activity, and tradition to have theological authority, it also receives a third (yet more defensive) pillar of support: such interpretation was not unrestrained. The medieval fourfold sense of Scripture could be seen, positively, as the means of spiritually extending the literal sense in accord with Scripture's story; negatively, as the means of restraining biblical polysemy.[68] Criteria for — or, better, limits upon — interpretation, then, would involve at least (1) the potential of the verbal sense, (2) the Rule of faith, and perhaps (3) fruitfulness in terms of Christian charity.

Advocates of this approach are often vexed by the Protestant insistence on Scripture's literal sense. On the one hand, Kathryn Greene-McCreight has recently argued that Calvin himself was a ruled reader (albeit differently than Augustine).[69] So too Luther's reading of Scripture, via *oratio-meditatio-tentatio,* was a religious activity; and with his embrace of the law-gospel tension as Scripture centered around Jesus Christ, he clearly read with a firmly religious sense of the Bible's scope. D. H. Williams, who wishes to recover the aforementioned closeness of Scripture and tradition, claims that "in many ways the basis of reform in the sixteenth century was over the rightful authority to claim the early church as its legitimate heir."[70] Certainly one cannot read Calvin's *Institutes* without noticing frequent appeals to the Fathers, especially Augustine, in addition to frequent arguments about who is appropriating them correctly.

Williams describes the Protestant legacy in a manner reminiscent of William Abraham, who was cited in chapter 1:

> In the name of rejecting ecclesiastical authority as 'hierarchy' or 'tradition' as theological manipulation and bondage, we have instead created a hermeneutic of suspicion and have invested every biblically informed conscience (instead of a pope) to speak ex cathedra. It is a Pyrrhic victory for Free church Protestantism when the net effect of its teaching results in the replacing of the tyranny of the magisterium with the tyranny of individualism.[71]

Johnson, in an interesting move, sees this individualism as a Reformation exacerbation of allegory: "The basic *premise* of allegory, that the vivifying power of Scripture is to be found in the reading *by an individual* was if anything made even more explicit by the Reformation." He concludes that "it seems impossible to combine a theology based on the literal sense, the principle of free individual interpretation, and a unified church."[72]

The Reformation is faulted not only for individualism but also for modern foundationalism. Again we hear echoes of Abraham's critique. Greer writes, "The early church would not be comfortable with any view that insisted upon Scripture alone as the authority for Christian belief and practice,"[73] which suggests that patristic exegesis and today's canonical criticism differ on whether the Rule of faith functions so as to exclude *sola scriptura*. Andrew Louth thinks that *sola scriptura* treats Scripture "as an arsenal rather than a treasury."[74] Moreover, *sola scriptura* reinforces the "abhorrence of allegory because of the way it seems to ignore the objective meaning of Scripture,"[75] and Louth discerns here "an alliance between the Reformation and the Enlightenment: not something that inspires confidence."[76] In other words, "our modern understanding of the Bible joins this principle [*sola scriptura*] with another: the principle of the *method*."[77]

Nevertheless Frei, himself no friend of modernity, seems to appreciate Calvin's approach to Scripture and to differentiate Calvin from his descendants:

> Conservative Protestants with their stress on the divine authorship and the verbal (or typological) structure and interconnectedness of texts as criteria for their meaning, had had no need for this assumption [human

authorial intention]. We miss the point if we think they considered the view mischievous. In a sense they did not, but it never occurred to them to substitute it for the divine authorship. More important is the difference in their imagination. The Bible was for the older Protestants a coherent world of discourse in its own right, whose depictions and teachings had a reality of their own, though to be sure, it was the reality into which all men had to fit, and in one way or another did fit.[78]

Frei contrasts modernity with pre-eighteenth-century hermeneutics in this way:

> Figural reading had been literalism extended to the whole story or the unitary canon containing it. But now figural sense came to be something like the opposite of literal sense. . . . Literal reading came increasingly to mean two things: grammatical and lexical exactness in estimating what the original sense of a text was to its original audience, and the coincidence of the description with how the facts really occurred.[79]

Now such a move to grammatical exactness, as G. R. Evans has chronicled, is in fact a legacy of medieval developments, not of the Reformation.[80]

The move to historical consciousness, on the other hand, seems more characteristically modern. Charles Taylor describes, in contrast, the pre-modern sense of time "as the locus for the recurrent embodiment of archetypes, not themselves temporally placed." For example,

> we feel the incongruity when Mary has the features of a thirteenth-century Tuscan rather than those of a first-century Jew, because to us she is this particular woman, whose placing in history is crucial to what she was. But in a mentality in which there were such, the Mother of God easily gravitates towards an archetype; and as such she is equidistant from, and hence equally belongs to, all ages.[81]

The upshot is that we have parallel historical problems in chapter 1 and here in chapter 4. In chapter 1, we saw that whether theology's love-knowledge split is blamed primarily on the medieval or the modern period, and how the Reformation is connected to these, depends significantly upon a constructive proposal for *sapientia* and *scientia*. Likewise here, whether Protestant exegesis is seen in greater continuity with the pre-modern or with the modern depends significantly upon a constructive proposal for theological interpretation.

Of course in both cases a hermeneutical circle obtains. But the point is that the question cannot be settled simply by reading the histories or historical claims. Rowan Williams comments,

> We have seen pleas for a return to allegory, a sophisticated deployment of modern literary theory to question any remaining obsession with authorial intentions, and the various forms of canonical criticism, insisting that we read scriptural texts in the context of their present and deliberate positioning in relation to each other as constituting a *single* book, settled once and for all in a community's history. With all this in mind, though, it has become difficult to see how what is also a central aspect of traditional and 'pre-critical' hermeneutics, the belief in the primacy of the 'literal' sense of Scripture, can now be understood. If we have become suspicious of a hermeneutic that looks for authorial meanings and treats them as normative, if — in literary theory in general — we have been taught a certain uneasiness about the whole notion of normative meaning, how are we to talk about a 'primary' or authoritative level of reading that is bound to history, in the way traditional exegesis conceived the *sensus literalis* to be?[82]

Given Frei's work, with its many and varied contemporary uses, the crucial underlying issue seems to be, in fact, a theological question: how to define "figural reading" (the literal sense extended canonically) in relation to allegory and typology. If one sees little difference between these two approaches,[83] then the modern fissure between the real and biblical worlds, into which figural reading collapsed, apparently stems from the Reformation's priority upon the humanly-authored literal sense. If, alternatively, one sees some distinction between typology and allegory, then the Reformers' rejection of allegory is not so problematic (if their typological, salvation-historical exegesis could be recovered).

Frei, for instance, wrote that "to view Christ as the subject matter of both testaments is quite a different matter from discerning this unity in the temporally distinct and ordered stages of the history of salvation. The two views may be held together, and so may the unity and difference between the two Testaments, through figural interpretation, as Calvin had done."[84] In a similar vein, according to Lindbeck, "Traditionally expressed, one could perhaps say that typological tropology or tropological typology was the chief interpretive strategy for making the Bible contemporary, for absorbing one's own world into the world of the text."[85] But "this is possible, however, only if the problem of canonical diversity, of which redactional criticism has made us vividly aware, can be solved." And the stakes are high:

> If it can be solved, the troping of our contemporary embattled worlds by the common symbolic universe of Scripture could generate for Christians a realm of discourse in which polarizations are attenuated, consensus-building facilitated, and conversation becomes civil even when disagreements remain. . . . Without a synthesis, however, it becomes impossible to appeal to Scripture as a whole for the contemporary guidance of the church. The canon threatens to become a grab-bag in which searchers pick and choose according to whim or, less pejoratively, in accordance with extrabiblical principles.[86]

D. H. Williams, in fact, claims that "one of the fundamental lessons about biblical exegesis learned as a result of the 'Arian' controversies . . . [is] that one must go outside of the Bible and biblical terms in order to interpret them."[87] At one level, of course, that claim is obviously true in light of creedal development. What we make of the claim, however, is very much tied to the relation between typology and allegory, and how that bears on the unity of Scripture vis-à-vis the discipline of "biblical theology."

B. Contemporary Warrant: Against "Biblical Theology" as Usual

Pre-modern interpreters were not unaware of the Bible's diversity: Marcion should make that fairly obvious. Moreover, it must be admitted that some pre-modern interpreters practiced allegory because they found the literal sense problematic in places. Nevertheless, biblical theology, as an academic discipline constituted by preoccupation with human authorship, has tended to canonize more extreme conclusions about that diversity than the church traditionally accepted. In response, scholars protective of Christian theology have tended to make one of three moves.

(1) Accepting "Biblical Theology" as Usual

Scholarship focused on the biblical texts as humanly authored tends to challenge the Bible's unity in literary or historical terms. Not incidentally, these have been the primary ways of approaching biblical theology.

First, there are more "synchronic" issues of genre and concept or, in Timothy Ward's terms, the "thematic" and "literary" issues.[88] Christian theologians would often, in bygone days following the Reformation, move rather straightforwardly by induction from the Bible as "propositional revelation" to doctrine in conceptual form. This generates problems connected to salvation history, which will be discussed below.

Prior theological problems arise, though. Portions of the Bible tend to be privileged at the expense of others, most especially the Pauline corpus at the expense of the Bible's dominant feature, narrative. This tends to privilege a "monolithic concept of revelation,"[89] which has polarized that doctrine (into, for example, "personal" versus "propositional"). Kelsey has demonstrated that such privilege is typically accorded due to a *discrimen* (or imaginative construal of what is authoritative) which is pre- or extra-textual.[90]

These problems are literary as well as theological. The monolithic concept of revelation has privileged a particular form of theological discourse, the propositional or conceptual. In Ricoeur's unflinching analysis, theologians are tempted thereby to "neutralize" biblical genres in order to "extract their theological content" and "transform these different forms of discourse into propositions." So to interpret is to treat the Bible's literary forms as a "rhetorical facade which it would be possible to pull down in order to reveal some thought content that is indifferent to its literary vehicle."[91]

This resonates with the work of John Goldingay, who links the concept of "revelation" to a particular biblical model, prophetic inspiration and dual authorship, a model which (in his view) pertains only to portions of Scripture. He claims that there are multiple models of authority within the biblical text, namely, witnessing tradition, authoritative canon, inspired word, and experienced revelation.[92]

If genres are relatively stable patterns of linking language and life; if "the confession of faith expressed in the biblical documents is directly modulated by the forms of discourse wherein it is expressed,"[93] then the very possibility of a unified biblical theology — at least upon moving to conceptual expression — seems doubtful. As noted in Ricoeur's essay on "Biblical Time," genre diversity makes it impossible simply to exchange a propositional for a purely narrative theology either.[94] However, if we grant all this, do we wind up viewing the Bible as "an accumulation of ambiguously related particulars . . . that remain unorganized until we apply the structuring principles of some extrabiblical prolegomenon or system," so that we are unable to say "our theological framework should reflect the unity of the revelation of God, which is itself a reflection of the unity of divine activity in history"?[95]

Second, therefore, are "diachronic" issues of sense and reference or, in Ward's terms, "chronological" and "religious" issues.[96] The revelationalist understanding of biblical theology, which faces such literary and theological problems, was summarized in this classic presentation by B. B. Warfield:

> The immediate work of exegesis may be compared to the work of a recruiting officer; it draws out from the mass of mankind the men who are to constitute the army. Biblical Theology organizes these men into companies and regiments and corps, arranged in marching order and accoutered for service. Systematic Theology combines these companies and regiments and corps into an army — a single and unitary whole, determined by its own all-pervasive principle.[97]

That understanding has fallen on hard times. In concert with the literary and theological difficulties already mentioned, salvation-historical problems surface.

Illustrations from Ps. 137 and Acts 10–15, already mentioned, suggest two of these. First, the manifest "sense" of OT texts cannot always be continually authoritative in the same way. For example, the attitude of Ps. 137 seems to be proscribed by our Lord's teaching about love for enemies in some fashion. Similarly, OT laws are rendered no longer binding for the early church, as recorded in Acts 15. Second, there are questions of "reference." How should OT references to God be read in light of Trinitarian doctrine? To whom or what do the Babylonians of Ps. 137 correspond in medieval France? And how do such questions of reference affect understandings of the textual sense and its authority?

These questions have been raised with regard to Christian readings of the OT. But distinct problems of salvation history relate to each Testament in its own right. For instance, salvation-historical approaches to OT theology are notorious for neglecting or excluding the Wisdom literature with its focus upon creation. An offbeat example comes in Walter Wangerin's *The Book of God: The Bible as a Novel,* which drops out Wisdom literature entirely.[98] Moreover, Christians must address whether or not the Acts 10–15 pattern of reading-against-a-canonical-text is an appropriate model for reading the NT today.

Accordingly, James Barr claims that reading the OT and NT together is simply an act of faith.[99] And Abraham, frequently appreciative of Barr, assesses the Warfield approach as follows: "This is a preposterous undertaking. It is ludicrous to think that this kind of territory can be studied, critically examined, and worked up into a coherent system with any measure of success. One would have to be virtually omniscient to execute such a project."[100] By contrast Warfield had written of biblical theology,

> Its chief object is not to find differences of conception between the various writers, though some recent students of the subject seem to think this

> is so much their duty, that when they cannot find differences they make them. It is to reproduce the theological thought of each writer or group of writers in the form in which it lay in their own minds, so that we may be enabled to look at all their theological statements at their angle and to understand all their deliverances as modified and conditioned by their own point of view.[101]

Warfield was undoubtedly right to blame scholarly ingenuity for some of the perceived biblical diversity. Still, by most measures, the revelationalist approach faces significant literary, theological, and salvation-historical challenges.

Therefore various definitions of biblical theology are encountered today: (1) as a branch of the theological disciplines; (2) as a complex interdisciplinary theological program; (3) as the regulative notion of a theology that accords with the Bible; or (4) as the notion of a theology that is found in the Bible and then brought to realization.[102] Furthermore, on the most optimistic view within biblical theology as an academic discipline, "dynamic concepts of unity are sought and developed — not ones set abstractly over against difference, but rather concepts of unity that distinguish between fruitful and creative differences and unfruitful and destructive differences."[103] However, the Barr-Abraham conclusion seems more dominant.

(2) Redefining "Biblical Theology"

Unfortunately, accepting the state of biblical theology "as usual" in Michael Welker's first definition would threaten the aspirations of the other definitions. Surely texts so diverse could be canonical only as a literary anthology:[104] they could not generate one theology, but many (contra definition 4); therefore they could not really adjudicate between theologies either (contra definition 3); and whether they could sustain an interdisciplinary program without question-begging is doubtful (contra definition 2). Lindbeck suggests that the canonical approaches of, for example, Childs and Hays suffer the following fate: "choices between alternative patterns of canonical construal are intratextually arbitrary; one must exit the text in order to find grounds for decision; and as to how one does that they seem to have no hermeneutically usable answers."[105]

Now it is a useful caution that, although the integrity of NT argument rests on its appropriations of the OT, this canonical integrity must be evaluated with appreciation of Christian witness rather than apologetic success.[106]

That is to say, the NT makes contextual claims, tied to witness of divine action, about properly recognizing and reading OT fulfillment; these — contested — claims cannot be expected to exclude all other possible readings, at least not on grounds satisfactory to the modern academic guild.

Such problems as the relation between the church and Israel are internal to the NT and its wrestling with the OT; that struggle has shaped the very texts themselves.[107] So aforementioned efforts toward an intratextual provider of canonical unity and adjudicator of authoritative teaching, such as law-gospel hermeneutics, head in the right direction, even if they remain problematic on present course.

Aside from these more diachronic or salvation-historical questions, the more synchronic or literary questions remain. Redefining biblical theology might involve different criteria for unity; Max Turner imagines the NT as "a discussion table (in Caird's terms, an 'apostolic conference')."[108] According to Robert Wall, "The canonical interpreter seeks to relate the different ideas of particular biblical writers and canonical units together in contrapuntal yet complementary ways, to expose the self-correcting (or 'prophetic') and mutually-informing (or 'priestly') whole of NT theology."[109] Suppose that such an understanding were fully developed and defended: would the result constitute biblical theology?

(3) Rejecting "Biblical Theology"?

Consider the following efforts to redefine biblical theology. Steve Motyer, writing in the same volume as Turner and Wall, defines it as "*that creative theological discipline whereby the church seeks to hear the integrated voice of the whole Bible addressing us today,*" with "*the contemporary theological agenda*" as its center.[110] D. A. Carson, by contrast, defines biblical theology as "that branch of theology whose concern it is to study each corpus of the Scripture in its own right, especially with respect to its place in the history of God's unfolding revelation."[111]

Carson's definition is more academically acceptable in focusing upon the human corpora of the Bible, but runs against the dominant grain of the discipline's conclusions about the extent of canonical unity.[112] Motyer's definition scarcely concerns that discipline; he has essentially redefined biblical theology as theologically-interested exegesis. Carson's moderate redefinition could be marginal in parts of the academic world because he wants to address divine action in history. Motyer's radical redefinition actually seems more suited to the move Fowl makes: abandoning "biblical theology" entirely.

Why so? Motyer is using academically-loaded terminology for an ecclesiastically-oriented approach, perhaps satisfying neither side. Barr, once again, epitomizes the state of the academic discipline: since the Bible itself is not theology (theology is what comes before and after the biblical text),[113] therefore biblical theology deals neither with "what it meant" nor with "what it means" but with "what it says." Biblical theology is not simply theological exegesis, because theology is not read off the text in that manner. Biblical theology's work is imaginative reconstruction of the (in the first instance human) theology that gave rise to the biblical texts.[114] Biblical theology is usually defined in contrast to something else, whether systematic theology or history of religions *or exegesis*, etc. The watershed concerns whether it is descriptive or normative;[115] for the academy, it must be the former — it is fundamentally historical work using literature.[116] Barr represents its standard locus: moving from texts to theology implied behind them. Moving the locus of biblical theology back and forth between texts and readers is academically unacceptable; in that case biblical theology is no longer essentially historical.

Hence Fowl believes that pursuing academic integrity precludes at least many appropriate interests involved in theological interpretation of Scripture. Therefore he rejects biblical theology, and advocates only *ad hoc* use of critical biblical scholarship by the church.[117]

By contrast, could this be "ecclesiastical positivism"[118] of the highest order? While, as accepted earlier, any Christian epistemology faces a certain scandal of particularity, it might be called at worst "revelatory positivism." Fowl's approach, however, risks positivism not so much of appeals to an authoritative Scripture but of appeals to what the church decides to do with Scripture.

The difference is important because of what Merold Westphal dubs the "law of inverse rationality": "the ability of human thought to be undistorted by sinful desire is inversely proportional to the existential import of the subject matter."[119] If determinate interpretation (so-called) fares badly against this law, does Fowl's version of underdetermined interpretation fare better? Perhaps not. Despite his denial (contra anti-determinate interpretation) that texts have ideologies, in parallel to a denial that texts have meanings, the law of inverse rationality remains a problem. Locating ideologies and meanings (and authority) in reading communities, as Fowl does, certainly requires "vigilant" reading. But is vigilance enough? Anthony Thiselton suggests, in fact, that we must address two key hermeneutical issues: not just self-deception, interest, and manipulation, but the corrigibility of interpretations as well.[120]

Moreover, should we make grace almost an entirely immanent matter of church practice? Or are a more interruptive possibility and a greater sense of transcendent otherness necessary in hearing Scripture as God's Word? Accordingly, we may have worries about a thoroughly underdetermined approach to biblical interpretation on grounds of *both* general *and* special hermeneutics.

IV. For the Word of God: Interpretation of the Bible as Scripture

To this point I have chronicled, in dialogue especially with Fowl, the concerns of those who advocate theological interpretation of Scripture. Notably, the chronicle of these concerns is amenable to an inverse parallel with the three quests of chapters 1 to 3. First, *the recovery of Christian practice and of theology as practical* suggests that theological interpretation is theoretically underdetermined. Second, theological interpretation must be done *in and for the church, involving somehow all its members.* But, third, the question of *recognizing divine action* must be addressed — especially of what it means to take the Bible as Scripture.

This follows from the argument so far. For advocates of theological exegesis do not so much disagree over determinate versus underdetermined interpretation, but over the ways in which theological interpretation is underdetermined. Moreover, disagreements over doctrines of inspiration and theories of hermeneutics manifest disagreements over pre-modern versus modern interpretation and the unity of Scripture. Fowl and others desire to recover pre-modern exegetical practices, so that interpretations are legitimate which (1) cohere with the Rule of faith, (2) are spiritually fruitful in lives that engage God and others, and perhaps (3) do not violate the potential of the verbal sense. Fowl does not advocate indeterminate interpretation; he engages critical scholarship and discusses the Bible's human authors or audiences at times. He seems to take for granted that the textual sense could only be made to go so far; his view is primarily concerned with how the Bible does (or does not) function as authoritative canon, rather than the impossibility of reconstructing what humans were doing.

Fowl has much to teach us. It is his failure, on occasion, to distinguish the issues mentioned above (as far as what is underdetermined), and to discern their important connections as well, with which we might disagree. This is especially true given the different politics of Bible reading — in short, its democratization: we must beware, to quote Erasmus, not to act "like the commonplace theologians who are wont to attribute to ecclesiastical authority whatever in any way has crept into public usage."[121]

While having advanced possibilities for discussion and consensus, I suggest that these latter issues make Fowl's views of inspiration and hermeneutics problematic. In a nutshell, a dogmatic deficiency — neglect of Scripture as "Word of God" — renders his proposal not only unrepresentative of the theological exegesis movement, but also vulnerable to (for lack of a better term) "ecclesiastical positivism." Against imperious claims from biblical theology as academic discipline, we may well opt for an alleged "revelatory positivism," for reasons of Christian identity; still, we dare not simply confuse church practice with revelation!

Indeed, it is questionable whether Barth, inspiration for many in the recovery of theological exegesis, would have guarded the freedom of God's Word from historical critics and philosophers only to hand it over to the church quite as Fowl does. While granting to some degree Reinhard Hütter's critique of Barth's revelationalism, that the recognition of God's action was insufficiently made public, on the opposite end God's action could be identified too immanently with church practice — either with doctrinal rules of faith (Hütter) or with religious readings of Scripture (Fowl).

Granted, God's action could also be identified too immanently or statically with the human texts of the Bible. With echoes of William Abraham, Joel Green criticizes a "pervasive biblical-theology hermeneutic" for thinking

> that the function of Scripture in theology was and is solely or primarily content oriented and boundary making. This way of conceiving the relationship between the Bible and theology is to construe the role of the Bible foundationally — i.e., it determines what we should and might believe. Lack of critical reflection on this assumption is remarkable since this way of thinking runs against the grain of some of our actual practices. . . . More telling, though, is how such readings assume that the primary or sole role of Scripture in theology is to provide theology's content.[122]

Or, in Dietrich Ritschl's apt expression, traditional models of biblical authority are commonly accused of "cryptic Deism."[123]

Yet in accepting that theological interpretation of Scripture must be a religious, performative activity, involving a dynamic aspect of biblical authority related to the Holy Spirit's presence in the event of reading, we need not render the text's stable properties irrelevant.[124] We must account for author and text, as well as reader, or else be content purely with functionalism, which does not do what its proponents might think: authority then becomes a "purely formal concept," leading us "to expect irreducible diversity at the level of actual textual interpretation." Moreover, there is neither theological nor ecclesiastical consensus on this matter of Scripture's authority being functional.[125] And if authority is a matter simply of how the church takes the text, what exactly keeps the interpretative argument going? How can God's action be recognized as speaking interruptively?

Indeed, if "Word of God" must be related to the event of reading, then this relation must still account for the Spirit's past action as well as the present. One might claim that precisely a doctrine of inspiration (or at least a notion of providence that does significant work) authorized the spiritual reading of bygone days. The Bible's human words were seen as bearing the Word of God, albeit in a complicated sense. The point of reading with the Spirit is not that the Spirit is a "hermeneutical tool" which contravenes the texts, but that the Spirit "is the 'presence' who finally renders the text 'authoritative' for faith," leading the church into the world of the text so that its story overlaps with our own.[126] Accordingly, this relation between a performative approach to biblical interpretation and the role of *phronēsis* in sapiential theology will occupy us in the next chapter. We can begin to reenact biblical *paideia* in public.

CHAPTER 5

Phronēsis and Theological Interpretation of Scripture

Chapter 4 began to develop the need for theological interpretation of Scripture, oriented to the practical concerns and spiritual formation of the church, guided by her Rule of faith, and in some sense theoretically underdetermined. While accepting this underdetermination, and some criticisms of critical biblical scholarship, I hinted that we should resist a purely functionalist understanding of Scripture's authority along with the attendant reader-response hermeneutics.

The church has traditionally taken the biblical texts to be spiritually formative, and to be consistent with (even to generate) the Rule of faith, because they are in some sense the Word of God. Uniquely "modern" preoccupation with the texts' human authorship can threaten the unity of the canon, and thwart the necessarily performative reading of Scripture "with the Spirit." However, some postmodern versions of performance interpretation, and the theoretical underdetermination of biblical meaning, turn the canon into a spiritual grab-bag. That response is dogmatically deficient, hushing the Word instead of recovering its Spirit; hushing the Spirit of the past and possibly hearkening to the spirit of the age; losing the possibility of distinguishing between the Word of the Spirit and the voice of the church.

Accordingly, theological interpretation of Scripture must face criticism not only via the church's own vigilance, and from an academic biblical scholarship which has been externalized. Criticism must also come from the relation between the biblical texts — already, as human writings — and divine transcendence, with the canon already being the action in and through which the Spirit speaks. The church must have a sense not only of reading Scripture against itself, but that the outcome of the reading does not depend entirely on a sense of the Spirit's present work. The texts may clearly say what we do not like.

At the same time, the church is rightly interested in reading the Bible for spiritual formation, with some settled judgments about telling the story to which the texts bear witness. The interests and assumptions of critical biblical scholarship, generated by its understandings of textuality and human authorship, may at times be irrelevant or contrary to the church. This tricky relation between Christian *paideia* and public truth is a driving concern in this chapter's discussion of theological hermeneutics.

The first step of the argument addresses general hermeneutics. While unfolding and defending any theory of textual meaning would be impossible here, a minimalist account will serve heuristic purposes in the argument that follows. The resulting thought experiment will explore the possibility that the Bible's theological use is underdetermined, yet to a significant degree constrained, by its human authorship. Neither may we ignore, however, that judgments about its human discourse already have a theological dimension.

Indeed, the second step will address the special questions raised by the Bible, as a collection of texts, yet a collection received by the church as the Word of God. Our historical distance from the human authors and audiences, and the hermeneutical distance between the human authors and the divine author, will be enfolded in a theological hermeneutical circle which relates Christian *phronēsis* to "figural reading." Because such *phronēsis* involves the theological performance, or communicative praxis, already being developed in this project, theological hermeneutics entail hermeneutical theology, and the two are mutually informing.

The final step of the larger argument about public truth, addressed in chapter 6, will be the relation of this Christian *phronēsis* to general understandings of rationality in our "postmodern" age. The intention is not a radical effort to defend Christian theological exegesis by deconstructing all "scientific" pretensions and practices. Instead, the effort will be more moderately post-critical: to demonstrate that Christians are appropriately "critical" to speak "publicly" (1) even when they accept a measure of theoretical underdetermination and uncertainty, (2) when they resist a thoroughly ahistorical approach to the Bible and seek to give textual reasons for their theological interpretations, (3) although such textual reasons will be at the level of canon and will appeal to the revelatory work of the Spirit in hearing the Word.

Christian faith is partially constituted by the latter understanding of how to read the Bible as one book, witnessing to one (variously told) story. Christians are being post-, not anti-critical, when they read the Bible figurally in accord with their Trinitarian Rule of faith that expresses who they are. Of course there will be a more critical dimension of theology (or even apologetics) that addresses objections, and encounters or assimilates alien viewpoints, more directly. Meanwhile, however, Christians may read the Bible as part of their communicative praxis, and engage in public witness thereby. To begin, then, textual exegesis must be located in hermeneutics, and human authorial discourse related to the "meaning" of the Bible.

I. The Bible as Text(s): Theological General Hermeneutics

Already in prior chapters we have seen the value of the concepts "communicative action" and "communicative praxis," coupled with the lacuna in some theological hermeneutics regarding the concept "Word of God." While a thorough theoretical defense of using speech-act philosophy would be impossible here, we may test whether it develops as a helpful working hypothesis. For the potential fit with sapiential theology seems snug, given wisdom's emphasis on hearing and speaking; besides, such a strategy already forms a significant segment of the literature on theological hermeneutics.

Kevin Vanhoozer follows George Steiner in accepting the argumentative power of deconstruction and neo-pragmatism on their own terms, but finding that one must "wager on transcendence" for texts to be meaningful.[1] On this account, "meaning" is an "emergent" property that "supervenes" on a text's written marks.[2] Texts themselves constitute communicative actions, of which authorial intention — in the sense of "attention" using public conventions, not in a Romantic or psychological sense of an inner "plan"[3] — is a defining component. The "result" of the author's intention fixes the illocutionary force applied to propositional content, and thus completes textual "meaning"; "consequences" of a text's reception relate to perlocutionary effects, or a text's "significance."[4] By "illocutionary" force we mean the action done *in* speaking: asserting, commanding, warning, promising, and so on — the most basic conceptual contribution of speech-act philosophy as it studies ordinary language use, or what we do with words in relation to the world.

Many have long maintained, following Jeffrey Stout, that stipulating such a definition of textual meaning is arbitrary. In reality, the word is used in all sorts of ways, to describe all sorts of interpretative interests.[5] Vanhoozer grants this, but claims that — whether or not the term "meaning" is used — we are obligated to textual authors, as "others," to do justice to their works. We ought not ascribe or impute actions to them which they did not commit;[6] beyond that fairly obvious point, we ought not use or apply texts in ways that are inconsistent with such actions. Significance is "recontextualized meaning" or meaning *"extended"*: "'Objectivity' with respect to significance is thus misplaced, even as an ideal. But relativity is not arbitrariness; it is still the same determinate meaning, or an aspect thereof, that is being extended or applied in new situations."[7]

If one permits the Christian theological assumption of transcendence, then this ontology of meaning is a possibility. To be convincing, however, the approach must do epistemological work, not necessarily establishing a goal that can be completely achieved but at least presenting a responsibility that can be fulfilled. Yet Stephen Fowl raises an important question: "if the felicity of speech-acts depends on properly observing the socio-linguistic conventions operative in specific contexts, how does one fix the particular context of a literary act in a non-arbitrary way?"[8]

A. The Possibility of Understanding a Text

Vanhoozer acknowledges the "main *problem* of literary knowledge, namely, the conflict of interpretations,"[9] but suggests that "often the text itself — the literary context — is sufficient evidence of the author's intention to engage in such and such a form of rule-governed communicative behavior."[10] He claims that "at least one context . . . remains relatively fixed: the literary context,"[11] that "the world of the text is indeed a shared world": this literary context is tied to genre, comprising "specific rules and conventions for discussing, describing, and discerning certain aspects of the real world."[12] Genre means that authors and readers share this real world to an extent.

Hans-Georg Gadamer's exploration of the ontological possibility of understanding has certainly dominated the hermeneutical conversation of recent decades. In Gadamer's understanding, a fusion of text and reader horizons occurs, as they undergo a sort of dialogue that negotiates commonality of subject matter. Somewhat different from Gadamer, Vanhoozer deploys various alternative resources, but most especially emphasizes genre in order to avoid a single fusion-of-horizons model.

Like Gadamer, the Russian Mikhail Bakhtin explored how language traditions over time, and emphasized dialogue as a model of understanding.[13] On his view, however, the author is involved, as well as the text, and in the dialogue of horizons "each retains its own unity and *open* totality, but they are mutually enriched."[14] Meaning has the character of an event (that continues to happen and embraces one's reception of a work), but the horizons are not fused. This is possible because genre relates language and life so as to foster creative, dialogical understanding. Genres arise because readers have "common conditions of life" with authors and prior readers, commonalities that evoke responses, from which the genres emerge.[15] Thus genres have "accumulated centuries of conceptualizations, and carry wisdom irreducible to any set of propositions."[16]

Accordingly, meaning involves "potentials" that are expected by authors; writers expect their texts to be extended appropriately into new contexts, so that a certain set of possibilities may be an aspect of the convention to which an author submits. In this sense, which Vanhoozer and other theological interpreters have perhaps underplayed, Bakhtin had a sense of meaning as an ongoing event-complex. But it still remains under obligation to authorial agency.[17] Indeed, for Bakhtin truth likewise develops *"on the boundary between two consciousnesses, two subjects,"* as meaning is actualized in a participant's "answerability."[18]

What then does it mean to speak of "potential" in relation to textual meaning? What are its constraints besides literary genre? This is perhaps the crucial question, at least for the interests of theological hermeneutics. When William Alston defines sentence meaning as "illocutionary act potential,"[19] this semantic priority upon language use could perhaps accord with a more pragmatically-oriented suggestion by Anthony Thiselton that the illocutionary actions of *texts* must be "actualized" on an ongoing basis.[20]

Vanhoozer would resist, it seems, because this might imply changing illocutionary actions — that, for example, promises could become warnings. Yet it is questionable whether this broad point, applicable at large-scale discursive or "utterance" levels, establishes the validity and value of a hard-and-fast epistemological distinction between the "description" of a text's meaning and its "significance," especially as one moves to the more particular details of "reference" in sentences and word usage. Indeed, such matters affect textual "sense," requiring us to rework[21] or even abandon[22] the latter distinction.

The key reason for this concerns the extension of texts into new contexts. Understanding always occurs against a background of collateral information; yet if we are not to suffer infinite regress, of information presupposing other information, which presupposes other information, *ad infinitum,* then the background must eventually be pre/extra-linguistic and pre/extra-cognitive, related to (for instance) embodied life, societal relations, and human experience.[23] The recent development of "relevance theory" illustrates this point: older "code" models of communication are deficient because semantics cannot entirely explain the contextually-related cognitive moves made in successful understanding.[24] We do not simply encode in writing or decode in reading as if language were a neutral tool in our hands; much of the meaning of discourse is not brought explicitly to the verbal level.[25]

The added complication is that authors of texts cannot presume the same stability of context (and thus of "background" which relates to the pragmatic component of "relevant" understanding) that speakers can. Genres provide a crucial element of relative contextual stability, but the stability is relative: genres therefore serve as a source of meaning potential. Thus we may not ignore the tie between text genres and institutions.[26] The communicative practices involved with genres are those of people and groups, and their relative stability occurs as the story of traditions engaged in maintaining, yet always defining, their identity. Laws evoke some form of communal judgment and enforcement; laments are performed in a worshiping community; apocalyptic literature resonates with a community that does not feel at home, but the resonance of its imagery also relies upon allusions to a shared stock of textual history. These forms offer a relative stability of literary context, partially as they are read in contexts of related social or institutional background. Accordingly, readers must attend to, and be related to, the context of a text's addressees as well as of its author(s).[27]

Re-contextualization, though, can affect the relative priority of a text's illocutionary actions,[28] and therefore that to which a text relates. It is intriguing that the founder of speech-act philosophy, J. L. Austin, did not have a standard definition of meaning because he brought issues of reference within it.[29] Forced to re-think the older hermeneutics of "sense" and "reference," we also need some sort of distinction between the "reference" of a textually-proposed world and "mimesis," the relation of that world to the actual world we inhabit.[30] Many of our most interesting interpretative questions will concern precisely what Nicholas Wolterstorff calls the "designative content" of a text and its extensions in so-called "application" or "significance." This is all the more true for the Bible as divine discourse.

B. The Actions of Understanding a Text

Can any worthwhile distinction be made, then, between a text's "meaning" (in the sense of, what did the author do?) and extensions thereof? Three actions involved in understanding, or appropriating meaning, might illuminate the lingering "epistemological," regulative significance of such an "ontological" distinction. If (once again) understanding involves a set of capacities for action in relation to something (in this case a text, and through the text a communicator), then how should we imagine the responsibilities of reading — if to understand means to "engage in speech"?[31]

(1) Question and Answer

Especially since Gadamer, the movement of question and answer has been a prime model for pursuing textual understanding. But on his model, fusion of text and reader horizons occurs, as the questioning is directed to common subject matter. This slides more toward dialectic than toward the dialogical understanding of Bakhtin,[32] who maintained that "without *one's own* questions one cannot creatively understand anything other," yet still "the questions must be serious and sincere," so as to encounter the text's potential as outside oneself.[33] Our questions surely reflect our own interests and conceptual frameworks, but the goal is to open ourselves to answers or other questions from the text — and, for Bakhtin, the text as a means of becoming answerable to authorial action. Those answers may well transform our interests and frameworks of understanding. Accordingly regarding Scripture, for Joel Green to say (without qualification) that the texts *and our questions* become the arbiters of meaning, may be an overstatement.[34]

(2) Directed Dialogue

Yet Bakhtin did recognize that there is a sense in which the author's action is realized or actualized with the help of the other.[35] Some reader-response theorists have proposed an aspect of textual effects as intrinsic to the "meaning" event. Paul Ricoeur also highlights the necessary interplay between individual effects (Iser's focus), and collective expectations (Jauß's focus), in a phenomenology of reading.[36] So readers, in a sense, follow instructions in appropriating a text.[37] This is true at two levels: to some extent, there is an open texture implicit in any writing;[38] to another extent, texts vary in the instructions that their particular genres send to readers, as to how closed or open they are to creativity in response.[39] To understand some literary acts, in Vanhoozer's playful sense of "standing under" them, is to follow the instructions fitting their illocutionary actions as one reads, as to how one takes the content at issue; or, put differently, one is to match a reading genre to the text's genre.[40]

(3) Provisional Monologue

If dialogical understanding involves the movement of question and answer, and of following instructions, then any absolute distinction between authorial discourse interpretation and performance interpretation would seem to be undermined,[41] in the sense that any re-description of authorial discourse is a performance involving significance. Nevertheless, Bakhtin thought that grasping a text's "strictly semantic aspect," its "*formal meaning,*" was largely possible. To be sure, this would be only the first stage of understanding, and fairly passive; active understanding of the "contextual meaning" really interested Bakhtin, involving "*assimilation*" of the "evaluative-semantic aspect."[42] Today many would be even less sanguine about such a semantic-pragmatic divide (as opposed to a rough and sometimes useful distinction). Nevertheless, "Bakhtin argues that provisional 'monologizations' may be useful and necessary as first steps in an ongoing dialogue, and Bakhtin is well aware that even he himself must inevitably resort to monologization in his own analysis of Dostoevsky's multi-voiced novels."[43]

To grant a first step of understanding that is significantly (though by no means exclusively) semantic, and to grant the necessity of such provisional re-descriptions of meaning, is to maintain a long-standing tradition of textual exegesis, centered around translation and commentary. With pretensions toward entirely semantic understanding, or disinterested and absolutely objective re-description, undone, we can perhaps rediscover this tradition as many in the pre-modern church undertook it. We must also separate the sometimes pathological pretensions of how historical criticism uses texts from the tradition of textual exegesis; this principle can likewise work in the other direction, against more radical reader-response excesses.[44] Various metaphors for the creative fidelity involved in performing texts — notably musical scores and dramatic scripts — have thus come into vogue for the practice of biblical interpretation.

II. The Bible as Canon and Special Hermeneutics

In what ways though, if any, is biblical interpretation a special case? What is its relation to theology? On the one hand, James Barr maintains that there should be no distinction between the exegesis undertaken by biblical theology and that undertaken by historical theology.[45] One should interpret Pauline texts, and move behind them to "Pauline theology," just as one would interpret Luther's writings, and move behind them to his theology. Of course this analogy is rather convenient; many biblical texts are far less directly related to the concepts of "theology" than are theological treatises such as Luther's, but the point is clear enough.

On the other hand, Fowl represents the view that theological exegesis of the Bible involves interpretative interests all its own. These interests may have nothing to do, at least in a theoretically meaningful sense, with interpreting the discourse of the Bible's human authors.

A. Hermeneutical Distance between the Bible and Theology

At first glance polar opposites appear, between public and private (or perhaps better, between universal — in the modern sense — and particular), between historical and theological, between academic and ecclesiastical interests. However, Barr and Fowl share a crucial premise: the human discourse of the Bible cannot be authoritative for Christian theology. Fowl seems to acknowledge many of modern criticism's historical judgments or at least the perceived problems, taken on such terms; moreover, he thinks necessary the church's resort to allegory or to communally-located reading strategies that unify canonical teaching and promote spiritual formation. The human discourse does not mediate divine discourse in a determinate fashion. Barr, likewise, thinks that critical exegesis cannot be initiatory for theology; while granting that biblical exegesis could be critical for theology,[46] he rather plainly adopts a philosophical locus of theological authority. The two representatives may head in theologically opposite directions, but they seem to agree on the point from which they depart.

When others such as D. A. Carson, by contrast, define exegesis with reference to the biblical texts' final form, with the Bible taken to be "an integral and self-referring literary object,"[47] they journey with neither Barr nor Fowl. For them, the line of thought moves neither straightforwardly nor simply from the Bible to theology, but the direction of authority finally does.[48] And so it must be asked: can this approach be developed and justified hermeneutically? To answer means facing two related problems of "distance" more directly.

(1) Historical Distance from Author and Audience?

First, does literary genre enable us to transcend adequately the problem of historical distance, as we now perceive it? Perhaps not entirely, but commitment to authorial agency must not be confused with necessity to offer an exhaustive account of textual origins. It is, in fact, inherent in canonical texts sometimes to erase particularities of their origin,[49] notably some subjective aspects. This is not problematic since the church recognizes the Bible's final form as authoritative, not any set of inner intentions at some stage along the way. Insofar as human agency is relevant to that final form, we are concerned with what communicative actions have been performed using the linguistic conventions now in the texts.

Furthermore, calling the Bible "Scripture" leads to a "presumptionist principle," in which "the authority of the Bible does not depend upon the results of historical scholarship," at least in the sense that "space is available for (1) concentrating upon other kinds of research on the biblical texts and, (2) doing historical research while accepting that most of its results will be tentative only."[50] The modern historian considers every possibility regarding both textual origins and truthfulness, except that s/he tends to elide the possibility of divine action (or at least the possibility of recognizing it and making it ingredient to a hypothesis). By contrast, the reader of Scripture tends to elide certain other possibilities just because s/he is committed to divine action that renders these texts truth-bearers.

So while Christians need not deny certain difficulties of ascribing communicative actions to biblical authors, they will tend to believe (as did pre-modern exegetes) that our disobedience poses a greater problem for biblical interpretation than historical distance.[51] Put differently, the most relevant hermeneutical distance is theological[52] or spiritual.[53]

Robert Jenson has highlighted that the church must, to some degree anyway, presume that her dogmatic teaching accords with Scripture, or else there is no church and the term "Scripture" becomes a misnomer.[54] This reminds us of the point made in chapter 3, concerning our linkage through doctrine (and other church practices) to the "canonical-linguistic world": contemporary preoccupation with historical distance should be replaced by a sense of connection in reading Scripture, because we are in one sense the same community as the original audience. The differences highlighted by historical criticism are to be seen as individual moments in a larger drama.[55]

Undoubtedly we know better, in some cases, what the human authors said than did our predecessors. It is possible, however, that pre-modern interpreters knew better in other cases: not only were they less historically distant, but they may have been less spiritually distant, all the while more attuned to the importance of that latter issue. Plus it is likely that along with our modern knowledge has come a penchant for minutiae: perhaps not all of the interpretative problems that concern biblical scholarship are theologically crucial.

The above considerations mitigate the problem of historical distance for theological interpretation of Scripture. To an extent such distance is inherent in canonical texts; certain modern understandings of history clash with any account of these texts' canonical status that shapes interpretative approaches and possibilities; and besides, not all the questions left open by such distance are important for knowing God. Christians must partially accept a kind of revelatory scandal, that being the church does keep us from fretting about historical distance according to the way of the modern world. The crucial point is that we are not finally interested in airtight reconstructions of the human discourse or the religious ideas behind the discourse; we are reading, instead, for the divine discourse and for theological judgments of our own. To what extent, then, do these interests relate to one another?

(2) Human Distance from the Authoritative Word?

This hints at a potential deficit in Vanhoozer's hermeneutical approach. Whatever the extent of our gratitude for his theologically-reinstated Christian humanism, we still must address the theological interpretation of the Bible, *as Scripture.* However intriguing is a reverse move from special to general hermeneutics — from biblical interpretation to reading any book — it threatens to underestimate the unique challenges and opportunities presented by the Bible.[56] For instance, how is one to regard the human discourse if convinced of its unique relation to the Spirit's action, its complex unity, and its use in authorizing theological proposals?

Once again, Vanhoozer is not unaware of this concern, and has taken first steps toward addressing it. In one sense "Word of God" refers to the Bible in terms of its locutionary acts, while Vanhoozer relates perlocutionary effects to the ongoing work of the Holy Spirit.[57] The locutionary dimension of the Bible as "Word of God" is a point about locus: God addresses us in the words *of just these texts.* The perlocutionary dimension of "Word of God" is a point about authoritative presence: *God addresses us* in the words of just these texts.

What then about the illocutionary dimension? What does it mean to say that God addresses us *in the words* of just these texts? Can or should a theoretical model be developed for determining the "divine discourse," with a methodological procedure for simply reading theology off the divine illocutionary acts?

Since the older, rather static "propositional revelation" model cannot fully account for the progress of redemptive history, or for the diverse forms of biblical literature as a unified canon, its proper concern should be addressed within another framework. On the other hand, dynamic foci — on revelation as "personal," or on God's present speaking, or on reader construction of "meaning," or perhaps even on "narrative" theologies — have problems of their own, threatening to privatize the Word of God or to make its reception only a matter of immanent church practice. Moreover, they tend to underestimate the ambiguities and failures of Christian communal discernment. While Acts 10–15 has become a popular locus supporting a pattern of discernment that can read with the Spirit against the canonical grain, such readings neglect details of the narrative. For instance, according to one reviewer, Fowl fails to recognize "that it is easier to find the Spirit's activity in the past than in the present," understating considerably "the resistance of Peter in Acts 10 as well as the resistance of the Jerusalem community in Acts 11 and again in Acts 15," so that he winds up with an (overly) "optimistic assessment of the capacity of humans to see the Spirit's work in those around them."[58]

Yet David Kelsey's classic *The Uses of Scripture in Recent Theology* (reissued as *Proving Doctrine*) demonstrates the inability of various models to hear the whole Bible as profitable Scripture. It is no accident that B. B. Warfield and descendants have tended to prioritize epistolary literature in authorizing doctrine, or that others privilege the Gospel narratives, still others the power of biblical expressions to generate experience, and so on. Christians have always found the theological use of the OT to be a problem for debate; for contemporaries the NT seems ever more problematic as well.

The words of 2 Tim. 3:14-17 are used for two contrasting emphases: the "house of authority" appeals to "all Scripture is inspired by God"; the newer functional approaches appeal to ". . . and profitable for teaching, rebuking, correcting, and training in righteousness." If profitability in "equipping us for good works" (which, by the way, entails a peculiarly substantive account of "shaping Christian identity" that a generic functional view neglects) ought to shape an account of the Bible as Scripture, so also profitability is tied to the divine Word in the texts. If, as established since chapter 2, we are not "made wise for salvation" apart from God's prevenient communicative action, then not just any account of "shaping Christian identity" will do for theological interpretation of Scripture.

Kelsey recognizes that accounts of shaping Christian identity are bound up with linking God to the Bible. His own view is that such an account should center on God as Sanctifier — the Third Person — rather than God as Revealer — the Second Person.[59] More must be said about a properly Trinitarian account of *phronēsis* in relation to God's self-communication, but Kelsey's related challenge concerns the variety of Scripture's possible uses as theological authority, which we shall explore here.

The virtue of a focus upon God's communicative action is its effort to receive all forms of biblical literature as profitable and authoritative for knowing God, which the Bible strongly connects to the metaphor of "hearing,"[60] a metaphor connected (like wisdom) to both knowledge and obedience. Virtue is always formed indirectly; direct attention, disconnected from a storied communal ethos regarding the true, the good, and the beautiful, thwarts its essential humility. The Bible sharpens that point: virtue is formed by attending to divine communication mediated to us. As the normative mediator of such communication through its witness to Christ, Scripture is the Word of wisdom that we must "hear" by the Spirit, and by which we must "hear" the Spirit. God sanctifies by speaking, and speaks by having spoken.

Yet the tempting vice of such a focus upon God's communicative action, perhaps, would be a lingering effort to offer an exhaustive theoretical, procedural account of such hearing, in particular an account that would not relate Scripture to the pedagogy of discipleship. Instead, we are tempted to confuse publicness and objectivity with the exhaustive methodological determination of biblical interpretation. This tension will come clear in a brief consideration of "Word of God" via speech-act philosophy rather than direct recourse to a concept of "revelation." Once the limitations of the theoretical options are exhausted, a role for *phronēsis* will come even clearer.

First, Vanhoozer speaks of the Bible having its divine "meaning" emerge at the level of canon, with God's illocutionary acts supervening on the human and specifying the "referent" of their witness, namely Christ.[61] Presumably this specification does not alter the human illocutionary acts, but could only add to them (in a rather broad way, at the large-scale discursive level of canon) as well as affecting judgments about the text's ongoing theological "significance."

Second, besides this "supervenience" model we might mention "actualization" again, the hint from Anthony Thiselton that textual illocutionary acts are instantiated by readers. This actualization could be related to the divine discourse of Scripture. Similarly, Stanley Grenz's account of biblical authority has the Spirit using the biblical texts as locutions to commit illocutionary acts as they are read. Grenz resists the notion that the Spirit could contradict the meaning of biblical texts, but seems to license greater interpretative freedom regarding the present divine discourse.[62]

Third, Nicholas Wolterstorff takes the view that biblical interpretation for the Word of God involves two hermeneutics: first, interpreting for the mediating human discourse; second, interpreting for the mediated divine discourse. The relevant dual authorship model for this mediation is "appropriation": the "second hermeneutic" requires judgments about how God appropriates the human discourse. The most fundamental principle is "the interpreter takes the stance and content of my [God's] appropriating discourse to be that of your [human] appropriated discourse, unless there is good reason to do otherwise. . . ."[63] Wolterstorff's approach seems to lie between the supervenience and actualization models; he does not use an "inspiration" model quite as Vanhoozer seems to do, but he offers a stronger account of "illocution" tied to the original text than Grenz seems to do.[64]

B. Transcending the Hermeneutical Distance Theologically

Since Wolterstorff has treated the problem in more detail than the others, his "appropriation" account helps to specify lacunae in their thought. John Goldingay highlights that we are presented with divine discourse more directly by prophetic oracle (God's action presented in first person) than by, for instance, a historical narrative (God's action presented in third person) or a psalm (God's action presented in second person).[65] In Wolterstorff's terms, the point is that divine illocutionary acts supervening on the human, at the level of canon, would not enable us fully "to arrive at the correct *rhetorico-conceptual structure* of the divine discourse,"[66] in the many (mostly!) biblical texts which do not directly fit the oracular model.

Conversely, in his minimalism regarding divine discourse Goldingay may not recognize the full significance of the NT putting all sorts of texts in God's mouth, as it were.[67] For an easy example, the shift of voice within Ps. 95 bothers Hebrews not one bit when citing the text (Heb. 3:7-11), which is God's locution, and its illocutionary stance or force remains stable. Yet as the "propositional content" of this discourse traverses redemptive history, a story unfolds not only of perlocutionary effects but also of growing theological import.

(1) The Transitive Aspect of Divine Discourse?

This point can be developed in two parts. First, if biblical texts are God's locutions, nonetheless Wolterstorff presents some compelling examples of what he calls *"transitive discourse,"* in which God must use the text as "*discourse-generating* discourse" in the service of "*discourse-generated* discourse." For instance, to what end does God present us with biblical narratives, or with the voices within such narratives (such as the dialogue in the Book of Job)?

Second, this point about transitive discourse could also be made in terms of types of speech acts, rather than in terms of discursive voices. To illustrate, Maarten Wisse reworks a philosophical notion of authority using speech-act theory and applies it to the Bible. Rather straightforwardly, authority sometimes deals with propositions believed, at other times with rules obeyed.[68] The former relates especially to speech acts labeled "constatives," and the latter to speech acts labeled "prescriptives."[69] But what about "commissives" and "expressives"?

Wisse argues that, strictly speaking, "The Bible itself cannot have commissive authority. When someone trusts in a promise made in the Bible, he does not rely on the fulfilment of the promise by the Bible, but he relies on the fulfilment of the promise by the person who made the promise in the Bible [God]."[70] To my mind, this helps him out of a quagmire created by his prior discussion: the reason that we obey only certain prescriptives of the Bible has to do with recognizing that some commands are presently related to God's speaking, versus understanding God's authority to stand behind others only in some particular time or place or manner. Speaking of the Bible's authority in any sense involves a claim about God's authority, implying divine communicative action.

What then about expressives? At one level, we take the Bible to give us appropriate sincerity of human expression. However, at the level of divine purpose in presenting us with such expressions, the theological judgments become complex: *de facto* authority would mean that "believers express their faith this way just because these words are used in Scripture." Interestingly enough, Wisse uses the frequently mentioned Ps. 137 as an example that might restrict this *de facto* authority of biblical expressions! He describes several potential strategies for this restriction: (1) we are allowed to express thoughts and feelings before God, but that does not make them morally acceptable; (2) we assess moral acceptability of thoughts and feelings in terms of fundamental human rights, not of biblical expression; or (3) we are allowed to express thoughts and feelings, and deem them acceptable, if they do not contradict canonical rules given elsewhere.[71] Once again, Wisse's helpful discussion is limited by his treatment of the biblical texts as texts *per se*, dislocated abstractly from an account of canon that relates them to the personal action of the triune God. Indeed, relating the progress of revelation to the progress of redemption might make the integration of all three strategies appropriate, although the third would have priority in the construal.

The point is that for speech acts which are neither constative nor prescriptive, in which God does not directly take a first-person speaking stance toward the locution, theological judgments are required to hear the divine discourse correctly in this transitive sense. They are not only required for us; they were required for the original audiences. And these judgments, if one holds to some kind of divine-human concursus in Scripture, would have certain implications for the possible meanings of the human discourse. To say with Vanhoozer, contra Grenz, that illocutionary acts supervene on locutions, so that God's illocutionary acts must be tied to the human locutions of the Bible, is a correct but incomplete account. Nor would the actualization model really help us to specify the nature of the judgment calls concerning transitive discourse. Moreover, it would turn an illocutionary act into a different concept by removing it one abstract step from a concrete locutionary act. Wisdom must take us farther than any theoretical model could.

(2) The Timeliness of Divine Discourse?

Wolterstorff makes a related point about the "relation of *specificity/generality* between the noematic content of the appropriated human discourse and that of the appropriating divine discourse."[72] Again, this concerns the propositional content of the illocution:

> Even without transitive discourse entering the picture, we human beings sometimes say several distinct things by uttering or inscribing one sentence; and those several distinct things sometimes — though not always — are said to distinct persons. There is every reason to suppose the same for divine discourse, every reason to suppose that God's discourse is in this way rich in its diversity.[73]

Thus it seems that, despite Vanhoozer's salutary preservation of the biblical discourse's illocutionary integrity, we still face theological judgment-making in the act of understanding the text with respect to God's voice. How does canonical divine discourse supervene on the human through time, especially in terms of the "transitive" and "designative" questions that are so crucial to theology as the text enters new contexts?

The actualization model, once again, would not rescue us. We probably should not say that the illocutionary acts change across time (in the sense of a command becoming a promise or a story, for instance); the concern is rather how the propositional content of the illocutionary act travels across time. And once again, the actualization model might be an unwieldy theoretical encumbrance (or mirage!) for matters that should be left to practical reason, because it tries out the concept "illocutionary act" for something that has no tangible existence (oral and written texts constitute — in one sense, they just are — actions; whereas "illocutionary action" on this account would be a purely theoretical abstraction, a step too removed from an aural or literary "locution").

(3) Two Hermeneutics or One?

So the larger point is that what Thiselton calls the *"directedness"* of communicative acts "implies either that they are addressed to a specific situation or that they apply to types or patterns of situation."[74] In the case of Scripture, this directedness varies with the type of speech act, and the relation God takes to the speaker's voice. God addresses us in all these literary acts, but their illocutionary integrity is relevant for authorizing theological judgments only to an extent. Although one could work at sketching some tendencies or guidelines for theological interpretations of particular genres and types of speech acts, advocacy of "underdetermined interpretation" becomes relevant just here: one could never cover all the cases in advance.[75] It is for this reason, perhaps, that Richard Briggs remains wary of attempts to globalize speech-act philosophy into a doctrine of Scripture that might entail one determinate, semantically-focused, hermeneutical procedure.[76] We must acknowledge, as Jorge Gracia argues, that theology is *necessarily* involved in the interpretation of revealed texts, even if (for literary and culturally-related reasons) theology should *not be sufficient* to determine their interpretation.[77]

The human discourse of biblical texts must be partially regulative in theological interpretation, unless their character as texts is ignored altogether. Thus a more semantically-oriented focus upon translation and commentary is one of the legitimate actions of "creative understanding." Yet if it is wrong to imply that readers of the Bible have no responsibilities to its human authors, we must still recognize a potential gap between Scripture as Word of God and our authoritative teaching today,[78] a gap requiring the exercise of practical reason. This gap, in its relation to the Bible's authority, complicates the distinctions between illocutionary and perlocutionary acts in interpretative practice and theological understanding.

As previously noted, Wolterstorff advocates a "first" and a "second" hermeneutic in response to this gap. The first hermeneutic interprets the mediating human discourse; the second moves to the mediated divine discourse, assuming divine appropriation of the human unless there is "good reason to do otherwise" — involving the "probabilities and improbabilities of what God would have been intending to say by appropriating this particular discourse-by-inscription."[79] These are matters for the Christian imagination, as Wolterstorff says in another place,[80] but an imagination formed by a vision of canonical teaching on the whole. Contra radical (mis)understandings of *sola scriptura,* without such inevitably theological-ecclesiastical visions or "rules of faith," interpretation could not even get off the ground,[81] which is not to say that the visions are incapable of reform during actual cases of discernment. At any rate, such matters of "good reason to do otherwise" have traditionally meant an "*exceptional* principle" focused on truth and love: God would neither speak falsely, nor say that which does not conduce to loving God and neighbor.[82]

Wolterstorff recognizes the implications of such a second hermeneutic: "has Scripture become a wax nose?"[83] While this is a genuine risk, the risk can be diminished:[84] (1) "we should shy away from the expectation of ever formulating a set of informative generalizations which catch all the cases; the relationships are much too subtle for that. But some persistent patterns there will be";[85] (2) we should remember that the exceptional principle is exceptional, operating within a presumption that God appropriates the human discourse as is; (3) we should be open to the possibility that we are wrong (vision may be reformed due to cases of discernment); (4) we must cultivate knowledge of ourselves and of the world, but most importantly of God.[86]

As reflection upon the warrant for, and criticism of, theological interpretations of Scripture, this double hermeneutic has its uses. As a description of Christian reading practices regarding Scripture, however, the double hermeneutic at least reverses a proper order, and perhaps tears asunder that which God joined together.

Mary Hesse notes the problematic (and oddly ironic, I would add, given Wolterstorff's other work) result of this double hermeneutic for biblical studies: its present practice in terms of the first hermeneutic remains largely unchanged.[87] Canon does little or no work as context until after the human discourse has been understood using essentially secular historical canons. As a useful example, the first hermeneutic might well leave open the possibility of conflict between Rom. 4 and Jas. 2. It is not that textual arguments cannot be made for complementarity rather than conflict in what they say about justification and faith, but the case is not open and shut. The second hermeneutic, faced with the challenge posed in this fashion, could resort either to seeking harmony or to privileging a voice (usually Paul's!).

Two crucial concerns from chapter 4 become relevant at this point: canonical unity and pre-modern interpretation. Pre-modern interpreters would have the order of reading priority regarding Scripture's authorship to move from divine to human rather than from human to divine, and this clearly related to their understanding of canonical unity. Such a reversal would not mean excluding the option of privileging one voice or the other, depending on circumstances (especially in more diachronic cases involving, say, suspension of something from the OT by the NT). But we might expect to hear a complementary harmony, especially in cases that are relatively synchronic in redemptive history.

In terms of reading practice, this would move the "exceptional principle" of divine discourse forward and allow it to do some — though by no means totalizing — work in sifting through possible interpretations. To anticipate, negatively, a crucial objection, this need not preclude responsible interpretation of the human discourse (1) if at least certain kinds of "allegory" are illegitimate, and (2) if "rules of faith" are in some sense subordinate derivations from Scripture itself. In other words, so long as churchly readers remain obligated not to impose a primarily external hermeneutical key on the interpretation of canonical texts, exegesis can play a significant critical role in what they make of Scripture. That is, of course, to stake a "faith" claim about a dialogical unity to the Bible, from which to seek a creative "understanding" of how that unity may be expressed and theologically useful. More in defense of these principles is forthcoming, but first, positively, another crucial claim: bringing the exceptional principle forward actually enhances responsible appropriation of the human discourse for theology, (1) by refusing to silence prematurely a canonical voice, and thus (2) by including all the voices somehow in a complex polyphony rather than hearing cacophony only to hush portions of the choir, in favor of an *analogia fidei* that sounds good solely to us.[88]

Thus a pre-critical principle, namely, the vital overlap of biblical interpretation and theology, must be recovered post-critically. Aspects of biblical interpretation preoccupied with the human discourse, particularly translation and commentary, must be undertaken with acknowledgment of their theological and performative character; aspects of theology preoccupied with the divine discourse and our own communicative praxis, must be undertaken with acknowledgment of their interpretative character. In both directions a *regula fidei* provides perspective on how to read the literal sense in terms of the canon as a whole — and how to read life through these "spectacles of faith" — while that *regula fidei* itself is opened to questioning and reform.

At this point a subtle transition must be made explicit. The focus must shift from divine discourse ("all Scripture is inspired by God") to Christian theological discourse and the attendant communicative praxis (". . . and is profitable") — from *sophia* to *phronēsis.* God's communicative act must be related to the effect of its reception or, put differently, the work of Word and Spirit must be distinguished rather than separated. Discussing divine discourse advanced us beyond the reader-response functionalism of Fowl and others, requiring that we listen to all biblical voices and do justice in hearing them. Otherwise the canon would not exert its rule, over church selectivity and in favor of relative stability for its theological reading. But we have also faced theoretical limits that require a stronger concept of *phronēsis* than

Vanhoozer's and a somewhat different notion of imagination than Wolterstorff's.

Thus we must develop and deploy a doctrine of Scripture in terms of the Trinitarian economy of salvation.[89] As the Word of God by which the Spirit bears witness to God's final Word, Jesus Christ, Scripture is divine and human somewhat analogously (Scripture is not a person) to the duophysite Christ.[90] Just as in Christ God's self-disclosure comes by way of Spirit-led human faithfulness, so Scripture "makes us wise unto salvation" as divine speech that comes by way of and elicits Spirit-led human faithfulness. Such an emphasis is compatible with the "wisdom" model of the present work: Scripture as divine discourse establishes a locus of communication, with integrity of textual illocutionary action, but properly transitive and timely hearing of its propositional content and perlocutionary force requires Spirit-led discernment. Moreover, to use a different emphasis, in its Spirit-led humanity Scripture is an instrument of both the *embodiment* and the *enablement* of the wisdom found in Christ, God's final Word. That is, in different genres and various ways Scripture communicates both theological judgments and patterns for theological judgment as an ongoing practice. Bluntly put, we read Scripture for how God says that we may or should speak about God.

III. The Bible as Canon and Hermeneutical Theology

Any Christian reading of the Bible, as Scripture, therefore has hermeneutical wholeness, which must not be lost amid necessary critical distinctions and discussions of interpretative warrant. Theology pervades this practice, as well as emerges from it, whether one is engaged with the human-to-divine focus of translation and commentary (which tends toward the church's teaching leadership), or with the divine-to-human order of most Christian reading (which essentially presumes translation, tending toward the everyday practice of the whole people of God). So to the character of theological judgment we must turn once again, addressing the role of Scripture in authorizing theological proposals — even or especially proposals about how to understand Scripture. Prior developments — the oscillatory relation of *sophia* and *phronēsis;* the relative adequacy and stability of doctrinal habits in communicative praxis — can further fulfill their promise by addressing the dilemmas of chapter 4.

A. Performing Theology with Diverse Canonical Voices

Vanhoozer already, addressing the diversity of biblical genres as imaginative ways of relating language and life, has spoken of looking "along" rather than "at" the Bible for developing theology as wisdom.[91] Addressing the deficiencies of the older "propositional revelation" model, and rejecting the notion that theology can be read off biblical concepts in a simple foundationalist fashion, he negotiates the tension between "canon" and "concept," between "sameness" and "otherness," by arguing for the possibility of "conceptual mimesis." Such mimesis would be an imaginative re-description of the theology in these genres, using conceptual forms without pretending to any absolute sameness. Again, genres speak theologically in ways that are not fully re-describable in concepts, without imaginative loss.[92] But that is not to say the diversity is a matter of conflicting canonical voices, or of voices that cannot talk with each other. Indeed, God speaks to us in all these voices put together; conceptual re-description helps to reach and teach a Christian vision of the whole, but does not replace the irreducible role of biblical literary forms for learning to inhabit the faith.

As with genres, so also the conceptual patterns within them can be diverse without forestalling biblical unity. David Yeago, as alluded to previously, demonstrates the possibility of similar theological judgments taking different conceptual forms. Conversely, a different question about diverse content arises when similar conceptual forms are involved. To return to Paul and James, they use the same vocabulary of "faith," and indeed the same OT passages regarding Abraham, in markedly different ways. Yet if each addresses different questions, it is plausible that their voices are complementary rather than contradictory. The lesson to learn, once again, is that the practical concerns surrounding theological judgments do shape how words and concepts are used, what they mean, and therefore their relevance for divinely-authorized theology in later contexts.

(1) Which Texts Should Be Heard and What Do They Say?

So a dialogical notion of truth, à la Bakhtin, is necessary to avoid the criticisms of Ricoeur and others against theology done with a traditional doctrine of biblical inspiration. Vanhoozer has helpfully addressed this synchronic question of coherence, especially regarding genre and conceptual diversity as an invitation rather than an impediment to systematic theology. But it is unclear whether or not his development of *phronēsis* in theology is fully consistent with his supervenience model of divine discourse. He distinguishes epistemologically, not just ontologically, between a text's meaning (redescribed) and significance, and this could lead to the eclipse of *phronēsis* by technical reason if not carefully discussed. The *technē* of exegesis threatens to overwhelm the dramatic nature of reading Scripture in Christian witness.

How then, in a dialogical model, would the earlier definition of doctrine's "relative adequacy" — Christian teaching has been adequately (not exclusively) stated so long as there are no more relevant questions to answer — hold in connection with biblical discourse? Relevant questions would, in the first instance, concern the discernment of theological habits in or authorized by Scripture, some of these habits more directly conceptual than others, depending on genre and voice. To authorize a theological judgment would mean establishing which biblical patterns of communicative action about God ought to become ours, or how those patterns might preclude some of our possibilities for action; this question would involve both the selection of relevant biblical texts, and the interpretation of those texts.

Kelsey has claimed that "a theologian who marshals his proposals under the emblem 'Let theology accord with scripture' does not thereby announce that he has made a methodological decision, but only that he has taken on an awesome array of methodological problems."[93] Certainly true to a point, this should not become a counsel of despair. Kelsey himself can offer an "anatomy" of a theological argument, demonstrating that Scripture may function not merely as "data" (an impoverished term anyway) but also as "warrant" or "qualifier," as "backing" for warrant or "rebuttal" for a qualifier, in staking a "claim."[94] Theological judgments, moreover, often order Scripture's particulars into larger patterns,[95] and these claims are capable of being studied and criticized.[96] Here I am suggesting that the "narrative coherence" between various biblical texts, as well as the contexts of our own reading, may be critically evaluated on literary, historical, and social-scientific grounds. Such judgment ought to be undertaken and refined theologically, as that narrative coherence is oriented to an understanding of God's communicative action in Christ, and the connections between the Spirit's shaping of Jesus' life and our own. The working out of such a criteriological approach, especially in more detail regarding communicative action,[97] would allow for greater sophistication in the selection and application of biblical texts than would more generic notions, such as recognizing the "spirit" of a text.[98]

(2) What Are the Implications of Performing These Texts?

Of course, as just noted, *interpretation* bears on the *selection* of relevant texts, and vice versa. Furthermore, the relevance of biblical texts, and their patterns of communicative action, involves more than explicit statements. Long ago Austin noted that successful speech acts often imply other truth claims. He mentioned three of many ways in which this could occur: a speech act could imply, entail, or presuppose some truth claim.[99] If this is true for biblical speech acts, and if this matter of implicature is related to situation as well as to semantics, then the possibilities for theology are exceedingly rich. At the same time, theology's task is a daunting one. Certainly we cannot read theology straight off the surface statements of the Bible; that would satisfy the demands neither of theology nor of the texts. Instead, theological exegesis will require engagement with the presuppositions and implications of potential interpretations for what we say about God.[100]

It must be clarified that these implicatures stem from what is said, not from what is thought. Obviously the two are related if one adopts a version of authorial discourse interpretation, but the distinction remains important (1) for avoiding the intentional fallacy; (2) for distinguishing human discourse, which God appropriates, from human thoughts and frameworks (e.g., ancient cosmology) which God by accommodation may speak within, but not appropriate; and (3) for relating properly to "biblical theology" as an academic pursuit. Reconstructions of Pauline theology "behind" the text may be informative for understanding the canonical writings, but they are not dogmatically authoritative. Not only is historical speculation involved, but not all of the apostles' or prophets' thoughts are canonical. God communicates to us in the theological judgments provided in the text, and in patterns and implicatures of those judgments, but the author or editor's mental framework itself is not authoritative — the wisdom of the canonical writings is. The distinction is subtle to apply, but vital to maintain.

Judgments about God and God's ways are very much exercises in inference and implication. Here the Protestant orthodox were right about the propriety of logically extending the divine discourse for Christian teaching, whether or not they always undertook such thinking or understood its limits appropriately.[101] Certain judgments do follow from what God has said in Scripture; other judgments are ruled out for inconsistency with what God has said. We must seek the wisdom to recognize the various cases for what they are.

B. Figural Reading with Development in Canonical History

If a dialogical, wisdom model thus begins to address the transitive aspect of Scripture as divine discourse and the synchronic dimension of its diversity, what about timeliness? How would the "relative adequacy" of doctrine relate to the claim that the unity of God's revelation "is itself a reflection of the unity of divine activity in history"?[102] And how can we "indwell" the worlds of biblical language so as to discern the theological habits therein and make "relatively stable" theological judgments? If biblical theology can be modeled (on NT terms) after an "apostolic conference table,"[103] to handle the diversity of genres and voices, that is defensible partly on analogy with today's cultural-linguistic approach: some differing uses of concepts can mask consistent or complementary judgments and practice, and vice versa.

Perhaps then the diachronic development of a cultural-linguistic approach can be handled on the model of the NT's use of the OT, even for reading the NT — although not in exactly the same fashion, since Christ is God's final Word and in that sense churchly readers share an eschatological context.[104] Again, dialogical truth — but a "drama" of creatively faithful understanding in which the Word and Spirit have the first and last words — is the pertinent notion. Now our role in this drama must be fleshed out with regard to the lingering questions of chapter 4.

(1) Must Scripture Be Read Allegorically?

First, the Protestant orthodox rejection of allegorical interpretation faces two challenges: (1) can typology and allegory be meaningfully distinguished on historical grounds, and (2) can typology be deemed adequate on theological grounds for legitimating a unified canon? Both of these questions elicit monographs in themselves, but a brief reformulation of the problem may at least be attempted here.

The history of interpretation mitigates an absolute distinction between typology and allegory. Despite, for instance, Antiochene and later Protestant perceptions of a distinction, at points both these groups engaged in forms of allegorical interpretation. If the differences between Luther and Calvin concerning Christ in the OT are instructive,[105] then so also would be the differences between various avowed practitioners of allegory (say, between Origen and Augustine). The terms must be defined very carefully any time a statement is made. But a blurry line is still a line, and to resist any essential distinction insults the perceptiveness of those who were party to the earlier and later disputes.

Frances Young argues for reformulating the unworkable traditional distinction along the lines of "iconic" and "symbolic" mimesis, with the difference being whether or not an interpretation offered "narrative coherence."[106] This might explain the historical issues more accurately, and also points toward a theological resolution.

In the first place, meeting a requirement of "narrative coherence" is easier to defend inductively than (at least the narrower versions of) strictly typological exegesis. E. Earle Ellis offers a concise definition of typology as relating "the past to the present in terms of a historical correspondence and escalation in which the divinely ordered prefigurement finds a complement in the subsequent and greater event."[107] Types in this strict sense have to do with persons, institutions, or events.[108] Not all scholars would agree with Richard Davidson that the prefiguration provides advance notice or leaves evidence in the typical text; neither do all scholars accept the historicity of the types, and so approaches to salvation history affect discussions about what would count as evidence for typological hermeneutics. For the moment, whatever contemporary convictions might be, we must admit that the NT authors took the precedents of the canonical salvation history to anticipate patterns of further divine action.

Whether or not, in terms of warrant for such early Christian interpretations, we narrow "typology" to having a salvation-historical dimension of prophetic anticipation and fulfillment, the notion of narrative coherence could also include a strongly ethical dimension — discovery not only of patterns to expect from God but also of patterns for us to emulate (or not). Indeed, this fits exactly our concern about the role of *phronēsis* in discerning the divine discourse from the human texts.

Without minimizing the importance of assessing warrant, we may consider this process of discovery. What if the early Christians did not think in terms of prophetic fulfillment and ethical application from OT texts as separate categories? In this connection, a significant "typological" passage is 1 Cor. 9–10, where Paul's rationale for ethical applications of OT laws and negative examples is grounded in the claim that they were written "for us, upon whom the ends of the ages have come." Clearly he did not do critical exegesis of the OT wilderness narratives, only to arrive directly at the Christian sacraments. Yet just as clearly Paul took the OT *historia* seriously, and it is possible to unpack the framework of theological assumptions by which he read, as a framework derived from canonical reading of the OT itself.

So, in the second place, (strictly speaking) typology may be only one model for reading in light of redemptive history, whereas narrative coherence can be manifest variously. But that does not leave us with a broadly defined, even unbridled "allegorical" approach as the only satisfying alternative for finding the canonical story to be "our story." Narrative coherence puts our focus upon the canonical context — divine action and authorship rather than human authorship — without ignoring "the way the words go." Sometimes such coherence would involve promise and fulfillment; at times, strict identity of reference (a statement may continue to refer not only to the same God but also simply to another generation of the same people of God); other times, typological fulfillment in the precise sense; at still other times, there would be some form of type-token narrative structure rather than a purely symbolic move, but the coherence might take a more unexpected form. Perhaps Paul's "allegory" in Gal. 3–4 is a classic example of such reading, susceptible to discovery only at the right redemptive-historical moment, yet defensible when theological deep structures cohere in terms of a canonically-connected narrative. Likewise R. T. France claims that the "typological" interpretations offered by Jesus, according to the Gospels, are often "most implicit," involving a "far looser method" than type and antitype: "more often the parallels, though present, are unexpressed, and the typological intention must be inferred from the selection of that particular Old Testament passage for that particular occasion."[109] These might be patterns for Christian reading of the Bible today, as we seek to connect our own lives with the canonical story and its subplots.

We are not left merely with metaphorical links to the Bible, in which we are sufficiently "other" to it that allegory makes our only connection. Rather, we make analogical moves grounded in our complex identity relation with Israel, the people of God now being re-constituted in Jesus Christ. The "is-not" dimension of these analogical connections can be discerned by taking the redemptive-historical whole of the entire canon as the framework for reading the parts; claims about the "is" of an analogical move may arise due to a variety of processes of discovery, but their warrants may be discussed and defended as critical scholars study — literarily and otherwise — the canonical connections on which they depend. We have to look ahead with eschatological expectation even when reading the NT, not invoking a modern myth of ever greater progress to relativize it (God's final Word has been spoken) but not ignoring its own forward look to the future either (God's final Word is still being received; humanity is still being re-created).[110] That will mean extrapolation by analogy, but such analogy entails a relationship involving identity — extended as the story goes on — not the emphasis on our "otherness" from the persons, institutions, and events of the text which characterizes allegorizing.[111]

Thus, in the third place, a negative claim: allegorical exegesis was often a problem-solving resort necessitated by an outmoded approach to language.[112] If one expects of Scripture theological profitability (1) from its literal rather than literalistic sense, (2) without a strict referential approach, (3) thus freed from a Platonic signs-things orientation (at the level of words, especially),[113] (4) with greater awareness of genre and discursive voice, and (5) with due regard for epochal change in redemptive history, then such a resort may be unnecessary.

And in the fourth place, a positive corollary: many of the "allegorical" or "spiritual" readings of the past were indeed fruitful extensions of the textual meaning on theological assumptions from a canonical context. In other words, the fourfold sense often guided the church to readings in tune with its understandings of salvation history; these need not be dubbed "allegorical." Conversely, flaws in its readings may have been due to a flawed understanding of salvation history.

The appropriate concept of reference with which to work, then, is a narrative concept of identity regarding textual "designations" that can inform theological judgments with a "narrative substructure." Back to the NT doctrines of justification and faith, just such a narrative substructure informed Paul's use of the Abraham story in Gal. 3:1–4:11,[114] which of course leads into his "allegory" of Hagar and Sarah. The question concerns how to figure our own situation — the characters in our act of the drama — into the canonical story line.

Certainly one could not claim that the early church always exegeted the OT text in accord with modern critical standards of "meaning" before appropriating its "significance." Instead, one might claim that their appropriations of the OT are consistent with its authorial actions, and openness to the future of redemptive history, when understood canonically with reference to anticipated divine action. Underlying this claim would be a now familiar narrative concept of identity, tied to personal constancy rather than exact sameness. The reference points of the original text regarding Israel may designate Jesus Christ and/or his church including Gentiles, depending on how the rest of the text's story seems to go.

So also theological judgments — whether those somehow implied by the biblical discourse or those we are trying to make anew amidst communicative praxis — involve personal agency, as do the questions that give rise to them. Yeago describes the comparison of such judgments: "We must ask (1) about the logical subjects of which predicates are affirmed and denied, (2) about the logical type of the particular predicates affirmed or denied within the conceptual idioms they employ, and (3) about the *point* or function of their affirmations or denials within their respective contexts of discourse."[115] If the NT's pattern of reading the OT may instruct our own, then we may thus engage in "figural reading," that extends literal sense interpretation to the canonical level, and the canonical story line to include our present interpretative contexts.

This fits a hint from Vanhoozer again, who linked "translation" of texts to "tradition": "*Like tradition, then, translation does not simply repeat the past but rather develops it.* Like tradition, interpretation helps the text survive the passing on of its original context in order to live on. The text does not preempt dialogue but opens it through an overture of meaning that invites a responsible response."[116] But this promising start must be carried further. The narrative identity of personal constancy does not simply pertain to translation, but to all sorts of textual performances (which of course imply translations[117] and indeed ascriptions of authorial action). The lesson of NT theological exegesis is that one could narrate the identity of past communicative action not simply by how the humanly-authored texts are translated, but also by how the faith community appropriates them in redemptive history.

Theological judgments are an unfolding story, that can be told in diverse literary and conceptual forms, responding to diverse questions of different times and places. Thus the different questions of practice, which shape the meaning of (roughly) synchronic theological statements and which already suggest a dialogical notion of truth, pertain to the diachronic question even more. The extension of a text into new contexts, because of the complex interplay of language and life, occurs dialogically and a measure of otherness pertains. In this sense narrative movement is always at stake, and the coherence often cannot be recognized until or after the new moment comes. Yet that may simply highlight the importance of divine authorship in history as well as the Bible, and the otherness is not absolute difference but rather that of narrative development.

Bakhtin recognized that dialogical, creative understanding is necessary because questions must be asked to appropriate a text in responsibility to an other. It is our ongoing theological questions — how to communicate regarding God and God's ways — that keep the practice of reading Scripture lively, even as past answers inform the practice. The former keeps "relative adequacy" from reifying static formulations, while the latter offers the "relative stability" that shapes the coherence of the tradition. But these questions must be asked in ways that respect the text's otherness and priority. If one took the biblical and contemporary dialogue partners to be equal others, or if one used a "fusion of horizons" hermeneutical model, then the subject matter of the dialogue would be mutually determined: a "correlationist" theological model ensues, in which text and culture — or their authority — are equated.[118] But Christians sense an obligation to indwell the biblical story, so that George Lindbeck and Hans Frei relate theology to "figural reading," in which one seeks to have "the text absorb the world" not the reverse.

Both approaches tend to misunderstand the reality of our own enculturation. The "text absorption" model is too sanguine about our ability to objectify the canonical story in terms of directly extending it to our own indwelling;[119] the "correlation" model is too sanguine about our ability to objectify the present culture while we indwell it.[120] Moreover, both models tend to ignore that we actually indwell a multiplicity of cultural-linguistic worlds (at least as these are often defined).[121]

Kathryn Tanner trenchantly details such "postmodern" criticisms of modern, anthropological understandings of "culture," which have tended to drive theological models such as "correlation" and "contextualization." She suggests that once we view theology as part of culture, the relation between academic and everyday theology must not be understood in terms of a distinction between first-order and second-order discourse — as I have argued throughout.[122] However, the church-as-culture metaphor that is so crucial to the "cultural-linguistic turn" also becomes problematic — as indeed I mentioned in chapter 3. This could possibly jeopardize the application of the concept of narrative identity to the coherence between canonical and post-canonical theological judgments.

In response, while finding Tanner's notion of "Christian identity as a task"[123] helpful — fitting, in fact, with the notion of a quest for wisdom developed here — I worry that its theological context is inadequately developed. Christian identity is a task, but the task is initiated in the story of Israel and of Jesus Christ, and therefore informed canonically. Furthermore, the task has a *telos,* so that eschatological orientation and accountability likewise frame inquiry into Christian identity. In other words, the task is not nearly as formless, or Christian identity as void, as more recent theories of culture might be taken to imply.

The inadequacy of models for working with culture should not really surprise us; a detailed model for such interactions would, like a detailed model for interpreting divine discourse, perhaps overrun the *phronēsis* — the situation-sensitive reasoning — we are intended to develop. Despite the inadequacy of "contextualization" and "correlation" models, then, we should not heed a counsel of despair, but try to depict theologically the broader framework of such Bible-and-culture theological interactions.

Accordingly, a sense of dialogical drama is vital. Bakhtin has also offered us a correlative concept named the "chronotope," which involves a time-and-space context being thematized within an utterance. The chronotope involves "the intrinsic connectedness of temporal and spatial relationships that are artistically expressed in literature" in which "time, as it were, thickens, takes on flesh, becomes artistically visible; likewise, space becomes charged and responsive to the movements of time, plot and history."[124] Time and space are thematized axiologically in relation to humanity.[125] Easy examples include the crossroads as used by novelist Thomas Hardy;[126] or, biblically, the pilgrimage idea as taken up in Hebrews or the significance of journey in Luke's Gospel. The notion is, however, more far-reaching and intricate than these examples might indicate. All meaning, Bakhtin claimed, comes through the gates of the chronotope;[127] as we read a text, the time-and-space contexts of its authorship or of its "world"[128] and of its past reception are put in dialogue with the context of our reading.

The chronotope is a particularly helpful notion for three reasons. First, a text's "significance" is not set free of its "meaning" in a sense which renders the former thoroughly relative. Yet we are not sent off on an endless search for reconstructions of what pertained "behind the text" either; as Francis Watson put it, "an initial 'contextual significance' is relevant for interpretation only if it leaves its explicit mark on the wording of the text."[129] The context is actually made literary, so that practical reason does not operate altogether independently of textual criteria: "the chronotope is a way to acknowledge that texts carry historical information in an indirect way."[130] Hence analogical moves from original to reader contexts remain open to assessment and criticism, in terms of answerable engagement with what is somewhat other. The chronotope deals with "*a field of possibilities* . . . the possibility *of* events" in relation to human agency.[131]

Second, insights of performance models for interpretation such as music and drama that lean toward "textual sense" are not ignored. If not all meaning is semantically manifest, nevertheless it is also true that pragmatic factors can take semantic shape. Language and life intermingle, not only at the level of genre, but more particularly in concrete utterances that carry aspects of their world along with them; hence understanding will attend to an author's background and audience context partly through semantic as well as formal features. Language is not dialogical simply as a system but because living people are; nevertheless, language itself becomes involved in dialogism, and the chronotope shapes our roles in performing texts.

Thus, third, Bakhtin suggested the possibility of layering chronotopes, of their having multiple levels with some chronotopes embedded in others.[132] They are tools related to genre, but enabling distinctions within such forms, to engage more robustly the literary configuration of time. This will be especially important in undertaking biblical interpretation with reference to the drama of redemption. Indeed, chronotopes hint that the drama metaphor, taken up by some who have followed Hans Urs von Balthasar, legitimates certain performative aspects of biblical interpretation and handles performance more completely than the music metaphor.[133] If creative understanding is dialogical, this is so not in providing for some transparent, subjective access to the historical author, but in establishing the answerability of relationship to an other. Granted, strictly speaking "the dead cannot answer back."[134] But close reading[135] plus the linguistic connectivity of genre and chronotope can approximate a kind of dialogue.

Our answerability occurs in concrete time-and-space contexts and involves a range of responses as readers understand. While music[136] offers a useful analogy for the faithful improvisation involved in semantically-focused aspects of understanding (certainly a dimension of translation), and for particular kinds of audience reception (such as liturgical readings of texts), drama[137] may offer more conceptual resources for full-orbed performance of biblical texts.[138] For we have multiple roles in understanding, roles in which we are answerable for doing justice to the otherness of authors (and prior readers): provisionally re-saying and clarifying what they have said; following the rules for reading the text they have composed; and sincerely asking serious questions about the implications of their communication.

So, again, using this notion of a chronotope, with context actually being literarily thematized, practical reason does not operate altogether independently of textual criteria. But neither are the criteria independent of character development in communal forms of life. Analogical moves of theological judgment are necessary to hear the divine discourse, as acknowledged in principle and intertextual practice by the Bible itself.[139] The chronotope helps us to see how they can remain open to assessment and criticism, with canonical, salvation-historical development addressed by the possibility of layering, of chronotopes having multiple levels with some embedded in others. Ricoeur had suggested that "narrative is not the whole story" with regard to biblical time; to opt for a purely narrative theology may simply replace the "concept" with a different dominant form.[140] On the other hand, there is always an "interweaving" of narrative and non-narrative elements; even non-narrative genres include "a specifically temporal dimension."[141] Bakhtin helps us to develop such an "intertextual" model of biblical time toward which Ricoeur presses.[142]

How does this intertextuality of time relate to multiple levels of chronotopes? Not only does the chronotope coordinate space with time, giving a sense of a theological judgment's place. Bakhtin also engages the worlds of author, text, and readers more robustly in terms of time's literary configuration: the chronotope provides a new tool for recognizing biblical diversity, related to genre but also enabling distinctions within it — distinctions especially related to the drama of redemption within which occurs the drama of reading Scripture. Such distinctions take a helpful but broad preoccupation with genre, and further work *phronēsis* into the nooks and crannies of particular theological judgments which raise narrower issues of canon, concept, and context. The largest chronotope that addresses canonical unity and linguistic commensurability (at some level) would pertain to creation and new creation, to the larger story told in the Rule of faith. The more particular chronotopes of authors and readers would then concern the time-and-places *within which* practice sharpens understanding of communication, *within which* practice helps us to appropriate particular tellings of the story or its subplots.

In short, to answer the query of this section, there is no need to defend a Christian right to allegorical interpretation. Granted, much of Christian typological or figural reading has at times been labeled "allegorical" — even by its practitioners. Yet the degree of otherness, between text and context, and between the text's plain sense and spiritual meaning, which is implied in most uses of the word (from the Greek *allos,* "other"), is neither necessary nor appropriate. (If we grant Northrop Frye's rather formalist claim that all commentary or interpretation is allegorical, we trivialize the word.)[143] To the degree that allegorical interpretation is taken to be "imposed," "abstract," "closed," and "ahistorical,"[144] Christians need not adopt it for explaining their figural reading.[145]

So now we can move on to a second major question, which can be answered more briefly in light of the foregoing discussion and in light of the oscillation between *sophia* and *phronēsis* in Christian wisdom: what is the role of the *Regula fidei* in theological hermeneutics?

(2) Must Scripture Be Read with the Rule of Faith?

First, "*regula fidei*" needs more precise definition. It is true both that the rule is intended to be one rule — hence we often speak of it as *the* Rule of faith — and that "the Rule exists as various 'rules' of faith that bear a striking family resemblance to each other"[146] — thus one could speak of *a* rule of faith. This accords with the sort of "critical realist" approach that was applied earlier to linguistic expressions of Christian doctrine.

So, second, the family resemblances of these rules lie in "classical Christian theology, insofar as it presents and argues and ponders certain central *judgments of identity* that span the divide between the two testaments";[147] as "the grammar of theological agreements which Christians confess to be true,"[148] the rules that seek to express the Rule lend a certain coherence to our renditions of their story of redemption. Yeago adds:

> The most important of these judgments are (i) that the one who sent Jesus, and raised him from the dead, is self-identically the God of Israel, the God attested in the Old Testament scriptures; (ii) that the church of Jesus Christ is continuous, to be sure across massive and radical transformation, with the covenant people of the Old Testament; and (iii) binding these together, that Jesus Christ is the *one* word that God speaks to his people, so that whatever is 'word of God' in the Old Testament must be read as a moment within the protracted utterance of what is conclusively articulated only in the paschal mystery of Good Friday and Easter — in 'the resurrection which has now taken place.'

It is true both that "there is no 'method' of a *formal* kind — historical or literary, critical or allegorical or typological — by which the unity of the Christian canon can be set forth in abstraction from theological argument and judgment,"[149] and that the rule is considered a derivation from and description of the Bible's own unity.[150]

Third, then, the interpretative function of the *Regula* must be considered more specifically. In fact, the part-whole or discernment-vision oscillation of *phronēsis* and *sophia* describes its use perfectly. One comes to a theological judgment — whether about understanding biblical texts or living virtuously before God, which are in fact inseparable — with a large-scale Christian vision or rule of faith. One then seeks to exercise prudent judgment in the particular situation, engaging in responsible Christian witness as part of redemption's unfolding drama. That particular discernment can work back on understanding of the vision; understanding particular biblical texts may lead to revision of one's rule, recognizing more fitting correspondence to the *Regula*.

This is no mere hermeneutical circle or spiral (although that is clearly involved), in either of its guises — textual parts-and-whole, or text-and-presuppositions[151] (although it would allow them to be thought together in the case of the Bible). Nor is it simply a principled understanding of salvation history (although, again, that is present). Christian *sophia* takes particular shape with reference to Jesus Christ, so that *phronēsis* must understand present contexts of obedience in the light of his work *pro nobis*, and in view of his pattern to which we are being conformed. Moreover, *phronēsis* must understand the OT not only in terms of its anticipating fulfillment in Christ's work, but also in terms of its shaping the pattern of his image. The ecclesiological and eschatological judgments of identity cited by Yeago are rooted in the Christological judgment that grounds the *Regula*'s Trinitarian focus. And the *sophia-phronēsis* pattern is apt for the figural reading of Scripture's literal sense because these judgments of identity relate knowing God to knowing ourselves, as this wisdom is found in the duophysite Christ and enabled by his Spirit. The Trinitarian Rule helps us to find ourselves in the story and to imagine its unfolding drama, offering not simply static or abstract doctrines of church or last things but patterns for living in the church during the last days, with assurance that God has acted communicatively in the Spirit-led Christ. More simply put, the connection between Israel and the church via the humanity of Christ authorizes the inclusion of sanctification — and hence ethical discernment — within the deployment of the Rule of faith.

The *Regula* unfolds Scripture's unity while remaining subject to understanding its parts appropriately. Yet this critical potential of exegesis neither suggests nor licenses dispensing with such a rule in favor of formal or methodological approaches to Scripture only. Not to read with the Rule is not to read as a Christian; not to read with some flexibility between one's understanding and the Rule itself is not to read with cruciform humility or openness to the eschatological Spirit. For the Bible is a book of divine discourse as Jesus Christ reveals God his Father by the witness of the Spirit, and makes us wise unto salvation by that same Spirit who led him. *Technē* must always be used within the personal and corporate ethos of *phronēsis* and *sophia.* That is not to reject public accountability for theology or critical biblical scholarship in theological exegesis, but to specify their roles in a post-critical, sapiential understanding of epistemology. To that relation of *phronēsis* and *Wissenschaft* chapter 6 now turns, before we conclude by returning to the beginning of our quest, the relation of theology to theological education — and thus of *phronēsis* to *paideia.*

PART III

Education and Interpretation: Synergy

CHAPTER 6

Phronēsis and *Wissenschaft*

Having advocated that Christians read the Bible as Scripture, employing the Rule of faith and seeking wisdom — in other words, that they read the Bible as Christians — have I simply opted for a theology of *paideia* over public truth? This might appear to be the case, but *phronēsis* is, according to many, one (or the) major category of a post-critical, instead of anti-critical, rationality.[1] Still, if we relate *phronēsis* very specifically to "the mind of Christ" who is the *sophia* which Scripture communicates by the Spirit, have we lost Christian theology's public presence again?

At this juncture navigation is required between a rock and a hard place. As James Buckley and David Yeago note, the burden on those who emphasize Christian publicness "is to do justice to what is essential for Christian communal identity, and avoid the reduction of Christian knowledge to a mere 'case in point' of some more general kind of knowing"; Bruce Marshall has established that allegiance to the self-disclosed triune God shapes the Christian understanding of what "truth" even is. Conversely, the burden on those who emphasize Christian particularity "is to relate the singular Christian knowledge of God to other human knowing, and avoid the isolation of the knowledge of God in a special 'religious' sphere."[2] If the focus of chapter 5 led to the appropriation of *sophia* and *phronēsis* for understanding theological interpretation of Scripture, I now intend to appropriate the role of critical reason in biblical interpretation for understanding the public possibilities of Christian *paideia*, and its relation to *phronēsis* more generally.

I. Uncertainty and Universality: The Public Importance of *Phronēsis*

First the revival of *phronēsis* in general epistemology must be considered. On the one hand, this can follow an uncoupling of everyday knowledge and knowledge in "the humanities" from the natural sciences.[3] What modernity insisted upon joining together, may now be put asunder. On the other hand, the natural sciences themselves have undergone a "paradigm shift," at least to some degree. Michael Polanyi and Thomas Kuhn, among others, have raised awareness of subjectivity in philosophy of science.[4]

Thus attempts to employ some kind of "fallibilism" from natural science to religious knowledge are promising, but "the move from participation in communicative social interaction to the relative abstraction of theoretical discourse" probably requires that some distinctions between "scientific" and "religious" knowledge remain.[5] Moreover, if theology (whether involving the communicative praxis of the church or the more intensified — and technical, critically reflective — practices of its leaders or of scholars) must be considered one discourse about God, as opposed to two discourses or a second-order discourse about religion, then scientific fallibilism will not immediately provide a complete religious epistemology.

Even so, all Christian witness ought to strive for "intersubjectivity" and "objectivity," since understanding truth dialogically does not mitigate the need to strive for a measure of systemic unity (or, perhaps better, wholeness).[6] While the differences of practice between scientific and other knowledge do not mitigate the chastening of rationality in general, especially via pragmatic concerns, the opposite extreme is not necessary either.[7] For instance, the reason Richard Rorty questions any use for an *"overall notion of rationality"* is *"because only a narrow range of possibilities is taken seriously into account for such a notion's relevance to the contingent starting points we all share."*[8]

The better way forward seems to be "understanding *phronēsis* as the most inclusive label for reason itself (all other 'types' of reasoning, so-called, being amplifications of one or another of its constitutive moments)," thus giving "our 'craving for generality' something useful to do without turning it into an obsession."[9] Communal accountability is important, but some penchants for working this out in a strictly transcendental and logical fashion unwisely cling to the Enlightenment.[10] Contra Jürgen Habermas, for example, we should not make communicative praxis a rational affair in such a way that everything becomes argument; rather, conversation is the better category to embrace what rationality means.[11]

Phronēsis addresses the reality of rules or laws of regularity, but also their seeming incapacity to account fully for human choice and behavior.[12] For *phronēsis* may be defined as "the historically founded, communally nurtured capacity to construe what is reasonable and right in relatively singular contexts, where general, formal, and systematic expertise is, when conceived only as such, insufficient, even where necessary . . . the capacity to make *good* sense of variations *as* variations."[13] Even theoretical knowledge must be addressed "primarily in terms of a moral commitment to certain ideals of human flourishing";[14] this precludes the formulation and use of "comprehensive universals" in the classic sense, but still deals with the "actualization" of *universals* in some fashion.[15]

Many, of course, take *phronēsis* in a very broad sense, to say that *"the abstract guides while the concrete governs,"*[16] if they grant even that much influence to the abstract and universal. In so doing they defect from Aristotle,[17] and it becomes questionable whether they can legitimately claim to appropriate his *phronēsis.*[18] For Aristotle set such "knowledge" within a larger framework of contemplating ultimate (and unchanging) reality. Charles Allen, in fact, blames Aristotle's overly staunch *theoria* for an improper corollary, the instrumentalization of *phronēsis* via English equivalents such as "prudence"[19] and hence relegation of it to the ethical or practical realm only. The point must be reinforced that *phronēsis* is not a kind of *technē;* it has to do with means *and ends.*[20] An added problem with using "prudence" as a gloss is its connotation of caution,[21] which again tends to reinforce an instrumental concept.

Martha Nussbaum points out that Aristotle did not adequately distinguish (at least not clearly) "the *general* from the *universal.*" The general is opposed to the concrete, in how many cases it covers and in how it covers them non-concretely; the universal might cover particular cases in very concrete ways. She adds that "rules could play an important role in practical reason without being prior to particular perceptions," if they are used for making good concrete judgments rather than as inflexible normative measures for perception.[22] As Al Wolters puts this point with regard to biblical interpretation, "it's not that there are no rules, it's just that the business of knowing and applying them is necessarily engaged in all the dimensions of being human."[23] This subtle distinction relates to the need, against generality, for taking into account (1) new and unanticipated features, (2) the context-embeddedness of relevant features, and (3) the ethical relevance of particular persons and relationships,[24] so that (4) emotions ought to be relevant to intellectual life as "discriminating responses closely connected with beliefs about how things are and what is important."[25]

Hence the turn to *phronēsis* means a recovery of virtue in epistemology, to counteract the possibility of a merely instrumental view of reason. Virtues are "dispositional properties, along with the concerns and capacities for judgment and action that constitute them . . . deeply embedded parts of character that readily dispose us to feel, to think and to act in morally appropriate ways as our changing circumstances require."[26] Prudence then is a "bridge virtue, with one foot in the camp of reason and the other in the camp of action."[27]

However, a problem arises in building this bridge. Aristotle does seem to treat *phronēsis* instrumentally at points (having to do with means), precisely in relation to some similarities with *technē* and connections to a concept of excellence — upon which its universal significance for rationality (in terms of the abstract-concrete relationship) might depend.[28] If one reacts to this diminution of *phronēsis* by emphasizing its moral character, then one threatens to divide it into two parts[29] or to divest its universal significance. We struggle further, from another angle, because there seems to be a distinction between moral and intellectual virtues, at least in terms of how they are learned, to which even Aristotle appealed.[30]

The virtue epistemologist's move toward a parallel between moral skills serving the morally virtuous, and intellectual skills serving the intellectually virtuous, is helpful if one can hold together the notion of "virtue" between the two, and, in particular, if a substantive account of "intellectual virtue" can be given which addresses the frequent self-referentiality of defining "virtue" in terms of success.[31] Otherwise we remain under the formal hegemony either of ("modern") method and means, or a thoroughly functional ("postmodern") neo-pragmatism.

It is not that methods are unimportant or indistinct; even a staunch virtue theorist such as Linda Zagzebski grants that the intellectually virtuous are committed to using the right skills and procedures.[32] Nevertheless the methodical cart must not drag the horse:

> The tragedy is that objectivism and relativist pluralism ('perspectivism' as MacIntyre calls it) find themselves driven onto the alternative horns of the modern/post-modern dilemma. When the notion of publicness is fused with an ideal of knowledge as demonstrable certainty (resulting in the search for a truth which is 'public' in the sense that it is equally accessible to all) and when the pluralist abandonment of this ideal results instead in a relativistic agnosticism (a loss of publicness of any sort), then, frankly, the dilemma seems to be insuperable.[33]

The lesson from the ascendancy of virtue epistemologies is not that they have given an exhaustively satisfactory account; there is no exclusive, universal epistemology against which Christianity or any other truth claim must be publicly measured. The lesson, rather, is that to some degree "it is the truth which is public rather than our mode of knowing or dealing with it."[34] Even in the operation of *technē,* skills, procedures, methods, and so on, trade on some end in view, and on whole-personed judgment and engagement before and during the testing process of critical reason. For studying public or social matters, whereupon even *technē* pushes toward *phronēsis,*[35] the end will have a moral component, and thus a substantive account is required that relates the True and the Good. Perhaps even *technē* hints, at a more basic level, that a substantive account is required regarding what is Beautiful or aesthetically whole — the form an epistemic product takes. Moreover, this substantive account must address the transformation of our very selves and communities: for we do not seem inclined to love even what we acknowledge as true, good, and beautiful, and this failure to love shapes what we will acknowledge and what we can know.

When it comes to hermeneutics, Merold Westphal has rightly criticized the tendency to see the exclusive objectivity of method as a (really Pelagian) means of purification, which substitutes for grace.[36] Furthermore, according to Roger Lundin we have privileged method because of a Cartesian predilection for focusing upon solitary subjects.[37] By contrast, *phronēsis* would recover the hermeneutical significance of Christian community, but also acknowledge its ongoing sinfulness. Critical tools therefore have some value, along with openness to transforming divine action as another aspect of objectivity.

At just this point it becomes possible, and indeed attractive, to proffer a specifically Christian version of *sophia* and *phronēsis* in the public square. Having learned the need to integrate rules, consequences, and virtues into an account of moral and intellectual life, we face considerations of reliability, internal coherence, and responsibility.[38] Having learned all over again that rationality involves a "conscientious rhetoricism"[39] — it is centered in dialogue and argument — we acknowledge that method can only be a heuristic guide; there will be no *de facto* universal consensus as to what rationality means.[40] Accordingly "faith" and "theology" must be considered much closer together[41] — as I have suggested throughout.

Indeed, that which a post-critical rationality attacks, and due to which the recovery of *phronēsis* is so crucial, might be aptly named "epistemology" (or some current perceptions thereof)! Making such a move, Charles Taylor describes this monster as centrally "the view that we can somehow come to grips with the problem of knowledge, and then later proceed to determine what we can legitimately say about other things: about God, or the world, or human life."[42] In its wake, we must admit the guiding role of background understanding, the possibility of rational interlocution without fully explicit positions, and the frequent need for comparative rather than absolute judgments.[43] In other words, we must return to what Taylor calls elsewhere "substantive reason,"[44] recognizing that decisions for or against, and about the shape of, "procedural reason" always trade on life experience and accounts thereof.

In a way we accept a lack of certainty, at least in the present postmodern climate. Joseph Dunne repeatedly stresses that "a desperate attempt to escape from the inherent vulnerability of human affairs"[45] led to the loss of *phronēsis* in the first place. But, ironically enough, lacking full certainty, and sometimes knowing better than we can say, are precisely why *phronēsis* is so important![46] Indeed, currently even *phronēsis* could still be used to authorize and buttress an instrumental or strictly procedural reason, unless we work with and toward a compelling account of the True, the Good, and the Beautiful, and their harmony.

So, by shaping its account of *phronēsis* in relation to the *sophia* found in Christ, the Christian faith makes a distinctive appeal: find the True, the Good, and the Beautiful in a person (!) who reveals and relates the nature of God and human flourishing. Moreover, the Christian faith answers the Aristotelian and neo-pragmatist dilemma about the origin of *phronēsis,* given its communal and habitual character:[47] where do the virtuous habits come from? We must be transformed by the Holy Spirit, who initiates us into a new communal praxis. Christians should not apologize (in one sense!) for the measure of epistemological uncertainty their claims encounter: it follows from the inescapable need for substantive reason, with (accordingly) competing social practices that attest to competing understandings of the True, the Good, and the Beautiful. There must be space for various communities to stage their dramas of *paideia* in the public square.

II. *Phronēsis* and the Parameters of Critical Reason

Is critical reflection unable to fit within post-critical plurality, a plurality of voices that must remain discontent with sheer pluralism? David Kelsey notes that such careful reflection must "find its criteria partly in the end to which the practice is ordered . . . and partly in the standards of excellence that partially define the practice. . . ." Nevertheless, beyond that "critical reflection must raise questions about the practice itself: Why become involved in it at all? Insofar as engagement in this practice brings with it commitment to certain claims about reality, are they true?"[48] Why, in other words, interpret the Bible to know God in Jesus Christ?

A. Recovering Theology from Apologetics

Kelsey's seemingly obvious distinction between sources of criteria suggests a two-part introductory response, providing for critical reflection in a post-Enlightenment fashion. First, with modernity this distinction, which was really the difference between theology and apologetics (and, in terms of biblical interpretation, a certain distinction between meaning and truth), was often lost. Hence apologetic concerns were allowed to reshape fundamentally how the Bible's meaning was understood, so that, second, the practice of theology itself was lost. Admittedly, a difference worth preserving exists between the critical dimension of theology, which apologetic concerns stimulate, and apologetics itself. When the latter overwhelms theological practice, Christians are tempted to teach something other than the Christian faith, changing its meaning to defend its plausibility.[49]

Historical perspective thus permits the recovery of Christian theology's voice, even if we are still in its throat-clearing stage.[50] (Post)critical reflection will no longer understand "criticism" to entail narrowly modern empiricism, or to absolutize the Enlightenment.[51] (Post)critical reflection will be suspicious of a predilection for discovery, invention, and novelty, which are characteristically modern expectations of theology, and perhaps pathological throughout the contemporary university.[52]

Yet it is not that all novelty is bad, or that all aspects of critical reason have been pathological. Kelsey reminds us how natural historical and philosophical work must have seemed for theology:

> Theological schooling was to have a movement from sources (history of Christianity or historical theology, including scripture) to a theoretical moment (philosophical theology) to the application of the theory to practice (practical theology). This is why *Wissenschaft* was so important. It meant, quite particularly, the disciplines of the academic *historian* to make sure the first moment was rigorously done, and the disciplines of the academic *philosopher* to make sure that the second, theoretical moment was rigorously done.[53]

Avery Dulles notes, in fact, that there had never been a pre-critical era in theology, except regarding the sources themselves, toward which modernity turned its critical gaze;[54] nevertheless, the application of academic disciplines to theology and then of their criticism to the sources themselves flowed somewhat innocently from a theory-to-practice orientation that had been increasingly latent within scholasticism. Only in the end has the criticism that almost inevitably confronted faith itself[55] (and its sources), seemed of a different character than previously, and this has resulted in the *paideia-Wissenschaft* tensions of contemporary theological education.[56]

Christian theology can recover its voice, and live with the tensions evoked by this new ideological criticism, only if we believe with pre-moderns that first- and second-order reflection can blur but still occur self-consciously.[57] To be "post-critical" still means to be wary of valorizing the pre-critical age and instituting the "subjectivism" of what Dulles calls a "para-critical" approach, which would "address only the private experience of believers."[58] Yet if we are historically aware, to be (post)critical will also mean being critical of modern critical reason itself, with (1) its bias toward doubt, (2) its failure to recognize even doubt's fiduciary basis, (3) its impossibility of applying criticism with absolute consistency, (4) its neglect of the social dimension of knowledge, and (5) its neglect of the tacit dimension of knowledge.[59] Whether or not from a non-Christian perspective, even some versions of "post-colonialism" illustrate the possibility of resisting the hegemony of critical reason without deposing or banishing it altogether, as in more radical versions of "postmodernism."[60]

B. Reforming Theological Disciplines

What then would the critical reflection of a (post)critical theology involve, in distinction from more apologetic tasks or engagements? Robert Jenson rightly suggests that in reading Scripture to authorize theological judgments, we must involve personal commitment but are still constrained from giving ahistorical interpretations.[61] This attention to history has been the burden of my effort to establish "narrative coherence" and "narrative identity" as textual criteria for figural readings of Scripture.

What qualifies as "ahistorical," negatively, or "public," positively, must be appropriate to the subject matter. Theologians sometimes borrow this criterion of propriety to the subject matter from Barth who borrowed the idea from a scientist. They seek to defend theology's "public" character by defining it in "scientific" terms. Yet it seems that *sapientia* may well eventuate in public truth claims without necessarily preserving such a contested label as "scientific" for them; in Dietrich Ritschl's terms, theology might not be a science but rather wisdom that can incorporate scientific methods.[62] This battle becomes terminological depending on one's agenda for theology vis-à-vis the university, which means that American, British, and German — let alone non-Western — theologians will perhaps make different judgments depending on their different contexts. It is for this reason that I do not labor over the important issue of whether or how to construe theology (or its submovements) as academic discipline(s) at a purely abstract level of general theory.

In any case theological interpretation of Scripture, on an account of *phronēsis* sketched in relation to narrative considerations of the Christian faith, would provide criteria of a-historicity: interpretations and theological claims could be challenged on textual grounds. These grounds would not simply involve speculative reconstructions of human authorship in isolation from the level of canon and the Rule of faith, but they would be textual nonetheless.[63] Interpretations and theological judgments would be subject to criticism in offering reasons distinct from solely the subjectivity of any interpreter, in being accountable regarding communication, in offering criteria that would unsubstantiate a claim.[64] Against wisdom's emphasis upon narrative and character leading straight to subjectivism and individualism,[65] a kind of suspicion is needed — what some particular text says, or how various texts fit together, could falsify an exegetical and/or theological proposal that "seems good to us." Conversely, such proposals will be stronger and deserve more conviction to the degree that they rely upon clear and converging textual evidence of what "seemed good to the Holy Spirit."

Two objections would be pertinent at this stage. First, John Goldingay worries that theological interpretation of Scripture is rather inclined toward agreement with current Christian doctrine.[66] Of course this reflects the concern that generated the academic discipline of biblical theology in the first place. While not being insensitive to it, we may plausibly respond, in light of the historical discussion above, by asking whether faith or doubt — trust or suspicion — ought to be the more fundamental posture. Valuing continuity in its doctrine, and accepting a slower pace of development and change, is probably ingredient to the church's self-understanding. Goldingay's worry may pathologically call for the church to give up being itself.

Nevertheless the criterion of "relative adequacy" leaves theology open to continual questioning. Second, then, one might worry that not all criteria can or should be "autonomously generated internally to the enterprise of *fides quaerens intellectum*."[67] Once again the issue concerns how this worry is construed. Recent treatments of ecclesiology, for example, have highlighted the need for the church to undergo prophetic critique from a host of sources, not least the social sciences and dialogue with other religions.[68] Yet in some sense the willingness to undergo, and perhaps embrace, such critique stems from Christian self-understanding, even if some of the critical practices themselves do not. Believing that the truthfulness of Scripture's plain sense must be tied to the truthfulness of God, Christians have persistently evaluated their theological understanding for its capacity to assimilate what is clearly true from outside, in God's other "book" of creation. This requires charitable interaction with the claims of other discourses and communities.[69]

The point is that the "narrative coherence" of Christian theology can be questioned from both sides — not only regarding its treatment of the biblical texts as humanly authored, but also regarding church praxis. Christian witness may be criticized as unwise either for incoherence with the biblical Rule of Christian faith, or for implausibility in terms of lived experience and human inquiry. The Christian story of redemption entails openness to both possibilities while we wait the eschaton.

The fact that we must not simply focus on moments of theological judgment as isolated decisions of analytic casuistry, devoid of narrative context and character formation, does not preclude some role for both first- and third-person accounts justifying such judgments.[70] Christians should be committed to these "best accounts"[71] of the logic implied in their communicative practice, and to *ad hoc* exegetical and social-scientific criticism of their *phronēsis,* because they realize that "if divinity is transcendent, then descriptions of divinity are most obviously inadequate; descriptions of divinity are brought first and foremost under a relativizing knife."[72] The Bible can remain subject to the full range of human inquiries, but their given results may be more or less relevant to theological interpretation.[73] Christian theology has in itself resources for self-criticism,[74] and for opening itself to other-criticism.

In terms of criteria, then, Christian theology *per se* — not to mention its apologetic task — seeks to use the Bible with a narrative coherence between text and history that is open to continual questioning of several kinds. On the surface, such a criterion ("narrative coherence between text and history") suggests that historical, literary, and theological methods will be especially crucial, and indeed these are widely cited as the chief components of biblical scholarship interested in "biblical theology."[75] Thus we briefly consider how *theologia* might appropriate them as moments within its communicative praxis.

(1) Biblical Theology and/or Theological Interpretation? Discovery versus Warrant

One aspect of theology's relation to university *Wissenschaft,* as explored previously, concerns the possibility of "biblical theology" vis-à-vis "theological interpretation of Scripture." On this point, a post-critical, *phronēsis*-oriented approach to theology in the university would need to distinguish process and result, or discovery versus warrant.[76] This is not quite as simple as a distinction between the aims of interpretation (including virtue) and the norms of interpretation (excluding virtue). As a discourse, the results of theological interpretation are invariably claims about the content or result of biblical theology. What the theologian says about the concept of humans as "image of God," for instance, must be at least consistent with anthropological judgments we find in the Bible. Yet normative, theological or philosophical[77] concerns inevitably intrude on the process or approach we use in arriving at such claims. The line of authority does move in a sense from the Bible to theology, but a sort of provisional authority must be granted to the analogy of faith — to theological understanding of the Bible's scope — to get interpretation going (to get us into the hermeneutical spiral). Furthermore, conceptual analysis will be required in making historical and literary judgments. To be sure, the process of biblical theology as a discipline (even as an interdisciplinary program) will involve a more *historical-and-literary* focus, whereas the process of systematic or philosophical theology (or an interdisciplinary program of "theological interpretation") will involve a more *literary-and-philosophical* focus. (This is not even to mention the non-academic dimensions shaping theological interpretation such as personal prayer, liturgical practice, participation in struggles for justice, and so on.) Still, the "philosophical" analysis and deep background beliefs of theology will be in play throughout these processes.

For example, theological interpretation would explore the issue of humans as the image of God not only on historical and literary grounds in Scripture, but also by asking questions of the biblical texts in terms of the history of Christian anthropology (with issues such as freedom, nature and grace surfacing); relevant aspects of evolutionary theories (not least, efforts to assess and explain the uniqueness of human language); philosophical interests regarding agency and selfhood; as well as contemporary concerns regarding bioethics, technology, social justice, environmental stewardship, and the like. If the content of biblical theology is to be a bridge between exegesis and theology, still the traffic must be two-way. And if a biblical theology enterprise is to travel into the public square, not just walking around a walled-off Christian enclosure, then we must not simply collapse strategies for public engagement or apologetic concerns (such as defending the Bible historically) into the commitments we use in understanding and teaching our faith (reading the Bible as our Word from God). Instead, theological interpretation of Scripture assumes that intentionally addressing the implications for the church's life in the world actually assists in recognizing what is the biblical teaching to start with. Compared to "biblical theology," then, "theological interpretation" opens up more conversational space, or opportunities for processes of *discovery*, between both Scripture and church practice, and the Bible and liberal learning. Historical and literary scholarship on the Bible will offer criticism of the questions that surface in these conversations, and scriptural *warrant* for the answers we seek. Because those questions open up ultimate concerns, however, and because integrating the biblical texts themselves obligates us to undertake conceptual analysis, philosophical/theological construction is integral to the process — essential to discovering warranted results.

(2) Historical, Literary, and Philosophical? Disciplines as Discourses with Textual Practices

Accordingly, from how to approach the Bible as Scripture, while open to the public square, Christians can discern more generally a particular relationship between historical, literary, and philosophical disciplines or approaches. If thus far we have navigated the rocky shores of what might be called the *material* question over how theology pursues its conversational role — how might Scripture's relevant content emerge in the process of interaction with wider learning? — may we also address (suggestively) the more general, *formal* question of how history, literature, and philosophy ought to relate, in light of Christian faith? If the two are consistent, that would strengthen the overall case made here for a Christian *phronēsis.*

With three small points we must be content: first, while dealing of course with the human, "the humanities" are also irreducibly textual; second, this textual dimension suggests a redefinition away from carefully-bounded academic "disciplines" toward communities of discourse that focus on somewhat fluid configurations of overlapping textual practices; and third, the "social sciences" must have greater say regarding the questions pursued by theology.

Historical inquiry in relation to the Bible — whether done as "biblical theology" or religious studies — illustrates the inevitable requirement of literary and philosophical sophistication: the literary, since even material evidence will be handled with a component of textual interpretation; the philosophical, since background and comparative studies will be pursued with certain expectations as well as commitments regarding ultimate questions. Moreover, conceptual analysis will be required if scholars are to be clear on the way that intended results correlate with interpretative practice itself. For instance, remember how much confusion in biblical theology may be due to methodological imprecision or even ineptitude about its locus (in the text or behind the text?) and its focus (words or concepts or judgments?).[78]

Literary scholarship, likewise, puts philosophical positions and practices constantly in play. Meanwhile, at worst philosophers (and theologians) tend to alternate between extremes of creative theoretical schemes that could use closer reading, and careful analyses of words that could use a lesson or two in broader aesthetic forms and concerns.

Admittedly, aesthetics is an area that could challenge my argument: for, indeed, we should not reduce art to text.[79] Yet it is a potential contribution of literary scholarship that our understanding of texts must better integrate appreciation of form with meaning and ultimate concerns. Furthermore, God has chosen to communicate personally — in the form of Jesus Christ — by means of a written text with quite diverse forms of its own.[80] If these Scriptures have any role as arbiter of truth for Christian thinking, then scholars need competence in historical, literary, and philosophical approaches to texts.

This suggests, then, that academic "disciplines" (at least in the humanities) should not function as closed communities which are exceedingly scrupulous about methodological distinctiveness and therefore simply generate ever more specialized studies and discourses. Instead, historians undertake the reading of texts with an interest in describing events and ascribing actions to agents; they will tend to interpret for the sake of offering explanations or partially causal narrative accounts, but will do so in relation to communicative agency in or behind the texts themselves. Literary scholars have some difficulty — or so my good friends in the field admit — defining what exactly they undertake in a coherent "disciplinary" way. But it seems fair to say that they undertake reading with an interest in describing texts as (in a sense) events, so that they will have aesthetic focus on form. Moreover, they must have (historical) interest in the actions of authors and readers both; at their best, they do not ascribe quasi-personal agency to texts or language in themselves.[81]

Each of these fields, then, clearly needs the other. So also do philosophers and theologians need such interaction, for they will have nothing to analyze in relation to God and/or ultimate human questions otherwise — their practices, so to speak, inhere within the textuality of the historical and literary. Each set of practices, while inescapably intertwined with the others, will be undertaken with a particular kind of rigor that generates a "discourse" — not only about the deliverables of the practices *per se* ("history" or "literature") but also concerning the nature and methods of its "best practices" ("doing history" or "studying literature"). Even so, we must resist the tendency of these discourses to inhere within social structures that float freely above the texts they read, and hence apart from the other necessary practices involved in human understanding — not least, diverse approaches to the act of reading itself.[82] Indeed, while these practices are pursued with more time, intensity, and rigor by scholars, they implicitly characterize the act of reading itself in communicative praxis.

Beyond the boundaries of the humanities as some corners of the university would draw them, theology must also engage the social sciences.[83] One might argue, in fact, that the historicity of textual engagement demands skill in cultural interpretation, as well as openness to the descriptions of oneself and one's community that come from others, and which the social sciences can particularly mediate. Perceived divisions between the humanities and social sciences might be neither essential nor even helpful. The "secular" premises and practices of social theory need not be denied to appreciate the value of *ad hoc* but deliberate theological engagement with them. No academic discipline or discourse is free at its core from challenges to Christian commitments. If, for example, history and the natural sciences pose the question of methodological naturalism, or literature and philosophy often presume a non-Christian anthropology, then the social sciences are no more or less worthy of theological attention.

Why theological interpretation of Scripture, then, to engage these academic communities of practice while preserving a degree of alienation from them and allegiance to "ordinary" Christian community? Not because something like biblical theology, to discern the texts' structural wholes and parts, is impossible or unimportant: rather, its best practice requires the widest possible set of questions to be asked before the God who communicates in the Bible. Questions of Christian life, churchly interest, and contemporary cultural concern are required to interpret Scripture as a whole, and to uncover its manifold implications. Merely "historical" or "literary" description, while essential in assessing interpretative warrant, will be insufficient for Christian discovery of the whole truth, which engages texts to pursue analysis of ultimate concerns. Furthermore, the practice of theological interpretation has greater integrative potential for Christian intellectual life *and public engagement:* if conversation or dialogue is taken seriously as a metaphor, then we will have to acknowledge how these dimensions of theology's interaction with Scripture (and accordingly any textually-involved university pursuit) — the historical, literary, philosophical, and so on — impinge on each other. Yet each must also respect the integrity of how the others ask questions. Perhaps Christians can learn, in Daniel Hardy's phrase, a *"polity of exploration and expression"* from their textual reasoning that will accept continued argument as a source of wisdom's "deeper meaning" — and, if so, our theological interpretation of Scripture might be pursued dialogically with outsiders, helping perhaps to show how the fractures of contemporary universities might be healed.[84] Wisdom is about the mysterious wholeness that emerges in movement and tension, rather than the maintenance of isolated static positions.[85]

C. Revisiting the Classroom

Would the drive for wholeness in sapiential epistemology demand the avoidance of Western theological academies? Would seeking wisdom lead to the annihilation, or fundamental alteration, of courses on the history of philosophy, literary theory, and the like? If so, has religion retreated and left university territory altogether to "science"? If not, how could such classes proceed without the inevitable distinctions, curricular sequence, and ultimately elitism (of a sort) that seem non-sapiential?

Contemporary appreciation of cultural density and difference must apply not only to the teachers and learners in universities, but also to their larger departmental structures, and even beyond to the arrangements of academies across the world. Among other realities, the dynamics of church and state interaction vary widely across cultures, with very concrete implications for how academic theology might function. This is true even within the West; note, as one illustration, the ramifications of free-standing American seminaries over against university divinity faculties in Great Britain.

Instead of a programmatic, one-size-fits-all vision for theology and the university, we must apply *phronēsis* regarding this issue as well. Particular arrangements for academic life themselves involve different possibilities and visions of cultural goods. Christians will need to discern what such arrangements offer by way of opportunity for theology to engage the academy, and also what they demand by way of resistance or alternative practice. Scholarly communities and their literature, round the world, must make space for such a plurality of arrangements and, indeed, the differing visions they imply regarding what even counts as rationality. It is true, on the one hand, that many attempt to abstract features of rationality common to all fields in all places;

usually this has meant privileging the natural sciences or perhaps analytic philosophy as intellectually paradigmatic. On the other hand, most such attempts have been subject to deconstruction or at least severe chastening. The middle way is *phronēsis,* eliciting standard features of rationality only via situated, shared efforts at argument and understanding. In saying this I do not embrace a playful "postmodern" cynicism, but extend soberly a flexible vision of rationality as conversation and argument to include everyone in dialogue about the academic forms that will take.

When it comes to curriculum and the classroom, then, the point is not to exclude a course on Hegel, for example — tempting though his exclusion might be — from theological study in favor of pedantic biblicism. No, the point is to distinguish (but not separate) such academic "theology" from sapientially-defined *theologia.* Therefore, the degree to which such a course contributes to *theologia* will depend on the public and private praxis of intending God in the midst of reflection, even when its character is quite demanding. Teachers can make public space for praxis in that direction, while learners can pursue it more privately as well. In various ways the shape of writing and other assignments, as well as reading practices in and outside the classroom, can create such space. The aims of education — and accordingly the degree to which background knowledge must be presumed upon either a class's entry or exit — are profoundly pluralistic. *Theologia* defined sapientially has no stake in legislating a particular arrangement that excludes study oriented historically, literarily, or otherwise. Rather, its aim would be to orient moments of such study toward personal formation and questions of corporate concern. Moreover, it is important to recognize — both for communities that have tended toward forms of biblicism and for others fearful of it — that theological interpretation of Scripture is not merely a matter of engaging exegetical intricacies. Its questions are wide-ranging, and its immediacy of engagement with the biblical text varies. Sapiential theology sometimes cannot constructively take place in the disoriented practices of the church, even as at other times it certainly could take place in the disparate pursuits of academic theology. It involves moments of grace in engagements with God and each other, moments for which we may seek to be disposed but which we cannot programmatically determine.

III. Summary: *Phronēsis* in Public

Phronēsis, in sum, offers not only the possibility that biblical interpretations remain subject to exegetical method, but also that in their theological dimensions they — and the theological judgments they authorize or rule out — are subject to other types of critical reason as well. Accordingly, Stephen Davis summarizes the theories that must be rejected in construing Scripture's normativity according to this hermeneutic of *phronēsis:* (1) the view that there are virtually no limitations on what counts as acceptably Christian; (2) the effort simply to conform the Christian faith to some other current theory; (3) the acceptance of a selective biblical authority limited by current taste; (4) openness to tradition's binding the faithful with theological proposals that have no biblical warrant; and (5) lack of openness to tradition's performance of Scripture, in an effort to do theology based merely upon proof-texting.[86] None of these views are acceptable because each neglects some aspect of what constitutes Christian wisdom.

So Christian communication about God, God's ways and will, is an enterprise of faith seeking understanding, understanding that arises from encountering various others — or else it is not *Christian* theology at all. The triune God who communicates in creating and redeeming us is, for Christian theology, "in place" so that faith becomes a principle of inquiry.[87] Thus logic *per se* will not be enough to determine Christian theological judgments, but the faith does have its own kind of logic.[88] Included in this logic of faith is eschatological space between the gospel and summary confessions thereof, which frees theology from dogmatism and focuses its work.[89] We are accountable, on this logic, for knowing God, not necessarily for exhaustively knowing how we know (at least contra some modern versions of procedural reason); that is to say, knowledge of God is a saving and sanctifying reality that may never fully satisfy the general canons of epistemology.

Yet neither William Abraham's important insight about unhealthy preoccupation with epistemology to the exclusion of soteriology, nor Bruce Marshall's Trinitarian focus regarding Christian truth claims, should legitimize the neglect of "taking every thought captive" to Christ. We must beware understanding that phrase in an uncritical, hegemonic sense. But it would be strange indeed to claim that everything holds together in Christ, and at the same time that the Spirit's witness to the Word has no canonical function whatsoever in most areas of knowledge. That points up the irony of leaving epistemology entirely to the philosophers, keeping Christian theology safely away. Might not epistemology need the revelation of the gospel too?[90]

Phronēsis is necessary because we must live with the uncertainty of competing versions of substantive reason. A Christian account of *phronēsis* addresses crucial aporias of other, more general versions, such as the origin of the virtuous habits or their community of formation noted earlier. It is tempting, of course, to try turning this into a transcendental argument. For instance, Nicholas Lash notes that the basic conditions for critical theology — there is a God, who is accessible by self-communicating action, with this contingently expressed in communal speech action — parallel the three articles of the Christian creed.[91] Yet Taylor reminds us that when it comes to transcendental arguments, "it is hard to know when you have [a valid] one, at least one with an interesting conclusion. But then that seems true of most arguments in philosophy."[92] So we are left with the responsibility of witnessing to the plausibility and appeal of the Christian story, all the while learning from engagements via critical reason and culture with how other communities construe wisdom.

In places the modern Western university has made Christian theology seem obscure and private unless constantly apologetic, because "once God is understood as a speculative (and, in other contexts, heteronomously threatening) accessory to autonomous human life, it is hardly surprising if the question of God recedes from the public agenda."[93] But there is no reason for this anymore; at least there is no reason for Christian theology to cooperate with such an agenda. As Hardy points out, "the search for wisdom is very closely related to the question of the purpose of a university today, and the identity of theology there."[94] It appears that the academy can be accused of "massive moral failure, a failure which is manifest in the visionlessness of current social life in such matters as the common good."[95] There will be no one-size-fits-all solution to this, but in many contexts Christians must neither abandon nor knuckle under the contemporary academy. We may instead communicate the beauty of wisdom, and discover it afresh by reading Scripture amid present-day challenges in our communities.

CHAPTER 7

Phronēsis and *Paideia:* The School of the Triune God

It is time to put education and interpretation together. This book has investigated the possibility of recovering, post-critically, an ancient understanding in which

> thought — reason! — was not merely *our act,* instigated by us and aimed at our mastery of data, and so of nature and history. Both Athens and Jerusalem (consider the wisdom literature) believed thought to be a process and a grace into which one was sometimes permitted to be carried; hence also a source of wonder, for such thought opened one to the *logos* of the universe, to sources of true *wisdom (sapientia)* beyond and behind the small victories of accumulated human *knowledge (scientia).*[1]

Chapter 1 narrated various efforts toward re-conceiving theology as such a sapiential enterprise, and noted quite diverse understandings of what wisdom might mean. To this diversity chapter 2 addressed a biblical theology of wisdom, undertaken via theological interpretation of Scripture.

I. Sapiential Interaction with Concerns for Theological Education

By this point it had been stressed that theology's theoretical dimension lies in prevenient divine communicative action which is ingredient to Christian wisdom. This communicative action invites everyone, not only a privileged few, into a transforming vocation of Christian witness. Theology is therefore communicative praxis, of response to God that enriches self and others by learning to live wisely.

Hence the need arose to construe carefully theology's practical character. With Edward Farley I agreed to construe *theologia* ambiguously so that it can refer to an activity and the knowledge that produces, so that "church education" and "theological education" may be construed together. But with Charles Wood I agreed that Farley does not characterize this ambiguity so as to capitalize on it, and that he remains too cognitively oriented in his understanding of education and theological process. Wood's understanding of theology in terms of "vision" and "discernment" helpfully captures the *sophia* and *phronēsis* oscillation of Christian wisdom, yet his understanding of Scripture's public and critical function (or its lack of such function) within that wisdom was deemed inadequate.

David Kelsey's analysis of divergent material understandings of "wisdom" was enormously helpful, as was his acceptance of tensions between theological education oriented to *paideia* and to *Wissenschaft*.[2] Yet I accepted Reinhard Hütter's critique of Kelsey's proposal concerning "pluralism" as, in fact, not pluralistic but preferential toward an account of theology (and of Christianity) that excludes particular, prevenient divine action. While appreciative of George Lindbeck's cultural-linguistic turn, I accepted Hütter's related critique thereof, that a formal preoccupation with ecumenism and religion in general can elide necessary material, soteriological considerations. Linguistic expressions of Christian doctrine must be related to divine action, and then will have an integral place within an account of theology.

At the same time, if from one side various accounts of theology as reflection on practice could distance it from the communicative praxis of Christian wisdom, Hütter's account could do so from the other side, in making theology a discrete practice undertaken by a select few rather than by all the people of God. Kelsey was right to see theology not as a discrete practice, but as a practice-encompassing discourse — which, in my view, has a particular relationship to the practice of teaching or doctrine, in which a few may take a God-given lead.

Sustaining this claim requires an account of Christian wisdom's critical dimension, and thus of theology's particular relationship to Scripture. Hence, in Part Two, I capitalized on recent discussion of interpreting Scripture theologically, to address the challenge of post-critical wisdom but also (in the process) to capitalize on wisdom for properly understanding the post-critical interpretation of Scripture.

Probably the most controversial claim underlying this move — the subtext of the narrative in chapter 4 and the argument of chapters 5 and 6 — is that theology and the interpretation of Scripture can be appropriately reflective and subject to critical reason even if everyone's witness has a place in the meta-discourse by which they are defined. I am happy to accept the controversy, with legitimate tensions and worries reflected therein, as ingredient to the need for this project and its recovery of substantively Christian wisdom. Theologians and the university in general must take more seriously educational literature in which a concept of praxis operates with "action and reflection . . . seen as being in a state of constant and productive tension."[3] Still, such a "transformative" and "critical" pedagogy should not be developed without primary reference to Christian doctrine; neither should the controversial claims about praxis herein be misunderstood, apart from qualifications that follow.

First, I have not denied the propriety of Hütter's concern, a binding aspect to doctrine and a teaching office or leadership role for some within the church, variously defined by different traditions of polity. Rather, the practice of such leaders has been viewed as an intensified undertaking of the doctrine or teaching practice of the church, in which God's maturing people are all still called to some participation at least in terms of the discernment involved in "reception."[4] The difference between leaders and laity should involve time and degree, not kind, of inquiry or reflection, with two primary exceptions: (1) only some will translate the Bible; (2) the leaders will have considerably more academic background knowledge (say, of the history of philosophy) to fund their reflection.

Nor is the particularity of doctrinal discussion and definition denied simply by admitting that the meaning of Christian language habits is enmeshed in praxis and much of their learning is "caught" as well as "taught." Indeed, much discourse about God takes up such habits and furthers them practically, rather than addressing them theoretically; critical evaluation of the language must address its relation to life as well. In other words, factual knowledge and analytic practices must not be isolated from the pragmatic dimensions of language and synthetic practices of doctrine. Thus theology can more adequately acknowledge a critical role for imagination and the social sciences, in addition to philosophical inquiry and its other traditional conversation partners.

Second, I have not denied the propriety of Kelsey's, Wood's, Farley's, and in a different way Hütter's, concern over against Lindbeck, that the truthfulness of Christian practice on the whole be subject to public criticism, and that dialogue across publics somehow be possible. Yet the distinction between theology and apologetics must be kept firmly in mind. Disputes about the propriety and practice of apologetics should not obscure best theological practice, which must be located within soteriology. Christians are within their epistemic rights to read the Bible figurally, as Scripture, in speaking about God, and to have those readings open to criticism on their own terms, while addressing the larger apologetic concerns about the legitimacy of Christian practice — and therein its approach to biblical texts — distinctly and otherwise.

Third, and perhaps the really controversial claim within some church constituencies, I believe it impossible for theology to transcend *Religionswissenschaft* and to recover an "ancient and post-modern sense of the *spirituality of thought*" unless spirituality is no longer regarded "as a quality essentially distinct from what transpires under the nomenclature of disciplined rationality and intellectual learning" — it will be impossible so long as "reasoning is something that is done in the classroom and the library whilst prayer is reserved for the chapel or meditation-centre!"[5] If Christian wisdom is to characterize theology, then it is at least as important, if not more so, for discursive reasoning to shape contemplation and "action" as it is for them to shape discursive reasoning. Wise Christian living depends upon habits of communicative praxis that develop from reflective, discerning thought about God and God's ways. If God gives the church leaders in its teaching, nevertheless all are to grow in the knowledge of God; no one is without vision or free from cultivating discernment.[6]

Thus the impulse seems right to reject the habit of "regarding the more 'theoretical' disciplines of the curriculum as though they could be, indeed, *should* be, undertaken at a once-remove from life."[7] Recent orientation to Christian practices,[8] as opposed to older understandings of a "practical theology" discipline[9] or preoccupations with a certain understanding of praxis, seems healthy and promising in this regard. Yet it is also right to see as perilous "the effective withdrawal of biblical, historical, and dogmatic theology from intimate contact with the churches."[10] The peril eventuates differently depending upon the church context, but the withdrawal has been perilous whatever its form.[11]

Having summarized my contribution about "theology" in relation to several key players in that conversation, I might seem close to Robert Banks's recent missional model.[12] Nevertheless, it may be questioned whether "mission" is sufficiently embracive for the knowledge of God to orient theological education. Admittedly, popular conceptions of the word that would narrow it to activism — of either conservative or liberal varieties — would be rejected by Banks; the recent rediscovery of a full-orbed concept of "mission" to orient the church has been a salutary development.[13] However, the calling that precedes mission; the personal knowledge of God that is not simply a matter of church practice; and the sense from Farley onward that theology's end must somehow be wrapped up in theology itself (as communicative praxis)

— all these elements must also be incorporated within understandings of theology and theological education.

Wisdom's various communicative dimensions handle this more holistically, with clarity in particular about prevenient divine communication in creation and redemption, and about the giving and receiving of communicative action in the praxis of human flourishing. Moreover, wisdom addresses both the particularity and universality of human knowing in relation to the gospel: sciences and skills offer particulars for living well but are to fit within the whole of fearing the Lord; conversely, many of these particulars may be more universally embraced than the fear of the Lord, which has particularity in the gospel. Mission is vital to the context and orientation of the practices by which God is known, but such knowledge might still be more integral to theological education on a sapiential model.[14] In fact, wisdom enables us to think about the nature of theology and theological education *together.*

II. Sapiential Concerns and Interaction with the Triune God

In the words of Bryan Pettifer, "Education is transmission of culture: theology is knowledge of God. Theological education is therefore, on the one hand, a specific aspect of cultural transmission and, on the other hand, initiation into knowledge of a reality which transcends human culture."[15] We must therefore address theological understanding as embracing the twin phenomena of discovery and transmission — a matter of participation and perception both. If Christian *phronēsis* bears partial formal correspondence to other versions, and merits a place in the public conversation because substantive reason is inescapable, nevertheless its material particularity may — indeed must — also be maintained. Central to this Christian specificity must be the doctrine of the Trinity, with hermeneutics the obvious bridge by which wisdom could connect the concerns of theological education and biblical interpretation.[16]

Most broadly, this means an effort to understand the nature of understanding. Often, though not necessarily always, hermeneutical approaches take the particular form of understanding the understanding of texts, or else understanding all forms of understanding in terms of "texts" — whether a person, poem, play, or painting, etc., is being understood, it is understood *as* a text. To engage hermeneutics as Christians, or with a view toward its relation to the triune God, is to engage the question of so-called "general" versus "special" hermeneutics: should we seek to cover understanding generally, and then apply this more specifically to how we understand God's communication? Or should we not assume that we read the Bible just like any other book but, at most, apply only select insights from that special case to texts in general? However we nuance, we tend to privilege one or the other; regardless, though, Christians must grapple with the relation of Word and Spirit as we respond to revelation, "the eloquence of divine action."[17]

Contemporary conversations about the roles of Son and Spirit in revealing God necessarily focus upon special hermeneutics at first. General hermeneutics, though, always foster our understanding of what is special about knowing God via the Bible, since they offer the languages within which we articulate, and the cultural "others" with reference to which we articulate, our Christian concerns. So as we attempt by "theological hermeneutics" to gather together the concerns and commitments of this quest for wisdom, such terminology may designate either or both (1) developing an account of text interpretation or even human understanding in interaction with Christian doctrine(s); (2) developing an account of how biblical interpretation should shape, and be shaped by, Christian theology. For the former project, the adjective "theological" designates the mode in which to pursue *general* hermeneutics; for the latter, "theological" designates not only a mode of pursuit, but also the material aims of *special* hermeneutics regarding the Bible. The two projects may be undertaken simultaneously, or distinctly, or even separately — as if the interpretative interests of each are uninteresting to the other. On a wisdom model that understands Christianity as *paideia,* however, such a separation would be unlikely or even unhealthy. Thus we must think about Word and Spirit with caution about general hermeneutics but also, I am arguing, with willingness to capitalize on such work.

A. Word and Spirit

To appreciate the contemporary conversation about Word and Spirit, we must concede its somewhat scandalous character. By no stretch of the imagination can either reason or experience lead us from the natural world to Trinitarian religion. Indeed, stretches of the imagination were exactly Ludwig Feuerbach's accusation against Christian theism; and, despite many noble attempts, no theologian seemed able to attain the Enlightenment's rational ideal while insisting upon an orthodox version of God's triunity as well. Friedrich Schleiermacher is representative or even paradigmatic: his achievement deserves much admiration, but it is no accident that his version of natural religion opted for something like Sabellian modalism. God is, in the end, only one apart from (the modes of) revelation, and this "doctrine of the Trinity" is placed in thirteen pages at the very end of Schleiermacher's dogmatics.

Karl Barth, by contrast, understood that no Christian response to "modernity" was possible which accepted *its* terms of rationality from the get-go. Instead, the Christian account of God as triune would have to unfold in terms of revelation. In fact, Barth understood the doctrine of the Trinity to unfold as the necessary interpretation of the biblical reality of revelation: that "God speaks." Barth's summary heading for this section unfolds that **"for the concept of revelation . . . God Himself in unimpaired unity yet also in unimpaired distinction is Revealer, Revelation, and Revealedness."**[18] The knowledgeable reader cannot help but hear a striking parallel to Augustine, for whom (at one point in *De Trinitate*) God is Lover, Beloved, and Love itself. In and against the modern age, Barth recovered the doctrine of the Trinity by uncovering its connection with the grammar of revelation. This core Christian conviction Barth unpacked in a number of ways.

1. *Three inseparable questions.* "The question of the self-revealing God which thus forces itself upon us as the first question cannot, if we follow the witness of Scripture, be separated in any way from the second question: How does it come about, how is it actual, that this God reveals Himself? Nor can it be separated from the third question: What is the result? What does this event do to the man to whom it happens? Conversely the second and third questions cannot possibly be separated from the first."[19]
2. *God reveals himself through himself.* The answer to these questions is that God reveals himself through himself. In answer to the first, Who reveals himself?, "*God* reveals Himself." In answer to the second, How does it come about?, "He reveals Himself *through Himself*." In answer to the third, What is the result?, "He reveals *Himself*."[20]
3. *Revealer/subject, act, and effect.* Thus Barth says that "if we really want to understand revelation in terms of its subject, i.e., God, then the first thing we have to realise is that this subject, God, the Revealer, is identical with His act in revelation and also identical with its effect."[21]
4. *Subject, predicate, and object.* Or, again thinking of God as the acting Subject, he is the subject, predicate, and object of the statement "God speaks" or of its equivalent "I show myself."[22]
5. *God as self-revealing (YHWH), revelation (Moses and the prophets; the angel of YHWH; Jesus Christ), and revealedness (Abraham; prophet, priest, and king; Israel; the Church).* On and on go Barth's triadic distinctions within the God of unimpaired unity. Indeed, this God's unity

> is not a matter of isolation or of simple singularity, for that would be a human conception of unity in which he would need a Second or a Third to be a One.[23] Thus it is appropriate for the self-revealing God YHWH to identify with his revelatory acts, whether we think of how Moses and the prophets come to represent God, or indeed the angel of YHWH figure, even as these point us ultimately to Jesus Christ.[24] Moreover, since revelation "is always a history" — whether we think of Abraham, or prophets, priests, and kings, or the nation of Israel, or ultimately the Church — in that light we have to do with the effects of God's being self-revealed. This effectiveness upon humanity has brought us not merely to a "second" but to a "third."[25] Accordingly, an order or distinction within God is appropriate, pertaining to the fact that God chooses not simply to be himself, but also his self-revealing.

If revelation were, as Barth puts it, a "minus" or "another over against God," then we would give in to modern skepticism of a most acute form: how could we know that revelation — if we claimed it — in fact corresponded to the real God? Or would that real God be hidden? Accordingly, for Barth revelation must be "the repetition of God."[26]

So Barth discussed as point I "The Place of the Doctrine of the Trinity in Dogmatics" and that place is, contra Schleiermacher, front and center — because, point II, "The Root of the Doctrine of the Trinity," is revelation. The doctrine of the Trinity is not revelation *per se,* but a necessary analysis or interpretation of its grammar or logic.[27]

Now because "revelation in the Bible means the self-unveiling, imparted to men, of the God who by nature cannot be unveiled to men," it follows that "the true theme of the biblical witness is the second" of our concepts, namely "God's action in His revelation, revelation in answer to the question what God does, and therefore the predicate in our statement." Revelation's theme is "primarily the second person of the Trinity, God the Son, the deity of Christ." *Materially* the questions are equally important that pertain to all three persons. *Formally,* however, the questions find their answer to be centered in Christ.[28] God's self-unveiling is a matter of "taking form"[29] before those to whom God cannot be unveiled — and that form is God's act in Jesus Christ.

Barth's achievement connects an Augustinian pattern of understanding God through a unified reality of divine action (in Augustine's case, love; in Barth's, revelation), with the post-Reformation pattern of knowing God through the unfolding reality of divine action in Word and Spirit. That pattern was torn apart in the modern age, perhaps due partly to internal weakness. It may be that other constructions could have preserved and promoted better than Barth's doctrine the verbal component of God's self-communication by Word and Spirit. For the Logos as God-man had knowledge of God appropriate by analogy to human creatures, an accurate archetype in which the Spirit may give us via Scripture a corresponding share.[30]

That said, Barth's account may nonetheless be better than the post-Reformation Protestant pattern in an Augustinian respect. He understood God's "essence" and his "work" not to be twofold, but one:

> God's work is His essence in its relation [a prominent Augustinian category] to the reality which is distinct from Him and which is to be created or is created by Him. The work of God is the essence of God as the essence of Him who . . . is revealer, revelation and being revealed, or Creator, Reconciler and Redeemer. In this work of His, God is revealed to us. All we can know of God according to the witness of Scripture are His acts. All we can say of God, all the attributes we can assign to God, relate to these acts of His; not, then, to His essence as such.[31]

Barth went on to distinguish God's essence and work in only one respect, namely with reference to God's freedom — to the fact that God chooses to be the God who is his act by "grace, a free divine decision."[32] Barth could have said more about God's communication being God's act, as well as the reverse (that God's act is communicative), which would strengthen the verbal constancy in his doctrine of Scripture.

Nonetheless, Barth recovered the overwhelmingly consistent conviction of Augustine and the Christian tradition that we do not know God *in se* simply via human language. *Yet* he simultaneously responded to the modern crisis of separation between God's essence and our knowledge of God — a separation that could only conclude in skepticism. If God has revealed choosing freely to constitute the divine essence by acting in Christ and the Spirit's effect, then only *that* freedom *distinguishes* God's essence from God's work — but we are free to conclude that they are not separate.[33]

By now this interaction with Barth has helped us to see the necessity of, in Kelsey's terms, housing "a 'doctrine of Scripture' in the context of a doctrine of God." The Christian tradition has handled this by appropriating the work of revelation especially to God the Son, "the principle of intelligibility and of communication between the Creator and creatures." Accordingly, "scripture's de jure authority for theology was grounded in the work of the Logos, the second person of the Triune Godhead": revelation was the "middle term" between Scripture and theology.[34]

However, in his influential essay "The Bible and Christian Theology," Kelsey argues this is impossible today. The traditional version of revelation, he claims, is docetic, unable to account for the "thoroughgoing historical and cultural conditioning of all human phenomena," even or especially Scripture. The modern version of revelation, in which Kelsey claims that Barth's personal focus aligns him with Rudolf Bultmann, Paul Tillich, et al., is "systematically elusive," unable to account for a "determinate content" about which we might undertake critical inquiry, and "incoherent" with the conviction that God's determinate self-revelation can be complete only at the end of history.[35] Since (in Kelsey's view) "neither the traditional nor the modern way of grounding the de jure authority of scripture in the revelatory work of the Second Person is available to us," he suggests instead that we ground it "in the relation to scripture that God assumes as sanctifier and transformer of human identity, traditionally appropriated to the Third Person."[36]

Rowan Williams similarly has critiqued the revelation model of the Trinity for marginalizing the Holy Spirit. His essay "Word and Spirit," after surveying the rather minimal significance of Western reflections on the Holy Spirit, suggests that revelation is the problem. Revelation addresses, "How is God heard or seen to be present to the human world?" With God and world as two terms, the revelation model has understood Word and Spirit as mediators between these, with the line running downward from God to world. Accordingly, the line upward from world to God is unspecified, and "the understanding of God as such is not affected by the 'bridge-concept'"; put more baldly, ". . . this scheme strictly requires one mediator only. If we are to speak of a third divine hypostasis at all, Spirit as well as Logos, there is an immediate awkwardness."[37] The awkward solutions for finding the Spirit something to do usually restrict that "to a mediatorial or an episodically inspirational role," namely, the Spirit is the person of the exceptional or the miraculous. This tends to "avoid the critical experience of Godlessness," and "run the risk of making Spirit a refuge from the critical rather than a pressure towards the critical."[38]

If that essay might seem to avoid revelation as the way of relating Word and Spirit, nevertheless another essay called "Trinity and Revelation" relates them precisely by tying together revelation as generating event (involving the Son) and as hermeneutical spiral interpreting the event (involving the Spirit).[39] Williams's difference from Barth and the Protestant tradition remains, however, as he rejects the idea of revelation imparting the "ultimate epistemological security" of participation in God's self-knowledge. Instead, he relates his view to Ricoeur, and relates revelation to never-ending questioning about the meaning of the church's generative events — the Spirit is at work in our "puzzlement" about the significance of the story of Jesus.[40]

Yet another Williams essay, "Trinity and Ontology," cites with appreciation an essay by John Milbank entitled "The Second Difference,"[41] which makes a parallel claim about the Spirit's action needing greater priority if we are to appreciate his personality. Milbank's transcendental argument for this from language and aesthetics is very dense, and at minimum is a bit dismissive of the dogmatic significance of God's salvation history in Jesus Christ. To quote a summation of sorts from Williams: "Not only Jesus' distance from the Father, but our distance, our critical 'absence', from Jesus is included in the eternal movement of God in and to himself."[42]

My point is not necessarily to admit the compelling character of Kelsey's, Williams's, or Milbank's arguments, at least not entirely, but to acknowledge their trajectory from the Logos toward the Holy Spirit. This trend in Trinitarian speculation correlates with three possibilities that hit closer to our hermeneutical home.

(1) Adopting a "Functional" View of the Bible's Authority?

First, Kelsey himself argued that the Bible is authoritative inasmuch as it serves the function of Christians shaping their identities by the Spirit. Stephen Fowl and L. Gregory Jones, as already seen, take this type of approach; at least somewhat like Williams, they construe Scripture as the foundational text about which the Christian community is an extended argument.[43] Clearly true in part, the approach will play out according to how it is theologically described. Commonly a doctrine of the Bible's inspiration is replaced with a doctrine of providence and reader-response hermeneutics correlated with a doctrine of the church. God gave the community these texts *for* shaping its identity *by* shaping its identity in the first place, but the character of this work is not decisively different in the two time periods. Hence, in parallel to early Christian reading of the OT, we today may read "with the Spirit" against the apparent sense of an earlier Word, as the Spirit presently shapes the narratives that inform our communal identity.

(2) Abandoning the Filioque?

Second, Williams alludes to the Eastern charge that our Trinitarian asymmetry or "Christomonism" in the West follows the *filioque* clause we added to the Nicene Creed, namely that the Holy Spirit proceeds from the Father "and the Son."[44] Many Western writers are attracted to the Eastern claim that the *filioque* de-personalizes the Spirit, who becomes largely an impersonal bond of union between Father and Son; the Spirit's activity lacks proper distinction, and consists largely in bringing believers to the Father through the Son.

Should this ancient and perhaps arcane controversy matter to us? Thomas Smail argues that it should: on the one hand, "we can understand the Pentecostal movement as a protest against the exclusive christocentricity of Western Christianity in both its Catholic and Protestant manifestations";[45] though he admits that, on the other hand, the "Christless mysticism" of some Eastern Orthodoxy, or the separation between spirituality and sound doctrine of some Pentecostalism and evangelicalism, or the religious experience tied to Spirit but not Christ within some versions of liberalism — all these may be understood as perversions of an Eastern-like centrality of the Father,[46] from whom Son and Spirit are two hands stretched toward creation.

On this account, the Western church downplayed the "living and immediate presence" of the Spirit, and the result was "authoritarianism" — either an infallible pope or an infallible Bible. Smail laments that "it was precisely such defects in the Western churches that led to the protest of liberalism on behalf of the freedom of the Spirit of man and to protests of pietism and Pentecostalism on behalf of the freedom [*sic*] the Spirit of God, but in ways that, once again, for the sake of the freedom of the Spirit, downgraded the normative authority of the work and person of Christ."[47] A modified Eastern approach becomes attractive on such a view.

(3) Appropriating Scripture to the Spirit?

Third, Stanley Grenz accented the Holy Spirit for Scripture's authority by locating his discussion of Scripture not at the beginning of dogmatics, but under his doctrine of the Holy Spirit.[48] He accordingly located authority in "the Spirit speaking through the Scriptures" — his frequent way of quoting the Westminster Confession of Faith, which actually speaks of "the Spirit speaking in the Scriptures." While not allowing that the Spirit would speak against the Scriptures, Grenz accepted that the Spirit speaks in some way through the cultural context of their reading, and seemed to adopt a notion of the Bible's inspiration that is not fundamentally different in character from the Spirit's illumination.[49]

Clearly this is not a turn to the church of an Eastern character, in which the Spirit is sufficiently prominent to accord infallibility to Tradition with a capital T (of which Scripture is only one component). Nor is it a turn to the church of a Roman Catholic character, in which the classic view of Trent started to accord infallibility by the Spirit to capital-T Tradition as a second revelatory source beside the Word, or in which contemporary views can still accord infallibility to Tradition or to the teaching office regarding certain churchly interpretations of the one Word. Nor is it a turn of an older Protestant liberal sort, to a Spiritual hermeneutic of cultural or communal experience — at least not intentionally.

The turn to the church and the Spirit does raise, however, questions about whether or how the canon functions as criterion for knowing God, in particular for hearing the Spirit as Christians, in churches, and within culture. Do we substitute for an infallible pope or Bible an unfalsifiable community or individual interpreter? The answer depends, in part, on careful contemporary hermeneutics of commitment to Scripture's inspiration — taking account of (1) Barth's Trinitarian call to connect God's being and act in self-communication, and hence the NT centrality of Jesus Christ the God-man as the final, personal Word we must hear (even as we articulate also Scripture's verbal, true correspondence to that Word); (2) the call of Kelsey and others to consider the freedom of the Spirit as a personal agent in God's self-communication (even as we articulate also the consistency of the Spirit's work with the form God takes in the Son); and (3) the call to acknowledge the human factors in Scripture's composition and canonization (even as we articulate these also in their theological context, not simply in a socio-cultural framework).

Such a formulation can and must be undertaken, while requiring care and attention to complexity that cannot be achieved here. At root a theological decision remains necessary in favor of describing canonization as obedient discovery or recognition, not baldly the church's decision, concerning which texts were sacred — by God the Spirit's prior action in and through humans. For the moment, though, we may more summarily formulate connections between the communicative action of God's Word and Spirit, and between general and special hermeneutics — centered around *phronēsis.*

B. General and Special Hermeneutics: The Christian Virtue of Understanding?

If the triune God chose to create others with whom to share the communion of the divine life, and if God communicates to these fallen creatures through redemptive self-giving action of the Son and Spirit, then human understanding will be a relational affair involving an intimate connection between knowledge and love. This claim was characteristic of ancients like Augustine

— for whom, A. N. Williams shows, knowledge and love were as inseparably related as were their parallel in the Word and Spirit of the Holy Trinity.[50] "Understanding" might then be characterized in terms of various "capacities for action in relation to something."[51]

Consequently, in a Christian version of virtue epistemology, understanding is communicative action, undertaken with our character formed in community — ultimately with the God whose being is in communion, with the God who is love. Consistent with the general yet Christianly-informed sensibilities of Mikhail Bakhtin, that understanding is "dialogical," these "virtue" categories emerge from NT texts on "discernment" or "judgment" as discussed earlier.

If we take this tack, we would not discuss God's revelation as a possibility tied to purely human phenomena, in prolegomena desiring outside permission to do theology. We would rather discuss revelation as the prior reality (in which we participate) that makes theological understanding possible. We would discuss Scripture within the triune God's communicative action, not the Bible as a set of books abstracted from God's personal accompaniment. Neither would we discuss the church's reading of Scripture or the Spirit's relation to culture as merely human realities of composition, canonization, or contextualization — as if there were no prior Word the Spirit leads cultural agents to acknowledge, hear and obey. Such an understanding of revelation largely traces John Webster's renewal of the Protestant dogmatic tradition, and Kevin Vanhoozer's work on Trinitarian theological hermeneutics, in light of both the problems of the Enlightenment and the possibilities of speech-act theory. These approaches tend to connect dogmatic discussion of the canon with the prophetic ministry of Christ the Logos.[52]

Even still, discussion of Scripture could be relocated primarily under the doctrine of the Holy Spirit, because that move follows the third article of the Nicene Creed: there the Spirit creates the church, yet gives this new life "having spoken through the prophets" — so that community is "one, holy, catholic, and apostolic" which hears God's Spirit correctly. More than one people (two, in fact, and a very pluriform "Protestant" multitude besides) claim this identity; church division is a difficult and distressing problem for theological hermeneutics. Yet Protestants, perhaps in light of all our failures, appropriately connect infallibility to Christ and Scripture, not the institutional church or any of its interpretations — except that in a sense the ecumenical creeds will not be revised. Infallibility deals with the prior Word of the Spirit, never tied down to our competing claims about the Spirit's present work.

This understanding of revelation requires Christian discernment *as* an account of how understanding accompanies revelation — education and interpretation together form a gracious development from God. Discernment is limited to the form of God's revelatory *act* in the Word (which addresses at least our finitude), but also involves freedom linked to the revelatory *effect* of the Spirit (who addresses further our fallen rejection of God's communication). Discernment means having "the mind of Christ," with this pattern for life set by the cross (Phil. 2:5-11). *Who we are to become in Christ* (a pattern of self-giving and other-receiving) is only possible because of *who Christ is for us* (a prior self-giving). But Christ not only died — he was raised, and exalted to pour out the Holy Spirit who gives us participation in the new pattern of life we need.

The Spirit helps to give the Word form. In *that* pattern of possibility we learn a lesson about the form the Christ-centered theological meaning of Scripture takes. The form of access is personal — holistic, embodied, and social — not strictly cognitive. David Tracy is probably right that the meaning of "Christo-morphism" (his term preferred over "Christ-centeredness") may be the most promising way to heal modern separations between feeling and thought, practice and theory, form and content — while of these three pairs the problem of form has been paid the least attention.[53] However, the interaction of form and freedom is quite important for understanding *phronēsis*.[54] So yes, the Spirit trans-forms us by the renewing of our minds in such a way that we are con-formed to Christ. Yet, although the Spirit's renewal always takes a *form* like Christ's and therefore fits within and extends the patterns of his mind in Scripture, two reminders balance this out with remaining *freedom* for interpretative practice.

First, who raised Christ from the dead so that he could ascend triumphantly as the God-man? The Spirit. Their relationship is not simply asymmetrical in favor of the Son, but always interpenetrating and mutually on the move. Second, what is the form of Christ? Not the form of God given from the Father only, but the Logos took human form that grew faithfully in the freedom of the Spirit as well. For the Spirit not only raised him from the dead but also led throughout his life and to the cross. Indeed, the Spirit superintended and strengthened the incarnate Son from conception onward. Moreover, as Telford Work reminds us, the Spirit spoke through the OT "prophets" even before that.[55] This means that the form of Israel's servanthood, which shaped the vocation Jesus Christ fulfilled, was shaped by the Holy Spirit's role in the economy of salvation.

Accordingly, while the Spirit's freedom in illuminating Scripture for us is always bound to take the form of the inspired Word, that says a lot! The Spirit helped give form to that Word in the first place — not simply in the testimony of "apostles" after the fact, but just as surely before in prophetic testimony to the form the Son would take. Worries about the doctrine of revelation resulting in Trinitarian imbalance, or de-personalization of the Spirit, are best addressed not by denying that in Christ all things hold together, but by developing the Spirit's salvation-historical role in proper Christomorphism. This may even be a development of Hardy's suggestion that we learn about "law" and "liberty" in wisdom by exploring their relations in the life and activity of God.[56] The Spirit's formation of a particular people (Israel, in part via law) and person (the Christ) paved the way for the most universal freedom, which can embrace rather than bypass cultural particularity (the church).

In this light, implications of the famous analogy between the divinity and humanity of the Logos, and the divinity and humanity of Scripture, may take appropriate shape.[57] God's self-communication does incorporate three forms — three human forms, in fact, which include both personal and verbal factors. In the primary form, Jesus Christ, the personal factor seems primary; in the tertiary form, church witness[58] and its forms of understanding, the personal factors also seem primary (the Spirit leads us to imitate others as they imitate Christ, à la, e.g., 1 Cor. 11:1); whereas, in the second form, Scripture, the verbal factor seems primary (it is the certain source for the Spirit's connection between the church and the mind of Christ).

We may recall here the connection between Christian discernment in the NT and Aristotle's virtue *phronēsis,* which regulates the combination of other virtues in particular situations, so that we see those settings for what they are and take appropriate action in light of a prior standard. Of course the Christian version is distinctive, requiring prayer and seeing humility as a virtue not a vice, because it takes Christ instead of "scientific knowledge" to be the ultimate reality that transforms our lives in contemplation. *Phronēsis* does not dismiss scientific practices at all — including critical scholarship involving texts — but does develop the significance of those skills within the framework of character shaped in community. Only then are sciences and skills appropriately deployed in particular situations. In fact, not to deploy them, nor to dialogue with outsiders, would mean failure to live a cruciform life: we must live out intellectually the virtue of humility, chastened by the cross about the Christian community's frequent failure to love, and therefore its lack of discernment.

So, to sum up this point about the form of Christian understanding, it involves action in relation — to God, in Christ, by the Spirit, then with others. It is only possible because of who Christ is for us, and his self-giving sets the pattern for our lives as well. We will discern rightly only as we develop at seeing situations — including the situations within and about which we read Scripture — with the mind of Christ. In this way we will not set knowledge and love in opposition, but in *perichoresis* — in a dance involving form and freedom dimly analogous to that of the Trinity.[59] Reminded that the Spirit gave form to the Word in the first place, we will not set our freedom over against the Word but rather will read with discernment about how the Spirit freely extends the form of its effect.

This Trinitarian understanding of revelation means that we are free to take human social realities very seriously in education and interpretation that are "Christ-centered." In fact we must. Not only does the verbal form of revelation — Christ's knowledge and Scripture's faithful correspondence to it — take full humanity. But the Spirit also frees us to receive revelation as human persons in communities, to realize our fallibility in responding to God *and* in relating to creation, yet also in our finitude to revel in created realities as vehicles for God's communicative action. Hence Christians must define truth distinctively to hold that "in Christ all things hold together." Truth is not simply intellectual correspondence with the reality of an external world, nor with Christ's knowledge of the Father and thus knowledge of that world. It is fitting correspondence to Jesus Christ as human beings who live in the freedom of the Spirit — who know what they love and love whom they know.

This Trinitarian reflection has not been a meandering detour, but directs our journey toward the two senses in which Christian hermeneutics for the Bible will be special. (1) God in the person of Jesus Christ freely communicates in Scripture, and forms our character through the active accompaniment of the Holy Spirit, as covenanted through no other book. (2) This communication takes the form of various human writings that were composed spanning a complex history of revelation and redemption, yet are collected as human forms faithfully speaking one Word. We read Scripture with a submissive, trusting expectation to encounter God in a way that the truth, goodness, and beauty of no other book can match.[60]

However, when it comes to general hermeneutics, Oliver O'Donovan's reminder is important that people outside the Christian faith may understand and even obey many divine ordinances because God created with order, and has re-affirmed this in Christ's resurrection[61] — hence the continuing significance of Wisdom literature and its connection to other cultures. But in terms of special hermeneutics, these others fail to understand and obey at the level of the moral whole — not responding with integrity (in the full Christomorphic sense Wisdom calls for) because they do not know specifically the God of cruciform wisdom. Yet non-Christians may have insight into many particulars, and help to recognize how beautiful and good patterns of Truth cohere in Scripture; often Christians will mistake these connections or need criticism when we do not connect our living with what we see.

The lesson is that strong similarity or overlap often obtains between the special and general. Often non-Christian interpreters will understand — that is, develop various capacities for action in relation to — texts and other realities far better than Christians will. They will perhaps read charitably to a degree, with various virtues, even Scripture. But if in Jesus Christ we come to love the One who is love, who is the form knowledge takes in its fullest connections and freest charity, then to the degree that whole shapes the parts, failures to know the Logos may entail misunderstanding — for Christians and non-Christians alike.

Now, such communicative action and reaction has not yet accounted fully for response to the Spirit over time and across place: God's communicative action takes human forms, with the Spirit giving freedom for our communicative actions to correspond fittingly with God's in Christ, through the Word. So the final aspect of this account concerns the form our corresponding reaction takes *in and as the church.*

Human persons are agents; communities are not, except in a more abstract and complex sense. Ultimately, however, the NT teaches that the Spirit effects the new creation of *one new humanity* — that the congregation, the concrete shape of catholicity, would correspond corporately to "the measure of the stature of the fullness of Christ" (Eph. 4:13). The goal is a church united in growth to maturity, maturity that connects truth and love. Given biblical texts regarding discernment, such as Phil. 1:9-11 for example, *phronēsis* must be a gift in which we pray to grow, while crucial indeed for both the unity and genuine maturity of a congregation.

The Spirit does not form individuals *per se,* but persons in and for communities, and communities as catholic stand-ins for and with the church as a whole — across not only place but time. Personal actions, and even the communication of Christian congregations, are but subplots in the one effect of God's one act, in the growing creation of a new humanity conformed to — with knowledge corresponding to — the Son. This does not disregard personal actions as unimportant, or deny that sometimes communities are unfaithful. Sometimes particular people such as Luther must read against the grain. But doctrinal development, cultural difference, and therefore ethical discernment in relation to Scripture are not to be treated simply as problems in light of disparate individual identities. Sometimes they may constitute part of what Vanhoozer would call (in a slightly different context) "Pentecostal plurality."[62] Diverse identities may cohere as parts of a corporate whole which is the ultimate measure that counts. We need not always deny that past understandings were appropriate to their context, or perhaps were the only options in their context, when we discern nevertheless a possibly new development.[63] Opposition to slavery might illustrate such a case, regarding what interpretations were realistically possible at certain times and places in social history. Surely the message of Philemon, in context, represents a more liberating theological judgment than the mistaken and sinful hermeneutics of Europe and America later on. Their meaning and the moral significance of their similarities and differences are properly assessed only in the story of the church overall — the slow sanctification of the still fallen new creation, till humanity corresponds to "the measure of the stature of the fullness of Christ" (Eph. 4).

We need not adopt simple pluralism to explain such differences. For such pluralism would actually exclude the possibility of discernment (there would be no standard to recognize situationally), entailing denial of revelation in favor of a form of relativism. The Spirit's new creation has developmental identity across time, and dialogical unity across place, that entails discernment — figuring out in what ways the church grows in faithfulness, free to take cultural form that grows in correspondence to the Word. If this is right, though, then "spiritual formation" is the "moral formation" of the church, of Christian persons within and as local communities of the whole.

Parallel to general hermeneutics, understanding and *moral* formation are possible in many particular ways for persons outside the Christian faith and communities outside the church. But parallel to special hermeneutics, the fullest sense of understanding and *spiritual* formation takes place in Christian community. While the many partial possibilities of unchurched virtue come gracefully from the Spirit, they do not constitute God's revelatory effect in quite the same way as the growth of the church does.

So my modest proposal, in brief, is that the form of Christian understanding can be Christ-centered yet appropriately creative if its freedom lies in our formation by the Spirit. God's Spirit educates in a tradition of wisdom incarnate in the form of Christ, inspired in the form of Scripture, and imparted in the form of the church. Thus wisdom involves the imitation of holy human persons, the interrelation of knowledge and love, the improvisation of freedom with fidelity to form, after the fashion of Word and Spirit. Wisdom connects epistemology and ethics by way of virtue, especially the virtue of discernment that regulates the others. Accordingly, we recognize the true shape of a particular situation in light of a prior standard set in Scripture, but also discover how to specify the prior standard more truly in light of each new cultural opportunity for recognizing reality — as a whole, yet only in part.

You may see in that description of practical reason a version of the famous "hermeneutical circle" or "spiral." The Christian difference is that the part-and-whole oscillation is concretely personal in a Trinitarian sense. What God is saying in a passage about new life in Christ must not only be discovered with the help of sciences and skills for interpretation, and with reference to clearer passages according to the analogy of Scripture. Not simply *theoria,* it takes human form that must also be recognized in and through praxis with the help of the Holy Spirit, according to the church's Rule of faith. Only such wisdom does justice to an ontology of God's Word in terms of act and relations. Put differently, the Chalcedonian analogy for Scripture is not extraneous or merely comparative, but an organic relation suggesting instead that God's communicative action takes particular human forms in reception. We must pay attention not merely to the issue of warrant or "norms" in theological interpretation of Scripture, but also to the matter of virtuous "aims"[64] and how they shape the reception of communication, the particular kinds of interpretative action we pursue, and how we prioritize their results. A certain pedagogy of discovery and transmission is internal to a doctrine of the Word of God, and gives rise to a particular construal of the Rule of faith and its function.

That Rule concerns the identity of God's work with the person of Jesus Christ, the essence of Scripture's Word on the whole. In him are hidden all the treasures of wisdom and knowledge — he is the version of truth, goodness, and beauty communicated in Scripture to which virtuous readers are conformed, as the Spirit transforms fractured humanity into one pluriform new creation. Different churchly versions of that Rule of faith — yes, theological traditions — give and take with the Bible necessary directions for finding and walking more faithfully in the ways of wisdom.

None of this precludes the church staging its "theodrama" of *paideia* in the public square. Quite the contrary, that drama of dialogue is necessary in view of the human and social realities ingredient to theological understanding. General and special hermeneutics will therefore share much overlapping territory, including many scholarly criteria and reading skills, even while for the church biblical interpretation constitutes a distinct province. Despite its church *polis,* Christian reading of Scripture may not have to address general hermeneutics either by "plundering the Egyptians" or else defending against a Trojan horse. No, since its entire realm concerns living virtuously in communion with God, all understanding will have a theological component — and so the interpretation of Scripture may have abundant hermeneutical gifts to share in fair trade.

III. Sapiential Understanding of Scripture

Theological education, therefore, will center on "the work of the Spirit in the practices of the church,"[65] itself the context of theological discovery and judgment. Theological schooling may serve various aspects of that work, and its institutional dynamics should be studied and configured carefully for effective service, so long as we do not become confused and think that schools are about *theologia* and the church about something else, or vice versa. *Theologia* ought to foster recognizable commonality between the two, whatever the institutional configurations. To foster that commonality, at minimum, will entail the recovery of reading practices within church and school that could bring them closer together, and thus the rejection of thoroughly "consumerist" approaches that currently dominate the West, albeit in very different versions.[66]

I have argued that theological judgments are subject to what God could possibly use the humanly-authored biblical texts to say when they are read "figurally," so that the study of the texts as historical, human discourse is one necessary aspect of the theological interpretation of Scripture. While siding with advocates of authorial discourse interpretation, and resisting the notion that canonical teaching be unified by the arbitrary imposition of churchly interpretative interests or extratextual criteria, I have nevertheless sought a fuller and clearer account of theology's role in biblical interpretation, of *phronēsis* in relation to Scripture as divine discourse. The Rule of faith, which according to the tradition is textually derived (and thus, in a certain sense, subordinate to Scripture), nonetheless can have a necessary pedagogical role, especially when its concreteness is maintained Christologically as done here.

This effort to mediate between the priorities of Vanhoozer and Nicholas Wolterstorff, on the one side, and Fowl on the other, would seem to align my proposal closely with Francis Watson's work. Two distinct contributions, however, should be highlighted. First, orienting theology and theological schooling around the "theological interpretation of Scripture" is not exactly the same as orienting it around "biblical theology." Watson is welcome to fight the hegemony of the specialization bequeathed to us by that discipline as often practiced, but the nature of this effort should be clear: he is advocating that biblical scholarship, in undertaking its historical task, be shaped by theological beliefs and concerns — an inescapably contested position. Moreover, Fowl rightly recognizes that biblical theology as a discipline could pursue a sort of clarity and integrity different from theological interpretation of Scripture.[67] Simply equating the two, in terms of a biblical scholar's identity, is likely to generate further confusion and relegate the church's theological interests to a subordinate place, by way of a backlash.

I am therefore inclined to draw a parallel between the integrity of theology, with its *ad hoc* but necessary relationship to philosophy and (thus) apologetics,[68] and the wholeness of theological interpretation of Scripture, with its *ad hoc* but necessary relationship to biblical theology. The latter should involve reconstructing the theological ideas explicit and implicit within the biblical texts as we have them, which can shed light upon the tasks of translation and commentary.[69] Taking the texts seriously as human discourse, biblical theology will inescapably generate various proposals about those ideas and their genesis in persons and communities. While Christians have every right to put forward their own understandings of the historical possibilities and probabilities shaped by divine action, these will be contestable.

Such openness to criticism will often result in valuable, fresh understanding. We have learned a great deal from efforts to understand the theologies of Paul and James in their historical contexts, despite much confusion and counterproductive speculation being generated as well. Theological interpretation of Scripture, a related but different enterprise which should not constantly jeopardize its mission by confusing theology with "history" or apologetics, thus has a sharper understanding of "the righteousness of God," "justification by faith," and other doctrinal foci. And this sharper understanding has probably contributed to legitimate ecumenical gains: for instance, widespread agreement now exists between Protestants and Roman Catholics regarding an initial "declaration of acquittal" in salvation, taught especially in the Pauline epistles, whatever the dogmatic language systems for its description.

However, for all the remaining items on biblical theology's research agenda, theological interpretation is not constantly hostage to that fortune. Whether or not consensus emerges on a proper historical interpretation of *pistis tou Christou,* at a certain level exposition of Romans and Galatians can be undertaken with clarity and confidence. The church is not required to suspend gospel witness out of fear that Paul and James will be found utterly irreconcilable, or out of hesitancy about *pistis tou Christou,* or out of admission that Luther may have altogether misconstrued the sense of *dikaiosunē tou Theou.* Biblical theology may need (or at least have a predilection) to countenance and argue these as possibilities, but theological interpretation may at times proceed differently, leaving apologetics for later. Of course, Christians themselves are free to differ over the exact nature of these procedures, in part due to substantive differences over divine action in relation to Scripture!

This is a reminder that, while from the side of criteria or warrant Wolterstorff's "double hermeneutic" — consideration of human and historical particularities as well as divine discursive possibilities — will be very helpful, the nature of reading practice for discovery is all important in theological interpretation. One will not be formed or informed to make the necessary judgments if theological exegesis is simply equated with biblical theology. Moreover, it may be salutary, at least for now, that some tensions between Christians over how the biblical texts are related to divine action — notably over what it means to read the OT Christianly — are preserved by the disciplinary integrity of biblical theology.[70] Just as philosophy and theology speak about much the same reality yet philosophy serves theology sometimes as its "indispensable opponent,"[71] so biblical theology may serve theological interpretation of Scripture.

A second distinction from Watson, therefore, concerns my effort to construe the Bible's theological authority with reference to a substantive account of wisdom. With many, Watson has rightly worried about the need to distinguish adequately between biblical and systematic theology, or to delineate a distinctive task for the latter besides contemporizing or "contextualizing" the former.[72] An account of the *Regula fidei* in terms of a particular *sophia-phronēsis* oscillation accomplishes this: (1) providing the substantive account of Christian virtue, and accountability for Christian *phronēsis* which, as Christopher Seitz points out, Fowl's account of the virtue of *phronēsis* lacks;[73] (2) while avoiding a construal of divine communicative action that makes theology exclusively propositional or biblical interpretation excessively theoretical and methodological; (3) especially by construing the Bible's narrative coherence around the God-man Jesus Christ, not only in terms of the Father's revelation or discourse but in terms of Spirit-led faithful humanity in the formation of reception. This gives wisdom an embodied, active, communicative, and fully Trinitarian character that other notions of biblical unity or functional descriptions of the *Regula fidei* can lack.

In other words, while attending to the theological interpretation of Scripture has completed a sapiential understanding of *theologia*, the "wisdom" of this project has also paid off for understanding the use of Scripture.[74] The interpretative practice of chapter 2 is supposed to authorize and illustrate this: an effort was made to develop a biblical theology of wisdom, via theological interpretation — with contemporary interests kept firmly in mind as a way into discovering the riches of Scripture. While subject to criticism regarding its basis in, and consistency with, the biblical texts, my theology of wisdom unapologetically works with Christian convictions and interests at stake, rather than arguing simply from (supposedly) neutral, "historical" criteria.

If theology would recover its sapiential, and thus "biblical," voice, then it must be undertaken as communicative responses to God's transforming voice, heard in and through Scripture. We must believe that by the Holy Spirit doctrine can be virtuous for us, linking our thinking and living to God's self-disclosure in Christ of which the Bible witnesses. As we gaze upon this "house of authority," we find not that it lies in rubble, but that it still stands — rather in need of shoring up, of structural change that gives it greater flexibility for withstanding the prevailing winds, but still tied to the church's one foundation, Jesus Christ. Contrary to temptation, we should not substitute the church *as* the foundation, nor should we suppose that the house of authority lies in rubble because (mistakenly) we had made the Bible the foundation *per se.* No, the wise builder looks to adorn the house with biblical materials — with gold, silver, and precious stones instead of wood, hay and stubble — seeking all the treasures of wisdom and knowledge hidden in Christ. Yet, by the Spirit, such a project takes shape only through human construction, and takes discernment to find the most fitting materials and use them for the common good.

Bibliography

Abraham, William J. *Canon and Criterion in Christian Theology.* Oxford: Clarendon, 1998.

Allen, Charles W. "The Primacy of *Phronēsis:* A Proposal for Avoiding Frustrating Tendencies in Our Conceptions of Rationality." *JR* 69 (July 1989): 359-74.

———. "The Recovery of *phronēsis:* Its Implications for the Role of Practical Reason in Theology." Ph.D. diss., University of Chicago, 1987.

Alonso-Schökel, Luis. "Sapiential and Covenant Themes in Genesis 2–3." In *Studies in Ancient Israelite Wisdom,* edited by James L. Crenshaw, 468-80. New York: Ktav, 1976.

Alston, Wallace M., Jr., ed. *Theology in the Service of the Church: Essays in Honor of Thomas W. Gillespie.* Grand Rapids: Eerdmans, 2000.

Alston, William P. *Illocutionary Acts and Sentence Meaning.* Ithaca, NY: Cornell University Press, 2000.

Apczynski, John V. *Doers of the Word: Toward a Foundational Theology Based on the Thought of Michael Polanyi.* Missoula, MT: Scholars Press, 1977.

Astley, Jeff, Leslie J. Francis, and Colin Crowder, eds. *Theological Perspectives on Christian Formation.* Grand Rapids: Eerdmans, 1996.

Augustine, St. *On Christian Teaching.* Translated by R. P. H. Green. Oxford: Oxford University Press, 1997.

Austin, J. L. *How to Do Things with Words.* Oxford: Oxford University Press, 1962.

Axtell, Guy. "Recent Work on Virtue Epistemology." *APQ* 34, no. 1 (January 1997): 1-26.

Ayres, Lewis, and Stephen E. Fowl. "(Mis)Reading the Face of God: *The Interpretation of the Bible in the Church.*" *TS* 60 (1999): 513-28.

Bacote, Vincent E., Laura C. Miguélez, and Dennis L. Okholm, eds. *Evangelicals and Scripture: Tradition, Authority, Hermeneutics.* Downers Grove, IL: IVP, 2004.

Baker, David L. *Two Testaments, One Bible.* Rev. ed. Downers Grove, IL: IVP, 1991.

Bakhtin, Mikhail Mikhailovich. *Art and Answerability: Early Philosophical Essays.* Translated by Vadim Liapunov and Kenneth Brostrom. Edited by Michael Holquist and Vadim Liapunov. Austin: University of Texas Press, 1990.

———. *The Dialogic Imagination.* Translated by Caryl Emerson and Michael Holquist. Edited by Michael Holquist. Austin: University of Texas Press, 1981.

———. *Problems of Dostoevsky's Poetics.* Edited and translated by Caryl Emerson. Theory and History of Literature, vol. 8. Manchester: Manchester University Press, 1984.

———. *Speech Genres and Other Late Essays.* Translated by Vern W. McGee. Austin: University of Texas Press, 1986.

———. *Toward a Philosophy of the Act.* Translated by Vadim Liapunov. Edited by Vadim Liapunov and Michael Holquist. Austin: University of Texas Press, 1993.

Banks, Robert. *Reenvisioning Theological Education: Exploring a Missional Alternative to Current Models.* Grand Rapids: Eerdmans, 1999.

Barr, James. *The Concept of Biblical Theology: An Old Testament Perspective.* Minneapolis: Fortress, 1999.

Barth, Karl. *The Word of God.* Vol. I/1 of *Church Dogmatics.* Translated by Thomas F. Torrance. 2d ed. Edinburgh: T&T Clark, 1975.

Barth, Markus. *Ephesians 4–6.* AB, vol. 34A. New York: Doubleday, 1974.

Bartholomew, Craig, Colin Greene, and Karl Möller, eds. *After Pentecost: Language and Biblical Interpretation.* Scripture and Hermeneutics, vol. 2. Grand Rapids: Zondervan, 2001.

———, eds. *Renewing Biblical Interpretation.* Scripture and Hermeneutics, vol. 1. Grand Rapids: Zondervan, 2000.

Bartholomew, Craig, Jonathan Chaplin, Robert Song, and Al Wolters, eds. *A Royal Priesthood? The Use of the Bible Ethically and Politically.* Scripture and Hermeneutics, vol. 3. Grand Rapids: Zondervan, 2002.

Bartholomew, Craig, C. Stephen Evans, Mary Healy, and Murray Rae, eds. *"Behind" the Text: History and Biblical Interpretation.* Scripture and Hermeneutics, vol. 4. Grand Rapids: Zondervan, 2003.

Barton, Stephen C. "New Testament Interpretation as Performance." *SJT* 52, no. 2 (1999): 179-208.

———, ed. *Where Shall Wisdom Be Found? Wisdom in the Bible, the Church and the Contemporary World.* London: T&T Clark, 1999.

Begbie, Jeremy S. *Theology, Music and Time.* Studies in Christian Doctrine. Cambridge: Cambridge University Press, 2000.

Bernstein, Richard J. *Beyond Objectivism and Relativism: Science, Hermeneutics, and Praxis.* Philadelphia: University of Pennsylvania Press, 1983.

Bevans, Stephen B., SVD. *Models of Contextual Theology.* Maryknoll, NY: Orbis, 1992.

Blenkinsopp, Joseph. *Wisdom and Law in the Old Testament: The Ordering of Life in Israel and Early Judaism.* Oxford Bible Series. Oxford: Oxford University Press, 1983.

Blocher, Henri. "The 'Analogy of Faith' in the Study of Scripture." In *The Challenge of Evangelical Theology,* edited by Nigel M. de S. Cameron, 17-37. Edinburgh: Rutherford House, 1987.

———. *In the Beginning: The Opening Chapters of Genesis.* Translated by David G. Preston. Downers Grove, IL: IVP, 1984.

Blowers, Paul M. "The *Regula Fidei* and the Narrative Character of Early Christian Faith." *Pro Ecclesia* 6 (1997): 199-228.

Boff, Clodovis. *Theology and Praxis: Epistemological Foundations.* Maryknoll, NY: Orbis, 1987.

Briggs, Richard S. *Words in Action: Speech Act Theory and Biblical Interpretation.* Edinburgh: T&T Clark, 2001.

Brookfield, Stephen D. *Becoming a Critically Reflective Teacher.* San Francisco: Jossey Bass, 1995.

Brown, William P. *Character in Crisis: A Fresh Approach to the Wisdom Literature of the Old Testament.* Grand Rapids: Eerdmans, 1996.

———. *The Ethos of the Cosmos: The Genesis of Moral Imagination in the Bible.* Grand Rapids: Eerdmans, 1999.

Browning, Don S. *A Fundamental Practical Theology: Descriptive and Strategic Proposals.* Minneapolis: Fortress, 1991.

———. "The Nature and Criteria of Theological Scholarship." *Theological Education* 32, no. 1 (1995): 1-11.

Browning, Don S., and Francis Schüssler Fiorenza, eds. *Habermas, Modernity, and Public Theology.* New York: Crossroad, 1992.

Bryce, Glendon E. *A Legacy of Wisdom: The Egyptian Contribution to the Wisdom of Israel.* Lewisburg, PA: Bucknell University Press, 1979.

Buckley, James J., and David S. Yeago, eds. *Knowing the Triune God: The Work of the Spirit in the Practices of the Church.* Grand Rapids: Eerdmans, 2001.

Callow, Kathleen. *Man and Message: A Guide to Meaning-Based Text Analysis.* Lanham, MD: Summer Institute of Linguistics & University Press of America, 1998.

Carroll, Jackson W., et al. *Being There: Culture and Formation in Two Theological Schools.* Oxford: Oxford University Press, 1997.

Carson, D. A. "Unity and Diversity in the New Testament: The Possibility of Systematic Theology." In *Scripture and Truth,* edited by D. A. Carson and John D. Woodbridge, 65-95. Grand Rapids: Baker, 1992.

Carson, D. A., and John D. Woodbridge, eds. *Hermeneutics, Authority and Canon.* Grand Rapids: Baker, 1995.

Cessario, Romanus, O.P. *Christian Faith and the Theological Life.* Washington, DC: Catholic University of America, 1996.

Charry, Ellen T. *By the Renewing of Your Minds: The Pastoral Function of Christian Doctrine.* Oxford: Oxford University Press, 1997.

———, ed. *Inquiring After God: Classic and Contemporary Readings.* Blackwell Readings in Modern Theology. Oxford: Blackwell, 2000.

Claassens, L. Juliana M. "Biblical Theology as Dialogue: Continuing the Conversation on Mikhail Bakhtin and Biblical Theology." *JBL* 122, no. 1 (2003): 127-44.

Clayton, Philip. *Explanation from Physics to Theology: An Essay in Rationality and Religion.* New Haven: Yale University Press, 1989.

———. *The Problem of God in Modern Thought.* Grand Rapids: Eerdmans, 2000.

Clements, R. E. *Wisdom in Theology.* Grand Rapids: Eerdmans, 1992.

Coates, Ruth. *Christianity in Bakhtin: God and the Exiled Author.* Cambridge: Cambridge University Press, 1998.

Colson, Charles, and Richard John Neuhaus, eds. *Your Word Is Truth: A Project of Evangelicals and Catholics Together.* Grand Rapids: Eerdmans, 2002.

Congar, Yves M.-J. *A History of Theology.* Edited and translated by Hunter Guthrie. Garden City, NY: Doubleday, 1968.

Contino, Paul J., and Susan M. Felch, eds. *Bakhtin and Religion: A Feeling for Faith.* Evanston, IL: Northwestern University Press, 2001.

Craigo-Snell, Shannon. "Command Performance: Rethinking Performance Interpretation in the Context of *Divine Discourse.*" *Modern Theology* 16, no. 4 (October 2000): 475-94.

Cunningham, David S. *Faithful Persuasion: In Aid of a Rhetoric of Christian Theology.* Notre Dame: Notre Dame University Press, 1991.

Cunningham, Mary Kathleen. *What Is Theological Exegesis? Interpretation and Use of Scripture in Barth's Doctrine of Election.* Valley Forge, PA: Trinity Press International, 1995.

Davidson, Richard M. *Typology in Scripture: A Study of Hermeneutical* Τυπος *Structures.* Berrien Springs, MI: Andrews University Press, 1981.

Davis, Ellen F. "Preserving Virtues: Renewing the Tradition." In *Character and Scripture,* edited by William P. Brown, 183-201. Grand Rapids: Eerdmans, 2002.

Davis, Ellen F., and Richard B. Hays, eds. *The Art of Reading Scripture.* Grand Rapids: Eerdmans, 2003.

Davis, Stephen T., ed. *Philosophy and Theological Discourse.* New York: St. Martin's, 1997.

Dawson, John David. *Christian Figural Reading and the Fashioning of Identity.* Berkeley: University of California Press, 2002.

Day, John, Robert P. Gordon, and H. G. M. Williamson, eds. *Wisdom in Ancient Israel: Essays in Honour of J. A. Emerton.* Cambridge: Cambridge University Press, 1995.

Dulles, Avery, S.J. *The Craft of Theology: From Symbol to System.* New York: Crossroad, 1992.

Dunn, James D. G. *Romans 1–8.* WBC, vol. 38A. Dallas: Word, 1988.

Dunne, Joseph. *Back to the Rough Ground: 'Phronesis' and 'Techne' in Modern Philosophy and in Aristotle.* Notre Dame: Notre Dame University Press, 1993.

Ebeling, Gerhard. *Studium der Theologie: Eine Enzyklopädische Orientierung.* Tübingen: J. C. B. Mohr (Paul Siebeck), 1975.

Elder, E. Rozanne, ed. *From Cloister to Classroom: Monastic and Scholastic Approaches to Truth.* Kalamazoo, MI: Cistercian Publications, 1986.

Ellingworth, Paul. *The Epistle to the Hebrews.* NIGTC. Grand Rapids: Eerdmans, 1993.

Ellis, E. Earle. *The Old Testament in Early Christianity.* Grand Rapids: Baker, 1991.

English, Edward D., ed. *Reading and Wisdom: The 'De Doctrina Christiana' in the Middle Ages.* Notre Dame: Notre Dame University Press, 1994.

Evans, G. R. *The Language and Logic of the Bible: The Earlier Middle Ages.* Cambridge: Cambridge University Press, 1984.

———. *The Language and Logic of the Bible: The Road to Reformation.* Cambridge: Cambridge University Press, 1985.

———. *Old Arts and New Theology: The Beginnings of Theology as an Academic Discipline.* Oxford: Clarendon, 1980.

Evans, G. R., Alister E. McGrath, and Allan D. Galloway. *The Science of Theology.* Vol. 1 of *The History of Christian Theology.* Grand Rapids: Eerdmans, 1986.

Farley, Edward. *Ecclesial Reflection: An Anatomy of Theological Method.* Philadelphia: Fortress, 1982.

———. *The Fragility of Knowledge: Theological Education in the Church and the University.* Philadelphia: Fortress, 1988.

———. *Theologia: The Fragmentation and Unity of Theological Education.* Philadelphia: Fortress, 1983.

Farmer, Kathleen A. *Who Knows What Is Good? A Commentary on Proverbs and Ecclesiastes.* ITC. Grand Rapids: Eerdmans, 1991.

Farrow, Douglas. "Is Theological Education Possible?" *Pro Ecclesia* 9, no. 4 (Fall 2000): 404-13.

Fee, Gordon D. *God's Empowering Presence: The Holy Spirit in the Letters of Paul.* Peabody, MA: Hendrickson, 1994.

———. *Paul's Letter to the Philippians.* NICNT. Grand Rapids: Eerdmans, 1995.

Feinberg, John S. "Rationality, Objectivity, and Doing Theology: Review and Critique of Wentzel Van Huysteen's [*sic*] *Theology and the Justification of Faith.*" *TrinJ* 10 NS (1989): 161-84.

Fink, Eugen. "Phronēsis und Theoria." In *Die Welt des Menschen,* edited by Walter Biemel and Jan Patocka, 134-58. The Hague: M. Nijhoff, 1976.

Fiorenza, Francis Schüssler. "Theory and Practice: Theological Education as a Reconstructive, Hermeneutical, and Practical Task." *Theological Education* 23, Supplement (1987): 113-41.

Ford, David F. *A Long Rumour of Wisdom: Redescribing Theology.* Cambridge: Cambridge University Press, 1992.

———. *Self and Salvation: Being Transformed.* Studies in Christian Doctrine. Cambridge: Cambridge University Press, 1999.

———. *Theology: A Very Short Introduction.* Oxford: Oxford University Press, 1999.

Ford, David F., and Graham Stanton, eds. *Reading Texts, Seeking Wisdom: Scripture and Theology.* Grand Rapids: Eerdmans, 2004.

Fowl, Stephen E. *Engaging Scripture.* Oxford: Blackwell, 1998.

———. Review of *Is There a Meaning in This Text?* by Kevin J. Vanhoozer. *Modern Theology* 16 (2000): 260-62.

———, ed. *The Theological Interpretation of Scripture: Classic and Contemporary Readings.* Oxford: Blackwell, 1997.

Fowl, Stephen E., and L. Gregory Jones. *Reading in Communion: Scripture and Ethics in Christian Life.* Grand Rapids: Eerdmans, 1991.

France, R. T. *Jesus and the Old Testament: His Application of Old Testament Passages to Himself and His Mission.* London: Tyndale, 1971.

Frei, Hans W. "Barth and Schleiermacher: Divergence and Convergence." In *Barth and Schleiermacher: Beyond the Impasse,* edited by James O. Duke and Robert F. Streetman, 65-87. Minneapolis: Fortress, 1988.

———. *The Eclipse of Biblical Narrative: A Study in Eighteenth and Nineteenth Century Hermeneutics.* New Haven: Yale University Press, 1974.

Fretheim, Terence E. "שׂכל." In *NIDOTTE,* edited by Willem A. Van Gemeren, vol. 3, p. 1243. Grand Rapids: Zondervan, 1997.

Gadamer, Hans-Georg. *Dialogue and Dialectic: Eight Hermeneutical Studies on Plato.* New Haven: Yale University Press, 1980.

———. *Truth and Method.* Translated by Joel Weinsheimer and Donald G. Marshall. 2d ed. New York: Continuum, 1989.

Gallagher, Shaun. *Hermeneutics and Education.* SUNY Series in Contemporary Continental Philosophy. Albany, NY: SUNY Press, 1992.

Gamble, Harry Y. *Books and Readers in the Early Church: A History of Early Christian Texts.* New Haven & London: Yale University Press, 1995.

Gammie, John G., et al., eds. *Israelite Wisdom: Theological and Literary Essays in Honor of Samuel L. Terrien.* Missoula, MT: Scholars Press, 1978.

Gammie, John G., and Leo G. Perdue, eds. *The Sage in Israel and the Ancient Near East.* Winona Lake, IN: Eisenbrauns, 1990.

Gaventa, Beverly Roberts. Review of *Engaging Scripture,* by Stephen E. Fowl. *Modern Theology* 16 (2000): 271-72.

Gerrish, Brian A. "The Nature of Doctrine." *JR* 68 (1988): 87-92.

———. "Tradition in the Modern World: The Reformed Habit of Mind." In *Toward the Future of Reformed Theology: Tasks, Topics, Traditions,* edited by E. David Willis and Michael Welker, 3-20. Grand Rapids: Eerdmans, 1999.

Gibbs, Raymond W., Jr. *Intentions in the Experience of Meaning.* Cambridge: Cambridge University Press, 1999.

Goldingay, John. *Models for Interpretation of Scripture.* Grand Rapids: Eerdmans, 1995.

———. *Models for Scripture.* Grand Rapids: Eerdmans, 1994.

Goodman, Martin. *State and Society in Roman Galilee, A.D. 132-212.* Oxford Centre for Postgraduate Hebrew Studies. Totowa, NJ: Rowman & Allanheld, 1983.

Goppelt, Leonhard. *TYPOS: The Typological Interpretation of the Old Testament in the New.* Translated by Donald H. Madvig. Grand Rapids: Eerdmans, 1982.

Grabner-Haider, Anton. *Theorie der Theologie als Wissenschaft.* Munich: Kösel-Verlag, 1974.

Gracia, Jorge J. E. *How Can We Know What God Means? The Interpretation of Revelation.* New York: Palgrave, 2001.

Green, Barbara. *Mikhail Bakhtin and Biblical Scholarship: An Introduction.* Atlanta: SBL, 2000.

Green, Garrett. *Imagining God: Theology and the Religious Imagination.* Grand Rapids: Eerdmans, 1989.

———, ed. *Scriptural Authority and Narrative Interpretation.* Reprint. Eugene, OR: Wipf & Stock, 2000.

———. *Theology, Hermeneutics, and Imagination: The Crisis of Interpretation at the End of Modernity.* Cambridge: Cambridge University Press, 2000.

Green, Joel B., and Max Turner, eds. *Between Two Horizons: Spanning New Testament Studies and Systematic Theology.* Grand Rapids: Eerdmans, 2000.

Greene-McCreight, Kathryn. *Ad Litteram: How Augustine, Calvin, and Barth Read the "Plain Sense" of Genesis 1–3.* New York: Peter Lang, 1999.

Greer, Rowan A. *Broken Lights and Mended Lives: Theology and Common Life in the Early Church.* University Park: Pennsylvania State University Press, 1986.

Grenz, Stanley J. "Beyond Foundationalism: Is a Nonfoundationalist Evangelical Theology Possible?" *Christian Scholar's Review* 30, no. 1 (Fall 2000): 57-82.

———. *Renewing the Center: Evangelical Theology in a Post-Theological Era.* Grand Rapids: Baker, 2000.

———. *Revisioning Evangelical Theology.* Downers Grove, IL: IVP, 1993.

———. "The Spirit and the Word: The World-Creating Function of the Text." *TToday* 57, no. 3 (October 2000): 357-75.

———. *Theology for the Community of God.* Nashville: Broadman & Holman, 1994.

Grenz, Stanley J., and John R. Franke. *Beyond Foundationalism: Shaping Theology in a Postmodern Context.* Louisville: Westminster John Knox, 2001.

Griffiths, Paul J. *Religious Reading: The Place of Reading in the Practice of Religion.* Oxford: Oxford University Press, 1999.

Grigg, Richard. *Theology as a Way of Thinking.* Atlanta: Scholars Press, 1990.

Groome, Thomas. *Sharing Faith: A Comprehensive Approach to Religious Education and Pastoral Ministry.* San Francisco: Harper Collins, 1991.

Guarino, Thomas. "Between Foundationalism and Nihilism: Is Phronesis the Via Media for Theology?" *TS* 54 (March 1993): 37-54.

Guder, Darrell L. "The Church as Missional Community." In *The Community of the Word: Toward an Evangelical Ecclesiology,* edited by Mark Husbands and Daniel J. Treier, 114-28. Downers Grove, IL: IVP, 2005.

Gunton, Colin E. *A Brief Theology of Revelation.* Edinburgh: T&T Clark, 1995.

———, ed. *The Cambridge Companion to Christian Doctrine.* Cambridge: Cambridge University Press, 1997.

———. "Dogma, the Church and the Task of Theology." *Neue Zeitschrift für Systematische Theologie und Religionsphilosophie* 40, no. 1 (1998): 66-69.

———. "Indispensable Opponent: The Relations of Systematic Theology and Philosophy of Religion." *Neue Zeitschrift für Systematische Theologie und Religionsphilosophie* 38, no. 3 (1996): 298-306.

———. "A Rose by Any Other Name? From 'Christian Doctrine' to 'Systematic Theology'." *IJST* 1, no. 1 (March 1999): 4-23.

Habermas, Jürgen. *Lifeworld and System: A Critique of Functionalist Reason.* Vol. 2 of *The Theory of Communicative Action.* Translated by Thomas McCarthy. Boston: Beacon, 1987.

———. *Reason and the Rationalization of Society.* Vol. 1 of *The Theory of Communicative Action.* Translated by Thomas McCarthy. Boston: Beacon, 1984.

Hafemann, Scott J., ed. *Biblical Theology: Retrospect and Prospect.* Downers Grove, IL: IVP, 2002.

Hall, Douglas John. "Theological Education as Character Formation." *Theological Education* 24, Supplement 1 (1988): 53-79.

Hamilton, Victor P. *The Book of Genesis: Chapters 1–17.* NICOT. Grand Rapids: Eerdmans, 1990.

Hart, Trevor. *Faith Thinking: The Dynamics of Christian Theology.* Downers Grove, IL: IVP, 1995.

Hauerwas, Stanley. *The Peaceable Kingdom: A Primer in Christian Ethics.* Notre Dame: Notre Dame University Press, 1983.

Hays, Richard B. *The Faith of Jesus Christ: The Narrative Substructure of Galatians 3:1–4:11.* 2d ed. Grand Rapids: Eerdmans, 2002.

———. *The Moral Vision of the New Testament: A Contemporary Introduction to New Testament Ethics.* San Francisco: Harper Collins, 1996.

Healy, Nicholas M. *Church, World and the Christian Life: Practical-Prophetic Ecclesiology.* Studies in Christian Doctrine. Cambridge: Cambridge University Press, 2000.

Heitink, Gerben. *Practical Theology.* Translated by Reinder Bruinsma. Grand Rapids: Eerdmans, 1999.

Hermisson, Hans-Jürgen. "Gottes Freiheit — Spielraum des Menschen: Alttestamentliche Aspekte eines Biblisch-Theologischen Themas." *ZTK* 82, no. 2 (1985): 129-52.

Heyduck, Richard. *The Recovery of Doctrine in the Contemporary Church: An Essay in Philosophical Ecclesiology.* Waco, TX: Baylor University Press, 2002.

Hodgson, Peter C. *God's Wisdom: Toward a Theology of Education.* Louisville: Westminster John Knox, 1999.

Holmer, Paul L. *The Grammar of Faith.* San Francisco: Harper & Row, 1978.

Holquist, Michael. *Dialogism: Bakhtin and His World.* New York: Routledge, 1990.

Horton, Michael S. *Covenant and Eschatology: The Divine Drama.* Louisville: Westminster John Knox, 2002.

Hughes, Graham. *Hebrews and Hermeneutics: The Epistle to the Hebrews as a New Testament Example of Biblical Interpretation.* SNTSMS, vol. 36. Cambridge: Cambridge University Press, 1979.

Hütter, Reinhard. *Suffering Divine Things: Theology as Church Practice.* Translated by Doug Stott. Grand Rapids: Eerdmans, 2000.

———. "Worth Discussing: Two Books by David Kelsey." *Currents in Theology and Mission* 22 (F 1995): 49-52.

Jaeger, Werner. *Paideia: The Ideals of Greek Culture.* Translated by Gilbert Highet. 2d ed. New York: Oxford University Press, 1939.

James, E. O. *The Tree of Life: An Archaeological Study.* Leiden: E. J. Brill, 1966.

Jaros, Karl. "Die Motive der Heiligen Bäume und der Schlange in Gen 2–3." *ZAW* 92, no. 2 (1980): 204-15.

Jeanrond, Werner G. "Criteria for New Biblical Theologies." *JR* 76, no. 2 (April 1996): 233-49.

———. *Text and Interpretation as Categories of Theological Thinking.* Translated by Thomas J. Wilson. New York: Crossroad, 1988.

———. *Text und Interpretation als Kategorien theologischen Denkens.* Tübingen: J. C. B. Mohr (Paul Siebeck), 1986.

———. *Theological Hermeneutics: Development and Significance.* New York: Crossroad, 1991.

Jeffrey, David L. *People of the Book: Christian Identity and Literary Culture.* Grand Rapids: Eerdmans, 1996.

Jennings, Theodore W., Jr., ed. *The Vocation of the Theologian.* Philadelphia: Fortress, 1985.

Jenson, Robert W. "The Religious Power of Scripture." *SJT* 52, no. 1 (1999): 89-105.

———. *The Triune God.* Vol. 1 of *Systematic Theology.* Oxford: Oxford University Press, 1997.

———. *The Works of God.* Vol. 2 of *Systematic Theology.* Oxford: Oxford University Press, 1999.

Johnson, Luke Timothy. "Fragments of an Untidy Conversation: Theology and the Literary Diversity of the New Testament." In *Biblical Theology: Problems and Perspectives,* edited by Steven Kraftchick, Charles D. Myers, Jr., and Ben C. Ollenburger, 276-89. Nashville: Abingdon, 1995.

———. *Scripture and Discernment in the Early Church.* 2d ed. Nashville: Abingdon, 1996.

Jones, L. Gregory, and James J. Buckley, eds. *Theology and Scriptural Imagination.* Oxford: Blackwell, 1998.

Jones, L. Gregory, and Stanley Hauerwas, eds. *Why Narrative? Readings in Narrative Theology.* Reprint. Eugene, OR: Wipf & Stock, 1997.

Jones, L. Gregory, and Stephanie Paulsell, eds. *The Scope of Our Art: The Vocation of the Theological Teacher.* Grand Rapids: Eerdmans, 2002.

Kaiser, Walter C., Jr. "The Nature and Criteria of Theological Scholarship: An Evangelical Critique and Plan." *Theological Education* 32, no. 1 (1995): 57-70.

Kasper, Walter. *The God of Jesus Christ.* Translated by Matthew J. O'Connell. New York: Crossroad, 1992.

Keck, Leander E. "Rethinking 'New Testament Ethics'." *JBL* 115, no. 1 (Spring 1996): 3-16.

Kelsey, David H. *Between Athens and Berlin: The Theological Education Debate.* Grand Rapids: Eerdmans, 1993.

———. "The Bible and Christian Theology." *JAAR* 48, no. 3 (September 1980): 385-402.

———. *Proving Doctrine.* Harrisburg, PA: Trinity Press International, 1999.

———. *To Understand God Truly: What's Theological About a Theological School.* Louisville: Westminster John Knox, 1992.

———. *The Uses of Scripture in Recent Theology.* Philadelphia: Fortress, 1975.

Kirk, J. Andrew. *The Mission of Theology and Theology as Mission.* Valley Forge, PA: Trinity Press International, 1997.

Kögler, Hans Herbert. *The Power of Dialogue: Critical Hermeneutics After Gadamer and Foucault.* Translated by Paul Hendrickson. Cambridge, MA: MIT Press, 1996.

Köpf, Ulrich. *Die Anfänge der theologischen Wissenschaftstheorie im 13. Jahrhundert.* Tübingen: Mohr, 1974.

Kübel, Paul. "Ein Wortspiel in Genesis 3 und sein Hintergrund: Die 'Kluge' Schlange und die 'Nackten' Menschen: Uberlegungen zur Vorgeschichte von Gen 2–3." *Biblische Notizen* 93 (1998): 11-22.

Kuhn, Thomas S. *The Structure of Scientific Revolutions.* Chicago: University of Chicago Press, 1962.

Lash, Nicholas. *Theology on Dover Beach.* New York: Paulist, 1979.

———. *Theology on the Way to Emmaus.* London: SCM, 1986.

Leclercq, Jean, O.S.B. *The Love of Learning and the Desire for God: A Study of Monastic Culture.* Translated by Catharine Misrahi. 3d ed. New York: Fordham University Press, 1982.

Lee, Jung Young. "Multicultural and Global Theological Scholarship: An Asian American Perspective." *Theological Education* 32, no. 1 (1995): 43-55.

Leith, John H. *Crisis in the Church: The Plight of Theological Education.* Louisville: Westminster John Knox, 1997.

Lincoln, Andrew T. *Ephesians.* WBC, vol. 42. Dallas: Word, 1990.

Lindbeck, George A. *The Nature of Doctrine: Religion and Theology in a Postliberal Age.* Philadelphia: Westminster, 1984.

Lindsey, William D. "'The Problem of Great Time': A Bakhtinian Ethics of Discourse." *JR* 73 (July 1993): 311-28.

Lints, Richard. *The Fabric of Theology: A Prolegomenon to Evangelical Theology.* Grand Rapids: Eerdmans, 1993.

Lobkowicz, Nicholas. *Theory and Practice: History of a Concept from Aristotle to Marx.* Notre Dame: Notre Dame University Press, 1967.

Louth, Andrew. *Discerning the Mystery: An Essay on the Nature of Theology.* Oxford: Clarendon, 1983.

———. "The Nature of Theological Understanding: Some Parallels Between Newman and Gadamer." In *Tradition Renewed,* edited by D. Rowell, 98-109. London: Darton, Longman, & Todd, 1986.

———. Review of *Biblical Exegesis and the Formation of Christian Culture,* by Frances M. Young. *SJT* 54, no. 2 (2001): 247-48.

Lubac, Henri de, S.J. *Exégèse Médiévale: Les Quatre Sens de l'Ecriture.* Paris, 1959-1964.

Luc, A. "ערמ." In *NIDOTTE,* edited by Willem A. Van Gemeren, vol. 3, pp. 539-41. Grand Rapids: Zondervan, 1997.

Lundin, Roger, ed. *Disciplining Hermeneutics: Interpretation in Christian Perspective.* Grand Rapids: Eerdmans, 1997.

Lundin, Roger, Clarence Walhout, and Anthony C. Thiselton, eds. *The Promise of Hermeneutics.* Grand Rapids: Eerdmans, 1999.

———. *The Responsibility of Hermeneutics.* Grand Rapids: Eerdmans, 1985.

MacIntyre, Alasdair. *After Virtue: A Study in Moral Theory.* 2d ed. Notre Dame: Notre Dame University Press, 1984.

Macovski, Michael, ed. *Dialogue and Critical Discourse: Language, Culture, Critical Theory.* Oxford: Oxford University Press, 1997.

Macquarrie, John. *Principles of Christian Theology.* New York: Scribner, 1977.

Maddox, Randy L. "The Recovery of Theology as a Practical Discipline." *TS* 51, no. 4 (December 1990): 650-72.

Mangina, Joseph L. "After Dogma: Reinhard Hütter's Challenge to Contemporary Theology: A Review Essay." *IJST* 2, no. 3 (2000): 330-46.

Marshall, Bruce D., ed. *Theology and Dialogue: Essays in Conversation with George Lindbeck.* Notre Dame: Notre Dame University Press, 1990.

———. *Trinity and Truth.* Studies in Christian Doctrine. Cambridge: Cambridge University Press, 2000.

McClendon, James Wm., Jr. *Doctrine.* Vol. 2 of *Systematic Theology.* Nashville: Abingdon, 1994.

McCormack, Bruce L. "Grace and Being: The Role of God's Gracious Election in Karl

Barth's Theological Ontology." In *The Cambridge Companion to Karl Barth*, edited by John Webster, 92-110. Cambridge: Cambridge University Press, 2000.

———. "What's at Stake in Current Debates over Justification? The Crisis of Protestantism in the West." In *Justification: What's at Stake in the Current Debates*, edited by Mark A. Husbands and Daniel J. Treier, ch. 3. Downers Grove, IL: IVP, 2004.

McGrath, Alister E. *The Genesis of Doctrine: A Study in the Foundation of Doctrinal Criticism.* Grand Rapids: Eerdmans, 1990.

McIntosh, Mark A. *Mystical Theology: The Integrity of Spirituality and Theology.* London: Blackwell, 1998.

McKane, William. *Proverbs: A New Approach.* OTL. Philadelphia: Westminster, 1970.

Meilaender, Gilbert C. *The Theory and Practice of Virtue.* Notre Dame: Notre Dame University Press, 1984.

Meinhold, Arndt. "Gott und Mensch in Proverbien III." *VT* 37 (October 1987): 468-77.

Melchert, Charles F. *Wise Teaching: Biblical Wisdom and Educational Ministry.* Valley Forge, PA: Trinity Press International, 1998.

Mihailovic, Alexandar. *Corporeal Words: Mikhail Bakhtin's Theology of Discourse.* Studies in Russian Literature and Theory. Evanston, IL: Northwestern University Press, 1997.

Milbank, John. *Theology and Social Theory: Beyond Secular Reason.* Oxford: Blackwell, 1993.

———. *The Word Made Strange: Theology, Language, Culture.* Oxford: Blackwell, 1997.

Millard, Alan R. *Reading and Writing in the Time of Jesus.* New York: New York University Press, 2000.

Moberly, R. W. L. *The Bible, Theology, and Faith: A Study of Abraham and Jesus.* Studies in Christian Doctrine. Cambridge: Cambridge University Press, 2000.

———. Review of *Is There a Meaning in This Text?* by Kevin J. Vanhoozer. *ExpTim* 110, no. 5 (Fall 1999): 154.

Morgan, Robert. "Can the Critical Study of Scripture Provide a Doctrinal Norm?" *JR* 76, no. 2 (April 1996): 206-32.

Morson, Gary Saul. *Narrative and Freedom: The Shadows of Time.* New Haven: Yale University Press, 1994.

Morson, Gary Saul, and Caryl Emerson. *Mikhail Bakhtin: Creation of a Prosaics.* Stanford: Stanford University Press, 1990.

Muller, Richard A. *Holy Scripture: The Cognitive Foundation for Theology.* Vol. 2 of *Post-Reformation Reformed Dogmatics.* Grand Rapids: Baker, 1993.

———. *Prolegomena to Theology.* Vol. 1 of *Post-Reformation Reformed Dogmatics.* Grand Rapids: Baker, 1987.

———. *The Unaccommodated Calvin: Studies in the Foundation of a Theological Tradition.* Oxford: Oxford University Press, 2000.

Murphy, Nancey. *Beyond Liberalism and Fundamentalism: How Modern and Postmodern Philosophy Set the Theological Agenda.* Valley Forge, PA: Trinity Press International, 1996.

———. *Theology in the Age of Scientific Reasoning.* Cornell Studies in the Philosophy of Religion. Ithaca and London: Cornell University Press, 1990.

Murphy, Roland E. *The Tree of Life: An Exploration of Biblical Wisdom Literature.* 2d ed. Grand Rapids: Eerdmans, 1996.

Newman, John Henry. *An Essay in Aid of a Grammar of Assent.* London & New York: Longmans, Green & Co., 1930.

———. *An Essay on the Development of Christian Doctrine.* 6th ed. London: Longmans, Green, & Co., 1890.

Newsom, Carol A. "Bakhtin, the Bible, and Dialogic Truth." *JR* 76, no. 2 (April 1996): 290-306.

Nussbaum, Martha C. *The Fragility of Goodness: Luck and Ethics in Greek Tragedy and Philosophy.* Cambridge: Cambridge University Press, 1986.

———. *Love's Knowledge: Essays on Philosophy and Literature.* New York: Oxford University Press, 1990.

O'Brien, Peter T. *The Epistle to the Philippians.* NIGTC. Grand Rapids: Eerdmans, 1991.

O'Collins, Gerald, and Daniel Kendall. *The Bible for Theology: Ten Principles for the Theological Use of Scripture.* New York & Mahwah, NJ: Paulist, 1997.

O'Connor, Kathleen M. *The Wisdom Literature.* Message of Biblical Spirituality. Wilmington, DE: Michael Glazier, 1988.

O'Donovan, Oliver. *Resurrection and Moral Order: An Outline for Evangelical Ethics.* 2d ed. Grand Rapids: Eerdmans, 1994.

Ogden, Schubert M. "Theology and Biblical Interpretation." *JR* 76, no. 2 (April 1996): 172-88.

Olson, Dennis T. "Biblical Theology as Provisional Monologization: A Dialogue with Childs, Brueggemann and Bakhtin." *BibInt* 6 (April 1998): 162-80.

O'Neill, Colman. "The Rule Theory of Doctrine and Propositional Truth." *Thomist* 49 (1985): 417-42.

Packer, J. I., and Sven K. Soderlund, eds. *The Way of Wisdom: Essays in Honor of Bruce K. Waltke.* Grand Rapids: Zondervan, 2000.

Pannenberg, Wolfhart. *Wissenschaftstheorie und Theologie.* Frankfurt am Main: Suhrkamp Verlag, 1973.

Patterson, David. "Bakhtin on Word and Spirit: The Religiosity of Responsibility." *Cross Currents* 41 (Spring 1991): 33-51.

Patterson, Sue. *Realist Christian Theology in a Postmodern Age.* Studies in Christian Doctrine. Cambridge: Cambridge University Press, 1999.

Pelikan, Jaroslav. *The Emergence of the Catholic Tradition (100-600).* Vol. 1 of *The Christian Tradition: A History of the Development of Doctrine.* Chicago: University of Chicago Press, 1971.

Perdue, Leo G. *Wisdom and Creation: The Theology of Wisdom Literature.* Nashville: Abingdon, 1994.

———. "Wisdom Theology and Social History in Proverbs 1–9." In *Wisdom, You Are My Sister: Studies in Honor of Roland E. Murphy, O.Carm., on the Occasion of His Eightieth Birthday,* edited by Michael L. Barre, S.S., 78-101. CBQMS, vol. 29. Washington, DC: Catholic Biblical Association of America, 1997.

Perry, T. A. *Wisdom Literature and the Structure of Proverbs.* University Park: Pennsylvania State University Press, 1993.

Petersen, Rodney L., and Nancy M. Rourke, eds. *Theological Literacy for the Twenty-First Century.* Grand Rapids: Eerdmans, 2002.

Peterson, Eugene H. "Eat This Book: The Holy Community at Table with the Holy Scripture." *TToday* 56, no. 1 (April 1999): 5-17.

Pettifer, Bryan. "Education and the Knowledge of God: Towards a Model of Theology as a Practical Discipline." In *The Foundations of Pastoral Studies and Practical Theology,* edited by Paul Ballard, 65-77. Cardiff: University College Faculty of Theology, 1986.

Phillips, Timothy R., and Dennis L. Okholm, eds. *The Nature of Confession: Evangelicals and Postliberals in Conversation.* Downers Grove, IL: IVP, 1996.

Polanyi, Michael. *Personal Knowledge: Towards a Post-Critical Philosophy.* London: Routledge & Kegan Paul, 1958.

———. *The Tacit Dimension.* London: Routledge & Kegan Paul, 1967.

Popkin, Richard H. *The History of Skepticism from Erasmus to Spinoza.* Rev. ed. Berkeley: University of California Press, 1979.

Rad, Gerhard von. *Wisdom in Israel.* Nashville & New York: Abingdon, 1972.

Radner, Ephraim. *The End of the Church: A Pneumatology of Christian Division in the West.* Grand Rapids: Eerdmans, 1998.

Reed, Walter L. *Dialogues of the Word: The Bible as Literature According to Bakhtin.* Oxford: Oxford University Press, 1993.

Reeve, C. D. C. *Practices of Reason: Aristotle's Nicomachean Ethics.* Oxford: Oxford University Press, 2000.

Reno, Russell. "'You Who Were Far Off Have Been Brought Near': Reflections on Theological Exegesis." *Ex Auditu* 16 (2000): 169-82.

Richards, Jay Wesley. "Truth and Meaning in George Lindbeck's *The Nature of Doctrine.*" *RelS* 33, no. 1 (March 1997): 33-53.

Ricoeur, Paul. *Figuring the Sacred: Religion, Narrative, and Imagination.* Translated by David Pellauer. Edited by Mark I. Wallace. Minneapolis: Fortress, 1995.

———. *Oneself as Another.* Translated by Kathleen McLaughlin Blamey. Chicago: University of Chicago Press, 1992.

———. "Practical Reason." Translated by Kathleen Blamey. In *From Text to Action: Essays in Hermeneutics,* II, 188-207. Evanston, IL: Northwestern University Press, 1991.

———. *Time and Narrative.* 3 vols. Translated by Kathleen McLaughlin Blamey and David Pellauer. Chicago: University of Chicago Press, 1984-1988.

———. "Toward a Hermeneutic of the Idea of Revelation." Translated by David Pellauer. In *Essays on Biblical Interpretation,* edited by Lewis S. Mudge, 73-118. Philadelphia: Fortress, 1980.

Ritschl, Dietrich. *The Logic of Theology: A Brief Account of the Relationship Between Basic Concepts in Theology.* Translated by John Bowden. Philadelphia: Fortress, 1987.

Rogers, Eugene F., Jr. "How the Virtues of an Interpreter Presuppose and Perfect Hermeneutics: The Case of Thomas Aquinas." *JR* 76, no. 1 (January 1996): 64-81.

Saffrey, H. D., O.P. "Theology as Science (3rd-6th Centuries)." In vol. XXX of *Studia Patristica,* edited by Elizabeth A. Livingstone, 321-39. Leuven: Peeters, 1997.

Satterthwaite, Philip E., and David F. Wright, eds. *A Pathway into the Holy Scripture.* Grand Rapids: Eerdmans, 1994.

Sauter, Gerhard. *Gateways to Dogmatics: Reasoning Theologically for the Life of the Church.* Grand Rapids: Eerdmans, 2003.

Schleiermacher, Friedrich. *Brief Outline on the Study of Theology.* Translated by Terrence N. Tice. Richmond, VA: John Knox, 1966.

———. *Kurze Darstellung des theologischen Studiums zum Behuf einleitender Vorlesungen.* Berlin: G. Reimer, 1830.

Schrag, Calvin O. *Communicative Praxis and the Space of Subjectivity.* Bloomington: Indiana University Press, 1986.

Schreiter, Robert J. *Constructing Local Theologies.* Maryknoll, NY: Orbis, 1985.

Schultz, Richard L. "Unity or Diversity in Wisdom Theology? A Canonical and Covenantal Perspective." *TynBul* 48, no. 2 (November 1997): 271-306.

Searle, John R. *Speech Acts: An Essay in the Philosophy of Language.* Cambridge: Cambridge University Press, 1970.

Seitz, Christopher R. "Christological Interpretation of Texts and Trinitarian Claims to Truth: An Engagement with Francis Watson's *Text and Truth.*" *SJT* 52, no. 2 (1999): 209-26.

———. *Figured Out: Typology and Providence in Christian Scripture.* Louisville: Westminster John Knox, 2001.

Seitz, Christopher R., and Kathryn Greene-McCreight, eds. *Theological Exegesis: Essays in Honor of Brevard S. Childs.* Grand Rapids: Eerdmans, 1999.

Shedinger, Robert F. "Kuhnian Paradigms and Biblical Scholarship: Is Biblical Studies a Science?" *JBL* 119, no. 3 (Fall 2000): 453-71.

Shults, F. LeRon. *The Postfoundationalist Task of Theology: Wolfhart Pannenberg and the New Theological Rationality.* Grand Rapids: Eerdmans, 2000.

Silva, Moisés, ed. *Foundations of Contemporary Interpretation.* Grand Rapids: Zondervan, 1996.

———. *Philippians.* WEC. Chicago: Moody, 1988.

Simon, Yves R. *The Definition of Moral Virtue.* Edited by Vukan Kuic. New York: Fordham University Press, 1986.

Sloan, Douglas. *Faith and Knowledge: Mainline Protestantism and American Higher Education.* Louisville: Westminster John Knox, 1994.

Smail, Thomas. "The Holy Spirit in the Holy Trinity." In *Nicene Christianity: The Future for a New Ecumenism,* edited by Christopher R. Seitz, 149-65. Grand Rapids: Brazos, 2001.

Smalley, Beryl. *The Study of the Bible in the Middle Ages.* 2d ed. Oxford: Blackwell, 1952.

Smith, James K. A. *The Fall of Interpretation: Philosophical Foundations for a Creational Hermeneutic.* Downers Grove, IL: IVP, 2000.

Snodgrass, Klyne. "Reading to Hear: A Hermeneutics of Hearing." *Horizons in Biblical Theology* 24, no. 1 (June 2002): 1-32.

Snyder, H. Gregory. *Teachers and Texts in the Ancient World.* London: Routledge, 2000.

Soskice, Janet Martin. *Metaphor and Religious Language.* Oxford: Clarendon, 1985.

Sperber, Dan, and Deirdre Wilson. "The Mapping Between the Mental and the Public Lexicon." *UCL Working Papers in Linguistics* 9 (1997): 1-19.

———. *Relevance: Communication and Cognition.* 2d ed. Oxford: Blackwell, 1995.

Springsted, Eric O. "Putnam, Plato and the Task of Theology." *Soundings* 73 (Spring 1990): 169-89.

———. "Theology and Spirituality: Or, Why Theology Is Not Critical Reflection on Religious Experience." In *Spirituality and Theology: Essays in Honor of Diogenes Allen,* edited by Eric O. Springsted, 49-62. Louisville: Westminster John Knox, 1998.

Stackhouse, John G., Jr., ed. *Evangelical Futures: A Conversation on Theological Method.* Grand Rapids: Baker, 2000.

Steiner, George. *After Babel.* Oxford: Oxford University Press, 1975.

———. *Real Presences.* Chicago: University of Chicago Press, 1989.

Stiver, Dan R. *Theology After Ricoeur: New Directions in Hermeneutical Theology.* Louisville: Westminster John Knox, 2001.

Stout, Jeffrey. "What Is the Meaning of a Text?" *New Literary History* 14 (1982): 1-11.

Stroup, George W. *The Promise of Narrative Theology: Recovering the Gospel in the Church.* Atlanta: John Knox, 1981.

Stuhlmacher, Peter. *Historical Criticism and Theological Interpretation of Scripture.* Translated by Roy A. Harrisville. Philadelphia: Fortress, 1977.

Suchocki, Marjorie. "The Symbolic Structure of Augustine's *Confessions.*" *JAAR* 50 (September 1982): 365-78.

Sugirtharajah, R. S. *The Bible and the Third World: Precolonial, Colonial and Postcolonial Encounters.* Cambridge: Cambridge University Press, 2001.

Tanner, Kathryn. *Theories of Culture: A New Agenda for Theology.* Minneapolis: Fortress, 1997.

Taylor, Charles. *Philosophical Arguments.* Cambridge, MA: Harvard University Press, 1997.

———. *Sources of the Self: The Making of the Modern Identity.* Cambridge, MA: Harvard University Press, 1989.

Terrien, Samuel L. *The Elusive Presence: Toward a New Biblical Theology.* Religious Perspectives, vol. 26. San Francisco: Harper & Row, 1978.

Thiel, John E. *Imagination and Authority: Theological Authorship in the Modern Tradition.* Minneapolis: Fortress, 1991.

Thiemann, Ronald F. *Constructing a Public Theology: The Church in a Pluralistic Culture.* Louisville: Westminster John Knox, 1991.

———. *Revelation and Theology: The Gospel as Narrated Promise.* Notre Dame: Notre Dame University Press, 1985.

Thiselton, Anthony C. *Interpreting God and the Postmodern Self: On Meaning, Manipulation and Promise.* Grand Rapids: Eerdmans, 1995.

———. *New Horizons in Hermeneutics: The Theory and Practice of Transforming Biblical Reading.* Grand Rapids: Zondervan, 1992.

———. "Speech-Act Theory and the Claim That God Speaks: Nicholas Wolterstorff's *Divine Discourse.*" *SJT* 50, no. 1 (1997): 97-110.

———. *The Two Horizons: New Testament Hermeneutics and Philosophical Description.* Grand Rapids: Eerdmans, 1980.

Thomson, Clive, ed. *Mikhail Bakhtin and the Epistemology of Discourse.* Critical Studies, vol. 2. Amsterdam-Atlanta: Rodopi, 1990.

Thornton, Martin. *The Function of Theology.* New York: Seabury, 1968.

Torrance, Thomas F. *Divine Meaning: Studies in Patristic Hermeneutics.* Edinburgh: T&T Clark, 1995.

Toulmin, Stephen. *Human Understanding: The Collective Use and Evolution of Concepts.* Princeton: Princeton University Press, 1972.

Tracy, David. *The Analogical Imagination: Christian Theology and the Culture of Pluralism.* New York: Crossroad, 1981.

———. "Can Virtue Be Taught? Education, Character, and the Soul." In *Theology and the University,* edited by John V. Apczynski, 131-48. Lanham, MD: University Press of America, 1990.

———. "Literary Theory and the Return of the Forms for Naming and Thinking God in Theology." *JR* 74 (July 1994): 302-19.

———. "Trinitarian Speculation and the Forms of Divine Self-Disclosure." In *The Trinity,* edited by Stephen Davis, Daniel Kendall, S.J., and Gerald O'Collins, S.J., 272-93. Oxford: Oxford University Press, 1999.

Treier, Daniel J. "The Superiority of Pre-Critical Exegesis?: Sic et Non." *TrinJ* 24 NS (2003): 77-103.

Vanderveken, Daniel. *Formal Semantics of Success and Satisfaction.* Vol. 2 of *Meaning and Speech Acts.* Cambridge: Cambridge University Press, 1990.

———. *Principles of Language Use.* Vol. 1 of *Meaning and Speech Acts.* Cambridge: Cambridge University Press, 1990.

Vanhoozer, Kevin J. "Body-Piercing, the Natural Sense, and the Task of Theological Interpretation: A Hermeneutical Homily on John 19:34." *Ex Auditu* 16 (2000): 1-29.

———, gen. ed. *Dictionary for Theological Interpretation of the Bible.* Grand Rapids: Baker Academic, & London: SPCK, 2005.

———. *The Drama of Doctrine: A Canonical-Linguistic Approach to Theology.* Louisville: Westminster John Knox, 2005.

———. *First Theology: God, Scripture, Hermeneutics.* Downers Grove, IL: IVP, 2002.

———. "From Canon to Concept: 'Same' and 'Other' in the Relation Between Biblical and Systematic Theology." *Scottish Bulletin of Evangelical Theology* 12, no. 2 (Autumn 1994): 96-124.

———. *Is There a Meaning in This Text? The Bible, the Reader, and the Morality of Literary Knowledge.* Grand Rapids: Zondervan, 1998.

———. "The Reader in New Testament Interpretation." In *Hearing the New Testament,* edited by Joel B. Green, 301-28. Grand Rapids: Eerdmans, 1995.

van Huyssteen, J. Wentzel. *Essays in Postfoundationalist Theology.* Grand Rapids: Eerdmans, 1997.

Van Leeuwen, Raymond C. "In Praise of Proverbs." In *Pledges of Jubilee: Essays on the Arts and Culture in Honor of Calvin G. Seerveld,* edited by Lambert Zuidervaart and Henry Luttikhuizen, 308-27. Grand Rapids: Eerdmans, 1995.

———. "Liminality and Worldview in Proverbs 1–9." *Semeia* 50 (1990): 111-44.

———. "Wealth and Poverty: System and Contradiction in Proverbs." *HS* 33 (1992): 25-36.

Volf, Miroslav, and Dorothy C. Bass, eds. *Practicing Theology: Beliefs and Practices in the Christian Life.* Grand Rapids: Eerdmans, 2002.

Volf, Miroslav, Carmen Krieg, and Thomas Kucharz, eds. *The Future of Theology: Essays in Honor of Jürgen Moltmann.* Grand Rapids: Eerdmans, 1996.

Wainwright, Geoffrey. *Doxology: The Praise of God in Worship, Doctrine and Life.* New York: Oxford University Press, 1980.

Walker, Larry L. "Tree of Life." In *NIDOTTE,* edited by Willem A. Van Gemeren, vol. 4, pp. 1260-61. Grand Rapids: Zondervan, 1997.

Ward, Timothy. *Word and Supplement: Speech Acts, Biblical Texts, and the Sufficiency of Scripture.* Oxford: Oxford University Press, 2002.

Warnock, G. J. *J. L. Austin.* London: Routledge, 1987.

Watson, Francis. "The Old Testament as Christian Scripture: A Response to Professor Seitz." *SJT* 52, no. 2 (1999): 227-32.

———, ed. *The Open Text: New Directions for Biblical Studies?* London: SCM, 1993.

———. *Text and Truth: Redefining Biblical Theology.* Grand Rapids: Eerdmans, 1997.

———. *Text, Church and World: Biblical Interpretation in Theological Perspective.* Grand Rapids: Eerdmans, 1994.

———. "What Does It Mean to Interpret the Bible Theologically?" Unpublished lecture presented at Trinity Evangelical Divinity School. Deerfield, IL, 2000.

Watson, Paul. "The Tree of Life." *Restoration Quarterly* 23, no. 4 (1980): 232-38.

Webb, William J. *Slaves, Women and Homosexuals: Exploring the Hermeneutics of Cultural Analysis.* Downers Grove, IL: IVP, 2001.

Webster, John. "Canon and Criterion: Some Reflections on a Recent Proposal." *SJT* 54, no. 2 (2001): 221-37.

———. "Criticism: Revelation and Disturbance." *Stimulus* 7, no. 1 (February 1999).

———. "The Dogmatic Location of the Canon." *Neue Zeitschrift für Systematische Theologie und Religionsphilosophie* 43, no. 1 (2001): 17-43.

———. *Word and Church: Essays in Christian Doctrine.* Edinburgh: T&T Clark, 2001.

Webster, John, and George P. Schner, eds. *Theology After Liberalism: A Reader.* Oxford: Blackwell, 2000.

Wells, David F. "Educating for a Countercultural Spirituality." In *Theological Education in the Evangelical Tradition,* edited by D. G. Hart and R. Albert Mohler, Jr., 290-99. Grand Rapids: Baker, 1996.

Wenham, Gordon J. *Genesis 1–15.* WBC, vol. 1. Dallas: Word, 1987.

Westberg, Daniel. *Right Practical Reason: Aristotle, Action, and Prudence in Aquinas.* Oxford: Clarendon, 1994.

Westphal, Merold. "Review Essay: Theology as Talking About a God Who Talks." *Modern Theology* 13, no. 4 (October 1997): 525-36.

———. "Taking Plantinga Seriously: Advice to Christian Philosophers." *Faith and Philosophy* 16, no. 2 (April 1999): 173-81.

———. "Taking St. Paul Seriously: Sin as an Epistemological Category." In *Christian Philosophy,* edited by Thomas P. Flint, 200-226. Notre Dame: Notre Dame University Press, 1990.

Whaling, Frank. "The Development of the Word 'Theology.'" *SJT* 34 (1981): 289-312.

Wheeler, Barbara G., and Edward Farley, eds. *Shifting Boundaries: Contextual Approaches to the Structure of Theological Education.* Louisville: Westminster John Knox, 1991.

Whitman, Jon, ed. *Interpretation and Allegory: Antiquity to the Modern Period.* Brill's Studies in Intellectual History, vol. 101. Leiden: Brill, 2000.

Whybray, R. N. *The Intellectual Tradition in the Old Testament.* BZAW, vol. 135. Berlin & New York: De Gruyter, 1974.

———. *Wisdom in Proverbs: The Concept of Wisdom in Proverbs 1–9.* Studies in Biblical Theology. Naperville, IL: Alec R. Allenson, 1965.

Wiles, Maurice F. *The Making of Christian Doctrine.* Cambridge: Cambridge University Press, 1967.

———. *The Remaking of Christian Doctrine.* Philadelphia: Westminster, 1978.

Wilken, Robert L., ed. *Aspects of Wisdom in Judaism and Early Christianity.* Notre Dame: Notre Dame University Press, 1975.

Williams, D. H. *Retrieving the Tradition and Renewing Evangelicalism: A Primer for Suspicious Protestants.* Grand Rapids: Eerdmans, 1999.

Williams, Rowan. "The Literal Sense of Scripture." *Modern Theology* 7, no. 2 (January 1991): 121-34.

———. *On Christian Theology.* Oxford: Blackwell, 2000.

Wilson, Gerald H. "Wisdom." In *NIDOTTE,* edited by Willem A. Van Gemeren, vol. 4, pp. 1276-85. Grand Rapids: Zondervan, 1997.

Wisse, Maarten. "The Meaning of the Authority of the Bible." *RelS* 36 (2000): 473-87.

Wolterstorff, Nicholas. *Divine Discourse: Philosophical Reflections on the Claim That God Speaks.* Cambridge: Cambridge University Press, 1995.

Wood, Charles M. *The Formation of Christian Understanding: Theological Hermeneutics.* 2d ed. Valley Forge, PA: Trinity Press International, 1993.

———. *An Invitation to Theological Study.* Valley Forge, PA: Trinity Press International, 1994.

———. "Scripture, Authenticity, and Truth." *JR* 76, no. 2 (April 1996): 189-205.

———. *Vision and Discernment: An Orientation in Theological Study.* Studies in Religious and Theological Scholarship. Atlanta: Scholars Press, 1985.

Wood, W. Jay. *Epistemology: Becoming Intellectually Virtuous.* Contours of Christian Philosophy. Downers Grove, IL: IVP, 1998.

Woodbridge, John D., and Thomas Edward McComiskey, eds. *Doing Theology in Today's World: Essays in Honor of Kenneth S. Kantzer.* Grand Rapids: Zondervan, 1991.

Woodhead, Linda. Review of *Interpreting God and the Postmodern Self,* by Anthony C. Thiselton. *Modern Theology* 13 (October 1997): 537-39.

———. "Theology and the Fragmentation of the Self." *IJST* 1, no. 1 (March 1999): 53-72.

Work, Telford. *Living and Active: Scripture in the Economy of Salvation.* Sacra Doctrina. Grand Rapids: Eerdmans, 2002.

Young, Frances M. *Biblical Exegesis and the Formation of Christian Culture.* Cambridge: Cambridge University Press, 1997.

———. *Virtuoso Theology: The Bible and Interpretation.* Cleveland: Pilgrim, 1993.

Zagzebski, Linda T. *Virtues of the Mind: An Inquiry into the Nature of Virtue and the Ethical Foundations of Knowledge.* Cambridge: Cambridge University Press, 1996.

Endnotes

Notes to Chapter 1

1. Friedrich Schleiermacher, *Brief Outline on the Study of Theology*, trans. Terrence N. Tice (Richmond, VA: John Knox, 1966). (German *Kurze Darstellung des theologischen Studiums zum Behuf einleitender Vorlesungen.* Berlin: G. Reimer, 1830.)

2. The importance — both symbolic and real — of Schleiermacher's pattern is demonstrated well in Charles M. Wood, *Vision and Discernment: An Orientation in Theological Study*, Studies in Religious and Theological Scholarship (Atlanta: Scholars Press, 1985).

3. See Edward Farley, *Theologia: The Fragmentation and Unity of Theological Education* (Philadelphia: Fortress, 1983); *The Fragility of Knowledge: Theological Education in the Church and the University* (Philadelphia: Fortress, 1988). Helpful introductions to the broader discussion include Barbara G. Wheeler and Edward Farley, eds., *Shifting Boundaries: Contextual Approaches to the Structure of Theological Education* (Louisville: Westminster John Knox, 1991); David H. Kelsey, *Between Athens and Berlin: The Theological Education Debate* (Grand Rapids: Eerdmans, 1993); Robert Banks, *Reenvisioning Theological Education: Exploring a Missional Alternative to Current Models* (Grand Rapids: Eerdmans, 1999), pp. 17-70; Jeff Astley, Leslie J. Francis, and Colin Crowder, eds., *Theological Perspectives on Christian Formation* (Grand Rapids: Eerdmans, 1996).

4. Wood criticizes Farley for lacking clarity on whether theology is a subjective *habitus* or an activity of inquiry, a charge to be discussed later. Compare Wood, *Vision*, p. 33, with Edward Farley, "Can Church Education Be Theological Education?" in *Theological Perspectives on Christian Formation*, pp. 31-44.

5. Frank Whaling, "The Development of the Word 'Theology'," *SJT* 34 (1981): 289-312.

6. George P. Schner, "Metaphors for Theology," in *Theology After Liberalism: A Reader*, ed. John Webster and George P. Schner (Oxford: Blackwell, 2000), p. 5; Gerhard Ebeling, *Studium der Theologie: Eine Enzyklopädische Orientierung* (Tübingen: J. C. B. Mohr [Paul Siebeck], 1975), p. 56.

7. Whaling, "Development," p. 297.

8. Whaling, "Development," pp. 298-99.

9. Whaling, "Development," p. 292.

10. Whaling, "Development," p. 299.

11. Andrew Louth, *Discerning the Mystery: An Essay on the Nature of Theology* (Oxford: Clarendon, 1983), p. 76.

12. G. R. Evans, *Old Arts and New Theology: The Beginnings of Theology as an Academic Discipline* (Oxford: Clarendon, 1980), p. 225.

13. Evans, *Old Arts,* p. 3.

14. Evans, *Old Arts,* pp. 29, 38. On the emergence of theology as a science, see H. D. Saffrey, O.P., "Theology as Science (3rd-6th Centuries)," in *Studia Patristica,* ed. Elizabeth A. Livingstone, vol. XXX, *1* (Leuven: Peeters, 1997), pp. 321-39; Edward D. English, ed., *Reading and Wisdom: The 'De Doctrina Christiana' in the Middle Ages* (Notre Dame: Notre Dame University Press, 1994); Ulrich Köpf, *Die Anfänge der theologischen Wissenschaftstheorie im 13. Jahrhundert* (Tübingen: Mohr, 1974). Köpf's charting of relevant sources on pp. 276-85 is especially helpful.

15. Schner, "Metaphors," p. 9; William J. Abraham, *Canon and Criterion in Christian Theology* (Oxford: Clarendon, 1998).

16. Yves M.-J. Congar, *A History of Theology,* ed. and trans. Hunter Guthrie (Garden City, NY: Doubleday, 1968), pp. 32-33.

17. Farley, *Theologia,* p. 31.

18. Evans, *Old Arts,* pp. 82-83, 93; Louth, *Discerning,* p. 5. Abelard, reading *intelligo* in 1 Cor. 14 to regard only discursive reasoning or dialectic questioning, departed from the Augustinian pattern and wove together *sapientia* and *scientia,* keeping *both* outside the context of contemplative illumination. See Eileen Kearney, "*Scientia* and *sapientia:* Reading Sacred Scripture at the Paraclete," in *From Cloister to Classroom: Monastic and Scholastic Approaches to Truth,* ed. E. Rozanne Elder (Kalamazoo, MI: Cistercian Publications, 1986), pp. 114-17.

19. Evans, *Old Arts,* p. 104. Augustine would be an exception worth considering as well (C. Clifton Black, "Augustinian Exegesis and the Nature of Christian Inquirers," in *Inquiring After God,* ed. Ellen T. Charry [Oxford: Blackwell, 2000], especially p. 229).

20. Jean Leclercq, O.S.B., *The Love of Learning and the Desire for God: A Study of Monastic Culture,* trans. Catharine Misrahi, 3d ed. (New York: Fordham University Press, 1982), pp. 15-16.

21. Leclercq, *Love of Learning,* p. 154; Schner, "Metaphors," p. 29.

22. Evans, *Old Arts,* p. 215.

23. Nicholas Lash, "Theologies at the Service of a Common Tradition," in *Theology on the Way to Emmaus* (London: SCM, 1986), p. 31.

24. Charles F. Melchert, *Wise Teaching: Biblical Wisdom and Educational Ministry* (Valley Forge, PA: Trinity Press International, 1998), p. 7.

25. Farley, *Theologia,* p. 60.

26. Beryl Smalley, *The Study of the Bible in the Middle Ages,* 2d ed. (Oxford: Blackwell, 1952), p. xvi.

27. Luke Anderson, O Cist., "Enthymeme and Dialectic: Cloister and Classroom," in *From Cloister to Classroom,* especially pp. 239, 244, 257, 268.

28. Randy L. Maddox, "The Recovery of Theology as a Practical Discipline," *TS* 51, no. 4 (December 1990): pp. 652-53.

29. Ebeling, *Studium der Theologie,* p. 119.

30. Richard A. Muller, "An Approach to Calvin: On Overcoming Modern Accommodations," in *The Unaccommodated Calvin* (Oxford: Oxford University Press, 2000), p. 15;

"Scholasticism in Calvin: A Question of Relation and Disjunction," in *The Unaccommodated Calvin*, p. 43.

31. Ellen T. Charry, *By the Renewing of Your Minds: The Pastoral Function of Christian Doctrine* (Oxford: Oxford University Press, 1997), pp. 176-221.

32. Maddox, "Recovery," pp. 652-53.

33. Bruce L. McCormack, "Setting the Mind on Things Above: The Immediate Practicality of Theoretical Knowledge of God," in *Theology in the Service of the Church*, ed. Wallace M. Alston, Jr. (Grand Rapids: Eerdmans, 2000), pp. 140-52.

34. Ellen T. Charry, "To What End Knowledge? The Academic Captivity of the Church," in *Theology in the Service of the Church*, p. 76.

35. Charry, "To What End Knowledge?" p. 79.

36. Charry, "To What End Knowledge?" p. 83.

37. Especially relevant to Thomas, Luther, and Calvin in Abraham's massive tome *(Canon and Criterion)* are chs. 5-7 (in particular, he cites Richard H. Popkin, *The History of Skepticism from Erasmus to Spinoza*, rev. ed. [Berkeley: University of California Press, 1979], on p. 164 n. 3).

38. Leclercq, *Love of Learning*, pp. 196, 200.

39. George A. Lindbeck, *The Nature of Doctrine: Religion and Theology in a Postliberal Age* (Philadelphia: Westminster, 1984).

40. Romanus Cessario, O.P., *Christian Faith and the Theological Life* (Washington, DC: Catholic University of America, 1996), p. 11.

41. Cessario, *Christian Faith*, p. 52.

42. Cessario, *Christian Faith*, pp. 75, 102, 115-17.

43. Nicholas Wolterstorff, "The Travail of Theology in the Modern Academy," in *The Future of Theology: Essays in Honor of Jürgen Moltmann*, ed. Miroslav Volf, Carmen Krieg and Thomas Kucharz (Grand Rapids: Eerdmans, 1996), p. 40.

44. Muller's assessment is that Calvin's polemic against "scholasticism" is related to the scholastic distinction over theology as a speculative or practical discipline, which he defines as whether theology's teachings "are to be known as a goal in themselves . . . [or] to be known insofar as they conduce to a particular goal" ("Scholasticism in Calvin," p. 48). Whereas intellectualism tends to view theology on the contemplative or speculative side, voluntarism tends to view theology as primarily practical ("*Fides* and *cognitio* in Relation to the Problem of Intellect and Will in the Theology of John Calvin," in *The Unaccommodated Calvin*, p. 162). Muller sees Calvin prioritizing the intellect temporally, the will causally, and leaning slightly to the voluntarist (and hence practical) side (p. 171).

45. Richard A. Muller, "The Study of Calvin: Contexts and Directions," in *The Unaccommodated Calvin*, p. 180.

46. Abraham, *Canon and Criterion*, p. 166.

47. Abraham, *Canon and Criterion*, p. 180.

48. Wolterstorff, "Travail," p. 41.

49. David F. Wells, "Educating for a Countercultural Spirituality," in *Theological Education in the Evangelical Tradition*, ed. D. G. Hart and R. Albert Mohler, Jr. (Grand Rapids: Baker, 1996), pp. 295-97.

50. Walter C. Kaiser, Jr., "The Nature and Criteria of Theological Scholarship: An Evangelical Critique and Plan," *Theological Education* 32, no. 1 (1995): 68-69.

51. Harold O. J. Brown, "On Method and Means in Theology," in *Doing Theology in To-*

day's World: Essays in Honor of Kenneth S. Kantzer, ed. John D. Woodbridge and Thomas Edward McComiskey (Grand Rapids: Zondervan, 1991), p. 153. See also Fred H. Klooster, "How Reformed Theologians 'Do Theology' in Today's World," in *Doing Theology in Today's World,* pp. 236-37.

52. Schner, "Metaphors."

53. Klooster, "How Reformed Theologians," p. 235.

54. Langdon Gilkey, "Theology as the Interpretation of Faith for Church and World," in *The Vocation of the Theologian,* ed. Theodore W. Jennings, Jr. (Philadelphia: Fortress, 1985), pp. 91, 93.

55. Richard Grigg, *Theology as a Way of Thinking* (Atlanta: Scholars Press, 1990), p. 13.

56. Theodore W. Jennings, Jr., "Theology as the Construction of Doctrine," in *The Vocation of the Theologian,* pp. 72-73.

57. Schubert M. Ogden, "Theology and Biblical Interpretation," *JR* 76, no. 2 (April 1996): 178.

58. Wolterstorff, "Travail," p. 41.

59. Edward Farley, *Ecclesial Reflection: An Anatomy of Theological Method* (Philadelphia: Fortress, 1982).

60. John Macquarrie, *Principles of Christian Theology* (New York: Scribner, 1977).

61. Wolfhart Pannenberg, *Wissenschaftstheorie und Theologie* (Frankfurt am Main: Suhrkamp Verlag, 1973), p. 424.

62. Compare F. LeRon Shults, *The Postfoundationalist Task of Theology: Wolfhart Pannenberg and the New Theological Rationality* (Grand Rapids: Eerdmans, 2000), with J. Wentzel van Huyssteen, *Essays in Postfoundationalist Theology* (Grand Rapids: Eerdmans, 1997).

63. Ronald F. Thiemann, *Constructing a Public Theology: The Church in a Pluralistic Culture* (Louisville: Westminster John Knox, 1991).

64. Nicholas Lash, "Theory, Theology, and Ideology," in *Theology on the Way to Emmaus* (London: SCM, 1986), p. 137.

65. Farley, *Fragility,* p. 133.

66. Farley, *Fragility,* p. 64.

67. Farley, *Theologia,* p. 35.

68. Farley, *Theologia,* pp. 46 n. 12, 47 n. 15.

69. Farley, *Theologia,* pp. 156, 170. See also Farley, *Ecclesial Reflection,* especially pp. 121-22.

70. Farley, *Theologia,* p. 164.

71. Farley, *Ecclesial Reflection,* pp. 180, 334.

72. Farley, *Theologia,* p. 181.

73. Craig R. Dykstra, "Reconceiving Practice," in *Shifting Boundaries,* p. 65 n. 28.

74. Banks, *Reenvisioning,* p. 41.

75. Banks, *Reenvisioning,* p. 32.

76. John E. Thiel, *Imagination and Authority: Theological Authorship in the Modern Tradition* (Minneapolis: Fortress, 1991), pp. 131-33.

77. Thiel, *Imagination and Authority,* pp. 158, 211-15.

78. Schner, "Metaphors."

79. Jung Young Lee, "Multicultural and Global Theological Scholarship: An Asian American Perspective," *Theological Education* 32, no. 1 (1995): 53.

80. Lee, "Multicultural and Global," p. 43.

81. Lee, "Multicultural and Global," pp. 54-55.

82. Mark A. McIntosh, *Mystical Theology: The Integrity of Spirituality and Theology* (London: Blackwell, 1998), p. 30.

83. McIntosh, *Mystical Theology,* p. 40.

84. David Tracy, *The Analogical Imagination: Christian Theology and the Culture of Pluralism* (New York: Crossroad, 1981), p. 5.

85. Wood, *Vision,* pp. 27-29.

86. Wood, *Vision,* p. 30.

87. Wood, *Vision,* p. 33.

88. Wood, *Vision,* pp. 21, 91.

89. Wood, *Vision,* p. 24.

90. Wood, *Vision,* p. 73.

91. Wood, *Vision,* pp. 84-88.

92. Wood, *Vision,* pp. 38-40.

93. For instance, Ebeling defines theology as "kritische Explikation . . . was auf Grund christlichen Glaubens in Konfrontation mit aller relevanten Überlieferung und Erfahrung über das Ineinander von Gotteserfahrung, Welterfahrung und Selbsterfahrung auszusagen ist" (*Studium der Theologie,* p. 171). Note Charles Wood's other works in the hermeneutical tradition: *The Formation of Christian Understanding: Theological Hermeneutics,* 2d ed. (Valley Forge, PA: Trinity Press International, 1993); *An Invitation to Theological Study* (Valley Forge, PA: Trinity Press International, 1994); "Theological Education and Education for Church Leadership," in *Theological Perspectives on Christian Formation,* pp. 303-14; "Theological Inquiry and Theological Education," in *Theological Perspectives on Christian Formation,* pp. 342-58.

94. Ogden, "Theology and Biblical Interpretation," p. 177. For a German instance of this standard breakdown, see Anton Grabner-Haider, *Theorie der Theologie als Wissenschaft* (Munich: Kösel-Verlag, 1974).

95. Ogden, "Theology and Biblical Interpretation," pp. 178-79.

96. See especially Wood, *Formation,* 20-29.

97. Don S. Browning, "Toward a Fundamental and Strategic Practical Theology," in *Shifting Boundaries,* p. 319.

98. Browning, "Toward a Fundamental and Strategic Practical Theology," p. 297.

99. Banks, *Reenvisioning,* p. 56.

100. Banks, *Reenvisioning,* pp. 58-59.

101. Banks, *Reenvisioning,* p. 168.

102. J. Andrew Kirk, *The Mission of Theology and Theology as Mission* (Valley Forge, PA: Trinity Press International, 1997), p. 50.

103. Kirk, *Mission of Theology,* pp. 8-10, 50.

104. Kirk, *Mission of Theology,* p. 21.

105. Geoffrey Wainwright, *Doxology: The Praise of God in Worship, Doctrine and Life* (New York: Oxford University Press, 1980), p. 9; "Theology as Churchly Reflection," in *The Vocation of the Theologian,* pp. 9-24.

106. Wainwright, *Doxology,* p. 217.

107. Wainwright, *Doxology,* pp. 175-77.

108. Martin Thornton, *The Function of Theology* (New York: Seabury, 1968), pp. 18, 21.

109. Clodovis Boff, *Theology and Praxis: Epistemological Foundations* (Maryknoll, NY: Orbis, 1987), ch. 1.

110. Boff, *Theology and Praxis*, p. 211. See also José Miguez-Bonino, "Theology as Critical Reflection and Liberating Praxis," in *The Vocation of the Theologian*, pp. 37-48.

111. Jaroslav Pelikan, *The Christian Tradition: A History of the Development of Doctrine*, vol. 1, *The Emergence of the Catholic Tradition (100-600)* (Chicago: University of Chicago Press, 1971), p. 5.

112. Maddox, "Recovery," pp. 665-69.

113. Maddox, "Recovery," pp. 670-71; Dykstra, "Reconceiving Practice," p. 40.

114. Alasdair MacIntyre, *After Virtue: A Study in Moral Theory*, 2d ed. (Notre Dame: Notre Dame University Press, 1984), pp. 186-87.

115. Dykstra, "Reconceiving Practice," pp. 44-45.

116. Dykstra, "Reconceiving Practice," p. 49.

117. Dykstra, "Reconceiving Practice," p. 35.

118. See Browning, "Toward a Fundamental and Strategic Practical Theology," especially p. 309; also, on "naming present practice," Thomas Groome, *Sharing Faith: A Comprehensive Approach to Religious Education and Pastoral Ministry* (San Francisco: Harper Collins, 1991).

119. Stanley Hauerwas, *The Peaceable Kingdom: A Primer in Christian Ethics* (Notre Dame: Notre Dame University Press, 1983), pp. 54-55.

120. James Wm. McClendon, Jr., *Systematic Theology*, vol. 2, *Doctrine* (Nashville: Abingdon, 1994), p. 46.

121. McClendon, *Doctrine*, pp. 28-29.

122. McClendon, *Doctrine*, p. 31.

123. David H. Kelsey, *To Understand God Truly: What's Theological About a Theological School* (Louisville: Westminster John Knox, 1992), p. 34.

124. Kelsey, *To Understand God Truly*, p. 46.

125. Kelsey, *Between Athens and Berlin*, p. 226.

126. Kelsey, *To Understand God Truly*, pp. 123-29.

127. Kelsey, *To Understand God Truly*, pp. 112, 135.

128. Kelsey, *To Understand God Truly*, pp. 200-201.

129. Kelsey, *To Understand God Truly*, pp. 206-7.

130. Kelsey, *To Understand God Truly*, pp. 232, 235.

131. Kelsey, *To Understand God Truly*, p. 216.

132. Kelsey, *To Understand God Truly*, p. 236.

133. Kelsey, *To Understand God Truly*, p. 179.

134. Kelsey, *To Understand God Truly*, p. 238.

135. Kelsey, *To Understand God Truly*, p. 214.

136. Reinhard Hütter, "Worth Discussing: Two Books by David Kelsey," *Currents in Theology and Mission* 22 (F 1995): 49-52.

137. McCormack, "Setting the Mind," pp. 150-51; Reinhard Hütter, *Suffering Divine Things: Theology as Church Practice*, trans. Doug Stott (Grand Rapids: Eerdmans, 2000), pp. 30-32, 37.

138. David F. Ford, *Self and Salvation: Being Transformed*, Studies in Christian Doctrine (Cambridge: Cambridge University Press, 1999), pp. 1, 17.

139. Ford, *Self and Salvation*, pp. 177-78.

140. Ford, *Self and Salvation,* p. 21; Rowan Williams, *On Christian Theology* (Oxford: Blackwell, 2000), pp. xii-iv.

141. Richard A. Muller, "The Study of Theology," in *Foundations of Contemporary Interpretation,* ed. Moisés Silva (Grand Rapids: Zondervan, 1996), p. 645.

142. Two different illustrations are Wood, *Formation,* especially pp. 20-29; Stephen E. Fowl, *Engaging Scripture* (Oxford: Blackwell, 1998), especially p. 30.

143. Chronicled afresh in "The Bible, the Question of God, and Christian Faith," ch. 1 in R. W. L. Moberly, *The Bible, Theology, and Faith: A Study of Abraham and Jesus,* Studies in Christian Doctrine (Cambridge: Cambridge University Press, 2000), pp. 1-44.

Notes to Chapter 2

1. Colin Crowder, "Wisdom and Passion: Wittgenstein, Kierkegaard, and Religious Belief," in *Where Shall Wisdom Be Found?* ed. Stephen C. Barton (Edinburgh: T&T Clark, 1999), pp. 363-80.

2. First suggested to me by Willem Van Gemeren.

3. As a survey of commentators would reveal, the somewhat self-contained 3:13-18 can be related to surrounding units in various ways. The mode of address is direct up to v. 13 (with a mild rheme in v. 5) and becomes direct again in v. 21, remaining so to the end of the chapter; conversely, the secure life of vv. 13-18 remains the theme through v. 26, at which point the subject switches. But this switch is not extreme even there, for the communal care encouraged in vv. 27-35 resonates with the kindness of v. 3 and the stewardship of vv. 9-10.

4. William P. Brown, *Character in Crisis: A Fresh Approach to the Wisdom Literature of the Old Testament* (Grand Rapids: Eerdmans, 1996), p. 35.

5. Gerald H. Wilson, "Wisdom," in *NIDOTTE,* ed. Willem A. Van Gemeren (Grand Rapids: Zondervan, 1997), 4:1283. Or it might even be that we should presuppose the Torah behind this discourse, as reader background that the Proverbial author-editor assumes: could it even be that the exhortations of Proverbs are meant to enable the son to live according to the Torah? So Stuart Weeks, "Wisdom in the Old Testament," in *Where Shall Wisdom Be Found?* p. 26.

6. Kathleen A. Farmer, *Who Knows What Is Good? A Commentary on Proverbs and Ecclesiastes,* ITC (Grand Rapids: Eerdmans, 1991), pp. 36-37.

7. Joseph Blenkinsopp, *Wisdom and Law in the Old Testament: The Ordering of Life in Israel and Early Judaism,* Oxford Bible Series (Oxford: Oxford University Press, 1983), p. 137. The motif is also found in Sirach, on which see Claudia V. Camp, "The Female Sage in Ancient Israel and in the Biblical Wisdom Literature," in *The Sage in Israel and the Ancient Near East,* ed. John G. Gammie and Leo G. Perdue (Winona Lake, IN: Eisenbrauns, 1990), p. 195. This has interesting implications for ch. 31, where we can no longer read of the excellent wife merely regarding marriage; there is apparently a connection to Wisdom. Luis Alonso-Schökel thinks Eve is in view ("Sapiential and Covenant Themes in Genesis 2–3," in *Studies in Ancient Israelite Wisdom,* ed. James L. Crenshaw [New York: Ktav, 1976], p. 473)! Kathleen M. O'Connor even wonders about canonical connections to the women of the two succeeding books, Ruth and the Song of Songs: could these women manifest Wisdom (*The Wisdom Literature,* Message of Biblical Spirituality [Wilmington, DE: Michael Glazier, 1988], pp. 81-83)?

8. William McKane, *Proverbs: A New Approach,* OTL (Philadelphia: Westminster, 1970), pp. 214-15, 295.

9. McKane, *Proverbs,* p. 296.

10. McKane, *Proverbs,* p. 295.

11. William P. Brown, *The Ethos of the Cosmos* (Grand Rapids: Eerdmans, 1996), p. 284. McKane thinks these verses, and their relation to Deutero-Isaiah, were instrumental to the development of 8:22 ff. (*Proverbs,* p. 297). Although, of note to the contrary, Arndt Meinhold finds 3:13-20 to be a development from ch. 8 ("Gott und Mensch in Proverbien III," *VT* 37 [October 1987]: 469-70). Wisdom is also personified as a woman in Prov. 1:20-33; 4:5-9; 31:11-31; Sir. 24; 51; Wis. 7–9; and perhaps Song of Songs, if one follows O'Connor, *Wisdom Literature,* p. 64.

12. Roland E. Murphy, *The Tree of Life: An Exploration of Biblical Wisdom Literature,* 2d ed. (Grand Rapids: Eerdmans, 1996), p. 139.

13. R. N. Whybray, *Wisdom in Proverbs: The Concept of Wisdom in Proverbs 1–9,* Studies in Biblical Theology (Naperville, IL: Alec R. Allenson, 1965), p. 104.

14. Judith M. Hadley, "Wisdom and the Goddess," in *Wisdom in Ancient Israel,* ed. John Day et al. (Cambridge: Cambridge University Press, 1995), p. 241.

15. R. W. L. Moberly, "Solomon and Job: Divine Wisdom in Human Life," in *Where Shall Wisdom Be Found?* p. 16.

16. Samuel L. Terrien, *The Elusive Presence: Toward a New Biblical Theology,* Religious Perspectives, vol. 26 (San Francisco: Harper & Row, 1978), pp. 357-58.

17. Brown, *Ethos,* p. 277.

18. Murphy, *Tree of Life,* p. 29.

19. Meinhold, "Gott und Mensch," p. 475.

20. Meinhold, "Gott und Mensch," p. 470.

21. Murphy, *Tree of Life,* p. 17.

22. A strong case has been made that Prov. 1–9 already qualifies "retribution" theology, in accord with much of the other wisdom literature such as Qohelet. For confirmation of this conclusion (perhaps downplaying the tension more than I have), see Raymond C. Van Leeuwen, "Liminality and Worldview in Proverbs 1–9," *Semeia* 50 (1990): 111-44; "Wealth and Poverty: System and Contradiction in Proverbs," *HS* 33 (1992): 25-36; "In Praise of Proverbs," in *Pledges of Jubilee: Essays on the Arts and Culture in Honor of Calvin G. Seerveld,* ed. Lambert Zuidervaart and Henry Luttikhuizen (Grand Rapids: Eerdmans, 1995), 308-27; also Richard L. Schultz, "Unity or Diversity in Wisdom Theology? A Canonical and Covenantal Perspective," *TynBul* 48, no. 2 (November 1997): 271-306.

23. O'Connor, *Wisdom Literature,* p. 76.

24. Later Jewish writings often locate the tree in Paradise, so that immortality is its fruit (Larry L. Walker, "Tree of Life," in *NIDOTTE,* 4:1260). However, while the mythic ancient Near Eastern parallels link the tree to immortality, they deny that immortality to humans (Leo G. Perdue, *Wisdom and Creation: The Theology of Wisdom Literature* [Nashville: Abingdon, 1994], p. 53). The zeal of scholars like Perdue for connecting the material in Proverbs with these myths seems to me overdone, despite connections between the symbol of a tree, the Canaanite Asherah, and Israel's high places according to E. O. James, *The Tree of Life: An Archaeological Study* (Leiden: E. J. Brill, 1966), especially pp. 16-17, 38.

25. T. A. Perry, *Wisdom Literature and the Structure of Proverbs* (University Park: Pennsylvania State University Press, 1993), p. 99.

26. Sirach 39:1-35 also seems to exemplify this. See Leo G. Perdue, "Cosmology and the Social Order in the Wisdom Tradition," in *The Sage in Israel,* p. 462.

27. Henri Blocher, *In the Beginning: The Opening Chapters of Genesis,* trans. David G. Preston (Downers Grove, IL: IVP, 1984), p. 125.

28. Blenkinsopp, *Wisdom and Law,* p. 37.

29. Alonso-Schökel, "Sapiential," pp. 472-73.

30. Alonso-Schökel, "Sapiential," pp. 478-80.

31. Gordon J. Wenham, *Genesis 1–15,* WBC, vol. 1 (Dallas: Word, 1987), p. 91.

32. Karl Jaros, "Die Motive der Heiligen Bäume und der Schlange in Gen 2–3," *ZAW* 92, no. 2 (1980): 215.

33. Paul Kübel, "Ein Wortspiel in Genesis 3 und Sein Hintergrund: Die 'Kluge' Schlange und die 'Nackten' Menschen: Uberlegungen zur Vorgeschichte von Gen 2–3," *Biblische Notizen* 93 (1998): 16.

34. Kübel, "Ein Wortspiel," p. 22.

35. Wenham, *Genesis 1–15,* p. 72.

36. Alonso-Schökel, "Sapiential," p. 479.

37. Blocher, *In the Beginning,* pp. 151-54.

38. Wenham, *Genesis 1–15,* p. 73.

39. Walker, "Tree of Life," 4:1259.

40. Brown, *Ethos,* pp. 155, 389, 222.

41. Wenham, *Genesis 1–15,* p. 75.

42. Brown, *Character in Crisis,* p. 41.

43. Brown, *Ethos,* p. 213.

44. Wenham, *Genesis 1–15,* p. 86.

45. Victor P. Hamilton, *The Book of Genesis Chapters 1–17,* NICOT (Grand Rapids: Eerdmans, 1990), p. 209; Paul Watson, "The Tree of Life," *Restoration Quarterly* 23, no. 4 (1980): 237.

46. Blocher, *In the Beginning,* pp. 122-23.

47. James, *Tree of Life,* p. 222.

48. Blocher, *In the Beginning,* pp. 125-26.

49. Hamilton, *Genesis 1–17,* p. 188.

50. A. Luc, "ערם," in *NIDOTTE,* 3:540.

51. Brown, *Ethos,* p. 155.

52. Terence E. Fretheim, "שׂכל," in *NIDOTTE,* 3:1243.

53. Brown, *Ethos,* pp. 155, 157.

54. Brown, *Ethos,* p. 223.

55. Leander E. Keck, "Rethinking 'New Testament Ethics'," *JBL* 115, no. 1 (Spring 1996): 3-16.

56. Henry A. Fischel, "The Transformation of Wisdom in the World of Midrash," in *Aspects of Wisdom in Judaism and Early Christianity,* ed. Robert L. Wilken (Notre Dame: Notre Dame University Press, 1975), pp. 70-71.

57. A hymnic fragment (106.20-28) from the *Teaching of Silvanus:* "For Christ is the Tree of Life. He is Wisdom. For he is Wisdom, he is also the Logos. He is Life and the Messenger and the Good Shepherd"; adduced in William R. Schödel, "Jewish Wisdom and the Formation of the Christian Ascetic," in *Aspects of Wisdom,* pp. 192-93. Reflecting on Job, Hans-Jürgen Hermisson argues that this particularity is necessary for wisdom to be experienced

concretely, in the face of a transcendent God: Christ and Torah were the only ways to maintain the ancient creation theology of wisdom ("Observations on the Creation Theology in Wisdom," in *Israelite Wisdom: Theological and Literary Essays in Honor of Samuel L. Terrien,* ed. John G. Gammie, et al. [Missoula, MT: Scholars Press, 1978], p. 55).

58. James, *Tree of Life,* pp. 106, 161-62.

59. Marjorie Suchocki, "The Symbolic Structure of Augustine's Confessions," *JAAR* 50 (September 1982): 370.

60. Suchocki, "Symbolic Structure," p. 366.

61. Suchocki, "Symbolic Structure," p. 374.

62. Murphy, *Tree of Life,* p. 147.

63. Perdue, *Wisdom and Creation,* pp. 332-33; R. N. Whybray, *The Intellectual Tradition in the Old Testament,* BZAW, vol. 135 (Berlin & New York: De Gruyter, 1974), p. 13.

64. Brown, *Character in Crisis,* p. 38.

65. Blenkinsopp, *Wisdom and Law,* pp. 130-31.

66. Perdue, *Wisdom and Creation,* p. 109.

67. Hans-Jürgen Hermisson, "Gottes Freiheit — Spielraum des Menschen: Alttestamentliche Aspekte eines Biblisch-Theologischen Themas," *ZTK* 82, no. 2 (1985): 152.

68. Perdue, *Wisdom and Creation,* p. 35. For a caution against overdoing order and creation theology in connection with wisdom, see Murphy, *Tree of Life,* pp. 115-21.

69. Roland E. Murphy, "Wisdom — Theses and Hypotheses," in *Israelite Wisdom,* p. 39.

70. Weeks, "Wisdom in the Old Testament," p. 29.

71. R. E. Clements, *Wisdom in Theology* (Grand Rapids: Eerdmans, 1992), p. 62.

72. Brown, *Character in Crisis,* p. 21.

73. Linda T. Zagzebski, *Virtues of the Mind: An Inquiry into the Nature of Virtue and the Ethical Foundations of Knowledge* (Cambridge: Cambridge University Press, 1996), pp. 211-31.

74. Brown, *Ethos,* p. 296.

75. Brown, *Character in Crisis,* p. 10 n. 43.

76. Wilson, "Wisdom," 4:1281.

77. Wilson, "Wisdom," 4:1283.

78. Murphy, *Tree of Life,* pp. 124-25.

79. Oliver O'Donovan, *Resurrection and Moral Order: An Outline for Evangelical Ethics,* 2d ed. (Grand Rapids: Eerdmans, 1994), p. 19. He notes on p. 85 that the ontological-epistemological distinction is one that the Western natural law tradition cannot keep clear.

80. O'Donovan, *Resurrection and Moral Order,* p. 88.

81. O'Donovan, *Resurrection and Moral Order,* p. 89.

82. Murphy, *Tree of Life,* p. 126.

83. Ellen F. Davis, "Preserving Virtues: Renewing the Tradition," in *Character and Scripture,* ed. William P. Brown (Grand Rapids: Eerdmans, 2002), pp. 183-201.

84. There is specialist disagreement over this, both in relation to quests for the historical Jesus (in what sense was he a wisdom teacher?) and quests for the origins of Paul's Christology. On the former, see the survey in James D. G. Dunn, "Jesus: Teacher of Wisdom or Wisdom Incarnate?" in *Where Shall Wisdom Be Found?* pp. 75-92. On the latter, we cannot be certain enough of Paul's or of certain "wisdom" concepts to connect them, so as to establish or exclude on this basis the preexistence of Jesus Christ as the divine Son. The danger, moreover, of fashioning a Jesus Christ according to our preferred image of wisdom is great; see

Gordon D. Fee, "Wisdom Christology in Paul: A Dissenting View," in *The Way of Wisdom,* ed. J. I. Packer and Sven K. Soderlund (Grand Rapids: Zondervan, 2000), pp. 251-79; Karen H. Jobes, "Sophia Christology: The Way of Wisdom?" in *The Way of Wisdom,* pp. 226-50. Yet Paul does not simply exclude wisdom vocabulary (as Fee's ardent exclusion of wisdom from the conceptual world of his Christology seems to do). Paul substitutes a person — and a cruciform pattern — for the prior concept(s) of wisdom, but still was willing to speak the language in a sense.

85. Ever since World War II, Christians have been rethinking Jewish-Christian relations and how they bear on theological interpretation of Scripture (indeed we should have been rethinking this long before that horrid episode). Christian theological interpretation makes an inescapably strong claim: "as Jesus cannot be understood apart from Jewish scripture, Jewish scripture cannot be understood apart from Jesus; what is needed is an interpretation which relates the two . . ." (R. W. L. Moberly, *The Bible, Theology, and Faith: A Study of Abraham and Jesus,* Studies in Christian Doctrine [Cambridge: Cambridge University Press, 2000], p. 51). But if both sides of that dialogue are given full weight, and if the claim is duly chastened as Moberly does ("to appeal to the privileged position of the Church as witness to Christ as a basis for ignoring, or persecuting, those who interpret the Bible differently will entail forfeiting that serendipitous sense that true understanding, like life and faith, is a gift"; p. 66), then Christians can perhaps proclaim Christ without doing violence either to his meaning or else to the meaning of Jewish lives.

86. σοφία and σοφός appear 34 times in the seven undisputed Pauline epistles; 26 of these occurrences come in 1 Cor. 1–3, where the term is negative except for Paul's play on a positive sense of the word in relation to the gospel. See Richard B. Hays, "Wisdom According to Paul," in *Where Shall Wisdom Be Found?* pp. 111-12.

87. Aristotle, *Nicomachean Ethics* 1141a.19-20.

88. Colin E. Gunton, "Christ, the Wisdom of God: A Study in Divine and Human Action," in *Where Shall Wisdom Be Found?* pp. 252-53.

89. Gordon D. Fee notes that this passage obviously influences Col. 1:9 and Eph. 1:17, two passages important to the subject. Paul's own ministry follows upon Daniel (4:8, 9, 18; 5:11, 14) to some extent, although he "takes all the 'mystery' out" by suggesting its availability to all Gospel believers via the Spirit. See Eph. 3:4, in addition to 1 Cor. 2, and the comments in Gordon D. Fee, *God's Empowering Presence: The Holy Spirit in the Letters of Paul* (Peabody, MA: Hendrickson, 1994), pp. 908-9.

90. Stephen C. Barton, "Gospel Wisdom," in *Where Shall Wisdom Be Found?* pp. 99, 109.

91. The difficulty of finding a suitable English gloss is well-known. In this context, I feel the freedom to alternate between "prudence" and "practical reason," capitalizing on connections between Proverbs, Aristotle, and Thomas Aquinas, rather than connoting any particular nuance.

92. Keck, "Rethinking," p. 15.

93. Brown, *Ethos,* p. 314.

94. Hays, "Wisdom According to Paul," p. 114.

95. The σοφία vocabulary is used for חָכָם words more than 150 times in the LXX; next is φρόνησις, 12 times. The verbal evidence is a bit more ambiguous. For wisdom, חָכְמָה and תְּבוּנָה/בִּינָה are the key Hebrew OT terms, as evidenced in Deut. 4:5-6.

96. Aristotle, *Nicomachean Ethics* 1139b.16.

97. Aristotle, *Nicomachean Ethics* 1140a.25-29.

98. Aristotle, *Nicomachean Ethics* 1140b.6-8.

99. Zagzebski, *Virtues*, pp. 211-31.

100. Dio Chrysostum, *Orationes* 3.6.7, 29.7.5, 59.1.3; Clement of Alexandria, *Stromata* 1.24.159.4.1, 2.5.24.2.2, 6.15.125.4.1; Plutarch, *De Virtute Morali* 441.A.1, 443.E9-10.

101. For a sampling of noun uses, Prov. 3:13, 19; 7:4; 8:1; 10:23; 16:16; 19:8; 24:5; of God, Isa. 40:28; Jer. 10:12. The verb's usage is positive; see Deut. 32:29 for an example. Occasionally, as already seen, the word translates a negative concept, of craftiness (Gen. 3:1) or of human wisdom endangered by self-inflation (Prov. 3:7), but the dominant usage is positive. Most negative uses are adjectival (φρόνιμος), but even here the majority of occurrences are positive (for instance, Prov. 11:12, 29; 15:1, 21; 17:10, 21, 27, 28; 19:7). A related word group is αἴσθησις, for which see the translation of Prov. 14:6, 10, and 30 in particular.

102. Gunton, "Christ, the Wisdom of God," p. 254.

103. John Milbank, *Theology and Social Theory: Beyond Secular Reason* (Oxford: Blackwell, 1993), pp. 5-6, 399, 410-17, and the entire ch. 11, "Difference of Virtue, Virtue of Difference" (pp. 327-79). Milbank thinks φρόνησις to be problematic, because how is one to acquire the needed dispositions for virtue in the first place? (On the Greek concept, one recollects, or is socialized into, habits of the good.) His discussion highlights the need for Christians to speak in this context of "conversion" (see especially p. 415), even if we would differ at other points.

104. Such an emphasis on Israel's unique wisdom from the Torah is a relatively frequent occurrence in rabbinic literature; a handy example in relation to Deut. 4:5-6 is *b. ʿAbod. Zar.* 4b, where Torah observance will produce Israel's vindication, over against idolaters, in the world to come. Of course the Torah required interpretation in order for Israel to be wise; so, for instance, in *CD* 6:3 Qumran seemed to limit wisdom within Israel to rightly interpreting and observing the Torah.

105. Opposite τὰ ἀδιάφορα, a contrast from which James D. G. Dunn detects a criticism of the Jewish expectation to distinguish essentials from non-essentials straight out of the Torah (this view seems to read in anticipation of Rom. 14) (*Romans 1–8*, WBC, vol. 38A [Dallas: Word, 1988], p. 111).

106. Harry Y. Gamble, *Books and Readers in the Early Church: A History of Early Christian Texts* (New Haven & London: Yale University Press, 1995), pp. 7-8. Although, according to Martin Goodman, primary education even in Galilee began by teaching literacy, it did not meet with universal success; about as many could not sign their names as could (and even that would be a fairly minimalist definition of literacy). Whatever secondary education there was in Galilee probably stuck to the laws of Judaism; "wisdom was defined as expertise in legal minutiae," whereas outside Palestine, classic texts would have followed on the Greek alphabet, etc. See Martin Goodman, *State and Society in Roman Galilee, A.D. 132-212*, Oxford Centre for Postgraduate Hebrew Studies (Totowa, NJ: Rowman & Allanheld, 1983), pp. 71-81. This is all the more striking if Gamble is correct, that the Jewish literacy rate was probably higher than the Gentile rate. A more recent survey of conclusions may be found in Alan R. Millard, *Reading and Writing in the Time of Jesus* (New York: New York University Press, 2000), especially ch. 6, pp. 154-84, "Who Read and Who Wrote?": it must be admitted that in principle every Jewish male was to read from the Scriptures in synagogue services, but probably this ideal was not fully realized; evidence is ambiguous in the Gospels (e.g., Jesus' "have you never read" versus "you have heard that it was said"), and generally inadequate.

107. The phrase λόγου δικαιοσύνης (5:13) is difficult, but best taken as an objective genitive referring to Scripture, especially in its ethical dimensions. This accords with τῶν λογίων τοῦ θεοῦ in 5:12 referring to Scripture as that which contains teaching, the στοιχεῖα τῆς ἀρχῆς which they need again. See Paul Ellingworth, *The Epistle to the Hebrews,* NIGTC (Grand Rapids: Eerdmans, 1993), 306-7. Moreover, it accords with the approach to theology and exhortation characteristic throughout the epistle, and especially in ch. 7. Graham Hughes helpfully writes, "The corrective word was hopefully to be administered by one member of the congregation to the others. . . . the author sees himself not as performing any specialist role but simply that of any Christian about his business within the fellowship." See Graham Hughes, *Hebrews and Hermeneutics: The Epistle to the Hebrews as a New Testament Example of Biblical Interpretation,* SNTSMS, vol. 36 (Cambridge: Cambridge University Press, 1979), especially p. 49.

108. So far I have not found this connection (φωτίζω, ὀφθαλμοί) mentioned in any commentaries, though it is hard for a theologian to keep up or be exhaustive. The discussion usually focuses upon non-canonical literature, such as Qumran (1QS 2:3); see Andrew T. Lincoln, *Ephesians,* WBC, vol. 42 (Dallas: Word, 1990), p. 58.

109. Translating δοκιμάζω is always tenuous, because it can shade from testing to approving/judging based on testing (*BAGD,* 2d ed., p. 202). It integrates "the transitive and intransitive meanings of 'probing' and 'testing'" always with moral overtones (Bernd Wannenwetsch, "'Members of One Another': *Charis,* Ministry and Representation: A Politico-Ecclesial Reading of Romans 12," in *A Royal Priesthood? The Use of the Bible Ethically and Politically,* ed. Craig Bartholomew et al., Scripture and Hermeneutics, vol. 3 [Grand Rapids: Zondervan, 2002], p. 207 n. 24). Lincoln's translation, "discovering," is a nice way to emphasize its connection to Christian experience and praxis in context. He rightly summarizes that "living as children of light will involve exercising a responsible freedom and developing an intuitive sense about how to act in a given situation" (Lincoln, *Ephesians,* pp. 328-29). The language of "pleasing the Lord" is sacrificial, particularly after 5:2; see Markus Barth, *Ephesians 4–6,* AB, vol. 34A (New York: Doubleday, 1974), pp. 559, 569.

110. The Stoic usage of this term may have led to the Fathers seeing here the ability to recognize heresy; so Moisés Silva, *Philippians,* WEC (Chicago: Moody, 1988), p. 63. Alternatively, Gordon D. Fee detects a contrast with *adiaphora* in anticipation of the warning about Judaizers in ch. 3: Paul prays for them to discover what is essentially Christian, contra circumcision and like matters (*Paul's Letter to the Philippians,* NICNT [Grand Rapids: Eerdmans, 1995], pp. 101-2). Further, Peter T. O'Brien seems to treat the phrase corporately (*The Epistle to the Philippians,* NIGTC [Grand Rapids: Eerdmans, 1991], pp. 77-78). These latter emphases are helpful in view of the epistle's thrust and circumstances: Paul prayed for a loving church, which required that they — as a church and as individuals therein — adopt a common mindset about what was truly essential, which would issue in discernment about particular occasions.

111. Cited in Lincoln, *Ephesians,* p. 341.

112. The language of God being "pleased," with its sacrificial tone, might imply degree: God could be pleased to varying extent, most pleased by supererogatory acts. Robert Song notes the problem conventional morality has in handling the supererogatory, and thinks this points the way toward wisdom (Robert Song, "Wisdom as the End of Morality," in *Where Shall Wisdom Be Found?* pp. 295-306). In something of a parallel concern, "As millions starve, ought anyone to be feasting? . . . Can we even sustain work of compassion and justice in the

right spirit if we are not also having some celebratory foretaste of the kingdom of God? Or, looking at the story of the early church in the Acts of the Apostles, in the light of the explosion of joy and gratitude that followed the resurrection and Pentecost is it not the most obvious thing in the world both to share with those in need and also to celebrate with them?" (David F. Ford, *Self and Salvation: Being Transformed,* Studies in Christian Doctrine [Cambridge: Cambridge University Press, 1999], p. 269). Thus we must recognize the legitimacy of our own joy amidst the teleology applied by Christian φρόνησις: the occasional Christian tendency toward a normative asceticism is hereby checked.

113. David H. Kelsey, *To Understand God Truly: What's Theological About a Theological School* (Louisville: Westminster John Knox, 1992), p. 238.

114. Paul Ricoeur, *Oneself as Another,* trans. Kathleen McLaughlin Blamey (Chicago: University of Chicago Press, 1992), p. 4.

115. Ricoeur, *Oneself as Another,* p. 3.

116. Charles Taylor, "Overcoming Epistemology," in *Philosophical Arguments* (Cambridge, MA: Harvard University Press, 1997), p. 18.

117. Ricoeur, *Oneself as Another,* pp. 3-16.

118. J. L. Austin, *How to Do Things with Words* (Oxford: Oxford University Press, 1962).

119. Ricoeur, *Oneself as Another,* pp. 16-17.

120. Narrative is not the exclusive form: "self-understanding is an interpretation; interpretation of the self, in turn, finds in the narrative, among other signs and symbols, a privileged form of mediation." See Ricoeur, *Oneself as Another,* pp. 114-15 especially n. 1.

121. From Ricoeur see especially "The Self and the Ethical Aim," pp. 169-202, which may be fruitfully read with MacIntyre on the "practice" and the "quest"; see Alasdair MacIntyre, *After Virtue: A Study in Moral Theory,* 2d ed. (Notre Dame: Notre Dame University Press, 1984), especially pp. 186-94, 219. According to the latter, the medievals had a "determinate goal" for their quest, but did not assume that the goal had already been "adequately characterized": they were still coming to know both themselves and their goal.

122. Anthony C. Thiselton, *Interpreting God and the Postmodern Self: On Meaning, Manipulation and Promise* (Grand Rapids: Eerdmans, 1995), p. 48.

123. Linda Woodhead, Review of *Interpreting God and the Postmodern Self,* by Anthony C. Thiselton, *Modern Theology* 13 (October 1997): 537-39.

124. Thiselton, *Interpreting God,* pp. 107, 113.

125. Thiselton, *Interpreting God,* p. 157.

126. Thiselton, *Interpreting God,* pp. 153, 160-61.

127. Ricoeur, *Oneself as Another,* p. 247.

128. Kevin J. Vanhoozer, "Human Being, Individual and Social," in *The Cambridge Companion to Christian Doctrine,* ed. Colin E. Gunton (Cambridge: Cambridge University Press, 1997), especially p. 179.

129. Andrew Louth, *Discerning the Mystery: An Essay on the Nature of Theology* (Oxford: Clarendon, 1983), pp. 76-77; David Tracy, "Can Virtue Be Taught? Education, Character, and the Soul," in *Theology and the University,* ed. John V. Apczynski (Lanham, MD: University Press of America, 1990), p. 132.

130. See Linda Woodhead, "Theology and the Fragmentation of the Self," *IJST* 1, no. 1 (March 1999): 53-72. Here she details her skepticism about what she calls the "fragmentation thesis" (that postmodernism is fragmenting the modern self, or that there was the modern self to break apart; pp. 54-57): "fragmentation may be viewed not so much as the result of

certain universal and unilinear modern processes, but as born from the confusion generated by the plural modes of selfhood available to modern men and women" (p. 58). Of these plural modes, the one detailed here is labeled "bestowed selfhood." While this view has much to commend it, its vulnerability to certain criticisms — chiefly, the worry that people are left subjugated — suggests caution and openness to blending in other modes (pp. 70-72).

Indeed, David Ford *(Self and Salvation)* has interacted recently not just with Ricoeur but with Emmanuel Lévinas and Eberhard Jüngel on this subject. Taking our encounter with God in worship as one of "joyful obligation" (p. 79), which relates to the joy we find in making others joyful (pp. 278-79), Ford points to the possibility of a "hospitable," non-idolatrous, neither oppressive nor oppressed self.

131. Gerhard Ebeling, *Studium der Theologie: Eine Enzyklopädische Orientierung* (Tübingen: J. C. B. Mohr [Paul Siebeck], 1975), p. 56.

132. Ellen T. Charry, "To What End Knowledge? The Academic Captivity of the Church," in *Theology in the Service of the Church*, ed. Wallace M. Alston, Jr. (Grand Rapids: Eerdmans, 2000), p. 74; George P. Schner, "Metaphors for Theology," in *Theology After Liberalism: A Reader*, ed. John Webster and George P. Schner (Oxford: Blackwell, 2000), pp. 4-5.

133. Luke Timothy Johnson, *Scripture and Discernment in the Early Church*, 2d ed. (Nashville: Abingdon, 1996), p. 109.

134. Edward Farley, *Theologia: The Fragmentation and Unity of Theological Education* (Philadelphia: Fortress, 1983), p. 55.

135. Moberly, *Bible, Theology, and Faith*, pp. 38-39.

136. Ellen T. Charry, "Introduction," in *Inquiring After God*, ed. Ellen T. Charry (Oxford: Blackwell, 2000), p. xvii.

137. Ellen T. Charry, "Inquiring After God Through Discernment," in *Inquiring After God*, p. 53.

138. David F. Ford, *A Long Rumour of Wisdom: Redescribing Theology* (Cambridge: Cambridge University Press, 1992), pp. 24-25.

139. Ford, *Long Rumour*, pp. 20-21.

140. Ford, *Long Rumour*, p. 4.

141. Ford, *Long Rumour*, p. 27.

142. Peter C. Hodgson, *God's Wisdom: Toward a Theology of Education* (Louisville: Westminster John Knox, 1999), p. 8.

143. Hodgson, *God's Wisdom*, pp. 12, 15-16, 90.

144. Hodgson, *God's Wisdom*, p. 48. See also the contrast between Paul and Plato in Douglas Farrow, "Is Theological Education Possible?" *Pro Ecclesia* 9, no. 4 (Fall 2000): 404-13.

145. Hodgson, *God's Wisdom*, p. 65.

146. Hodgson, *God's Wisdom*, p. 134.

147. Hodgson, *God's Wisdom*, p. 20.

148. Hays, "Wisdom According to Paul."

Notes to Chapter 3

1. See, e.g., Nancey Murphy, *Beyond Liberalism and Fundamentalism: How Modern and Postmodern Philosophy Set the Theological Agenda* (Valley Forge, PA: Trinity Press International, 1996).

2. Colman O'Neill, "The Rule Theory of Doctrine and Propositional Truth," *Thomist* 49 (1985): 419; Brian A. Gerrish, "The Nature of Doctrine," *JR* 68 (1988): 87-88.

3. George A. Lindbeck, *The Nature of Doctrine: Religion and Theology in a Postliberal Age* (Philadelphia: Westminster, 1984), p. 8.

4. John Milbank, *Theology and Social Theory: Beyond Secular Reason* (Oxford: Blackwell, 1993), p. 386.

5. Hans W. Frei, *Types of Christian Theology,* ed. George Hunsinger and William C. Placher (New Haven: Yale University Press, 1992), pp. 20-21; John Webster, "Theology After Liberalism?" in *Theology After Liberalism: A Reader,* ed. John Webster and George P. Schner (Oxford: Blackwell, 2000), pp. 52-61.

6. David Tracy, "The Uneasy Alliance Reconceived: Catholic Theological Method, Modernity and Postmodernity," in *Theology After Liberalism: A Reader,* pp. 335-57.

7. Lindbeck, *Nature of Doctrine,* pp. 12, 132-34.

8. Lindbeck, *Nature of Doctrine,* pp. 63-69.

9. At least so it seems; this position must be qualified by the statement that "the issue is not whether there are universal forms of reasonableness, but whether these can be formulated in some neutral, framework-independent language." See Lindbeck, *Nature of Doctrine,* pp. 130-31.

10. The religion/theology distinction seems hard and fast on p. 10, for example, and seems to be demanded by the logic of the project. But Lindbeck's acceptance of the realities in academic theology cannot be entirely sanguine once his vision of "theological competence" is considered.

11. Lindbeck is following Frei concerning the recovery of figural reading, of treating the biblical story as realistic narrative. Compare pp. 113-24 with Hans W. Frei, *The Eclipse of Biblical Narrative: A Study in Eighteenth and Nineteenth Century Hermeneutics* (New Haven: Yale University Press, 1974).

12. Lindbeck, *Nature of Doctrine,* p. 123.

13. Lindbeck, *Nature of Doctrine,* p. 135.

14. David H. Kelsey, *To Understand God Truly: What's Theological About a Theological School* (Louisville: Westminster John Knox, 1992), pp. 123, 232.

15. David H. Kelsey, "Church Discourse and Public Realm," in *Theology and Dialogue,* ed. Bruce D. Marshall (Notre Dame: Notre Dame University Press, 1990), pp. 29-30.

16. Bruce D. Marshall, *Trinity and Truth,* Studies in Christian Doctrine (Cambridge: Cambridge University Press, 2000), pp. 17-49, especially p. 48.

17. Marshall, *Trinity and Truth,* p. 24.

18. Marshall, *Trinity and Truth,* p. 6.

19. Marshall, *Trinity and Truth,* pp. 240-41.

20. Marshall, *Trinity and Truth,* pp. 269-70.

21. One of many points on which Marshall follows certain recent analytic philosophers, notably Donald Davidson (p. 87).

22. Marshall, *Trinity and Truth,* p. 216.

23. Marshall, *Trinity and Truth,* p. 267.

24. Marshall, *Trinity and Truth,* p. 123.

25. Marshall, *Trinity and Truth,* p. 277.

26. Marshall, *Trinity and Truth,* p. 278.

27. Marshall, *Trinity and Truth,* p. 142.

28. Marshall, *Trinity and Truth,* pp. 145-46.
29. Marshall, *Trinity and Truth,* pp. 152-53.
30. Marshall, *Trinity and Truth,* p. 157.
31. Marshall, *Trinity and Truth,* p. 204.
32. Marshall, *Trinity and Truth,* p. 211.
33. Marshall, *Trinity and Truth,* p. 204.
34. Marshall, *Trinity and Truth,* p. 192.
35. Marshall, *Trinity and Truth,* p. 194.
36. Marshall, *Trinity and Truth,* p. 216.
37. Marshall, *Trinity and Truth,* p. 267.
38. David S. Cunningham, *Faithful Persuasion: In Aid of a Rhetoric of Christian Theology* (Notre Dame: Notre Dame University Press, 1991), pp. 208-212.
39. Cunningham, *Faithful Persuasion,* p. 226.
40. Sue Patterson, *Realist Christian Theology in a Postmodern Age,* Studies in Christian Doctrine (Cambridge: Cambridge University Press, 1999), p. 31.
41. This covers the fivefold typology of the relation between theory and practice cited in Robert Banks, *Reenvisioning Theological Education: Exploring a Missional Alternative to Current Models* (Grand Rapids: Eerdmans, 1999), p. 164 n. 43. A fourfold typology related to theology may be found in Francis Schüssler Fiorenza, "Theory and Practice: Theological Education as a Reconstructive, Hermeneutical, and Practical Task," *Theological Education* 23, Supplement (1987): 113-41. A standard general history, though now a bit dated, is Nicholas Lobkowicz, *Theory and Practice: History of a Concept from Aristotle to Marx* (Notre Dame: Notre Dame University Press, 1967).
42. Webster, "Theology After Liberalism?" p. 60.
43. Kevin J. Vanhoozer, "The Voice and the Actor: A Dramatic Proposal About the Ministry and Minstrelsy of Theology," in *Evangelical Futures,* ed. John G. Stackhouse, Jr. (Grand Rapids: Baker, 2000), p. 77; see also (though it is not without some weaknesses) Alister E. McGrath, *The Genesis of Doctrine: A Study in the Foundation of Doctrinal Criticism* (Grand Rapids: Eerdmans, 1990), ch. 2.
44. McGrath, *Genesis of Doctrine,* p. 197.
45. Ronald F. Thiemann, *Revelation and Theology: The Gospel as Narrated Promise* (Notre Dame: Notre Dame University Press, 1985), p. 80.
46. Thiemann, *Revelation and Theology,* p. 143.
47. Thiemann, *Revelation and Theology,* pp. 151-54. See also several recent works by Stanley Grenz, a former student of Wolfhart Pannenberg, as well as Michael S. Horton, *Covenant and Eschatology: The Divine Drama* (Louisville: Westminster John Knox, 2002).
48. Stanley J. Grenz, "Articulating the Christian Belief-Mosaic: Theological Method After the Demise of Foundationalism," in *Evangelical Futures,* p. 136.
49. Stanley J. Grenz, "Beyond Foundationalism: Is a Nonfoundationalist Evangelical Theology Possible?" *Christian Scholar's Review* 30, no. 1 (Fall 2000): 77-82; *Renewing the Center: Evangelical Theology in a Post-Theological Era* (Grand Rapids: Baker, 2000), chs. 5-6.
50. This can be manifest either in the trend of functionalist approaches to biblical authority, discussed elsewhere, or else in the tendency to take away with one hand theological statements that are given in the other — for example, commitment to eschatology is laudable, but accompanied by some lack of clarity; see Gerhard Sauter, *Gateways to Dogmatics: Reasoning Theologically for the Life of the Church* (Grand Rapids: Eerdmans, 2003).

51. Thiemann, *Revelation and Theology,* p. 61.

52. Grenz, "Articulating," pp. 127-28. See also Stanley J. Grenz, "The Spirit and the Word: The World-Creating Function of the Text," *TToday* 57, no. 3 (October 2000): 357-75.

53. For further discussion of the issue surrounding these figures, see Daniel J. Treier, "Canonical Unity and Commensurable Language: On Divine Action and Doctrine," in *Evangelicals and Scripture: Tradition, Authority, Hermeneutics,* ed. Vincent E. Bacote, Laura C. Miguélez, and Dennis L. Okholm (Downers Grove, IL: IVP, 2004), pp. 211-28.

54. Colin E. Gunton, *A Brief Theology of Revelation* (Edinburgh: T&T Clark, 1995), pp. 3-4, 7.

55. Philip Kenneson, "The Alleged Incorrigibility of Postliberal Theology," in *The Nature of Confession,* ed. Timothy R. Phillips and Dennis L. Okholm (Downers Grove, IL: IVP, 1996), p. 273 n. 12.

56. Miroslav Volf, "Theology, Meaning, and Power," in *The Nature of Confession,* p. 264 n. 44.

57. Gunton, *Brief Theology of Revelation,* pp. 4, 15.

58. Reinhard Hütter, *Suffering Divine Things: Theology as Church Practice,* trans. by Doug Stott (Grand Rapids: Eerdmans, 2000), p. 24. A shorter (and more accessible) presentation of his proposal is Reinhard Hütter, "The Church: The Knowledge of the Triune God: Practices, Doctrine, Theology," in *Knowing the Triune God,* ed. James J. Buckley and David S. Yeago (Grand Rapids: Eerdmans, 2001), pp. 23-47.

59. Hütter, *Suffering Divine Things,* pp. 27-28.

60. Hütter, *Suffering Divine Things,* p. 29.

61. Hütter, *Suffering Divine Things,* p. 32.

62. Hütter, *Suffering Divine Things,* p. 34.

63. Hütter, *Suffering Divine Things,* p. 37.

64. Hütter, *Suffering Divine Things,* p. 30.

65. Hütter, *Suffering Divine Things,* p. 31.

66. Hütter, *Suffering Divine Things,* p. 34.

67. Hütter, *Suffering Divine Things,* pp. 45-46.

68. Hütter, *Suffering Divine Things,* pp. 54-55.

69. Hütter, *Suffering Divine Things,* pp. 58, 60-61.

70. Hütter, *Suffering Divine Things,* p. 108.

71. Hütter, *Suffering Divine Things,* p. 109.

72. Hütter, *Suffering Divine Things,* p. 113.

73. Hütter, *Suffering Divine Things,* pp. 114-15.

74. Hütter, *Suffering Divine Things,* p. 115.

75. Hütter, *Suffering Divine Things,* p. 133.

76. Hütter, *Suffering Divine Things,* p. 138.

77. Hütter, *Suffering Divine Things,* p. 141.

78. Hütter, *Suffering Divine Things,* p. 148.

79. Hütter, *Suffering Divine Things,* p. 153.

80. Hütter, *Suffering Divine Things,* p. 156.

81. Hütter, *Suffering Divine Things,* p. 168.

82. Hütter, *Suffering Divine Things,* p. 172.

83. Hütter, *Suffering Divine Things,* p. 175.

84. Hütter, *Suffering Divine Things,* p. 178.

85. Hütter, *Suffering Divine Things,* pp. 189-91.

86. Hütter, *Suffering Divine Things,* p. 192.

87. Hütter, *Suffering Divine Things,* p. 193.

88. They simply see the standard for a truth claim to be met differently, so that doctrines must be claims to express experience whereas philosophy, science, and the like may claim to know reality beyond the individual human. See, e.g., Richard Heyduck, *The Recovery of Doctrine in the Contemporary Church: An Essay in Philosophical Ecclesiology* (Waco, TX: Baylor University Press, 2002), pp. 26-27.

89. Gerrish, "Nature of Doctrine," pp. 91-92.

90. Jay Wesley Richards, "Truth and Meaning in George Lindbeck's *The Nature of Doctrine,*" *RelS* 33, no. 1 (March 1997): 33-53.

91. Hütter, *Suffering Divine Things,* p. 80.

92. Hütter, *Suffering Divine Things,* pp. 85-86.

93. Joseph L. Mangina, "After Dogma: Reinhard Hütter's Challenge to Contemporary Theology: A Review Essay," *IJST* 2, no. 3 (2000): 330-46. Mangina also highlights the relative lack of biblical exegesis in Hütter's work, which may lend further support to this complaint.

94. Ephraim Radner, *The End of the Church: A Pneumatology of Christian Division in the West* (Grand Rapids: Eerdmans, 1998), pp. 11, 15.

95. Radner, *End of the Church,* pp. 26-27.

96. Radner, *End of the Church,* p. 48.

97. Radner, *End of the Church,* p. 36.

98. Nicholas M. Healy, *Church, World and the Christian Life: Practical-Prophetic Ecclesiology,* Studies in Christian Doctrine (Cambridge: Cambridge University Press, 2000), p. 164.

99. See John Webster, "Hermeneutics in Modern Theology: Some Doctrinal Reflections," in *Word and Church: Essays in Christian Doctrine* (Edinburgh: T&T Clark, 2001), pp. 80-86.

100. Kathryn Tanner, "Self-Critical Cultures and Divine Transcendence," in *Theology After Liberalism: A Reader,* pp. 223-56.

101. Webster, "Theology After Liberalism?" p. 60.

102. Colin E. Gunton, "Dogma, the Church and the Task of Theology," *Neue Zeitschrift für Systematische Theologie und Religionsphilosophie* 40, no. 1 (1998): 74 n. 15.

103. David K. Clark, "Relativism, Fideism and the Promise of Postliberalism," in *The Nature of Confession,* p. 113.

104. Clark, "Relativism," p. 276 n. 26.

105. David F. Ford, "System, Story, Performance: A Proposal About the Role of Narrative in Christian Systematic Theology," in *Why Narrative?* ed. Stanley Hauerwas and L. Gregory Jones (reprint, Eugene, OR: Wipf & Stock, 1997), p. 211.

106. Calvin O. Schrag, *Communicative Praxis and the Space of Subjectivity* (Bloomington: Indiana University Press, 1986), p. 88.

107. Schrag, *Communicative Praxis,* p. 145.

108. Schrag, *Communicative Praxis,* p. 121.

109. At points Schrag seems overly resistant to ontology or metaphysics at all, so that Taylor's work might be a useful supplement.

110. Schrag, *Communicative Praxis,* p. 41.

111. Matthew Lamb, "Communicative Praxis and Theology: Beyond Modern Nihilism

and Dogmatism," in *Habermas, Modernity, and Public Theology*, ed. Don S. Browning and Francis Schüssler Fiorenza (New York: Crossroad, 1992), p. 97.

112. Schrag, *Communicative Praxis*, p. 187.

113. Schrag, *Communicative Praxis*, p. 193.

114. Schrag, *Communicative Praxis*, pp. 203-4.

115. Charles Taylor, *Sources of the Self: The Making of the Modern Identity* (Cambridge, MA: Harvard University Press, 1989), p. 204.

116. Taylor, *Sources of the Self*, p. 491.

117. Schrag, *Communicative Praxis*, p. 208.

118. In obvious relation to Ricoeur, Schrag, *Communicative Praxis*, p. 207. Compare this with Philip Clayton's discussion of the need for a theory of epistemic justification to work along with the process of communication (*The Problem of God in Modern Thought* [Grand Rapids: Eerdmans, 2000], pp. 351-54).

119. Jürgen Habermas, *The Theory of Communicative Action*, vol. 1, *Reason and the Rationalization of Society*, trans. Thomas McCarthy (Boston: Beacon, 1984), p. 8.

120. Habermas, *Reason and Rationalization*, p. 17.

121. Maurice F. Wiles, *The Remaking of Christian Doctrine* (Philadelphia: Westminster, 1978), pp. 13-14.

122. Maurice F. Wiles, *The Making of Christian Doctrine* (Cambridge: Cambridge University Press, 1967), p. 173. It is somewhat striking but indicative of our difficulties with precision on such matters, that Grenz and John Franke also suggest "it is the *intent* of the creeds, confessions, and formulations, and not the specific construction and order of their wording, that is significant" (*Beyond Foundationalism: Shaping Theology in a Postmodern Context* [Louisville: Westminster John Knox, 2001], p. 124).

123. Kevin J. Vanhoozer, "From Canon to Concept: 'Same' and 'Other' in the Relation Between Biblical and Systematic Theology," *Scottish Bulletin of Evangelical Theology* 12, no. 2 (Autumn 1994): 96-124.

124. John S. Feinberg, "Rationality, Objectivity, and Doing Theology: Review and Critique of Wentzel Van Huysteen's [*sic*] *Theology and the Justification of Faith*," *TrinJ* 10 NS (1989): 177-78.

125. A view attributed to Lyotard by James K. A. Smith, *The Fall of Interpretation: Philosophical Foundations for a Creational Hermeneutic* (Downers Grove, IL: IVP, 2000), p. 166. See also the grudging response about translation from Merold Westphal, "Taking Plantinga Seriously: Advice to Christian Philosophers," *Faith and Philosophy* 16, no. 2 (April 1999): 177.

126. Healy, *Church, World*, p. 120.

127. Tracy, "Uneasy Alliance," p. 349; *The Analogical Imagination: Christian Theology and the Culture of Pluralism* (New York: Crossroad, 1981).

128. Referring to a concern of Dallas Willard, "Hermeneutical Occasionalism," in *Disciplining Hermeneutics: Interpretation in Theological Perspective*, ed. Roger Lundin (Grand Rapids: Eerdmans, 1997), pp. 167-72.

129. Walter Kasper, *The God of Jesus Christ*, trans. Matthew J. O'Connell (New York: Crossroad, 1992), pp. 311-13.

130. McGrath, *Genesis of Doctrine*, pp. 37-52.

131. Heyduck, *Recovery of Doctrine*, ch. 1.

132. Horton, *Covenant and Eschatology*.

133. This, along with the analytic power of details from drama theory itself, looks to be a strength of Kevin J. Vanhoozer, *The Drama of Doctrine: A Canonical-Linguistic Approach to Theology* (Louisville: Westminster John Knox, 2005).

134. Gerrish, "Nature of Doctrine," p. 92.

135. Vanhoozer, "Canon to Concept."

136. David S. Yeago, "The New Testament and the Nicene Dogma: A Contribution to the Recovery of Theological Exegesis," in *The Theological Interpretation of Scripture,* ed. Stephen E. Fowl (Oxford: Blackwell, 1997), especially pp. 93-96.

137. Feinberg, "Rationality, Objectivity," p. 183.

138. Kathleen Callow, *Man and Message: A Guide to Meaning-Based Text Analysis* (Lanham, MD: Summer Institute of Linguistics & University Press of America, 1998), p. 20.

139. Callow, *Man and Message,* pp. 53, 55. Dan Sperber and Deirdre Wilson, famous for "relevance theory," discuss concepts similarly, as stabilized meanings constructed *ad hoc.* They suggest that the rejection of a "code" model of communication removes dilemmas about whether concepts and meanings are exactly the same. See Dan Sperber and Deirdre Wilson, "The Mapping Between the Mental and the Public Lexicon," *UCL Working Papers in Linguistics* 9 (1997): 1-19; *Relevance: Communication and Cognition,* 2d ed. (Oxford: Blackwell, 1995).

140. Compare Callow, *Man and Message,* pp. 57, 64, and Paul L. Holmer, *The Grammar of Faith* (San Francisco: Harper & Row, 1978), p. 139.

141. Callow, *Man and Message,* p. 65.

142. Kelsey, *To Understand God Truly,* p. 169.

143. Edward Farley, *Ecclesial Reflection: An Anatomy of Theological Method* (Philadelphia: Fortress, 1982), pp. 305, 334.

144. Hans W. Frei, "Barth and Schleiermacher: Divergence and Convergence," in *Barth and Schleiermacher: Beyond the Impasse,* ed. James O. Duke and Robert F. Streetman (Minneapolis: Fortress, 1988), p. 73.

145. Milbank, *Theology and Social Theory,* pp. 341-43.

146. Rowan Williams, *On Christian Theology* (Oxford: Blackwell, 2000), pp. xii-xiv.

147. Theodore W. Jennings, Jr., "Theology as the Construction of Doctrine," in *The Vocation of the Theologian,* ed. Theodore W. Jennings, Jr. (Philadelphia: Fortress, 1985), pp. 72-73.

148. Milbank, *Theology and Social Theory,* p. 413; Patterson, *Realist.*

149. Westphal, "Taking Plantinga Seriously," pp. 179-80.

150. Trevor Hart, *Faith Thinking: The Dynamics of Christian Theology* (Downers Grove, IL: IVP, 1995), p. 91.

151. Jaroslav Pelikan, *The Christian Tradition: A History of the Development of Doctrine,* vol. 1, *The Emergence of the Catholic Tradition (100-600)* (Chicago: University of Chicago Press, 1971), p. 1.

152. Pelikan, *Emergence,* p. 7.

153. Colin E. Gunton, "A Rose by Any Other Name? From 'Christian Doctrine' to 'Systematic Theology,'" *IJST* 1, no. 1 (March 1999): 4-23.

154. Stanley Hauerwas, "On Doctrine and Ethics," in *The Cambridge Companion to Christian Doctrine,* ed. Colin E. Gunton (Cambridge: Cambridge University Press, 1997), pp. 21-40.

155. Pelikan, *Emergence,* p. 2.

156. Yeago, "New Testament and the Nicene Dogma," p. 93.

157. Jeremy S. Begbie, *Theology, Music and Time,* Studies in Christian Doctrine (Cambridge: Cambridge University Press, 2000), p. 280.

158. Kelsey, *To Understand God Truly,* pp. 124-29.

159. In this vein, Kelsey cites Stephen Toulmin's understanding of philosophy as "field-encompassing." See Kelsey, *To Understand God Truly,* pp. 124-29.

160. Healy's summary is apt: "that form of reflection that situates all other forms of reflection" (*Church, World,* p. 67).

161. Milbank, *Theology and Social Theory,* p. 354.

162. Gunton, *Brief Theology of Revelation,* p. 102.

Notes to Chapter 4

1. The issue of a possible distinction between "doctrine" and "dogma" in some church polities is left to the side.

2. Colin E. Gunton, "Indispensable Opponent: The Relations of Systematic Theology and Philosophy of Religion," *Neue Zeitschrift für Systematische Theologie und Religionsphilosophie* 38, no. 3 (1996): 298-306.

3. Walter L. Reed, *Dialogues of the Word: The Bible as Literature According to Bakhtin* (Oxford: Oxford University Press, 1993), p. 167.

4. Gerald Bray, "Scripture and Confession: Doctrine as Hermeneutic," in *A Pathway into the Holy Scripture,* ed. Philip E. Satterthwaite and David F. Wright (Grand Rapids: Eerdmans, 1994), p. 224.

5. George A. Lindbeck, "Spiritual Formation and Theological Education," in *Theological Perspectives on Christian Formation,* ed. Jeff Astley, Leslie J. Francis and Colin Crowder (Grand Rapids: Eerdmans, 1996), p. 300.

6. Richard A. Muller, "The Study of Theology," in *Foundations of Contemporary Interpretation,* ed. Moisés Silva (Grand Rapids: Zondervan, 1996), pp. 556-57.

7. John H. Leith, *Crisis in the Church: The Plight of Theological Education* (Louisville: Westminster John Knox, 1997), p. 18.

8. E. David Willis, "The Relation of Historical to Systematic Theology," in *Theology in the Service of the Church,* ed. Wallace M. Alston, Jr. (Grand Rapids: Eerdmans, 2000), p. 246.

9. Werner G. Jeanrond, "Criteria for New Biblical Theologies," *JR* 76, no. 2 (April 1996): 238.

10. Werner G. Jeanrond, *Text und Interpretation als Kategorien theologischen Denkens* (Tübingen: J. C. B. Mohr [Paul Siebeck], 1986), p. 125.

11. Jeanrond, "Criteria," p. 245.

12. Schubert M. Ogden, "Theology and Biblical Interpretation," *JR* 76, no. 2 (April 1996): 172-88.

13. Robert Morgan, "Can the Critical Study of Scripture Provide a Doctrinal Norm?" *JR* 76, no. 2 (April 1996): 208.

14. Stephen E. Fowl, *Engaging Scripture* (Oxford: Blackwell, 1998), p. 8.

15. Fowl, *Engaging Scripture,* pp. 8-9.

16. Among other examples, Francis Watson, *Text, Church and World: Biblical Interpretation in Theological Perspective* (Grand Rapids: Eerdmans, 1994); *Text and Truth: Redefining*

Biblical Theology (Grand Rapids: Eerdmans, 1997), chs. 2, 6, 7; also Kevin J. Vanhoozer, "Body-Piercing, the Natural Sense, and the Task of Theological Interpretation: A Hermeneutical Homily on John 19:34," *Ex Auditu* 16 (2000): 1-29.

17. Fowl, *Engaging Scripture,* p. 1.

18. Fowl, *Engaging Scripture,* p. 16.

19. Fowl, *Engaging Scripture,* p. 18.

20. Fowl, *Engaging Scripture,* pp. 32-61.

21. Christopher R. Seitz, "Christological Interpretation of Texts and Trinitarian Claims to Truth: An Engagement with Francis Watson's *Text and Truth,*" *SJT* 52, no. 2 (1999): 210.

22. Fowl, *Engaging Scripture,* pp. 21-31.

23. Werner G. Jeanrond, *Theological Hermeneutics: Development and Significance* (New York: Crossroad, 1991).

24. Jeanrond, *Theological Hermeneutics,* p. 77.

25. Jeanrond, *Theological Hermeneutics,* p. 158.

26. Fowl, *Engaging Scripture,* p. 32.

27. Fowl, *Engaging Scripture,* p. 34.

28. Fowl, *Engaging Scripture,* p. 35.

29. E.g., Fowl, *Engaging Scripture,* pp. 60, 74.

30. Fowl, *Engaging Scripture,* p. 47.

31. Fowl, *Engaging Scripture,* p. 183.

32. Fowl, *Engaging Scripture,* p. 35.

33. Fowl, *Engaging Scripture,* pp. 8, 33, 40-56, 179.

34. Fowl, *Engaging Scripture,* p. 8.

35. Stephen E. Fowl and L. Gregory Jones, *Reading in Communion: Scripture and Ethics in Christian Life* (Grand Rapids: Eerdmans, 1991), p. 90.

36. St. Augustine, *On Christian Teaching,* trans. R. P. H. Green (Oxford: Oxford University Press, 1997), I.86-88.

37. Augustine, *On Christian Teaching,* II.9, III.4.

38. David C. Steinmetz, "The Superiority of Pre-Critical Exegesis," in *The Theological Interpretation of Scripture,* ed. Stephen E. Fowl (Oxford: Blackwell, 1997), p. 29.

39. Hans W. Frei, *The Eclipse of Biblical Narrative: A Study in Eighteenth and Nineteenth Century Hermeneutics* (New Haven: Yale University Press, 1974), pp. 104, 132.

40. Frei, *Eclipse,* p. 227.

41. Francis Watson, "What Does It Mean to Interpret the Bible Theologically?" Unpublished lecture presented at Trinity Evangelical Divinity School, Deerfield, IL, 2000.

42. Luke Timothy Johnson, *Scripture and Discernment in the Early Church,* 2d ed. (Nashville: Abingdon, 1996), p. 112.

43. Johnson, *Scripture and Discernment,* p. 37.

44. Watson, "What Does It Mean?"

45. Kevin J. Vanhoozer, *Is There a Meaning in This Text? The Bible, the Reader, and the Morality of Literary Knowledge* (Grand Rapids: Zondervan, 1998), ch. 7.

46. Vanhoozer, "Body-Piercing."

47. George A. Lindbeck, "Postcritical Canonical Interpretation: Three Modes of Retrieval," in *Theological Exegesis: Essays in Honor of Brevard S. Childs,* ed. Christopher R. Seitz and Kathryn Greene-McCreight (Grand Rapids: Eerdmans, 1999), pp. 26-51.

48. Kevin J. Vanhoozer, "The Voice and the Actor: A Dramatic Proposal About the

Ministry and Minstrelsy of Theology," in *Evangelical Futures,* ed. John G. Stackhouse, Jr. (Grand Rapids: Baker, 2000), pp. 61-106; Nicholas Wolterstorff, "Response to Trevor Hart," in *Renewing Biblical Interpretation,* ed. Craig Bartholomew, Colin Greene and Karl Möller, Scripture and Hermeneutics, vol. 1 (Grand Rapids: Zondervan, 2000), pp. 336-37.

49. James J. Buckley, "Beyond the Hermeneutical Deadlock," in *Theology After Liberalism: A Reader,* ed. John Webster and George P. Schner (Oxford: Blackwell, 2000), pp. 187-203.

50. Fowl, *Engaging Scripture,* pp. 2-8.

51. Fowl and Jones, *Reading in Communion,* pp. 38-40. The text, they say, need not have come from the "mouth of God."

52. Fowl, *Engaging Scripture,* pp. 161-62.

53. Fowl, *Engaging Scripture,* pp. 64-65, 203.

54. Fowl, *Engaging Scripture,* pp. 36, 126 n. 59.

55. Stephen E. Fowl, "The Role of Authorial Intention in the Theological Interpretation of Scripture," in *Between Two Horizons,* ed. Joel B. Green and Max Turner (Grand Rapids: Eerdmans, 2000), pp. 81-82.

56. Steinmetz, "Superiority," p. 28; Fowl, *Engaging Scripture,* p. 37.

57. Fowl, *Engaging Scripture,* pp. 113-26; Johnson, *Scripture and Discernment,* pp. 68-108, 144-48.

58. For another example, see John Christopher Thomas, "Reading the Bible from Within Our Traditions: A Pentecostal Hermeneutic as a Test Case," in *Between Two Horizons,* p. 119.

59. Watson, *Text, Church and World,* part 3.

60. Steinmetz, "Superiority," p. 37.

61. Kathryn Greene-McCreight, *Ad Litteram: How Augustine, Calvin, and Barth Read the "Plain Sense" of Genesis 1–3* (New York: Peter Lang, 1999), p. 80.

62. Eugene F. Rogers, Jr., "How the Virtues of an Interpreter Presuppose and Perfect Hermeneutics: The Case of Thomas Aquinas," *JR* 76, no. 1 (January 1996): 64.

63. Rogers, "Virtues of an Interpreter," p. 75.

64. Rogers, "Virtues of an Interpreter," p. 76.

65. Rogers, "Virtues of an Interpreter," pp. 80-81.

66. Rowan A. Greer, *Broken Lights and Mended Lives: Theology and Common Life in the Early Church* (University Park: Pennsylvania State University Press, 1986), p. 7.

67. Following Frei, George A. Lindbeck, "The Story-Shaped Church: Critical Exegesis and Theological Interpretation," in *The Theological Interpretation of Scripture,* p. 41.

68. Following Umberto Eco, John Milbank, "The Linguistic Turn as a Theological Turn," in *The Word Made Strange: Theology, Language, Culture* (Oxford: Blackwell, 1997), p. 94.

69. Greene-McCreight, *Ad Litteram,* especially pp. 148-49.

70. D. H. Williams, *Retrieving the Tradition and Renewing Evangelicalism: A Primer for Suspicious Protestants* (Grand Rapids: Eerdmans, 1999), p. 176.

71. Williams, *Retrieving the Tradition,* p. 201.

72. Johnson, *Scripture and Discernment,* p. 49.

73. Rowan A. Greer, "The Good Shepherd: Canonical Interpretations in the Early Church?" in *Theological Exegesis,* p. 328.

74. Andrew Louth, *Discerning the Mystery: An Essay on the Nature of Theology* (Oxford: Clarendon, 1983), p. 103.

75. Louth, *Discerning,* p. 98.

76. Louth, *Discerning,* p. 101.

77. Louth, *Discerning,* p. 103.

78. Frei, *Eclipse,* p. 90. He describes Calvin's position, of which he seems to approve even if it is not his own, this way: "Interpretation or the gathering of meaning is in no sense a material contribution on the part of the interpreter or a unique perspective he might represent" (p. 34).

79. Frei, *Eclipse,* p. 7.

80. G. R. Evans, *The Language and Logic of the Bible: The Earlier Middle Ages* (Cambridge: Cambridge University Press, 1984).

81. Charles Taylor, *Sources of the Self: The Making of the Modern Identity* (Cambridge, MA: Harvard University Press, 1989), p. 288.

82. Rowan Williams, "The Literal Sense of Scripture," *Modern Theology* 7, no. 2 (January 1991): 121.

83. E.g., Greer, *Broken Lights,* p. 7; Milbank, "Linguistic Turn," p. 118. The latter claims to follow Henri de Lubac in his magisterial *Exégèse Médiévale: Les Quatres Sens de L'Écriture* (Paris: Aubier, 1959-64; the first two volumes are translated into English as *Medieval Exegesis* [Eerdmans]). Lubac in fact distinguishes *allegoria facti* (of the "deed") from *allegoria verbi* (of the "word"), tying Christian allegory to *mysterium* or a sense of sacramental event, rather than solely the textual or verbal symbol. This might roughly correspond to the distinction Frances Young presses regarding narrative (see below), although we should not minimize the significance of the deed being presented to us in the word (Lubac puts it, "Plus précisément, elle [biblical allegory] est *allegoria facti et dicti*"; see especially 2:495-98).

84. Frei, *Eclipse,* p. 47.

85. Lindbeck, "Postcritical Canonical Interpretation," p. 31.

86. Lindbeck, "Postcritical Canonical Interpretation," pp. 38-39.

87. Williams, *Retrieving the Tradition,* p. 233.

88. Timothy Ward, *Word and Supplement: Speech Acts, Biblical Texts, and the Sufficiency of Scripture* (Oxford: Oxford University Press, 2002), pp. 208-9.

89. Paul Ricoeur, "Toward a Hermeneutic of the Idea of Revelation," trans. David Pellauer, in *Essays on Biblical Interpretation,* ed. Lewis S. Mudge (Philadelphia: Fortress, 1980), pp. 75, 90-91.

90. David H. Kelsey, *The Uses of Scripture in Recent Theology* (Philadelphia: Fortress, 1975). Now reissued as *Proving Doctrine* (Harrisburg, PA: Trinity Press International, 1999).

91. In addition to citations of Ricoeur and Kelsey above, see David Tracy, "Literary Theory and the Return of the Forms for Naming and Thinking God in Theology," *JR* 74 (July 1994): 302-19; Kevin J. Vanhoozer, "The Semantics of Biblical Literature: Truth and Scripture's Diverse Literary Forms," in *Hermeneutics, Authority and Canon,* ed. D. A. Carson and John D. Woodbridge (Grand Rapids: Baker, 1995), pp. 49-104.

92. Compare Ricoeur, "Toward a Hermeneutic," p. 72, with John Goldingay, *Models for Scripture* (Grand Rapids: Eerdmans, 1994); *Models for Interpretation of Scripture* (Grand Rapids: Eerdmans, 1995).

93. Ricoeur, "Toward a Hermeneutic," p. 91.

94. Paul Ricoeur, *Figuring the Sacred: Religion, Narrative, and Imagination,* trans. David Pellauer, ed. Mark I. Wallace (Minneapolis: Fortress, 1995), pp. 167-80.

95. Richard Lints, *The Fabric of Theology: A Prolegomenon to Evangelical Theology* (Grand Rapids: Eerdmans, 1993), p. 74.

96. Ward, *Word and Supplement,* pp. 208-9.

97. Warfield, *Idea of Systematic Theology,* pp. 65-68, cited in William J. Abraham, *Canon and Criterion in Christian Theology* (Oxford: Clarendon, 1998), pp. 325-26.

98. As noted in Charles F. Melchert, *Wise Teaching: Biblical Wisdom and Educational Ministry* (Valley Forge, PA: Trinity Press International, 1998), p. 281 n. 14.

99. James Barr, *The Concept of Biblical Theology: An Old Testament Perspective* (Minneapolis: Fortress, 1999), p. 187.

100. Abraham, *Canon and Criterion,* p. 326.

101. Warfield, *Idea of Systematic Theology,* pp. 65-68, cited in Abraham, *Canon and Criterion,* pp. 325-26.

102. Michael Welker, "Biblical Theology and the Authority of Scripture," in *Theology in the Service of the Church,* p. 232.

103. Welker, "Biblical Theology," p. 239.

104. Reed, *Dialogues of the Word,* p. ix.

105. Lindbeck, "Postcritical Canonical Interpretation," p. 44.

106. Douglas J. Moo, "The Problem of *Sensus Plenior,*" in *Hermeneutics, Authority and Canon,* pp. 186-87, 203.

107. Lindbeck, "Story-Shaped," p. 44.

108. Max Turner, "Historical Criticism and Theological Hermeneutics of the New Testament," in *Between Two Horizons,* p. 54.

109. Robert W. Wall, "Canonical Context and Canonical Conversations," in *Between Two Horizons,* p. 180.

110. Steve Motyer, "Two Testaments, One Biblical Theology," in *Between Two Horizons,* pp. 158, 160.

111. D. A. Carson, "Unity and Diversity in the New Testament: The Possibility of Systematic Theology," in *Scripture and Truth,* ed. D. A. Carson and John D. Woodbridge (Grand Rapids: Baker, 1992), p. 69.

112. Carson is obviously not unaware of this, making his case in a discussion of Dunn's significant work. He argues that the canonical dimension can be helpful to scholarship by breaking down textual isolation, and that despite "great diversity in emphasis, formulation, application, genre of literature, and forms of ecclesiastical administration," there is also a "unity of teaching that makes systematic theology not only possible but necessary. . . ." See Carson, "Unity and Diversity," pp. 91, 94-95.

113. Barr, *Concept of Biblical Theology,* p. 360. More staunchly, Barr does not think that most of the Bible even "contains" theology in any "direct or authentic sense" (p. 251).

114. Barr, *Concept of Biblical Theology,* pp. 203-4.

115. Barr, *Concept of Biblical Theology,* pp. 5-6.

116. Barr, *Concept of Biblical Theology,* pp. 204-5.

117. Abraham's qualified position is somewhat similar: "I am not here claiming that no good is to be gained from engaging in the development of 'biblical theology'. There can well be a place for this kind of work in the economy of scholarship and in the life of the Church. What is at stake here is the precariousness of such work in itself and the oddity of making this work essential to the very existence of systematic theology. We need an entirely different

way of conceiving the relationship between biblical material and systematic theology" (*Canon and Criterion,* p. 326).

118. Gordon D. Kaufman, "Theology as a Public Vocation," in *The Vocation of the Theologian,* ed. Theodore W. Jennings, Jr. (Philadelphia: Fortress, 1985), p. 50.

119. Merold Westphal, "Taking St. Paul Seriously: Sin as an Epistemological Category," in *Christian Philosophy,* ed. Thomas P. Flint (Notre Dame: Notre Dame University Press, 1990), p. 205.

120. Contrast Fowl, *Engaging Scripture,* ch. 3, entitled "Vigilant Communities and Virtuous Readers," with Anthony C. Thiselton, "Authority and Hermeneutics: Some Proposals for a More Creative Agenda," in *A Pathway into the Holy Scripture,* especially pp. 134-41.

121. *Opus Epistolarum,* ed. P. S. Allen, II.90-114, cited in G. R. Evans, *The Language and Logic of the Bible: The Road to Reformation* (Cambridge: Cambridge University Press, 1985), p. 79 n. 49.

122. Joel B. Green, "Scripture and Theology: Uniting the Two So Long Divided," in *Between Two Horizons,* pp. 34-35.

123. Dietrich Ritschl, "Is There Anything 'New' in Theology? Reflections on an Old Theme," in *The Future of Theology,* ed. Miroslav Volf, Carmen Krieg and Thomas Kucharz (Grand Rapids: Eerdmans, 1996), p. 54; *The Logic of Theology: A Brief Account of the Relationship Between Basic Concepts in Theology,* trans. John Bowden (Philadelphia: Fortress, 1987), p. 71.

124. Trevor Hart, "Tradition, Authority, and a Christian Approach to the Bible as Scripture," in *Between Two Horizons,* p. 202.

125. Ronald F. Thiemann, *Revelation and Theology: The Gospel as Narrated Promise* (Notre Dame: Notre Dame University Press, 1985), pp. 66-67.

126. Hart, "Tradition, Authority," p. 203.

Notes to Chapter 5

1. See George Steiner, *Real Presences* (Chicago: University of Chicago Press, 1989).

2. Kevin J. Vanhoozer, *Is There a Meaning in This Text? The Bible, the Reader, and the Morality of Literary Knowledge* (Grand Rapids: Zondervan, 1998), p. 249.

3. Vanhoozer, *Is There a Meaning?* pp. 246-48. This seems not to fall afoul of the necessary strictures discussed in Stephen E. Fowl, "The Role of Authorial Intention in the Theological Interpretation of Scripture," in *Between Two Horizons,* ed. Joel B. Green and Max Turner (Grand Rapids: Eerdmans, 2000), pp. 71-87. See also Raymond W. Gibbs, Jr., *Intentions in the Experience of Meaning* (Cambridge: Cambridge University Press, 1999).

4. Vanhoozer, *Is There a Meaning?* pp. 251, 262.

5. Jeffrey Stout, "What Is the Meaning of a Text?" *New Literary History* 14 (1982): 1-11.

6. Discussion of ascription or "imputation" is much more pronounced in Kevin J. Vanhoozer, "From Speech Acts to Scripture Acts: The Covenant of Discourse and the Discourse of Covenant," in *After Pentecost,* ed. Craig Bartholomew, Colin Greene and Karl Möller, Scripture and Hermeneutics, vol. 2 (Grand Rapids: Zondervan, 2001), pp. 1-49.

7. Vanhoozer, *Is There a Meaning?* p. 423.

8. Stephen E. Fowl, Review of *Is There a Meaning in This Text?* by Kevin J. Vanhoozer, *Modern Theology* 16 (2000): 261.

9. Vanhoozer, *Is There a Meaning?* p. 282.

10. Vanhoozer, *Is There a Meaning?* p. 251.

11. Vanhoozer, *Is There a Meaning?* pp. 338-39.

12. Vanhoozer, *Is There a Meaning?* pp. 345-46.

13. For resources on Bakhtin's thought in addition to those cited below, particularly its religious and theological dimensions, see Paul J. Contino and Susan M. Felch, eds., *Bakhtin and Religion: A Feeling for Faith* (Evanston, IL: Northwestern University Press, 2001); Alexandar Mihailovic, *Corporeal Words: Mikhail Bakhtin's Theology of Discourse,* Studies in Russian Literature and Theory (Evanston, IL: Northwestern University Press, 1997); William D. Lindsey, "'The Problem of Great Time': A Bakhtinian Ethics of Discourse," *JR* 73 (July 1993): 311-28; David Patterson, "Bakhtin on Word and Spirit: The Religiosity of Responsibility," *Cross Currents* 41 (Spring 1991): 33-51; Clive Thomson, ed., *Mikhail Bakhtin and the Epistemology of Discourse,* Critical Studies, vol. 2 (Amsterdam-Atlanta: Rodopi, 1990). A brief overview appears in Susan Felch, "Dialogism," in *Dictionary for Theological Interpretation of the Bible,* ed. Kevin J. Vanhoozer (Grand Rapids: Baker Academic, & London: SPCK, 2005).

14. Mikhail Mikhailovich Bakhtin, *Speech Genres and Other Late Essays,* trans. by Vern W. McGee (Austin: University of Texas Press, 1986), p. 7.

15. Bakhtin, *Speech Genres,* p. 69.

16. Gary Saul Morson and Caryl Emerson, *Mikhail Bakhtin: Creation of a Prosaics* (Stanford: Stanford University Press, 1990), p. 285.

17. Gary Saul Morson and Caryl Emerson, "Extracts from a *Heteroglossary,*" in *Dialogue and Critical Discourse,* ed. Michael Macovski (Oxford: Oxford University Press, 1997), pp. 262-64.

18. Bakhtin, *Speech Genres,* p. 106. Also Mikhail Mikhailovich Bakhtin, *Toward a Philosophy of the Act,* trans. Vadim Liapunov, ed. Vadim Liapunov and Michael Holquist (Austin: University of Texas Press, 1993), p. 58; *Art and Answerability: Early Philosophical Essays,* trans. Vadim Liapunov and Kenneth Brostrom, ed. Michael Holquist and Vadim Liapunov (Austin: University of Texas Press, 1990), p. 2. Moreover, Bakhtin distinguishes between two types of truth, the useful abstraction of "theoretical knowledge" versus *pravda* which *"answerably obligates me"* (*Toward a Philosophy of the Act,* p. 49).

19. William P. Alston, *Illocutionary Acts and Sentence Meaning* (Ithaca, NY: Cornell University Press, 2000).

20. Anthony C. Thiselton, "Communicative Action and Promise in Interdisciplinary, Biblical, and Theological Hermeneutics," in *The Promise of Hermeneutics,* ed. Roger Lundin, Clarence Walhout and Anthony C. Thiselton (Grand Rapids: Eerdmans, 1999), pp. 200-201.

21. Nicholas Wolterstorff, *Divine Discourse: Philosophical Reflections on the Claim That God Speaks* (Cambridge: Cambridge University Press, 1995), pp. 138-39.

22. Werner G. Jeanrond, *Theological Hermeneutics: Development and Significance* (New York: Crossroad, 1991), p. 76.

23. John R. Searle, "Conversation as Dialogue," in *Dialogue and Critical Discourse,* ed. Michael Macovski (Oxford: Oxford University Press, 1997), p. 254.

24. Dan Sperber and Deirdre Wilson, *Relevance: Communication and Cognition,* 2d ed. (Oxford: Blackwell, 1995).

25. Max Turner, "Historical Criticism and Theological Hermeneutics of the New Testament," in *Between Two Horizons,* pp. 48-49.

26. Werner G. Jeanrond, *Text und Interpretation als Kategorien theologischen Denkens* (Tübingen: J. C. B. Mohr [Paul Siebeck], 1986), p. 100.

27. Thiselton, "Communicative Action and Promise," p. 161.

28. Anthony C. Thiselton, "Reader-Response Hermeneutics, Action Models, and the Parables of Jesus," in *The Responsibility of Hermeneutics,* ed. Roger Lundin, Clarence Walhout and Anthony C. Thiselton (Grand Rapids: Eerdmans, 1985), p. 113.

29. G. J. Warnock, *J. L. Austin* (London: Routledge, 1987), pp. 121-22.

30. Clarence Walhout, "Narrative Hermeneutics," in *The Promise of Hermeneutics,* p. 74.

31. George W. Stroup, *The Promise of Narrative Theology: Recovering the Gospel in the Church* (Atlanta: John Knox, 1981), p. 208.

32. Admittedly, "dialogue" vocabulary is frequent in Gadamer and also his followers; e.g., Hans-Georg Gadamer, *Dialogue and Dialectic: Eight Hermeneutical Studies on Plato* (New Haven: Yale University Press, 1980); Hans Herbert Kögler, *The Power of Dialogue: Critical Hermeneutics After Gadamer and Foucault,* trans. Paul Hendrickson (Cambridge, MA: MIT Press, 1996). At the least, though, I would claim that they often mean something different than Bakhtin does, despite Kögler's apparent compatibility with much said here.

33. Bakhtin, *Speech Genres,* p. 7.

34. Joel B. Green, "Rethinking History (and Theology)," in *Between Two Horizons,* p. 241.

35. Ruth Coates, *Christianity in Bakhtin: God and the Exiled Author* (Cambridge: Cambridge University Press, 1998), pp. 109, 161.

36. Paul Ricoeur, *Time and Narrative,* 3 vols., trans. Kathleen McLaughlin Blamey and David Pellauer (Chicago: University of Chicago Press, 1984-1988), 3.166-79. More generally on reader theories, see Mark G. Brett, "The Future of Reader Criticisms?" in *The Open Text,* ed. Francis Watson (London: SCM, 1993), pp. 13-31; Kevin J. Vanhoozer, "The Reader in New Testament Interpretation," in *Hearing the New Testament,* ed. Joel B. Green (Grand Rapids: Eerdmans, 1995), pp. 301-328; Robin Parry, "Reader-Response Criticism," in *Dictionary for Theological Interpretation.*

37. Ricoeur, *Time and Narrative,* 1.77.

38. Francis Watson, *Text and Truth: Redefining Biblical Theology* (Grand Rapids: Eerdmans, 1997), pp. 118-19.

39. Discussed at length, and with reference to Bakhtin, in Thiselton, "Communicative Action and Promise," pp. 138, 142, 160-61, 169-71, 180-81.

40. Werner G. Jeanrond, *Text and Interpretation as Categories of Theological Thinking,* trans. Thomas J. Wilson (Dublin & New York: Gill & Macmillan; Crossroad, 1988), pp. 94-118.

41. Westphal makes this point with reference to Wolterstorff. See Merold Westphal, "Review Essay: Theology as Talking About a God Who Talks," *Modern Theology* 13, no. 4 (October 1997): 534-36.

42. Bakhtin, *Speech Genres,* pp. 125, 166.

43. Dennis T. Olson, "Biblical Theology as Provisional Monologization: A Dialogue with Childs, Brueggemann and Bakhtin," *BibInt* 6 (April 1998): 174. Olson notes that "Bakhtin rejects relativists who simply leave us with an infinity of monologizations" (p. 175). So "on this point there is simply no way to reconcile what he is up to with much of what is said these days in the name of 'deconstruction'" (Wayne Booth, introduction to Mikhail Mikhailovich Bakhtin, *Problems of Dostoevsky's Poetics,* ed. and trans. Caryl Emerson, Theory and History of

Literature, vol. 8 [Manchester: Manchester University Press, 1984], p. xxvi). Perhaps this should give pause about some conclusions of Carol A. Newsom, "Bakhtin, the Bible, and Dialogic Truth," *JR* 76, no. 2 (April 1996): 290-306.

44. For this I am indebted broadly to the work of Watson.

45. James Barr, *The Concept of Biblical Theology: An Old Testament Perspective* (Minneapolis: Fortress, 1999), pp. 212-13.

46. Barr, *Concept of Biblical Theology,* p. 79.

47. D. A. Carson, "The Role of Exegesis in Systematic Theology," in *Doing Theology in Today's World: Essays in Honor of Kenneth S. Kantzer,* ed. John D. Woodbridge and Thomas Edward McComiskey (Grand Rapids: Zondervan, 1991), p. 46.

48. Carson, "Role of Exegesis," p. 58.

49. Francis Watson, *Text, Church and World: Biblical Interpretation in Theological Perspective* (Grand Rapids: Eerdmans, 1994), p. 40.

50. Maarten Wisse, "The Meaning of the Authority of the Bible," *RelS* 36 (2000): 479.

51. Stephen E. Fowl and L. Gregory Jones, *Reading in Communion: Scripture and Ethics in Christian Life* (Grand Rapids: Eerdmans, 1991), p. 81.

52. Joel B. Green, "Scripture and Theology: Uniting the Two So Long Divided," in *Between Two Horizons,* p. 42.

53. Russell Reno, "'You Who Were Far Off Have Been Brought Near': Reflections on Theological Exegesis," *Ex Auditu* 16 (2000): 169-82.

54. Robert W. Jenson, *Systematic Theology,* vol. 2, *The Works of God* (Oxford: Oxford University Press, 1999), p. 281.

55. Jenson, *Works of God,* pp. 277-82. A similar viewpoint energizes McClendon's "baptist vision"; in the broad sense, such a view is simply Christian and points to the Rule of faith; while in a narrower sense, the view may have distinctive contours of a particular tradition (as to the church's identity, at present and in relation to Israel) and points to the Rule's existence in multiple rules (on which see below).

56. As noted in R. W. L. Moberly, Review of *Is There a Meaning in This Text?* by Kevin J. Vanhoozer, *ExpTim* 110, no. 5 (Fall 1999): 154. Vanhoozer introduces the Holy Spirit into general hermeneutics in "The Spirit of Understanding: Special Revelation and General Hermeneutics," in *Disciplining Hermeneutics: Interpretation in Christian Perspective,* ed. Roger Lundin (Grand Rapids: Eerdmans, 1997), pp. 131-65. But this may leave unclear that not all texts are equal; they merit different types and levels of trust (see Brian D. Ingraffia and Todd E. Pickett, "Reviving the Power of Biblical Language: The Bible, Literature and Literary Language," in *After Pentecost,* pp. 243-48).

57. See especially Vanhoozer, *Is There a Meaning?* ch. 7; "From Speech Acts to Scripture Acts," pp. 40-43.

58. Beverly Roberts Gaventa, Review of *Engaging Scripture,* by Stephen E. Fowl, *Modern Theology* 16 (2000): 271-72.

59. David H. Kelsey, "The Bible and Christian Theology," *JAAR* 48, no. 3 (September 1980): 385-402.

60. Klyne Snodgrass, "Reading to Hear: A Hermeneutics of Hearing," *Horizons in Biblical Theology* 24, no. 1 (June 2002): 1-32.

61. See especially Vanhoozer, *Is There a Meaning?* p. 423.

62. See especially Stanley J. Grenz, "The Spirit and the Word: The World-Creating Function of the Text," *TToday* 57, no. 3 (October 2000): 357-75.

63. Wolterstorff, *Divine Discourse,* p. 204.

64. Wolterstorff, *Divine Discourse,* pp. 54, 283-84. The thrust of his account emphasizes how speech "counts as" various actions in terms of assuming a normative stance, as noted in Anthony C. Thiselton, "Speech-Act Theory and the Claim That God Speaks: Nicholas Wolterstorff's *Divine Discourse,*" *SJT* 50, no. 1 (1997): 104. Nevertheless, we may worry that Wolterstorff seems to leave aside questions of divine action in the composition of the texts, embracing some instabilities or tensions thereby, according to I. Howard Marshall, "'To Find Out What God Is Saying': Reflections on the Authorizing of Scripture," in *Disciplining Hermeneutics,* especially pp. 50-52.

65. John Goldingay, *Models for Scripture* (Grand Rapids: Eerdmans, 1994); *Models for Interpretation of Scripture* (Grand Rapids: Eerdmans, 1995).

66. Wolterstorff, *Divine Discourse,* p. 208. The tradition was not as unaware of this as we might think, which is pointed out in Michael S. Horton, *Covenant and Eschatology: The Divine Drama* (Louisville: Westminster John Knox, 2002), p. 137. An illustration might be Origen's insistence on the proper *prosōpon,* mentioned in Frances M. Young, *Biblical Exegesis and the Formation of Christian Culture* (Cambridge: Cambridge University Press, 1997), p. 165 n. 15. But the importance of the point was surely eclipsed in some modern accounts of theology's work with revelation.

67. His discussion seems inadequate to handle texts such as Heb. 4:4-5; see Goldingay, *Models for Scripture,* pp. 219-21.

68. Wisse, "Meaning of Authority," p. 480.

69. Wisse, "Meaning of Authority," pp. 481-82. For different classification schemes prior to Alston's recent work, see John R. Searle, *Speech Acts: An Essay in the Philosophy of Language* (Cambridge: Cambridge University Press, 1970); Daniel Vanderveken, *Meaning and Speech Acts,* vol. 1, *Principles of Language Use* (Cambridge: Cambridge University Press, 1990); *Meaning and Speech Acts,* vol. 2, *Formal Semantics of Success and Satisfaction* (Cambridge: Cambridge University Press, 1990).

70. Wisse, "Meaning of Authority," p. 483.

71. Wisse, "Meaning of Authority," p. 484.

72. Wolterstorff, *Divine Discourse,* p. 215.

73. Wolterstorff, *Divine Discourse,* p. 216.

74. Anthony C. Thiselton, *New Horizons in Hermeneutics: The Theory and Practice of Transforming Biblical Reading* (Grand Rapids: Zondervan, 1992), p. 597.

75. Wolterstorff, *Divine Discourse,* p. 208. For further illustrations of this, note various types of uses for Scripture — ten from Avery Dulles, S.J., *The Craft of Theology: From Symbol to System* (New York: Crossroad, 1992), pp. 71-85; or Gerald O'Collins and Daniel Kendall, *The Bible for Theology: Ten Principles for the Theological Use of Scripture* (New York & Mahwah, NJ: Paulist, 1997).

76. Richard S. Briggs, *Words in Action: Speech Act Theory and Biblical Interpretation* (Edinburgh: T&T Clark, 2001).

77. Jorge J. E. Gracia, *How Can We Know What God Means? The Interpretation of Revelation* (New York: Palgrave, 2001), especially pp. 142-43.

78. Colin E. Gunton, *A Brief Theology of Revelation* (Edinburgh: T&T Clark, 1995), p. 67.

79. Wolterstorff, *Divine Discourse,* p. 204.

80. Nicholas Wolterstorff, "Response to Trevor Hart," in *Renewing Biblical Interpreta-*

tion, ed. Craig Bartholomew, Colin Greene and Karl Möller, Scripture and Hermeneutics, vol. 1 (Grand Rapids: Zondervan, 2000), pp. 336-37; Trevor Hart, "Imagination and Responsible Reading," in *Renewing Biblical Interpretation,* pp. 307-34.

81. Wolterstorff, *Divine Discourse,* p. 206.

82. Wolterstorff, *Divine Discourse,* pp. 207, 227-28.

83. Wolterstorff, *Divine Discourse,* ch. 13.

84. Wolterstorff, *Divine Discourse,* p. 236.

85. Wolterstorff, *Divine Discourse,* p. 208.

86. Wolterstorff, *Divine Discourse,* pp. 236-39.

87. Mary Hesse, "How to Be a Postmodernist and Remain a Christian: A Response to Nicholas Wolterstorff," in *After Pentecost,* pp. 91-96.

88. Richard B. Hays, *The Moral Vision of the New Testament: A Contemporary Introduction to New Testament Ethics* (San Francisco: Harper Collins, 1996), pp. 187-89. From another angle, Henri Blocher, "The 'Analogy of Faith' in the Study of Scripture," in *The Challenge of Evangelical Theology,* ed. Nigel M. de S. Cameron (Edinburgh: Rutherford House, 1987), pp. 17-37.

89. Telford Work, *Living and Active: Scripture in the Economy of Salvation,* Sacra Doctrina (Grand Rapids: Eerdmans, 2002).

90. To a large degree this is simply a recovery of a post-Reformation theme, on which see Richard A. Muller, *Post-Reformation Reformed Dogmatics,* vol. 1, *Prolegomena to Theology* (Grand Rapids: Baker, 1987), especially pp. 146-50.

91. Kevin J. Vanhoozer, "The Voice and the Actor: A Dramatic Proposal About the Ministry and Minstrelsy of Theology," in *Evangelical Futures,* ed. John G. Stackhouse, Jr. (Grand Rapids: Baker, 2000), especially pp. 81-85.

92. Kevin J. Vanhoozer, "From Canon to Concept: 'Same' and 'Other' in the Relation Between Biblical and Systematic Theology," *Scottish Bulletin of Evangelical Theology* 12, no. 2 (Autumn 1994): 96-124.

93. David H. Kelsey, *Proving Doctrine* (Harrisburg, PA: Trinity Press International, 1999), p. 111.

94. Kelsey, *Proving Doctrine,* pp. 125-29.

95. Kelsey, *Proving Doctrine,* p. 137.

96. As Kelsey admits (e.g., on p. 171), but he does seem to equivocate (Briggs, *Words in Action,* p. 125 n. 55).

97. As Briggs suggests (*Words in Action,* p. 125).

98. William J. Webb, *Slaves, Women and Homosexuals: Exploring the Hermeneutics of Cultural Analysis* (Downers Grove, IL: IVP, 2001).

99. J. L. Austin, *How to Do Things with Words* (Oxford: Oxford University Press, 1962), pp. 47-48; also discussed briefly in Thiselton, *New Horizons,* p. 362.

100. I explore this in some different detail elsewhere (Daniel J. Treier, "Model," and "Proof Text," in *Dictionary for Theological Interpretation*).

101. Richard A. Muller, *Post-Reformation Reformed Dogmatics,* vol. 2, *Holy Scripture: The Cognitive Foundation for Theology* (Grand Rapids: Baker, 1993), pp. 522-23.

102. Richard Lints, *The Fabric of Theology: A Prolegomenon to Evangelical Theology* (Grand Rapids: Eerdmans, 1993), p. 74.

103. Turner, "Historical Criticism and Theological Hermeneutics," p. 54.

104. Vanhoozer, "From Speech Acts to Scripture Acts," pp. 38-39 n. 76.

105. Muller, *Holy Scripture,* p. 490.

106. Young, *Biblical Exegesis,* pp. 2, 162. Andrew Louth criticizes Young's argument precisely for maintaining some distinction, but does not defend his own view or develop a plausible alternative view of the Antiochene reaction against Origen (in Review of *Biblical Exegesis and the Formation of Christian Culture,* by Frances M. Young, *SJT* 54, no. 2 [2001]: 247-48).

107. E. Earle Ellis, *The Old Testament in Early Christianity* (Grand Rapids: Baker, 1991), p. 106.

108. David L. Baker, *Two Testaments, One Bible,* rev. ed. (Downers Grove, IL: IVP, 1991), ch. 7; Richard M. Davidson, *Typology in Scripture: A Study of Hermeneutical* τύπος *Structures* (Berrien Springs, MI: Andrews University Press, 1981); Leonhard Goppelt, *TYPOS: The Typological Interpretation of the Old Testament in the New,* trans. Donald H. Madvig (Grand Rapids: Eerdmans, 1982).

109. R. T. France, *Jesus and the Old Testament: His Application of Old Testament Passages to Himself and His Mission* (London: Tyndale, 1971), p. 76.

110. The parallel between "proclamation" and "promise" in the OT, and "fulfillment" and "final consummation" in the NT, is suggestive in Charles Scobie, *The Ways of Our God: An Approach to Biblical Theology* (Grand Rapids: Eerdmans, 2003). (I regret this work came into my hands late in time, so that more substantial interaction with it proved impossible.)

111. It is helpful to point out the parallel between the OT as foundational text for Jesus' life and reading, and the NT (or even Jesus' own life) as foundational text for Christian readers; so David L. Jeffrey, *People of the Book: Christian Identity and Literary Culture* (Grand Rapids: Eerdmans, 1996), especially pp. 68-70. But this *imitatio Christi* model need not be deemed allegorical, if in an important respect Jesus' own life and reading are rendered within the text, even of the OT. I shall return to this point later.

112. Reno has characterized pre-modern interpretation as having "figural" and "intensive" aspects in "'You Who Were Far Off.'" The latter involved a belief, at least for some (e.g., Origen, Augustine), that God intended Scripture to be ambiguous at points, as a challenge for the sake of spiritual development. As an associated diminution of the literal sense was once (rather graphically) put forth, "the letter still seemed to some to be a 'harlot' *(omnis quippe litera meretrix est),* because it exposes itself freely to everyone"; so G. R. Evans, *The Language and Logic of the Bible: The Road to Reformation* (Cambridge: Cambridge University Press, 1985), p. 40. Can a sound theological basis be found to favor this view (distance from Scripture can be part of the pedagogy of salvation without it)?

113. For instance, Evans attributes to (the relatively late) John Wycliffe the (obviously important) shift in focus from word to sentence (Evans, *Road to Reformation,* p. 85). Whereas "the very hypothesis that Scripture has a multiplicity of senses rests on the assumption that it is a property of words to be capable of more than one signification" (pp. 114-15). Moreover, William Tyndale exemplifies the broadening of the "literal sense" to include figurative language, thus embracing much of what had passed for "allegorical" or "spiritual" previously (p. 49). By contrast, Lubac points out that Origen had used "the letter" *très étroite,* so that he deems non-literal what we would deem "un sens littéral figuré ou métaphorique" (Henri de Lubac, S.J., *Exégèse Médiévale: Les Quatre Sens de l'Ecriture* [Paris, 1959-1964], 2.390).

Again, Young emphasizes that the fathers were overwhelmingly preoccupied with identifying reference of words/symbols rather than sense (*Biblical Exegesis,* p. 117). This is exemplified by Origen (p. 137). And Thomas F. Torrance criticizes certain forms of allegorical interpretation for reflecting a dualism that abstracts God completely from creaturely and human being (in *Divine Meaning: Studies in Patristic Hermeneutics* [Edinburgh: T&T Clark, 1995], 34-35).

114. Richard B. Hays, *The Faith of Jesus Christ: The Narrative Substructure of Galatians 3:1–4:11*, 2d ed. (Grand Rapids: Eerdmans, 2002). The Antiochene Theodore's discussion of Gal. 3-4 bears out Young's point; he was not concerned about debating Paul's use of "allegorical" language, but about unfolding the canonical propriety of what Paul did; see Young, *Biblical Exegesis*, p. 180.

115. David S. Yeago, "The New Testament and the Nicene Dogma: A Contribution to the Recovery of Theological Exegesis," in *The Theological Interpretation of Scripture*, ed. Stephen E. Fowl (Oxford: Blackwell, 1997), p. 94.

116. Vanhoozer, *Is There a Meaning?* p. 392.

117. This is not to deny that all textual understanding is at root a matter of translation (George Steiner, *After Babel* [Oxford: Oxford University Press, 1975], p. 28). But I suggest that the translation is often implied rather than explicit, and may not be a discrete step in a methodical process. It is interesting that "'interpretation' meant much the same as 'translation' to the Greek who used the same word, *hermeneia*, for both," according to Young, *Biblical Exegesis*, p. 119. The liturgical and lay reading of the Bible (at minimum) presumes upon prior acts of translation (and often commentary), thus specifying it as a major role of the church's teaching leadership (along with catechesis in doctrinal habits) in shaping the subsequent Christian practice of Scripture reading and communication about God.

118. The influence of Gadamer and Ricoeur upon David Tracy and Don Browning (for example) is no accident.

119. Miroslav Volf, "Theology, Meaning, and Power," in *The Future of Theology*, ed. Miroslav Volf, Carmen Krieg and Thomas Kucharz (Grand Rapids: Eerdmans, 1996), especially p. 101.

120. Nicholas M. Healy, *Church, World and the Christian Life: Practical-Prophetic Ecclesiology*, Studies in Christian Doctrine (Cambridge: Cambridge University Press, 2000), pp. 22, 175-76.

121. "Contextualization" models for theological understanding — more popular among conservatives, when understood along the lines of "translation" — are problematic not only given the complexities of "culture" just mentioned, but also given their tendency to reify "transcultural" abstract entities. Kelsey also details problems with the associated "translation" metaphor used in this way, in *Proving Doctrine*, especially pp. 185-92. Other "contextual" models are detailed in Stephen B. Bevans, SVD, *Models of Contextual Theology* (Maryknoll, NY: Orbis, 1992); Robert J. Schreiter, *Constructing Local Theologies* (Maryknoll, NY: Orbis, 1985).

122. Kathryn Tanner, *Theories of Culture: A New Agenda for Theology* (Minneapolis: Fortress, 1997), pp. 71-86.

123. Tanner, *Theories of Culture*, especially pp. 151-55.

124. Mikhail Mikhailovich Bakhtin, *The Dialogic Imagination*, trans. Caryl Emerson and Michael Holquist, ed. Michael Holquist (Austin: University of Texas Press, 1981), pp. 84-85.

125. Michael Holquist, *Dialogism: Bakhtin and His World* (New York: Routledge, 1990), p. 152.

126. John P. Farrell, "Crossroads to Community: *Jude the Obscure* and the Chronotope of Wessex," in *Dialogue and Critical Discourse*, pp. 65-78.

127. Morson and Emerson, *Mikhail Bakhtin,* p. 432.

128. Note the distinction between reference and mimesis in Walhout, "Narrative Hermeneutics," pp. 71-79.

129. Watson, *Text and Truth,* p. 105.

130. Barbara Green, *Mikhail Bakhtin and Biblical Scholarship: An Introduction* (Atlanta: SBL, 2000), p. 62.

131. Gary Saul Morson, *Narrative and Freedom: The Shadows of Time* (New Haven: Yale University Press, 1994), p. 106.

132. Bakhtin, *The Dialogic Imagination,* p. 252.

133. Performance interpretation is not so opposed to Wolterstorff's authorial discourse interpretation as he alleges, particularly if drama instead of music becomes the preferred model; see Shannon Craigo-Snell, "Command Performance: Rethinking Performance Interpretation in the Context of *Divine Discourse,*" *Modern Theology* 16, no. 4 (October 2000): 475-94. Then questions of human action in the world outside the story are inextricably bound up with appropriating the text (as discussion of background and context has already hinted). We need not understand "performance" simply as the reader standing in place of the author. Lindbeck uses the analogy of performing Shakespeare (George A. Lindbeck, "Postcritical Canonical Interpretation: Three Modes of Retrieval," in *Theological Exegesis: Essays in Honor of Brevard S. Childs,* ed. Christopher R. Seitz and Kathryn Greene-McCreight [Grand Rapids: Eerdmans, 1999], p. 42). The script needs interpretation as would a musical score, but for drama the questions of interpretation do broaden, as Craigo-Snell points out. This need not preclude a concern with "getting it right": the "world" of Scripture is a historical one of action and encounter, so that our reading is a "generative moment in which there may be a *discovery* of what the primal text may become (and so of what it is)" — but it is the *church's* critical self-discovery, according to Rowan Williams, "Postmodern Theology and the Judgement of the World," in *Theology After Liberalism: A Reader,* ed. John Webster and George P. Schner (Oxford: Blackwell, 2000), pp. 322-23. Actually, hard-nosed "intratextuality" seems to preclude good drama; like Craigo-Snell, Westphal similarly finds Wolterstorff's theory to require practical reason and to minimize distance from performance interpretation (in "Theology as Talking," pp. 527, 534-35).

134. Nicholas Lash, "Understanding the Stranger," in *Theology on Dover Beach* (New York: Paulist, 1979), p. 75.

135. David Tracy, "The Uneasy Alliance Reconceived: Catholic Theological Method, Modernity and Postmodernity," in *Theology After Liberalism: A Reader,* p. 345.

136. Frances M. Young, *Virtuoso Theology: The Bible and Interpretation* (Cleveland: Pilgrim, 1993).

137. Vanhoozer, "Voice and Actor"; Craigo-Snell, "Command Performance"; Horton, *Covenant and Eschatology.*

138. Stephen C. Barton, "New Testament Interpretation as Performance," *SJT* 52, no. 2 (1999): 179-208.

139. R. W. L. Moberly, *The Bible, Theology, and Faith: A Study of Abraham and Jesus,* Studies in Christian Doctrine (Cambridge: Cambridge University Press, 2000), p. 41.

140. Ricoeur, *Time and Narrative,* 3.272.

141. Paul Ricoeur, "Biblical Time," trans. David Pellauer, in *Figuring the Sacred: Religion, Narrative, and Imagination,* ed. Mark I. Wallace (Minneapolis: Fortress, 1995), pp. 170-71.

142. Ricoeur, "Biblical Time," p. 178.

143. Jon Whitman, "A Retrospective Forward: Interpretation, Allegory, and Historical Change," in *Interpretation and Allegory: Antiquity to the Modern Period,* ed. Jon Whitman (Leiden: Brill, 2000), pp. 16-20.

144. Jon Whitman, "Present Perspectives: Antiquity to the Late Middle Ages," in *Interpretation and Allegory,* p. 34.

145. John David Dawson shows that the "allegorizing" of Paul and even Origen, which offends so many like Daniel Boyarin, may not be as guilty as charged, whereas the danger of protecting "history" in figural reading may lie in a reverse spiritualizing of the Christian story — it becomes about the spiritual reactions of disciples in history, not about the redemptive acts of God (see his comparison of Erich Auerbach and Frei; *Christian Figural Reading and the Fashioning of Identity* [Berkeley: University of California Press, 2002]). My sympathies lie more with Frei's approach, although I do think that Dawson's charge sticks regarding Frei's inattention to the spiritual transformation involved in receiving the story.

146. Robert W. Wall, "Reading the Bible from Within Our Traditions: The 'Rule of Faith' in Theological Hermeneutics," in *Between Two Horizons,* p. 102. Also Paul M. Blowers writes that "the Rule appears in retrospect to be larger than any one of its individual renditions," which were catholic in giving "the impression of a viable harmony, not a cacophony" ("The *Regula Fidei* and the Narrative Character of Early Christian Faith," *Pro Ecclesia* 6 [1997]: 226).

147. David S. Yeago, "The Bible: The Spirit, the Church, and the Scriptures: Biblical Inspiration and Interpretation Revisited," in *Knowing the Triune God,* ed. James J. Buckley and David S. Yeago (Grand Rapids: Eerdmans, 2001), p. 72.

148. Wall, "Reading the Bible," p. 88.

149. Yeago, "Bible," p. 72.

150. Blowers criticizes Young for "overstating the extrinsic, particularistic, and nonnarrative nature of the *regula fidei* by insisting that it in no way represented interpretative canons rooted in Scripture or a 'sense of context within the flow of an overarching narrative history,'" appealing to Irenaeus ("*Regula Fidei,*" p. 210).

151. Watson, *Text, Church and World,* p. 325 n. 1.

Notes to Chapter 6

1. E.g., Richard J. Bernstein, *Beyond Objectivism and Relativism: Science, Hermeneutics, and Praxis* (Philadelphia: University of Pennsylvania Press, 1983).

2. James J. Buckley and David S. Yeago, "Introduction: A Catholic and Evangelical Theology?" in *Knowing the Triune God,* ed. James J. Buckley and David S. Yeago (Grand Rapids: Eerdmans, 2001), p. 7; Bruce D. Marshall, *Trinity and Truth,* Studies in Christian Doctrine (Cambridge: Cambridge University Press, 2000).

3. To which Andrew Louth provides an example of a theologian's appeal, in *Discerning the Mystery: An Essay on the Nature of Theology* (Oxford: Clarendon, 1983), pp. 47-48, 98. In many ways the classic case for this, despite a diverse *Wirkungsgeschichte,* is Hans-Georg Gadamer, *Truth and Method,* trans. Joel Weinsheimer and Donald G. Marshall, 2d ed. (New York: Continuum, 1989). See also Andrew Louth, "The Nature of Theological Understanding: Some Parallels Between Newman and Gadamer," in *Tradition Renewed,* ed. D. Rowell (Lon-

don: Darton, Longman, & Todd, 1986), pp. 98-109. With his "illative sense," John Henry Newman recovered *phronēsis* and anticipated the demise of a purely procedural or technical reason; see *An Essay in Aid of a Grammar of Assent* (London & New York: Longmans, Green & Co., 1930).

4. Michael Polanyi, *Personal Knowledge: Towards a Post-Critical Philosophy* (London: Routledge & Kegan Paul, 1958); *The Tacit Dimension* (London: Routledge & Kegan Paul, 1967); Thomas S. Kuhn, *The Structure of Scientific Revolutions* (Chicago: University of Chicago Press, 1962). In addition to Thomas F. Torrance, John V. Apczynski has proclaimed Polanyi's theological relevance (see *Doers of the Word: Toward a Foundational Theology Based on Thought of Michael Polanyi* [Missoula, MT: Scholars Press, 1977], especially pp. 175-80). The utility of Kuhn's paradigm for explaining biblical studies has been challenged in Robert F. Shedinger, "Kuhnian Paradigms and Biblical Scholarship: Is Biblical Studies a Science?" *JBL* 119, no. 3 (Fall 2000): 453-71.

5. Relative, not absolute, distinctions — apparently contra Ricoeur, according to Dan R. Stiver, *Theology After Ricoeur: New Directions in Hermeneutical Theology* (Louisville: Westminster John Knox, 2001), p. 227. For examples of fallibilist approaches, see Nancey Murphy, *Theology in the Age of Scientific Reasoning,* Cornell Studies in the Philosophy of Religion (Ithaca and London: Cornell University Press, 1990); *Beyond Liberalism and Fundamentalism: How Modern and Postmodern Philosophy Set the Theological Agenda* (Valley Forge, PA: Trinity Press International, 1996); "The Role of Virtue in Epistemic Practices," in *Philosophy and Theological Discourse,* ed. Stephen T. Davis (New York: St. Martin's, 1997), pp. 224-28; Philip Clayton, *Explanation from Physics to Theology: An Essay in Rationality and Religion* (New Haven: Yale University Press, 1989), p. 101.

6. Philip Clayton, *The Problem of God in Modern Thought* (Grand Rapids: Eerdmans, 2000), ch. 1, pp. 351-54. The point that interpretative locality and diversity, or particularity and plurality, have often been resisted due to neglecting the Christian doctrine of creation (in relation to the event of Pentecost), is well-taken (James K. A. Smith, *The Fall of Interpretation: Philosophical Foundations for a Creational Hermeneutic* [Downers Grove, IL: IVP, 2000]). However, Smith could be clearer about how a plurality of particular understandings is different from the relativism he excludes (e.g., on p. 163). Or, if "interpretative norms" are to be affirmed absent "normative interpretations" (p. 169), then not all striving for the goal of a correct interpretation can be caricatured as viewing plurality to be fallenness (a position from which Smith's interlocutors, such as Vanhoozer, demur).

7. As demonstrated, for instance, by Clayton. In the arena of theology, again, Charry is right to oppose the exclusion of technical knowledge or the eclipse of all universality in truth claims, but a Christian *phronēsis* may still be the embracing category within which *technē* has its place and through which truth claims are made and manifest. For differing perceptions of *phronēsis* in this regard, see Donald Marshall, "Truth, Universality, and Interpretation," in *Disciplining Hermeneutics: Interpretation in Christian Perspective,* ed. Roger Lundin (Grand Rapids: Eerdmans, 1997), pp. 69-84; Ellen T. Charry, "Cure of Body and Soul: Interpretation as Art and Science," in *Disciplining Hermeneutics,* pp. 85-95. My understanding of doctrine in chapter 3, and of a critical role for biblical scholarship in chapters 4 through 6, is an effort to address Charry's objections to a project such as Marshall's.

8. Charles W. Allen, "The Recovery of *phronēsis:* Its Implications for the Role of Practical Reason in Theology" (Ph.D. diss., University of Chicago, 1987), p. 33.

9. Allen, "Recovery of *phronēsis,*" p. 36.

10. Charles W. Allen, "The Primacy of *Phronēsis:* A Proposal for Avoiding Frustrating Tendencies in Our Conceptions of Rationality," *JR* 69 (July 1989): 364-66.

11. Compare Jürgen Habermas, *The Theory of Communicative Action,* vol. 1, *Reason and the Rationalization of Society,* trans. Thomas McCarthy (Boston: Beacon, 1984); *The Theory of Communicative Action,* vol. 2, *Lifeworld and System: A Critique of Functionalist Reason,* trans. Thomas McCarthy (Boston: Beacon, 1987), with critics such as Matthew Lamb and Robert Wuthnow in Don S. Browning and Francis Schüssler Fiorenza, eds., *Habermas, Modernity, and Public Theology* (New York: Crossroad, 1992). There Tracy, in particular, makes the contrast between "conversation" and "argument."

12. This has long been recognized, as much discussion of the relation between natural sciences and the humanities would demonstrate; see Wolfhart Pannenberg, *Wissenschaftstheorie und Theologie* (Frankfurt am Main: Suhrkamp Verlag, 1973).

13. Allen, "Recovery of *phronēsis,*" p. 14.

14. Allen, "Primacy of *Phronēsis,*" p. 369.

15. Allen may follow Gadamer in overstating the point at some places, but is broadly correct to follow Toulmin's rather than Rorty's line.

16. Allen, "Recovery of *phronēsis,*" p. 49.

17. E.g., Allen, "Primacy of *Phronēsis,*" p. 369. He follows especially Stephen Toulmin, *Human Understanding: The Collective Use and Evolution of Concepts* (Princeton: Princeton University Press, 1972).

18. John Milbank, for instance, questions the accuracy of MacIntyre's appropriation of Plato and Aristotle, partially on this basis of a defection from their emphases on participation and contemplation, and their relative diminution of life in the polis (see *Theology and Social Theory: Beyond Secular Reason* [Oxford: Blackwell, 1993], ch. 11). For treatments of Aristotle and the Greek context, see Martha C. Nussbaum, *The Fragility of Goodness: Luck and Ethics in Greek Tragedy and Philosophy* (Cambridge: Cambridge University Press, 1986); C. D. C. Reeve, *Practices of Reason: Aristotle's Nicomachean Ethics* (Oxford: Oxford University Press, 2000); Eugen Fink, "Phronēsis und Theoria," in *Die Welt des Menschen,* ed. Walter Biemel and Jan Patocka (The Hague: M. Nijhoff, 1976), pp. 134-58. For a comparison with Thomas, see Daniel Westberg, *Right Practical Reason: Aristotle, Action, and Prudence in Aquinas* (Oxford: Clarendon, 1994).

19. Allen, "Recovery of *phronēsis,*" p. 11.

20. Allen, "Recovery of *phronēsis,*" p. 22.

21. Thomas Groome, "Wisdom for Life: The Horizon of Theological Literacy," in *Theological Literacy for the Twenty-First Century,* ed. Rodney L. Petersen and Nancy M. Rourke (Grand Rapids: Eerdmans, 2002), p. 361.

22. Martha C. Nussbaum, *Love's Knowledge: Essays on Philosophy and Literature* (New York: Oxford University Press, 1990), pp. 67-68.

23. Al Wolters, "Confessional Criticism and the Night Visions of Zechariah," in *Renewing Biblical Interpretation,* ed. Craig Bartholomew, Colin Greene and Karl Möller, Scripture and Hermeneutics, vol. 1 (Grand Rapids: Zondervan, 2000), p. 104.

24. Nussbaum, *Love's Knowledge,* p. 38.

25. Nussbaum, *Love's Knowledge,* p. 41.

26. W. Jay Wood, *Epistemology: Becoming Intellectually Virtuous,* Contours of Christian Philosophy (Downers Grove, IL: IVP, 1998), p. 45. A good basic introduction may be

found in Gilbert C. Meilaender, *The Theory and Practice of Virtue* (Notre Dame: Notre Dame University Press, 1984).

27. Wood, *Epistemology,* p. 70.

28. This is discussed at great length in Joseph Dunne, *Back to the Rough Ground: 'Phronēsis' and 'Technē' in Modern Philosophy and in Aristotle* (Notre Dame: Notre Dame University Press, 1993), especially ch. 8.

29. Perhaps reflecting the societal loss that sunders virtue into "integrity of motive" on the one hand and "measurement of consequence" on the other; so John Milbank, "A Critique of the Theology of Right," in *The Word Made Strange: Theology, Language, Culture* (Oxford: Blackwell, 1997), p. 30.

30. Brian A. Gerrish, "Tradition in the Modern World: The Reformed Habit of Mind," in *Toward the Future of Reformed Theology: Tasks, Topics, Traditions,* ed. E. David Willis and Michael Welker (Grand Rapids: Eerdmans, 1999), p. 6.

31. Linda T. Zagzebski, *Virtues of the Mind: An Inquiry into the Nature of Virtue and the Ethical Foundations of Knowledge* (Cambridge: Cambridge University Press, 1996), pp. 113, 135-37.

32. As noted in Murphy, "Role of Virtue," p. 225.

33. Trevor Hart, *Faith Thinking: The Dynamics of Christian Theology* (Downers Grove, IL: IVP, 1995), p. 90.

34. Hart, *Faith Thinking,* p. 91.

35. Again, see Dunne, *Back to the Rough Ground.*

36. Merold Westphal, "Taking St. Paul Seriously: Sin as an Epistemological Category," in *Christian Philosophy,* ed. Thomas P. Flint (Notre Dame: Notre Dame University Press, 1990), pp. 211-20.

37. Roger Lundin, "Interpreting Orphans: Hermeneutics in the Cartesian Tradition," in *The Promise of Hermeneutics,* ed. Roger Lundin, Clarence Walhout and Anthony C. Thiselton (Grand Rapids: Eerdmans, 1999), p. 41. It is for this reason that modern hermeneutical theories have tended to follow either Hegel or Schleiermacher (p. 5).

38. Guy Axtell, "Recent Work on Virtue Epistemology," *APQ* 34, no. 1 (January 1997): 15, 19.

39. Allen, "Recovery of *phronēsis,*" p. 61.

40. David Tracy, "The Uneasy Alliance Reconceived: Catholic Theological Method, Modernity and Postmodernity," in *Theology After Liberalism: A Reader,* ed. John Webster and George P. Schner (Oxford: Blackwell, 2000), pp. 342, 346, 348.

41. Allen, "Recovery of *phronēsis,*" p. 243. One of few authors to maintain this persistently (against the first/second-order distinction) is Eric O. Springsted, "Putnam, Plato and the Task of Theology," *Soundings* 73 (Spring 1990): pp. 169-89; "Theology and Spirituality: Or, Why Theology Is Not Critical Reflection on Religious Experience," in *Spirituality and Theology: Essays in Honor of Diogenes Allen,* ed. Eric O. Springsted (Louisville: Westminster John Knox, 1998), pp. 49-62.

42. Charles Taylor, *Philosophical Arguments* (Cambridge, MA: Harvard University Press, 1997), p. vii.

43. Taylor, *Philosophical Arguments,* pp. 54-55, 60, 179-80.

44. Charles Taylor, *Sources of the Self: The Making of the Modern Identity* (Cambridge, MA: Harvard University Press, 1989).

45. Dunne, *Back to the Rough Ground,* p. 12.

46. Shaun Gallagher, *Hermeneutics and Education,* SUNY Series in Contemporary Continental Philosophy (Albany, NY: SUNY Press, 1992), p. 342.

47. Milbank, *Theology and Social Theory,* especially p. 413.

48. David H. Kelsey, *To Understand God Truly: What's Theological About a Theological School* (Louisville: Westminster John Knox, 1992), p. 123.

49. Gerard Loughlin comments about Christian doctrine never having been able to win the modern war: "This was not just because reason is never impartial — because always the reason of particular people with particular interests — but also because Enlightenment reason was conceived in opposition to Christian faith, claiming to exist in its own right as pure reason. . . . Theology not only accepted philosophy's right to rule its own domain, but its right to rule everything else, including God. . . . As a consequence, the legitimate foundations of doctrine — scripture and tradition — were transformed in subtle and not so subtle ways into history and experience, which individually and together were to prove unstable and too weak for anything other than a liberal theology that is finally no theology at all" ("The Basis and Authority of Doctrine," in *The Cambridge Companion to Christian Doctrine,* ed. Colin E. Gunton [Cambridge: Cambridge University Press, 1997], p. 42).

50. The ubiquity of this once brilliant metaphor from Jeffrey Stout attests to the depth of the modern epistemological problem for Christian theology.

51. Edward Farley, *The Fragility of Knowledge: Theological Education in the Church and the University* (Philadelphia: Fortress, 1988), pp. 15, 24.

52. George P. Schner, "Metaphors for Theology," in *Theology After Liberalism: A Reader,* p. 12.

53. Kelsey, *To Understand God Truly,* p. 243.

54. Avery Dulles, S.J., *The Craft of Theology: From Symbol to System* (New York: Crossroad, 1992), pp. 3-4.

55. Edward Farley, *Ecclesial Reflection: An Anatomy of Theological Method* (Philadelphia: Fortress, 1982), p. 134.

56. David H. Kelsey, *Between Athens and Berlin: The Theological Education Debate* (Grand Rapids: Eerdmans, 1993), pp. 226-27.

57. Ellen T. Charry, "Inquiring After God When Meditating on Scripture," in *Inquiring After God,* ed. Ellen T. Charry (Oxford: Blackwell, 2000), p. 208; also, "Reviving Theology in a Time of Change," in *The Future of Theology: Essays in Honor of Jürgen Moltmann,* ed. Miroslav Volf, Carmen Krieg and Thomas Kucharz (Grand Rapids: Eerdmans, 1996), pp. 114-26.

58. Dulles, *Craft of Theology,* p. 13. "Personal responsibility" for interpretation is not the same as "private judgment" (Nicholas Lash, "Performing the Scriptures," in *Theology on the Way to Emmaus* [London: SCM, 1986], p. 43).

59. Dulles, *Craft of Theology,* pp. 5-6.

60. Especially with regard to the ethically perspectival aspect of criticism; see R. S. Sugirtharajah, *The Bible and the Third World: Precolonial, Colonial and Postcolonial Encounters* (Cambridge: Cambridge University Press, 2001), ch. 8 ("Postcolonializing Biblical Interpretation"), p. 266 in particular.

61. Robert W. Jenson, "The Religious Power of Scripture," *SJT* 52, no. 1 (1999): 104.

62. Dietrich Ritschl, "Is There Anything 'New' in Theology? Reflections on an Old Theme," in *The Future of Theology,* p. 54.

63. Even Charles Wood qualifies Kelsey's claim that use of Scripture is determined by

an imaginative *discrimen,* noting that although it is "imaginative, it is hardly arbitrary or inexplicable, as a rule" ("Hermeneutics and the Authority of Scripture," in *Scriptural Authority and Narrative Interpretation,* ed. Garrett Green [reprint, Eugene, OR: Wipf & Stock, 2000], p. 12). "To call something scripture is to affirm a critical principle . . . by which the authenticity of tradition may be evaluated and by which the development of tradition may be guided" (p. 9).

64. Pannenberg, *Wissenschaftstheorie und Theologie,* pp. 168, 348; Allen, "Primacy of *Phronēsis,*" p. 364. The danger is that "reasons" will be confused with a strictly procedural reason, as in the following quote: "We must demand of exegesis that its treatment of texts be scientifically verifiable, and that means capable of scrutiny as to method. Otherwise, historical interpretation of scripture would become an intuitive vision, limited to an individual or group, scarcely or no longer communicable" (Peter Stuhlmacher, *Historical Criticism and Theological Interpretation of Scripture,* trans. Roy A. Harrisville [Philadelphia: Fortress, 1977], p. 86). The either-or presented here obscures the substantive dimensions of methodology and the locality as well as transferability of communication.

65. David Tracy, "Can Virtue Be Taught? Education, Character, and the Soul," in *Theology and the University,* ed. John V. Apczynski (Lanham, MD: University Press of America, 1990), p. 132.

66. John Goldingay, "Biblical Narrative and Systematic Theology," in *Between Two Horizons,* ed. Joel B. Green and Max Turner (Grand Rapids: Eerdmans, 2000), p. 133. Maurice Wiles (characteristically) writes, "All authorities have a tendency to overreach themselves. . . . So there was a rapid expansion of the range of issues on which scripture was expected to speak. The history of early biblical exegesis shows scripture being asked to give precise answers to questions with which it was hopelessly ill suited to deal. The result was an overexegesis, which, since the answers it was being expected to produce had to come from somewhere, inevitably took the form of eisegesis" ("Scriptural Authority and Theological Construction: The Limitations of Narrative Interpretation," in *Scriptural Authority and Narrative Interpretation,* p. 43). He argues for reconfiguring the role of Scripture in the church, instead of reconfiguring the definition of critical study employed on the Bible (p. 50), having recognized that "what the scholar does is only a more concentrated form of what is involved in any reflective reading of scripture — and it cannot be the church's goal to exclude that" (p. 54). This analysis, spot on in a certain respect, thus presents the church with a clear choice about whether or not to maintain a "canonical" role for Scripture, tied to divine-human concursus therein.

67. Nicholas Lash, "The Remaking of Doctrine: Which Way Shall We Go?" in *Theology on Dover Beach* (New York: Paulist, 1979), p. 110.

68. Nicholas M. Healy, *Church, World and the Christian Life: Practical-Prophetic Ecclesiology,* Studies in Christian Doctrine (Cambridge: Cambridge University Press, 2000).

69. Bruce D. Marshall, "Absorbing the World: Christianity and the Universe of Truths," in *Theology and Dialogue,* ed. Bruce D. Marshall (Notre Dame: Notre Dame University Press, 1990), pp. 69-102.

70. For which Axtell maintains the need, again regarding virtue ethics and epistemology (Axtell, "Recent Work on Virtue," p. 19).

71. Taylor, *Sources of the Self,* p. 69.

72. Kathryn Tanner, "Self-Critical Cultures and Divine Transcendence," in *Theology After Liberalism: A Reader,* p. 248.

73. James J. Buckley, "Beyond the Hermeneutical Deadlock," in *Theology After Liberalism: A Reader*, p. 199.

74. John Webster, "Theology After Liberalism?" in *Theology After Liberalism: A Reader*, p. 58.

75. Recently these are related to theological interpretation of Scripture as well; for example, Robert Morgan suggests it "has always had *doctrinal, literary* and *historical* components"; see "Jesus Christ, the Wisdom of God (2)," in *Reading Texts, Seeking Wisdom: Scripture and Theology*, ed. David F. Ford and Graham Stanton (Grand Rapids: Eerdmans, 2004), p. 27, and essays throughout the volume.

76. I use this word in a generic sense, without engaging specific debates over defining "warrant" vis-à-vis "justification" in epistemology (which are especially due to the work of Alvin Plantinga).

77. Interchangeable use of these terms, *as academic disciplines*, should make sense in light of their competition for a significantly shared space, a point by Colin Gunton briefly discussed later. Both involve conceptual analysis with ultimate concerns in view.

78. E.g., David S. Yeago, "The New Testament and the Nicene Dogma," in *The Theological Interpretation of Scripture*, ed. Stephen E. Fowl (Oxford: Blackwell, 1997).

79. The tendency for hermeneutical inquiries to dominate everything else is well-documented; see, e.g., the cautions in Shaun Gallagher, *Hermeneutics and Education*, SUNY Series in Contemporary Continental Philosophy (Albany, NY: SUNY Press, 1992).

80. On the importance of form, see David Tracy, "Trinitarian Speculation and the Forms of Divine Self-Disclosure," in *The Trinity*, ed. Stephen Davis, Daniel Kendall, S.J. and Gerald O'Collins, S.J. (Oxford: Oxford University Press, 1999), pp. 272-93. My final chapter reflects on this at some length.

81. A point on which reminders come continually from Kevin Vanhoozer's work; see also Clarence Walhout, "Narrative Hermeneutics," in *The Promise of Hermeneutics*, ed. Roger Lundin, Clarence Walhout and Anthony C. Thiselton (Grand Rapids: Eerdmans, 1999), pp. 65-131.

82. For examples of the formation that modern reading practices in the Western university have lost, see Paul J. Griffiths, *Religious Reading: The Place of Reading in the Practice of Religion* (Oxford: Oxford University Press, 1999).

83. So, among others, Nicholas Healy, as cited earlier.

84. Daniel W. Hardy, "Reason, Wisdom and the Interpretation of Scripture," in *Reading Texts, Seeking Wisdom*, p. 81.

85. On which see further Daniel J. Treier, "Wisdom," in *Dictionary for Theological Interpretation of the Bible*, ed. Kevin J. Vanhoozer (Grand Rapids: Baker Academic, & London: SPCK, 2005).

86. Stephen T. Davis, "Tradition, Scripture and Religious Authority," in *Philosophy and Theological Discourse*, ed. Stephen T. Davis (New York: St. Martin's, 1997), p. 64.

87. J. Augustine DiNoia, "Theology in Dialogue," in *Theology After Liberalism: A Reader*, p. 166.

88. Colin E. Gunton, "Dogma, the Church and the Task of Theology," *Neue Zeitschrift für Systematische Theologie und Religionsphilosophie* 40, no. 1 (1998): 75.

89. Gunton, "Dogma," p. 79.

90. John Webster, "Canon and Criterion: Some Reflections on a Recent Proposal," *SJT* 54, no. 2 (2001): 221-37.

91. Nicholas Lash, "Doing Theology on Dover Beach," in *Theology on Dover Beach,* pp. 14-22.

92. Taylor, *Philosophical Arguments,* p. 33.

93. R. W. L. Moberly, *The Bible, Theology, and Faith: A Study of Abraham and Jesus,* Studies in Christian Doctrine (Cambridge: Cambridge University Press, 2000), p. 237.

94. Daniel W. Hardy, "The Grace of God and Earthly Wisdom," in *Where Shall Wisdom Be Found?* ed. Stephen C. Barton (Edinburgh: T&T Clark, 1999), p. 231.

95. Hardy, "Grace of God," p. 243.

Notes to Chapter 7

1. Douglas John Hall, "Theological Education as Character Formation," *Theological Education* 24, Supplement 1 (1988): 68.

2. For the classic history of the *paideia* to which Kelsey refers, see Werner Jaeger, *Paideia: The Ideals of Greek Culture,* trans. Gilbert Highet, 2d ed. (New York: Oxford University Press, 1939). On "culture and formation" in contemporary theological education, see Jackson W. Carroll, et al., *Being There: Culture and Formation in Two Theological Schools* (Oxford: Oxford University Press, 1997).

3. Stephen D. Brookfield, *Becoming a Critically Reflective Teacher* (San Francisco: Jossey Bass, 1995), p. 209.

4. On which see, e.g., Richard Heyduck, *The Recovery of Doctrine in the Contemporary Church: An Essay in Philosophical Ecclesiology* (Waco, TX: Baylor University Press, 2002), p. 76.

5. Hall, "Theological Education," p. 69.

6. Charles Wood rightly notes that "every Christian, under normal circumstances, inevitably is called to make judgements as to what constitutes valid Christian witness . . . a Christian community has no choice as to whether theological education, for all its members, will be an element of its educational work; it only has a choice as to the kind of theological education it will be" ("Theological Education and Education for Church Leadership," in *Theological Perspectives on Christian Formation,* ed. Jeff Astley, Leslie J. Francis and Colin Crowder [Grand Rapids: Eerdmans, 1996], pp. 307-8). The reminder is important that *habitus* is not habit in a "mechanical" sense, but rather it is "thought that is truly alive," grasped so as to generate creativity (Yves R. Simon, *The Definition of Moral Virtue,* ed. Vukan Kuic [New York: Fordham University Press, 1986], p. 60).

7. Hall, "Theological Education," p. 70.

8. E.g., Miroslav Volf and Dorothy C. Bass, eds., *Practicing Theology: Beliefs and Practices in the Christian Life* (Grand Rapids: Eerdmans, 2002).

9. In addition to the work of Don Browning, Gerben Heitink's configuration of this discipline (on those terms) around a theological theory of action seems promising; see *Practical Theology,* trans. Reinder Bruinsma (Grand Rapids: Eerdmans, 1999).

10. Hall, "Theological Education," p. 72.

11. The American consequences, centered around a split between faith and knowledge, are chronicled in Douglas Sloan, *Faith and Knowledge: Mainline Protestantism and American Higher Education* (Louisville: Westminster John Knox, 1994).

12. Robert Banks, *Reenvisioning Theological Education: Exploring a Missional Alternative to Current Models* (Grand Rapids: Eerdmans, 1999).

13. See the resources on a missional model of church in, e.g., Leanne Van Dyk, "The Formation of Vocation — Institutional and Individual," in *The Scope of Our Art*, ed. L. Gregory Jones and Stephanie Paulsell (Grand Rapids: Eerdmans, 2002), pp. 225-39, or the overview in Darrell L. Guder, "The Church as Missional Community," in *The Community of the Word: Toward an Evangelical Ecclesiology*, ed. Mark Husbands and Daniel J. Treier (Downers Grove, IL: IVP, 2005), pp. 114-28.

14. Banks rightly criticizes a "vocational" (read: "professional," I think) model for wrongly locating "the unity of theological education in its goal rather than its actual dynamics." However, by linking the knowledge of God a bit too directly with "the work of ministry," has he done likewise? Nevertheless, his work is helpful, and the "communicative praxis" of wisdom in the present work could certainly be a cousin of his model. Banks is right that we must not simply "locate the fragmentation of theological education in the rise of modern critical methodologies, post-Reformation theological encyclopedias, or medieval university structures," but in "the earlier separation of learning from active service of God and neighbor" (*Reenvisioning*, p. 144). However, this might be co-opted for an overly practical agenda unless "active service of God" embraces contemplation, as other vocabulary (rooted in wisdom) can accomplish. Seeing theology as a "research project" (p. 168) amidst Christian mission may make the questions of its discourse too immanent, and neglect the ongoing formation and enactment occurring in personal and corporate liturgical practices, and other ways of fellowship with God via Scripture.

15. Bryan Pettifer, "Education and the Knowledge of God: Towards a Model of Theology as a Practical Discipline," in *The Foundations of Pastoral Studies and Practical Theology*, ed. Paul Ballard (Cardiff: University College Faculty of Theology, 1986), p. 65.

16. See also Daniel J. Treier, "Theological Hermeneutics, Contemporary," in *Dictionary for Theological Interpretation of the Bible*, ed. Kevin J. Vanhoozer (Grand Rapids: Baker Academic, & London: SPCK, 2005).

17. John Webster, "Criticism: Revelation and Disturbance," *Stimulus* 7, no. 1 (February 1999).

18. Karl Barth, *Church Dogmatics*, vol. I/1, *The Word of God*, trans. Thomas F. Torrance, 2d ed. (Edinburgh: T&T Clark, 1975), p. 295.

19. Barth, *CD I/1*, pp. 295-96.

20. Barth, *CD I/1*, p. 296.

21. Barth, *CD I/1*, p. 296.

22. Barth, *CD I/1*, p. 296.

23. Barth, *CD I/1*, p. 354.

24. Barth, *CD I/1*, p. 298.

25. Barth, *CD I/1*, p. 298.

26. Barth, *CD I/1*, p. 299.

27. Barth, *CD I/1*, especially pp. 308-312.

28. Barth, *CD I/1*, pp. 314-15.

29. Barth, *CD I/1*, pp. 320-24.

30. See the discussions of the post-Reformation scholastics and the Princetonians in Timothy Ward, *Word and Supplement: Speech Acts, Biblical Texts, and the Sufficiency of Scripture* (Oxford: Oxford University Press, 2002).

31. Barth, *CD I/1*, p. 371.

32. Barth, *CD I/1,* p. 371.

33. The relation of being and act grows quite complex, in Barth and contemporary thought generally. Bruce McCormack even alleges inconsistency between Barth's later articulation regarding the doctrine of election and his earlier doctrine of the Trinity ("Grace and Being: The Role of God's Gracious Election in Karl Barth's Theological Ontology," in *The Cambridge Companion to Karl Barth,* ed. John Webster [Cambridge: Cambridge University Press, 2000], pp. 92-110). I ignore that matter here; on the doctrine of Scripture, though assessing the relative achievements of Barth and Warfield a bit differently, I am also informed by McCormack ("The Being of Holy Scripture Is in Becoming: Karl Barth in Conversation with American Evangelical Criticism," in *Evangelicals and Scripture: Tradition, Authority, Hermeneutics,* ed. Vincent E. Bacote, Laura C. Miguélez, and Dennis L. Okholm [Downers Grove, IL: IVP, 2004], pp. 55-75), as well as Ward, *Word and Supplement.*

34. David H. Kelsey, "The Bible and Christian Theology," *JAAR* 48, no. 3 (September 1980): 396.

35. Kelsey, "Bible," p. 397.

36. Kelsey, "Bible," p. 398.

37. Rowan Williams, "Word and Spirit," in *On Christian Theology* (Oxford: Blackwell, 2000), p. 110.

38. Williams, "Word and Spirit," p. 126.

39. Rowan Williams, "Trinity and Revelation," in *On Christian Theology,* p. 142.

40. Williams, "Trinity and Revelation," especially pp. 142, 147.

41. John Milbank, "The Second Difference," in *The Word Made Strange* (Oxford: Blackwell, 1997), pp. 171-93.

42. Rowan Williams, "Trinity and Ontology," in *On Christian Theology,* p. 165.

43. Stephen E. Fowl and L. Gregory Jones, *Reading in Communion: Scripture and Ethics in Christian Life* (Grand Rapids: Eerdmans, 1991), especially pp. 38-40; Stephen E. Fowl, *Engaging Scripture* (Oxford: Blackwell, 1998), pp. 2-8, 161-62.

44. Williams, "Word and Spirit," p. 109.

45. Thomas Smail, "The Holy Spirit in the Holy Trinity," in *Nicene Christianity: The Future for a New Ecumenism,* ed. Christopher R. Seitz (Grand Rapids: Brazos, 2001), p. 161.

46. Smail, "Holy Spirit," pp. 157-58.

47. Smail, "Holy Spirit," p. 162.

48. Stanley J. Grenz, *Theology for the Community of God* (Nashville: Broadman & Holman, 1994).

49. See especially Stanley J. Grenz, "Articulating the Christian Belief-Mosaic: Theological Method After the Demise of Foundationalism," in *Evangelical Futures,* ed. John G. Stackhouse, Jr. (Grand Rapids: Baker, 2000), pp. 127-28. This is a fairly consistent development from the earlier *Revisioning Evangelical Theology* (Downers Grove, IL: IVP, 1993). Also relevant are "Beyond Foundationalism: Is a Nonfoundationalist Evangelical Theology Possible?" *Christian Scholar's Review* 30, no. 1 (Fall 2000): 57-82; "The Spirit and the Word: The World-Creating Function of the Text," *TToday* 57, no. 3 (October 2000): 357-75; Stanley J. Grenz and John R. Franke, *Beyond Foundationalism: Shaping Theology in a Postmodern Context* (Louisville: Westminster John Knox, 2001).

50. A. N. Williams, "Contemplation: Knowledge of God in Augustine's *De Trinitate,*" in *Knowing the Triune God,* ed. James J. Buckley and David S. Yeago (Grand Rapids: Eerdmans, 2001), pp. 121-46.

51. Werner Jeanrond prefers the term "interpretation" rather than "understanding," to embrace a critical dimension of approaching texts, contra Gadamer (*Text und Interpretation als Kategorien theologischen Denkens* [Tübingen: J. C. B. Mohr (Paul Siebeck), 1986], pp. 18ff., 69ff.). And I would opt for a reconfigured version of Ricoeur's hermeneutical arch, with a more critical "understanding" than Gadamer's that can nevertheless be called phronetic (see Dan R. Stiver, *Theology After Ricoeur* [Louisville: Westminster John Knox, 2001], pp. 75, 210). Still, Kelsey's description of theological understanding is helpful. And Shaun Gallagher is right that hermeneutics — especially as it interfaces with the subject of education — should not be swallowed up into simply studying the interpretation of texts (*Hermeneutics and Education* [Albany: SUNY Press, 1992] shows that "understanding" must be broader than what often passes for critical inquiry or reflection).

52. See especially John Webster, "The Dogmatic Location of the Canon," *Neue Zeitschrift für Systematische Theologie und Religionsphilosophie* 43, no. 1 (2001): 17-43; Kevin J. Vanhoozer, *First Theology: God, Scripture, Hermeneutics* (Downers Grove, IL: IVP, 2002); *The Drama of Doctrine: A Canonical-Linguistic Approach to Theology* (Louisville: Westminster John Knox, 2005).

53. David Tracy, "Trinitarian Speculation and the Forms of Divine Self-Disclosure," in *The Trinity*, ed. Stephen Davis, Daniel Kendall, S.J. and Gerald O'Collins, S.J. (Oxford: Oxford University Press, 1999), pp. 272-93.

54. See, e.g., on "freedom" and "law" (and hence "institutions") Paul Ricoeur, "Practical Reason," trans. Kathleen Blamey, in *From Text to Action: Essays in Hermeneutics, II* (Evanston, IL: Northwestern University Press, 1991), pp. 188-207.

55. See Telford Work, *Living and Active: Scripture in the Economy of Salvation*, Sacra Doctrina (Grand Rapids: Eerdmans, 2002). The point is also made, in the slightly different context of the *filioque* discussion, by Smail, "Holy Spirit."

56. Daniel W. Hardy, "The Grace of God and Earthly Wisdom," in *Where Shall Wisdom Be Found?* ed. Stephen C. Barton (Edinburgh: T&T Clark, 1999), p. 246.

57. This analogy is helpfully considered *as an analogy* — neither more nor less — with reference to the economy of salvation, in Lewis Ayres and Stephen E. Fowl, "(Mis)Reading the Face of God: *The Interpretation of the Bible in the Church*," *TS* 60 (1999): 513-28. They may overdo the extent of our freedom from historical criticism, however (not only with reference to the Bible, but also Christology).

58. Perhaps broader than Barth's categorization; again, I use the word "witness" in the now current sense of Wood and others.

59. I take the point about "creeping perichoresis" (Bruce L. McCormack, "What's at Stake in Current Debates over Justification? The Crisis of Protestantism in the West," in *Justification: What's at Stake in the Current Debates*, ed. Mark Husbands and Daniel J. Treier [Downers Grove, IL: IVP, 2004], ch. 3). But I am not developing a full anthropology here.

60. Although, as admitted elsewhere, the need for a proper hermeneutic of intracanonical criticism remains pressing; for brief discussion of some options, see Daniel J. Treier, "Scripture, Unity of," in *Dictionary for Theological Interpretation*.

61. Oliver O'Donovan, *Resurrection and Moral Order: An Outline for Evangelical Ethics*, 2d ed. (Grand Rapids: Eerdmans, 1994).

62. Kevin J. Vanhoozer, *Is There a Meaning in This Text? The Bible, the Reader, and the Morality of Literary Knowledge* (Grand Rapids: Zondervan, 1998), pp. 419-21. See also the broad point of James K. A. Smith, *The Fall of Interpretation* (Downers Grove, IL: IVP, 2000).

63. See this developed elsewhere in Daniel J. Treier, "Canonical Unity and Commensurable Language: On Divine Action and Doctrine," in *Evangelicals and Scripture,* pp. 211-28. Also see the updating of a discussion connecting the NT and Nicene dogma in David S. Yeago, "The Bible: The Spirit, the Church, and the Scriptures: Biblical Inspiration and Interpretation Revisited," in *Knowing the Triune God,* pp. 64-65, n. 22.

64. The terminology is from Kevin J. Vanhoozer, "Body-Piercing, the Natural Sense, and the Task of Theological Interpretation: A Hermeneutical Homily on John 19:34," *Ex Auditu* 16 (2000): 1-29.

65. James J. Buckley and David S. Yeago, eds., *Knowing the Triune God: The Work of the Spirit in the Practices of the Church* (Grand Rapids: Eerdmans, 2001).

66. Compare Paul J. Griffiths, *Religious Reading: The Place of Reading in the Practice of Religion* (Oxford: Oxford University Press, 1999); Robert W. Jenson, "The Religious Power of Scripture," *SJT* 52, no. 1 (1999): 89-105; H. Gregory Snyder, *Teachers and Texts in the Ancient World* (London: Routledge, 2000). More specifically on the church, see Eugene H. Peterson, "Eat This Book: The Holy Community at Table with the Holy Scripture," *TToday* 56, no. 1 (April 1999): 5-17.

67. Stephen E. Fowl, "The Conceptual Structure of New Testament Theology," in *Biblical Theology: Retrospect and Prospect,* ed. Scott J. Hafemann (Downers Grove, IL: IVP, 2002), pp. 225-36.

68. Colin E. Gunton, "Indispensable Opponent: The Relations of Systematic Theology and Philosophy of Religion," *Neue Zeitschrift für Systematische Theologie und Religionsphilosophie* 38, no. 3 (1996): 298-306.

69. I. Howard Marshall, "Climbing Ropes, Ellipses and Symphonies: The Relation Between Biblical and Systematic Theology," in *A Pathway into the Holy Scripture,* ed. Philip E. Satterthwaite and David F. Wright (Grand Rapids: Eerdmans, 1994), p. 218.

70. E.g., Christopher R. Seitz, "Christological Interpretation of Texts and Trinitarian Claims to Truth: An Engagement with Francis Watson's *Text and Truth,*" *SJT* 52, no. 2 (1999): 209-26; Francis Watson, "The Old Testament as Christian Scripture: A Response to Professor Seitz," *SJT* 52, no. 2 (1999): 227-32.

71. Gunton, "Indispensable Opponent." Incidentally, philosophy has just been compared to biblical scholarship regarding the relative dearth of assured "*knowledge*" in both fields, by a philosopher (Peter van Inwagen, "Do You Want Us to Listen to You?" in *"Behind" the Text: History and Biblical Interpretation,* ed. Craig Bartholomew et al., Scripture and Hermeneutics, vol. 4 [Grand Rapids: Zondervan, 2003], p. 125 n. 24)!

72. Francis Watson, *Text, Church and World: Biblical Interpretation in Theological Perspective* (Grand Rapids: Eerdmans, 1994), p. 13.

73. Christopher R. Seitz, "The Theological Crisis of Serious Biblical Interpretation," in *Renewing Biblical Interpretation,* ed. Craig Bartholomew, Colin Greene and Karl Möller, Scripture and Hermeneutics, vol. 1 (Grand Rapids: Zondervan, 2000), p. 58.

74. Very recently "theological interpretation" and "wisdom interpretation" have been equated in David F. Ford, "Jesus Christ, the Wisdom of God (1)," in *Reading Texts, Seeking Wisdom,* ed. David F. Ford and Graham Stanton (Grand Rapids: Eerdmans, 2004), p. 6. Figural reading, or attention to a certain multiplicity of scriptural senses, is also discussed there, as well as in Ellen F. Davis and Richard B. Hays, eds., *The Art of Reading Scripture* (Grand Rapids: Eerdmans, 2003): in particular see the nine theses in the latter book.

Index of Names and Subjects

Index of Scripture References